The Science of Good Cooking

The Cook's Illustrated Cookbook

The America's Test Kitchen Menu Cookbook

The America's Test Kitchen Quick Family Cookbook

The America's Test Kitchen Healthy Family Cookbook

The America's Test Kitchen Family Baking Book

The America's Test Kitchen Family Cookbook

THE AMERICA'S TEST KITCHEN LIBRARY SERIES AND THE TEST KITCHEN HANDBOOK SERIES

Comfort Food Makeovers

The America's Test Kitchen D.I.Y. Cookbook

Pasta Revolution

Simple Weeknight Favorites

Slow Cooker Revolution

The Best Simple Recipes

Pressure Cooker Perfection

THE COOK'S COUNTRY SERIES

From Our Grandmothers' Kitchens

Cook's Country Blue Ribbon Desserts

Cook's Country Best Potluck Recipes

Cook's Country Best Lost Suppers

Cook's Country Best Grilling Recipes

The Cook's Country Cookbook

America's Best Lost Recipes

THE TV COMPANION SERIES

The Complete Cook's Country TV Show Cookbook

The Complete America's Test Kitchen TV Show Cookbook 2001–2013

America's Test Kitchen: The TV Companion Cookbook (2002–2009, 2011, 2012, and 2013 Editions)

AMERICA'S TEST KITCHEN ANNUALS

The Best of America's Test Kitchen (2007–2013 Editions)

Cooking for Two (2010–2013 Editions)

Light & Healthy (2010–2012 Editions)

THE BEST RECIPE SERIES

The New Best Recipe

More Best Recipes

The Best One-Dish Suppers

Soups, Stews & Chilis

The Best Skillet Recipes

The Best Slow & Easy Recipes

The Best Chicken Recipes

The Best International Recipe

The Best Make-Ahead Recipe

The Best 30-Minute Recipe

The Best Light Recipe

The Cook's Illustrated Guide to Grilling and Barbecue

Best American Side Dishes

Cover & Bake

Steaks, Chops, Roasts & Ribs

Baking Illustrated

Italian Classics

American Classics

FOR A FULL LISTING OF ALL OUR BOOKS OR TO ORDER TITLES

CooksIllustrated.com

AmericasTestKitchen.com

or call 800-611-0759

America's
TEST KITCHEN

Cooking
for Two

2013

THE YEAR'S BEST RECIPES CUT DOWN TO SIZE

BY THE EDITORS OF
AMERICA'S TEST KITCHEN

PHOTOGRAPHY BY
CARL TREMBLAY, KELLER + KELLER, AND DANIEL J. VAN ACKERE

AMERICA'S TEST KITCHEN
17 Station Street, Brookline, MA 02445

AMERICA'S TEST KITCHEN COOKING FOR TWO 2013:
The Year's Best Recipes Cut Down to Size

1st Edition

Hardcover: $35 US
ISBN-13: 978-1-936493-43-2 ISBN-10: 1-936493-43-8
ISSN: 2162-6863

Manufactured in the United States of America

10 9 8 7 6 5 4 3 2 1

Distributed by America's Test Kitchen
17 Station Street, Brookline, MA 02445

EDITORIAL DIRECTOR: Jack Bishop
EXECUTIVE DIRECTOR, BOOKS: Elizabeth Carduff
EXECUTIVE EDITOR: Lori Galvin
EXECUTIVE FOOD EDITOR: Julia Collin Davison
SENIOR EDITOR: Suzannah McFerran
ASSOCIATE EDITORS: Kate Hartke, Alyssa King, Christie Morrison, Adelaide Parker
TEST COOKS: Danielle DeSiato-Hallman, Rebecca Morris, Kate Williams
DESIGN DIRECTOR: Amy Klee
ART DIRECTOR: Greg Galvan
ASSOCIATE ART DIRECTOR: Beverly Hsu
DESIGNER: Allison Pfiffner
STAFF PHOTOGRAPHER: Daniel J. van Ackere
ADDITIONAL PHOTOGRAPHY: Keller + Keller, Carl Tremblay
FOOD STYLING: Marie Piraino, Mary Jane Sawyer
PHOTOSHOOT KITCHEN TEAM:
    ASSOCIATE EDITOR: Chris O'Connor
    TEST COOKS: Daniel Cellucci, Sara Mayer
PRODUCTION DIRECTOR: Guy Rochford
SENIOR PRODUCTION MANAGER: Jessica Lindheimer Quirk
SENIOR PROJECT MANAGER: Alice Carpenter
PRODUCTION AND TRAFFIC COORDINATOR: Brittany Allen
WORKFLOW AND DIGITAL ASSET MANAGER: Andrew Mannone
SENIOR COLORING AND IMAGING SPECIALIST: Lauren Pettapiece
PRODUCTION AND IMAGING SPECIALISTS: Heather Dube, Lauren Robbins
COPYEDITOR: Barbara Wood
PROOFREADER: Ann-Marie Imbornoni
INDEXER: Elizabeth Parson

PICTURED ON THE FRONT COVER: Pan-Roasted Chicken Breasts with Root Vegetables (page 49)
PICTURED OPPOSITE TITLE PAGE: Vegetable Pot Pie (page 122)
PICTURED ON BACK OF JACKET: Smoky Indoor Ribs (page 23), Risotto Primavera (page 132), Grilled Spicy Shrimp Masala with Zucchini and Couscous Salad (page 167), Individual Chocolate Fudge Cakes (page 284)

Contents

THE SMART SHOPPER'S GUIDE

MAKING THE MOST OF THE RECIPES IN THIS BOOK

LET'S FACE IT—WE ALL WASTE FOOD. AND WHEN you're cooking for two, this is an even bigger problem. Sure, there are some stores where you can buy loose leafy greens or a handful of Brussels sprouts, but usually you're stuck with prepackaged produce sold in large quantities. The same is true for canned goods and many other items used in everyday recipes. So what's the solution to this problem? Careful planning and shopping. To that end, we've prepared this guide to key ingredients, both perishable and canned, that are used throughout the book. So if you're making one recipe with half of a red bell pepper or half a can of chickpeas, you can see which other recipes in the book call for them so you don't have to toss the extras.

BEANS, Black	AMOUNT	PAGE
Chunky Black Bean Dip	¾ cup	180
Turkey Taco Salad	¾ cup	180

BEANS, Pinto		
Five-Alarm Chili	¾ cup	73
Mexican-Style Pinto Bean Salad	¾ cup	72

CHICKPEAS		
Crispy Spiced Chickpeas	¾ cup	135
Moroccan-Style Quinoa with Chickpeas and Kale	¾ cup	129
Slow-Cooker Moroccan Chicken Stew	¾ cup	221

BELL PEPPER, Green		
Cajun-Style Eggs in Purgatory with Cheesy Grits	½	59

BELL PEPPER, Red		
Beef Lo Mein with Broccoli and Bell Pepper	½	113
Chinese Chicken Salad	½ small	175
White Bean Salad	½	256

BUTTERMILK	AMOUNT	PAGE
Cinnamon Streusel Coffee Cake	¼ cup	266
Skillet Summer Vegetable Tamale Pie	⅓ cup	124
Vegetable Pot Pie	⅓ cup	122

CAULIFLOWER		
Cauliflower Gratin	10 ounces florets	246
Thai Vegetable Green Curry with Jasmine Rice Cakes	6 ounces florets	134

COCONUT MILK, Light		
Glazed Caribbean Tofu with Rice and Pigeon Peas	¾ cup	137

COCONUT MILK, Regular		
Slow-Cooker Red Lentil Stew	¾ cup	214
Thai Vegetable Green Curry with Jasmine Rice Cakes	¾ cup	134

COCONUT MILK, Light or Regular		
Easy Coconut Kulfi	¾ cup	12
Filipino Chicken Adobo	¾ cup	13

EGGPLANT		
Soba Noodles with Roasted Eggplant and Sesame	1 pound	115
Vegetable Lasagna	8 ounces	105

FENNEL		
Fennel, Olive, and Goat Cheese Tarts	½ bulb	126
Pan-Roasted Chicken Breasts with Fennel and Parsnips	½ bulb	50
Vegetable Pot Pie	½ small bulb	122

FETA CHEESE		
Campanelle with Roasted Garlic, Shrimp, and Feta	1½ ounces	90
Greek Meatballs with Herbs and Feta	1 ounce	33
Grilled Spicy Shrimp Masala with Zucchini and Couscous Salad	2 ounces	167
Lentil Salad with Olives, Mint, and Feta	2 tablespoons	259

STOCKING THE COOKING-FOR-TWO KITCHEN

IN GENERAL, WHEN YOU'RE COOKING FOR TWO, you really don't need special equipment—the usual battery of pots, pans, knives, and tools will work just fine. (Although if your kitchen isn't stocked with smaller skillets—8- and 10-inch—or a small saucepan, you'll need them for certain recipes in this book.) But for some scaled-down entrées and desserts, we found we needed small baking dishes, pie plates, and more. Even a small slow cooker came in handy for our scaled-down slow-cooked recipes (but note that a large slow cooker works fine for the recipes in this book). Fortunately, this equipment is inexpensive and widely available both online and at many retail stores. Plus, when it comes to things like ramekins and small pie plates, you'll never need more than two (and sometimes just one will suffice). Here's a list of the cookware we found most useful for the recipes in this book.

SMALL BAKING DISHES

A small baking dish, such as this 8½ by 5½-inch ceramic dish (with straight sides no higher than 2 inches to expose the surface of the food), came in handy when we wanted to scale down our Cauliflower Gratin (page 246) and Tomato Gratin (page 248). We also use it to roast the garlic for our Campanelle with Roasted Garlic, Shrimp, and Feta (page 90). For our Smoky Sausage and Polenta Bake (page 199) and Peach Melba Crisp (page 274), we reached for an even smaller 3-cup baking dish (measuring approximately 7¼ by 5¼ inches). Note that dishes of a comparable size or of a different material can be used in place of these dishes.

GRATIN DISHES

To make two servings of our Tortellini Gratin with Fire-Roasted Tomatoes (page 205), we needed a pair of 2-cup gratin dishes (measuring approximately 9 by 6 inches), although dishes of comparable size work, too.

RAMEKINS

Ramekins, in various sizes, are handy for making scaled-down desserts and savory dishes. We found that 4-ounce ramekins gave us two indulgent Crème Caramels (page 281), while a pair of 6-ounce ramekins were perfect for our petite but rich Individual Chocolate Fudge Cakes (page 284). Two 12-ounce ramekins were ideal for our mini Vegetable Pot Pie (page 122).

SMALL SLOW COOKER

For our slow-cooker suppers for two, such as Slow-Cooker Black Bean Soup (page 215) and Slow-Cooker Smothered Steak (page 231), we found a 3- to 3½-quart oval slow cooker easier to maneuver and clean and less space-hogging than the standard 6-quart slow cookers (but the recipes in this book will work equally well with either size).

LOAF PANS

We use both traditional loaf pans (either 8- or 9-inch) and mini loaf pans (which measure approximately 5½ by 3 inches) in the for-two kitchen. We reach for the larger loaf pan for small casseroles, such as our Vegetable Lasagna (page 105). The mini loaf pans are ideal for scaled-down baked goods, such as our Cream Cheese Pound Cake (page 276).

SMALL CAKE PAN

With a 6-inch round cake pan, you can make a perfectly sized coffee cake for two people (see our Cinnamon Streusel Coffee Cake on page 266).

SMALL PIE PLATE

For both sweet and savory pies, we rely on 6-inch pie plates. Our Chicken and Cheese Quesadilla Pies (page 194) call for a pair of these dishes for two servings, but our Banana Cream Pie (page 279) requires just one for a perfectly scaled-down dessert.

PRIME RIB FOR TWO

CHAPTER 1

THE MAIN COURSE

WEEKNIGHT ROAST CHICKEN

✓ **WHY THIS RECIPE WORKS:** To get a beautifully browned, perfectly roasted chicken on the table for two any night of the week, we skipped the brining and the V-rack. Instead we roasted a small chicken, thigh side down, on a preheated skillet. This gave the longer-cooking dark meat a head start so both thighs and breasts cooked through in sync. Starting with a hot oven to crisp the skin, then turning it off to cook the breast meat gently through, gave us flawless results every time. While the chicken rested, we simply moved the skillet to the stovetop to turn the flavorful pan juices into a tasty sauce.

IF THERE'S ONE THING WE'VE LEARNED FROM YEARS of experience in the test kitchen, it's that the best way to guarantee a juicy, well-seasoned roast chicken is to brine or salt the bird before it hits the oven. The salt in both methods buffers the meat against overcooking by restructuring its proteins, enabling it to retain more of its natural juices. While we stand by these methods, they require an investment in time (at least 30 minutes for brining and as much as 24 hours for salting) and usually work best with large 5-pound chickens (out of the question for two). We loved the idea of creating a foolproof method for roast chicken that not only worked for smaller chickens but also was fast and easy enough for a Wednesday night dinner.

We figured that the best approach would be to modify our standard method for roasting chicken, which calls for submerging the bird in a salt-sugar brine (the sugar encourages good browning) for an hour, brushing it with melted butter, and roasting it in a 375-degree oven on a V-rack, flipping the chicken periodically to get the skin crisp and browned on all sides. We would call for a 3-pound chicken (just enough for two), skip the brine, and then put every other step under the microscope—from the roasting pan, to the V-rack, to the oven temperature, to whether or not to flip.

We started our testing by eliminating the V-rack. This piece of equipment elevates the bird so the oven's heat can circulate evenly around it and the skin can get crisp and browned. We definitely wanted crisp skin, but we also knew that we could use the hot surface of the roasting pan to our advantage. If we preheated the pan and added the chicken breast side up, the thighs would get a jump start on cooking, much as they would if we seared them first in a skillet. And skipping the V-rack would mean we'd also get to skip flipping the bird (placing the breast directly on the pan's hot surface would only dry out the lean meat). The pan-seared bird was surprisingly good; the thigh meat had a head start in the pan, giving us perfectly cooked dark meat before the light meat dried out, and we even shaved a few minutes off the cooking time. The V-rack and flipping were out; preheating the roasting pan was in.

Now what about oven temperature? Since the 375-degree oven wasn't doing the breast meat any favors, we reasoned our next move should be lowering the heat to cook that delicate meat more gently. We readied a few more birds and experimented with dropping the temperature down as far as 300 degrees, but the results were disappointing. Though the white meat became marginally juicier, the skin had gone from patchy brown to pale. Cranking the heat above 375 degrees improved the skin but, not surprisingly, reversed the slight gains we'd made with the juicier breast meat.

Perhaps we needed a two-temperature method: a high, hot oven to crisp the skin and a lower, cool oven to gently cook the white meat. It can be tricky to get a home oven to hit a targeted low temperature; what if we started the chicken at a relatively hot temperature (in a preheated pan) to brown the skin, then turned off the oven midway through cooking? We set the dial to 400 degrees, brushed the chicken with melted butter, seasoned it aggressively with salt and pepper, and lowered it into the hot pan breast side up so that the thighs would start cooking immediately. Then, after about 40 minutes, we shut off the heat and let the bird idle in the oven until both the breast and thigh meat hit their target temperatures, another 40 minutes or so later.

This latest bird was a huge success: Beneath the nicely tanned skin was white meat so tender and moist that even the dark meat loyalists among us were reaching for seconds. We were thrilled with the progress we'd made with the meat, but we wondered if we could brown the skin on the breast even more (and shorten our lengthy cooking time) by increasing the oven's heat. We tested temperatures up to 500 degrees; at 475 degrees and above, the oven filled with smoke, but we found a sweet spot at 450. This bird was ready to eat in under an hour, with beautifully dark amber skin and tender, juicy meat.

Still, all was not perfect. The higher heat forced more of the chicken's juices to evaporate, leaving us with less for a pan sauce. We reasoned that if we replaced the roasting pan with a 12-inch skillet, the juices would pool in the smaller space and evaporate less quickly. And as an added bonus, we'd be able to move the skillet straight from the oven to the stovetop to whip up a simple pan sauce. Next, we swapped the melted butter for olive oil, which, thanks to its higher smoke point, gave us equally good results with even less chance of burning. We also broke with our original recipe by trussing the legs. In the past, we have avoided this technique because tying the legs together can slow down the cooking of the inner thigh, but now that we were relying on carryover cooking, trussing could help keep the heat in.

The only item left on the checklist? Making good use of the pan drippings. We spooned out and discarded all but 1 tablespoon of the fat, making sure to leave the flavorful browned bits in the pan, and worked up a simple sauce with mustard, tarragon, and lemon juice.

As we pulled our crisp, golden brown chicken out of the oven, we looked at the clock—we had started cooking only an hour beforehand. Thanks to our faster, foolproof, dead-simple technique, roast chicken for two was back on the weeknight menu.

Weeknight Roast Chicken

SERVES 2

Cooking the chicken in a preheated skillet will ensure that the breast and thigh meat finish cooking at the same time.

CHICKEN

- 1 **tablespoon kosher salt**
- ½ **teaspoon pepper**
- 1 **(3- to 3½-pound) whole chicken, giblets discarded**
- 1 **tablespoon olive oil**

PAN SAUCE

- 1 **shallot, minced**
- 1 **cup low-sodium chicken broth**
- 2 **teaspoons Dijon mustard**
- 2 **tablespoons unsalted butter**
- 2 **teaspoons minced fresh tarragon**
- 2 **teaspoons lemon juice**
  Pepper

1. FOR THE CHICKEN: Adjust oven rack to middle position, place 12-inch ovensafe skillet on rack, and heat oven to 450 degrees. Combine salt and pepper in bowl. Pat chicken dry with paper towels. Rub entire surface with oil. Sprinkle evenly all over with salt mixture and rub in mixture with hands to coat evenly. Tie legs together with kitchen twine and tuck wingtips behind back.

2. Transfer chicken, breast side up, to preheated skillet in oven. Roast chicken until breast registers 120 degrees and thighs register 135 degrees, 25 to 35 minutes. Turn off oven and leave chicken in oven until breast registers 160 degrees and thighs register 175 degrees, 25 to 35 minutes. Transfer chicken to carving board and let rest, uncovered, for 20 minutes.

3. FOR THE PAN SAUCE: While chicken rests, remove all but 1 tablespoon fat from skillet (handle will be very hot) using large spoon, leaving any fond and jus

NOTES FROM THE TEST KITCHEN

HOW TO GET GREAT ROAST CHICKEN IN ONE HOUR
Our unique high-heat/no-heat method ensures crisp skin and super-moist breast meat.

1. Place empty 12-inch skillet in oven and preheat to ensure chicken with nicely browned, well-rendered skin.

2. Place chicken breast side up in preheated skillet to sear thighs, giving them head start on cooking with delicate breast meat. Cook chicken at 450 degrees until breast registers 120 degrees and thighs register 135 degrees.

3. Once chicken is cooked halfway, turn off oven and let chicken cook in gentle heat until breast registers 160 degrees and thighs register 175 degrees, 25 to 35 minutes longer. Transfer chicken to carving board to rest for 20 minutes.

in skillet. Place skillet over medium-high heat, add shallot, and cook until softened, about 2 minutes. Stir in broth and mustard, scraping up browned bits. Simmer until reduced to ¾ cup, about 3 minutes. Off heat, whisk in butter, tarragon, and lemon juice. Season with pepper to taste; cover and keep warm. Carve chicken and serve with pan sauce.

CHICKEN MARBELLA

✔ WHY THIS RECIPE WORKS: This Moroccan-inspired cookbook classic from the 1980s had potential—but needed an update. The chicken was braised in a sauce flavored with bold ingredients (prunes, olives, and capers), but the sauce never melded with the chicken. To make the dish more cohesive, we made a quick, flavorful paste that coated the chicken and brought the rich flavors into every bite. Instead of whole chickens or chicken parts, we used just two bone-in chicken breasts; the bones helped to insulate the meat and keep it moist. A pat of butter, a little red wine vinegar, and a sprinkling of parsley finished the sauce, bringing this flavor-packed dish up-to-date.

IN 1977, A GOURMET SHOP CALLED THE SILVER Palate opened on Manhattan's Upper West Side and introduced New Yorkers to their first bite of chicken Marbella. The original recipe, which was published in the shop's eponymous cookbook, was inspired by the bold flavors and slow cooking of northern Africa: Chicken breasts and legs were marinated overnight in a potent prune, olive, and caper sauce; transferred to shallow baking dishes; moistened with white wine; topped with a cup of brown sugar; and baked (with frequent basting) in a 350-degree oven for about an hour.

When we made this modern classic in the test kitchen, it was easy to see why its unique balance of flavors has made it such an enduring hit. But there were also a number of problems. While the chicken was juicy, its flavor was very subtle. The skin remained pale and flabby, and the sauce, though well seasoned, was too sweet. On top of these issues, the recipe made

enough to serve a large party. But we knew that this essentially simple dish of richly flavored baked chicken breasts was a perfect candidate for scaling down for just two. Along with the scaling, we would need to update and simplify the recipe to make Marbella a weeknight staple.

To make the dish work for two, we decided to start with two bone-in chicken breasts and make a sauce of (mostly) pantry staples: olive oil, red wine vinegar, olives, prunes, garlic, capers, oregano, bay leaves, and plenty of salt and pepper. We also decided to skip the overnight marinade. We've found that regardless of how long a marinade remains in contact with meat, its flavor never penetrates more than a few millimeters into the flesh. What's more, an excess of acidic marinade ingredients can actually overtenderize meat, making its surface mushy. And the lengthy soak waterlogs poultry skin, inhibiting rendering and browning.

Instead of marinating, we tried salting the chicken before cooking. This method worked well for getting juicy, well-seasoned breast meat, but it took at least 6 hours to have an impact (with better results after 24 hours). Reluctantly, we scratched salting off of our list and turned our attention to the cooking method, hoping to find an alternative path to moist, flavorful meat.

Perhaps we could sear the chicken before baking to jump-start browning, then build a sauce from the fond. We seasoned our chicken breasts with salt and pepper and placed them, skin side down, in a smoking-hot 10-inch skillet. Once the skin turned golden, we flipped the parts over, transferred them to a small, shallow baking dish, and began building the sauce in the empty skillet. We browned our sauce components in olive oil, deglazed the skillet with white wine, poured the sauce around the chicken, and transferred everything to a 400-degree oven, leaving the skin on top of the chicken exposed. In the hope of allowing the skin to continue browning, we scrapped the brown sugar coating and didn't baste, since moist skin doesn't brown well.

 The good news was that the sauce was more flavorful, albeit still a little thin. But despite our efforts, the chicken skin hadn't rendered or colored much more than it had after the initial browning. We realized the problem: The straight sides of the baking dish were

CHICKEN MARBELLA

trapping moisture. Could we take further advantage of our skillet's shallow walls and cook the chicken through right in the pan? We gave it a shot, returning the seared chicken to the skillet after building the sauce and then placing the skillet in the oven to finish cooking in the oven's even heat. Sure enough, the skillet's low, flared sides allowed more steam to escape, resulting in well-browned skin and a more concentrated sauce. Finally we were getting somewhere.

But there was still more work to do. Tasters complained that none of the sauce's flavor had transferred to the chicken. Perhaps a more concentrated sauce was the answer. We ramped up the amount of olives, capers, prunes, and garlic, and to boost meatiness and complexity, we added minced anchovies and a pinch of pepper flakes. These changes helped the sauce, but its flavors still hadn't merged with the chicken. While mulling over how we could get the flavor to "stick" to the chicken, we hit on the solution: We'd make a paste that would literally adhere to the skin.

We prepped another batch, pureeing half of the prunes and olives with garlic, capers, anchovy, oregano, pepper flakes, and olive oil. After searing the chicken, we spread an even layer of paste on each piece before transferring the skillet to the oven. Things looked promising during the first half of cooking, but by the time the meat was cooked through, the paste was charred and the skin was, once again, flabby. The only upside was that the chicken tasted juicier than it had in previous batches. Could we keep this benefit without suffering the shortcomings of the paste? For the next test, we waited until the chicken was about half-cooked and the skin crisp before adding the paste. After another 10 minutes in the oven, the paste had caramelized and the flavors had bloomed, making this the best-tasting chicken yet.

Wondering if we could use the paste to deepen the flavor of the sauce as well, we caramelized some of the paste in the skillet after browning the chicken. Just as we had hoped, the sauce was deeply flavorful and had a velvety texture thanks to the pureed prunes. A last-minute pat of butter, a splash of red wine vinegar, and a sprinkle of fresh parsley pulled everything into balance. With these changes, we agreed that we'd made a good dish even better—and a unique weeknight meal perfect for two.

Chicken Marbella

SERVES 2

Be sure not to overseason the chicken; this dish can easily become too salty.

PASTE

- ¼ cup pitted green olives, rinsed
- ¼ cup pitted prunes
- 2 tablespoons extra-virgin olive oil
- 2 garlic cloves, peeled
- 1 tablespoon capers, rinsed
- 1 anchovy fillet, rinsed
- ¼ teaspoon dried oregano
- ¼ teaspoon pepper
- ⅛ teaspoon kosher salt
- Pinch red pepper flakes

CHICKEN

- 2 (12-ounce) bone-in split chicken breasts, trimmed
- Kosher salt and pepper
- 2 teaspoons olive oil
- ½ cup low-sodium chicken broth
- ¼ cup white wine
- ¼ cup pitted green olives, rinsed and halved
- 2 teaspoons capers, rinsed
- 1 bay leaf
- ¼ cup pitted prunes, chopped coarse
- 1 tablespoon unsalted butter
- ¾ teaspoon red wine vinegar
- 1 tablespoon minced fresh parsley

1. FOR THE PASTE: Adjust oven rack to middle position and heat oven to 400 degrees. Pulse all ingredients in food processor until mostly smooth, about 30 pulses, scraping down bowl every few pulses. Transfer to bowl. (Paste can be refrigerated for up to 24 hours.)

2. FOR THE CHICKEN: Pat chicken dry with paper towels. Sprinkle chicken breasts with ¾ teaspoon salt and season with pepper.

3. Heat oil in 10-inch ovensafe skillet over medium-high heat until just smoking. Add chicken, skin side down, and cook without moving until well browned, 5 to 8 minutes. Transfer chicken to large plate. Drain off all but 1 teaspoon fat from skillet and return to medium-low heat.

4. Add ⅓ cup paste to skillet and cook, stirring constantly, until fragrant and fond forms on bottom of pan, 1 to 2 minutes. Stir in broth, wine, olives, capers, and bay leaf, scraping up any browned bits. Return chicken to pan, skin side up (skin should be above surface of liquid), transfer to oven, and roast, uncovered, for 15 minutes.

5. Remove skillet from oven and use back of spoon to spread remaining paste evenly over chicken breasts; sprinkle prunes around chicken. Continue to roast until paste begins to brown and chicken registers 160 degrees, 7 to 12 minutes longer.

6. Transfer chicken to serving platter and tent loosely with aluminum foil. Remove bay leaf from sauce and whisk in butter, vinegar, and 1½ teaspoons parsley; season with salt and pepper to taste. Pour sauce around chicken, sprinkle with remaining 1½ teaspoons parsley, and serve.

NOTES FROM THE TEST KITCHEN

OUR FAVORITE TRADITIONAL SKILLET

We use our skillets all the time, for everything from searing steaks to braising chicken to cooking pasta. While nonstick skillets can be purchased at a reasonable price, traditional skillets cost anywhere from $30 to $150 or more. Preliminary tests of traditional skillets confirmed our suspicion that cheap was not the way to go, but how much do you really need to spend? We tested eight pans from well-known manufacturers. All of the pans we tested had flared sides, and most had uncoated stainless steel cooking surfaces, which we prize for promoting fond (the browned, sticky bits that cling to the bottom of the pan when food is sautéed and help flavor sauces).

We concluded that medium-weight pans (not too heavy and not too light) are ideal—they brown food beautifully and are easy to handle. These pans have enough heft for heat retention and structural integrity, but not so much that they are difficult to manipulate. For its combination of excellent performance, optimum weight and balance, and overall ease of use, the **All-Clad Stainless Steel Fry Pan**, which comes in 8-inch ($90), 10-inch ($105), and 12-inch ($140) sizes, was the hands-down winner.

FILIPINO CHICKEN ADOBO

✓ **WHY THIS RECIPE WORKS:** *Filipino adobo* is a quick-cooking braise with bold, tangy flavors and tender meat. To perfect our recipe, we needed a way to tone down the tartness of the traditional soy sauce and vinegar braise. Creamy coconut milk worked perfectly to balance the flavors and add richness to the sauce. For chicken that was moist and well seasoned but not mealy, we marinated it in soy sauce—just 30 minutes in the salty liquid gave us tender, flavorful meat. Braising the thighs didn't expose them to enough heat to render their fat, making the final dish greasy, so we added the chicken to a cold skillet, then slowly turned up the heat until the fat had rendered and the skin was crisp.

ADOBO MAY BE CONSIDERED THE NATIONAL DISH OF the Philippines, but thanks to the country's melting-pot ancestry, the formulas for making it are remarkably varied. The core concept is meat marinated and braised in vinegar and soy sauce, with lots of garlic, bay leaves, and black pepper. Everything from that point on, from vinegar and protein choice to the inclusion of coconut milk, is open to interpretation. Recipes do agree on a few counts, though: This dish is easy to prepare, and the finished product—tender meat napped in a reduction of the tangy braising liquid—boasts bold, well-developed flavors. The vibrant flavors and simple procedure made adobo perfect for a cooking-for-two makeover.

We armed ourselves with Filipino cookbooks and tried a bunch of recipes based on chicken, our protein of choice. These dishes were predictably varied, but unfortunately all were problematic, with unbalanced, aggressively tart and salty sauces that were too runny to cling to the meat. Most troubling of all was the meat itself, which more often than not sported a tough, mealy outer layer.

Using the best elements of our research recipes, we built a working formula using bone-in, skin-on chicken thighs. With more fat and collagen than breasts and more meat on the bone than drumsticks, thighs are rich, flavorful, and particularly well suited to braising, and two thighs per person made a perfect dinner portion. We picked cider vinegar for its round, fruity flavor; marinated for a reasonable 30 minutes (some recipes called for marinades as long as 24 hours); braised the chicken in the marinade for about 40 minutes; removed the meat to rest; and reduced the braising liquid until it had thickened slightly into a sauce.

We weren't surprised when tasters panned the adobo as too tart; we'd worry about evening out the flavors later. It was the tough, mealy texture of the meat that was more troubling. While we know that soaking meat in moderately acidic marinades makes the meat's surface mushy, strongly acidic mixtures like this one cause surface proteins to bind together and squeeze out moisture, drying out and toughening the meat's exterior.

USE IT UP: COCONUT MILK

Easy Coconut Kulfi
SERVES 2

Kulfi is a cardamom-spiced frozen dessert similar to ice cream—but you don't need an ice cream maker to make it. The kulfi made with cream will be richer and less icy, and the kulfi made with half-and-half will be similar to a granita. The vodka is crucial to maintaining a scoopable texture; do not omit it.

¾ **cup coconut milk or light coconut milk**
¾ **cup heavy cream or half-and-half**
⅓ **cup corn syrup**
1 **tablespoon vodka**
¼ **teaspoon lime zest**
¼ **teaspoon ground cardamom**
⅛ **teaspoon salt**

1. Whisk all ingredients together in medium bowl. Transfer to large bowl, cover with plastic wrap, and freeze until mixture begins to freeze around edges, 1½ to 2 hours.

2. Vigorously stir mixture until smooth and slightly frothy. Transfer to 2-cup container with tight-fitting lid and freeze until firm, 4 to 5 hours. To serve, scoop into individual bowls.

Instead of risking bland chicken by skipping the marinade altogether, we decided to strip it down to just the salty soy sauce, knowing that salt is one of the few marinade ingredients that actually makes its way to the interior of the meat. Sure enough, when we repeated the marinade test using only soy sauce, the flavor and tenderness of the meat improved radically. And as a boon to our plan for making this a weeknight dinner, thighs marinated for only 30 minutes were just as good as those that we'd left in the soy bath for much longer.

But the tartness of the sauce was still way off base, and it lacked enough body to cling to the meat. We tried diluting the braising liquid with water to tame the tartness, but this test was a bust; rather than balancing out the acidity, the water merely dulled the overall flavor of the dish. Instead, we turned to a common adobo ingredient we had yet to test: coconut milk. We'd shied away from the super-rich milk in our earlier tests, fearing that it would muddy the flavor of the braise, but perhaps its richness could work in our favor by taming the harsh acidity in our sauce.

We returned to the test kitchen and whisked some coconut milk into the braising liquid of our next batch. Tasters praised the balanced flavors and declared this the best adobo yet, save for one objection: The double dose of fat from the chicken skin and the coconut milk had rendered the sauce a little greasy. In addition, the chicken skin was too soft to grip the sauce.

Fortunately, the explanation behind both problems was obvious: Our one-step cooking method wasn't exposing the chicken to any high, dry heat, so there was no opportunity for the skin's gummy fat layer to render or for the skin to crisp. Easy fix, right? Just throw the thighs skin side down into a ripping-hot skillet for a few minutes before moving them into the braising liquid. Wrong. Sure, the skin looked crisp and nicely browned, but slicing below the surface revealed that the thick fat pad was still there. The chicken needed more time to render its fat.

For our next test, we started the chicken in a cold pan and slowly brought it up to medium-high heat. As the pan gradually grew hotter, the fat under the skin melted away before the exterior began to brown. In about 10 minutes the skin on our thighs was not only sheer but also gorgeously browned. Even better, we were able to remove several tablespoons of rendered fat from the pan. Greasiness problem solved. Finally, we employed one last trick to keep as much of the skin's crackly texture as possible. When we returned the chicken thighs to the skillet with the braising liquid, we started them skin side down to absorb flavor and then flipped them halfway through so that they finished skin side up to crisp.

Once the chicken cooked through, we briefly reduced the cooking liquid until it thickened. We poured the tangy, coconut milk–enriched sauce over the tender pieces of chicken, sprinkled on a handful of sliced scallion for color and freshness, and dug in, admiring how nicely these bold flavors had melded together—and how we'd finally created a version of adobo that we could proudly call our own.

Filipino Chicken Adobo

SERVES 2

Light coconut milk can be substituted for regular coconut milk. For more information on trimming chicken thighs, see page 15. Serve this dish over rice. See page 12 for a recipe to use up the leftover coconut milk.

- 4 (5- to 7-ounce) bone-in chicken thighs, trimmed
- 2 tablespoons soy sauce
- ¾ cup coconut milk
- ½ cup water
- ⅓ cup cider vinegar
- 4 garlic cloves, peeled
- 2 bay leaves
- 1 teaspoon pepper
- 1 scallion, sliced thin

1. Toss chicken with soy sauce in large bowl. Refrigerate for at least 30 minutes or up to 1 hour.

2. Remove chicken from soy sauce, allowing excess to drip back into bowl. Transfer chicken, skin side down, to 10-inch nonstick skillet; set aside soy sauce.

3. Place skillet over medium-high heat and cook until chicken skin is browned, 7 to 10 minutes. While chicken is browning, whisk coconut milk, water, vinegar, garlic, bay leaves, and pepper into soy sauce.

4. Transfer chicken to plate and discard fat in skillet. Return chicken to skillet skin side down, add coconut milk mixture, and bring to boil. Reduce heat to medium-low and simmer, uncovered, for 15 minutes. Flip chicken skin side up and continue to cook,

NOTES FROM THE TEST KITCHEN

BALANCING ACT

The two core components of Filipino adobo—vinegar and soy sauce—add up to a predictably sharp, salty braising liquid. To even out the acidity and salt, we took a cue from a regional variation and added coconut milk. The thick, rich milk mellows those harsher flavors while still allowing for plenty of tanginess. It also adds welcome body to the sauce.

SALTY AND SOUR
Soy sauce and vinegar are staples in Filipino adobo.

THICK AND CREAMY
We add coconut milk for body and richness.

THE BEST READY RICE

It doesn't get easier than precooked ready rice—just two minutes in the microwave and it's done. But we wanted to know if ready rice could deliver tasty results, so we tasted five national brands of white rice. Tasters preferred the long-grain samples, which were less sticky. Our two favorites were also both parboiled. This process steams rice kernels in their husks, which makes the grains firm and smooth. Our winner was the only brand to add salt and had the most fat, giving it a "buttery" taste. **Minute Ready to Serve White Rice** is fluffy and fast. Will we quit making rice the usual way? No, but it was a surprisingly close second choice in a taste-off; we'll definitely keep some in the pantry for busy weeknights.

uncovered, until chicken registers 175 degrees, 15 to 20 minutes longer. Transfer chicken to platter and tent loosely with aluminum foil.

5. Remove bay leaves. Return sauce to simmer and cook until slightly thickened and reduced to ¾ cup, about 2 minutes. Pour sauce over chicken, sprinkle with scallion, and serve.

QUICK BRAISED CHICKEN THIGHS WITH TOMATOES AND OLIVES

✔ **WHY THIS RECIPE WORKS:** To transform the classic French braise Chicken Provençal into a quick dinner for two, we started by ditching the whole chicken in favor of easy, quick-cooking chicken thighs. Browning the thighs for just 4 minutes gave us enough fond to build a richly flavored sauce without the chicken ending up dry and overdone after braising. For an intensely flavored tomato sauce with bright Provençal notes, we turned to canned diced tomatoes, white wine, lots of garlic, anchovy, briny niçoise olives, and aromatic herbes de Provence. The clean flavors of fresh parsley and lemon zest provided balance.

BRAISED CHICKEN WITH TOMATOES AND OLIVES IS a Provençal staple, representing the best of French peasant cooking. The chicken is meltingly tender, moist, and flavorful, napped in an aromatic, garlicky tomato sauce that is mopped up with a good loaf of crusty bread. Unfortunately, the dish usually requires a whole chicken and a whole afternoon of cooking. We knew this richly flavored dish was worth updating—could we streamline chicken Provençal to make it quick and easy enough for a weeknight dinner for two?

The chicken was our starting point. Most recipes we found consisted of browning a cut-up whole chicken; setting the chicken aside; sautéing some aromatic vegetables; deglazing the pot with white wine or dry vermouth; adding stock, tomatoes, olives, and herbs; and then simmering the chicken in the liquid until cooked through. Cutting a whole chicken into parts was out of the question for our two-person braise; we wanted an easy-prep, quick-cooking cut to facilitate our goal of a quick weeknight dinner. For this reason, we chose to work with boneless chicken thighs—they're quicker-cooking than bone-in thighs. And to cut the cooking time even further, we cut the thighs in half. We also wouldn't need to worry about taking the time to properly render the chicken skin, since the boneless cut comes with its skin removed—another step in the right direction.

We first addressed the browning step. While we know that browning before braising is a traditional technique, we wondered if we needed to brown the chicken at all since we were already doing away with the skin. We compared a batch of chicken well browned before braising to a batch simply seasoned before braising. We also threw in a batch of chicken browned lightly (for only 4 to 5 minutes) out of curiosity. We cooked each batch in a simple tomato-based braising liquid in a covered 10-inch skillet (just the right size for four thighs) for about 15 minutes or until they were cooked through.

As it turned out, the thin, small thighs didn't need a thorough browning; in fact, the well-browned thighs emerged from the braise a little dried out. The raw thighs lacked complexity, and the time saved by skipping the browning just wasn't worth the lost flavor. Our lightly browned thighs had great flavor, added a little fond to our skillet, and were still perfectly succulent by the end of the braise.

With our chicken perfectly cooked, we moved on to the sauce. Many recipes call for sautéing some onions after the chicken is browned and taken out of the pot. Tasters approved of the onion but commented that a modest amount of the onion's pungent flavor was enough to balance the sweetness of the tomatoes. Garlic is usually added next; we sautéed it briefly to bring out its flavor. To deglaze the pan, we relied on dry white wine. Both crushed and pureed canned tomatoes produced a thick, sweet, overbearing sauce reminiscent of bad Italian restaurant food. Canned diced tomatoes, though more promising, presented the opposite problem: Even when drained, they contain a fair amount of liquid, and the resulting sauce was too thin. Adding chicken broth rounded out the flavors, but the sauce was still thin. We added a few tablespoons of tomato paste to the diced tomatoes, and the texture improved dramatically. Stirring in a couple of teaspoons of flour with the tomato paste thickened it even more—now the sauce coated the chicken without overwhelming it. Reducing the braising liquid for just 2 minutes after removing the chicken from the pot perfected the sauce's consistency and intensified the flavors.

Whole niçoise olives appeared in nearly every recipe, and we liked their distinctive flavor. Though they're less authentic in this dish, kalamata olives are often easier to find, and we found that they made a good substitute. As for seasonings, herbes de Provence (a combination of dried lavender, marjoram, basil, fennel seeds, rosemary, sage, summer savory, and thyme) was a shoo-in. A sprinkling of fresh parsley added brightness to the dried herb mix. Inspired by a traditional recipe we found, we tried adding a teaspoon of minced anchovies before deglazing the pot. Although tasters could not identify the ingredient, everyone agreed that the sauce tasted richer and fuller. The final item on our list was lemon zest, a common and, as it turned out, welcome addition.

Our braised chicken dish now had all of the flavors of Provence but was ready to eat in record time. Inspired by our quick and easy method, we devised an earthy variation with porcini and shallots, giving our chicken dish an entirely different, but just as delicious, profile.

Quick Braised Chicken Thighs with Tomatoes and Olives

SERVES 2

Be sure to crumble any large pieces of rosemary in the herbes de Provence before adding it to the pot. Serve with mashed potatoes or polenta. See page 55 for a recipe to use up the leftover canned diced tomatoes.

- 4 (3-ounce) boneless, skinless chicken thighs, trimmed and halved
  Salt and pepper
- 1 tablespoon olive oil
- 1 small onion, chopped fine
- 1 teaspoon herbes de Provence
- 3 garlic cloves, minced
- 1 tablespoon tomato paste
- 2 teaspoons all-purpose flour
- 1 anchovy fillet, rinsed and minced
- ¾ cup low-sodium chicken broth
- ¼ cup dry white wine
- ½ cup canned diced tomatoes, drained
- ¼ cup pitted niçoise or kalamata olives, halved
- ½ teaspoon grated lemon zest
- 1 tablespoon minced fresh parsley

1. Pat chicken dry with paper towels and season with salt and pepper. Heat oil in 10-inch nonstick skillet over medium-high heat until just smoking. Brown chicken lightly on one side, about 4 minutes; transfer to plate.

2. Add onion and herbes de Provence to fat left in skillet and cook over medium heat until onion is softened, about 5 minutes. Stir in garlic, tomato paste, flour, and anchovy and cook until fragrant, about 30 seconds. Slowly whisk in broth and wine, scraping up any browned bits and smoothing out any lumps.

3. Add browned chicken with any accumulated juices and tomatoes, cover, and simmer gently until chicken is very tender, about 15 minutes. Transfer chicken to platter and tent loosely with aluminum foil.

4. Add olives and lemon zest to sauce, return to simmer, and cook until slightly thickened, about 2 minutes. Season with salt and pepper to taste. Pour sauce over chicken, sprinkle with parsley, and serve.

VARIATION

Quick Braised Chicken Thighs with Porcini and Shallots

Omit diced tomatoes, olives, and lemon zest. Add ½ ounce dried porcini mushrooms, rinsed and minced, to skillet along with onion in step 2. Add 4 shallots, peeled and quartered, to skillet with browned chicken in step 3.

NOTES FROM THE TEST KITCHEN

TRIMMING CHICKEN THIGHS

Trimming and removing excess fat from chicken thighs before adding them to the braising liquid reduces the amount of fat that can be rendered and helps to prevent the dish from becoming greasy.

Holding 1 hand on top of chicken thigh, trim off any excess fat with sharp knife.

FRENCH-STYLE POT-ROASTED PORK

FRENCH-STYLE POT-ROASTED PORK

✔ **WHY THIS RECIPE WORKS:** *Enchaud Périgourdin* is a French specialty that transforms lean pork loin into supremely tender and flavorful meat. We wanted to achieve the same result with pork tenderloin, which yields just the right amount for two. Butterflying the tenderloin gave us extra surface area for seasoning the pork with salt, a little sugar, and caramelized garlic. Roasting our pork at a low temperature ensured that the meat cooked gently and came out of the pot juicy and tender. And we used the rich jus from the pork along with some wine and apple to make a quick sauce that perfectly complemented our French-style pork.

FRENCH CUISINE IS WELL KNOWN FOR ITS MANY dishes featuring a lackluster cut of meat turned sumptuous and flavorful by surprisingly simple methods, but the one that impresses us most is *enchaud Périgourdin*. A specialty in the Périgord region of southwest France, it consists of a pork loin—one of the least promising cuts for slow cooking—thrown into a covered casserole with garlic to bake for several hours. You'd expect that a roast with so little fat or collagen to protect it would emerge from the pot dried out and tasteless. Instead, the finished meat is astonishingly moist and flavorful, with plenty of rich-tasting, viscous jus to drizzle on top. We'd recently developed a test kitchen recipe for this delicious roast pork loin, and we wanted to see if we could scale it back to work with the more size-appropriate pork tenderloin.

When developing our original recipe for pot-roasted pork using a loin, we encountered a problem common to cooking with American pork. The French method for pot-roasted pork relies on the fact that French pigs are bred to contain plenty of fat. American pigs, on the other hand, contain far less marbling, especially in the loin. To counter the leanness of the meat, we employed a couple of tricks: First, we butterflied the roast so that we could season it all the way to the center without taking the time to brine the meat. Second, we seared the roast on only the top and sides so that the bottom of the roast would not overcook while sitting on the hot surface of the pot. Finally, after testing a wide range of oven temperatures for cooking the roast, we landed on a low 225-degree oven. In this very low oven, the outer layers of the loin absorbed less heat (and consequently squeezed out less moisture) during the time it took the center to climb to 140 degrees. And not only was it far juicier than any of our previous attempts, but a small pool of concentrated jus had accumulated at the bottom of the pot.

We knew we'd want to make use of these tricks in our scaled-down version. If they worked on a larger, more finicky roast, they'd surely work on tenderloin. Butterflying the relatively skinny tenderloin was as simple as making one cut lengthwise through the roast and then using a meat pounder to ensure that the butterflied tenderloin was an even thickness. We gave the pork a liberal shake of salt and spread it with ¼ teaspoon of sugar and some sliced garlic caramelized in butter (we also tested both bacon fat and rendered salt-pork fat, but tasters preferred the subtle sweetness of butter). Next, we rolled up the seasoned tenderloin, tied it with a bit of kitchen twine, and sprinkled it with some herbes de Provence. We browned our tenderloin on just three sides, then cooked it in a covered saucepan (mimicking the original recipe's Dutch oven) in a 225-degree oven.

Now we just needed to build our sauce. Knowing that the sauce would be enriched with jus from the pork as it roasted gave us a head start. After we transferred the browned roast to a plate, we sautéed some apple and shallot in the saucepan. Then we deglazed the saucepan with white wine and added thyme and a bay leaf before returning the pork to the pot and moving it to the oven. After roasting, we let the pork rest while we finished the sauce with some chicken broth, a pat of butter for richness, and a handful of fresh parsley. This simple sauce was an easy inclusion in our scaled-down recipe. Once our pot-roasted tenderloin was ready for carving, we were pleased to find that this smaller roast was just as good as (and, thanks to the tenderloin, even a little more tender than) the original.

SERVES 2

We strongly prefer the flavor of natural pork in this recipe, but if enhanced pork (injected with a salt solution) is used, reduce the salt to ½ teaspoon (¼ teaspoon per side) in step 2. You will need a large ovensafe, heavy-bottomed saucepan for this recipe.

- **2 tablespoons unsalted butter, cut into 4 pieces**
- **4 garlic cloves, sliced thin**
- **1 (12-ounce) pork tenderloin, trimmed**
  Kosher salt and pepper
- **¼ teaspoon sugar**
- **¾ teaspoon herbes de Provence**
- **2 teaspoons vegetable oil**
- **½ Granny Smith apple, peeled, cored, and cut into ¼-inch pieces**
- **1 shallot, minced**
- **¼ cup water**
- **¼ cup dry white wine**
- **1 sprig fresh thyme**
- **1 bay leaf**
- **⅓ cup low-sodium chicken broth**
- **1 teaspoon minced fresh parsley**

1. Adjust oven rack to lower-middle position and heat oven to 225 degrees. Melt 2 pieces butter in 8-inch skillet over medium-low heat. Add half of garlic and cook, stirring frequently, until golden, 5 to 7 minutes. Transfer mixture to bowl and refrigerate.

2. Butterfly tenderloin by slicing lengthwise through side; do not cut through meat completely. Open tenderloin like book and place between 2 pieces of plastic wrap. Gently pound to even thickness. Sprinkle 1 teaspoon salt over both sides of tenderloin (½ teaspoon per side) and rub into pork until slightly tacky. Sprinkle sugar over inside of pork, then spread pork with cooled toasted garlic mixture. With shorter side facing you, roll pork away from you into tight cylinder and tie with kitchen twine at 1-inch intervals. Sprinkle tied pork evenly with herbes de Provence and season with pepper.

3. Heat oil in large ovensafe saucepan over medium heat until just smoking. Add pork, seam side up, and brown on top and sides (do not brown seam side, or bottom, of roast), about 5 minutes. Transfer pork to large plate.

4. Melt 1 piece butter in now-empty saucepan. Add apple, shallot, and ⅛ teaspoon salt. Cook, stirring frequently, until apple and shallot are softened and lightly browned, 5 to 7 minutes. Add water, scraping up any browned bits, and continue to cook until saucepan is dry and dark brown fond has formed on bottom, about 5 minutes longer. Stir in remaining sliced garlic and cook until fragrant, about 30 seconds. Stir in wine, thyme, and bay leaf and cook for 30 seconds, scraping up any browned bits. Return pork, seam side down, to saucepan; place large sheet of aluminum foil over saucepan and cover tightly with lid. Transfer saucepan to oven and cook until pork registers 140 degrees, 25 to 30 minutes.

NOTES FROM THE TEST KITCHEN

PREPARING THE PORK

1. Butterfly pork tenderloin by slicing lengthwise through side; do not cut completely through meat. Open tenderloin like book and place between 2 pieces of plastic wrap.

2. Using meat pounder, gently pound tenderloin into flat, even rectangle. Sprinkle pork with salt and sugar and spread garlic butter over surface of roast to enrich flavor of roast.

3. With short end facing you, roll tenderloin away from you into short, tight log.

4. Tie rolled tenderloin at 1-inch intervals so that the roast maintains its shape and cooks evenly.

5. Transfer pork to carving board, tent loosely with foil, and let rest for 10 minutes. While pork rests, remove thyme sprig and bay leaf from jus and discard. Add chicken broth and bring to brief simmer over medium-high heat. Off heat, whisk remaining 1 piece butter and parsley into sauce and season with salt and pepper to taste; cover to keep warm. Snip twine and slice pork into ½-inch-thick slices, adding any accumulated juices to sauce. Serve pork, passing sauce separately.

VARIATION

French-Style Pot-Roasted Pork with Port and Figs
Substitute ⅓ cup chopped dried figs for apple and ¼ cup port for white wine. Add 1 teaspoon balsamic vinegar to sauce with butter in step 5.

RED WINE–BRAISED PORK CHOPS

✔️ **WHY THIS RECIPE WORKS:** For juicy braised pork chops, we started with blade chops, which, like other braising cuts, have a good amount of fat and connective tissue. To prevent the chops from buckling when seared, we trimmed the excess fat, then, instead of ditching the trimmings, we seared them to build a flavorful fond. We deglazed the pot with red wine, then added chicken broth, onion, and the pork trimmings to the braise along with the chops. When the chops were perfectly tender, we reduced the braising liquid into a rich, glossy sauce, adding a little red wine vinegar and fresh parsley for brightness at the end.

WHEN WE THINK OF PORK CHOPS, WE THINK OF A simple, no-frills cut that's easy to buy in small quantities and that we can just toss into a hot skillet and have on the table in minutes. But lately we've been hearing talk of braised pork chops. The more we considered this option, the better it seemed. Not only did the slow, gentle approach of braising promise flavorful, tender chops, but we'd end up with a rich, glossy sauce. Braising seemed like a perfect way to dress up the simple, small-household-friendly pork chop.

Before fiddling with the cooking method, we had an important decision to make at the supermarket: exactly which type of pork chops to buy. Most of the recipes we found in our research called for center-cut loin chops, but we wondered if this was the best choice. There are actually four types of pork chops, each with varying levels of fat and connective tissue: blade, rib, center-cut, and sirloin. To test the cuts side by side, we brined a pair of each cut, patted them dry, and browned them in a large saucepan (the perfect size for two chops). Then we browned some aromatics garlic, thyme, and a bay leaf—and deglazed the pot with red wine to temper the meaty richness of the chops. Finally, we poured in chicken broth, covered the pot, and pushed it into a 275-degree oven to simmer for about 90 minutes.

Unfortunately, all but one of the cuts cooked up stringy and bland, officially disqualifying the center-cut, rib, and sirloin contenders from the running. But the blade chops were promising; they contain a good bit of marbling and connective tissue, both of which were breaking down during cooking, lending the meat flavor and juiciness. The drawback was that the chops buckled considerably during searing and, as a result, didn't take on much browning or supply much fond to the bottom of the pot. Without that foundation of flavor, the sauce was lackluster and the wine's contribution one-dimensional and a bit harsh. For the sake of both aesthetics and flavor, we had to figure out a way to keep the chops from curling.

We realized the problem was the connective tissue on the side of the chop; it was contracting like a rubber band as soon as the chop came in contact with the hot pan surface. What would happen if we trimmed away the offending portion of fat and connective tissue before searing? After making a few quick cuts, we placed a new batch of chops in the hot saucepan, where they stayed flat and took on an even layer of color. This was great news, we thought, until we took a peek at the bottom of the pot. Where we expected to find a thick, crusty layer of fond we found a few faint patches of browning. Where had all the fond gone? We glanced over to the cutting board and realized the real ingredient for fond was that pile of fatty scraps we were about to pitch into the trash.

That gave us an idea: Rather than toss the fatty trimmings, we chopped them into 1-inch pieces and seared them to generate fond. In less than 10 minutes, we had the most substantial layer of browning yet, thanks to the increased surface area of the smaller pieces. In fact, the fond was so impressive that we wondered if we needed to bother searing the chops themselves. One side-by-side test gave us our answer: The braise made with unseared chops was every bit as meaty as the seared batch. To take full advantage of the flavor of the fat trimmings, we left them in the pot during braising, where their rich fat would add to the meaty flavor and unctuousness of the sauce.

The fat trimmings offered one final benefit by helping to raise the pork chops out of the braising liquid. After searing the trimmings, sautéing the aromatics, deglazing the pan, and adding the broth, we nestled the chops on top of the chunks, where they rested well above the liquid line. When we pulled this batch out of the oven roughly 90 minutes later, the sauce was richer and more flavorful and the chops were noticeably juicier than when they'd cooked more thoroughly submerged in the liquid. Elevated out of the liquid, the chops were cooking at a lower temperature than the submerged chops, allowing them to produce more gelatin and retain more moisture than before. And just to ensure that they held on to every bit of their flavorful juices, we let the chops rest for 30 minutes before slicing into them, giving the juices ample time to redistribute throughout the meat.

Thanks to the trimmings and the aromatics, the braising liquid now had good meaty flavor, but a few tasters remarked that it could use body, further depth, and some brightness. Fixing the first problem was easy; we simply strained and defatted the liquid and reduced it for about five minutes. A pat of butter whisked in off

the heat added silkiness and viscosity. As for the latter critiques, we added brightness by stirring in a one-two punch of sugar and red wine vinegar. Then we tossed in a knob of crushed fresh ginger and a pinch of allspice, both of which lent this final batch a rich, spicy aroma and depth of flavor.

Just before serving, we added a final splash of vinegar and a handful of minced parsley, spooned the sauce over the tender, juicy chops, and knew we had finally done right by this classic technique.

Red Wine–Braised Pork Chops

SERVES 2

Look for chops with a small eye and a large amount of marbling, as these are the best suited to braising. The pork trimmings can be removed when straining the sauce in step 4 and served alongside the chops. (They taste great.) If the pork is enhanced (injected with a salt solution), do not brine in step 1, and season with salt after trimming the chops in step 2. You will need a large ovensafe, heavy-bottomed saucepan for this recipe.

  Salt and pepper
2 (10- to 12-ounce) bone-in pork blade chops,
  1 inch thick
1 teaspoon vegetable oil
1 onion, halved and sliced thin
3 sprigs fresh thyme plus ⅛ teaspoon minced
1 garlic clove, peeled
1 bay leaf
1 (¼-inch) piece ginger, peeled and crushed
  Pinch ground allspice
¼ cup red wine
1 tablespoon plus ¼ teaspoon red wine vinegar
1 teaspoon sugar
½ cup low-sodium chicken broth
1 tablespoon unsalted butter
2 teaspoons minced fresh parsley

1. Dissolve 3 tablespoons salt in 1½ quarts cold water in large container. Submerge pork chops in brine, cover, and refrigerate for 30 minutes to 1 hour.

2. Adjust oven rack to lower-middle position and heat oven to 275 degrees. Remove chops from brine and pat dry with paper towels. Trim off meat cap and any fat and cartilage opposite rib bones. Cut trimmings into

1-inch pieces. Heat oil in large ovensafe saucepan over medium-high heat until shimmering. Add trimmings and brown on all sides, 6 to 9 minutes.

3. Reduce heat to medium and add onion, thyme sprigs, garlic, bay leaf, ginger, and allspice. Cook, stirring occasionally, until onion is golden brown, 5 to 10 minutes. Stir in wine, 1 tablespoon vinegar, and sugar and cook, scraping up any browned bits, until mostly evaporated, 5 to 7 minutes. Add chicken broth, spread onion and pork trimmings into even layer, and bring to simmer. Arrange pork chops in single layer on top of pork trimmings.

4. Cover saucepan, transfer to oven, and cook until meat is tender, 1¼ to 1½ hours. Remove from oven and let chops rest in saucepan, covered, for 30 minutes. Transfer chops to serving platter and tent with aluminum foil. Strain braising liquid through fine-mesh strainer; discard solids. Transfer braising liquid to fat separator and let stand for 5 minutes.

5. Wipe out now-empty saucepan with wad of paper towels. Return defatted braising liquid to saucepan and cook over medium-high heat until reduced to ½ cup, 3 to 7 minutes. Off heat, whisk in butter, minced thyme, and remaining ¼ teaspoon vinegar. Season with salt and pepper to taste. Pour sauce over chops, sprinkle with parsley, and serve.

SMOKY INDOOR RIBS

✔ WHY THIS RECIPE WORKS: Smoked ribs take as much as a day in a smoker to become fall-off-the-bone tender. This low-and-slow method is effective, but it isn't very convenient when cooking for two, so we sought to move our ribs indoors. We braised the ribs in the oven until the meat was tender, then brushed them with a simple barbecue sauce and roasted them until they had a crusty exterior like the "bark" of real barbecue. But the ribs were light on smoky flavor. Adding liquid smoke and espresso powder to both our braising liquid and barbecue sauce and swapping regular paprika for smoked paprika in the sauce solved the problem. Now our indoor ribs boasted intense smokiness and depth and tasted as if they'd been in the smoker all day long.

PORK RIBS ARE A BARBECUE FAVORITE FOR A reason—they're a sweet, rich, and meaty finger food that is fun to eat and easily adaptable to taste. Recipes abound for ribs cooked every which way, from the grill to the oven to the slow cooker. But for the ultimate in barbecue ribs, we prefer the superior taste and texture of a long, slow smoke. The only problem with smoking ribs is that the time, effort, and equipment needed to do a proper job make them seem like a waste when cooking just enough for two. We didn't want to cut ribs from our cooking-for-two repertoire, so we decided to develop a recipe for cooking an authentic smoky rack indoors.

We gathered a representative sampling of recipes for indoor "smoked" ribs and got cooking. The recipes used three approaches to try to introduce smoke flavor: placing wood chips on the oven floor, rubbing the raw ribs with smoked paprika, and broiling a liquid smoke–enhanced barbecue sauce onto cooked ribs. Fail, fail, and fail. The chips never smoked, the rubs didn't add much, and the smoky sauce didn't get inside the meat. If we wanted deeply smoky, tender ribs with a sticky, saucy crust, we'd have to start from scratch.

First we tackled our rib choice. Pork ribs come in three distinct cuts: whole spareribs, baby backs, and St. Louis ribs. Spareribs are cut close to the belly of the pig; whole spareribs contain both the brisket bone and the surrounding meat. These huge cuts can weigh upward of 5 pounds—far too unwieldy for a two-person dinner. Baby back ribs are cut from the section of the rib cage closest to the backbone and tend to come in smaller cuts. However, baby backs are also fairly lean and have less meat per bone, so they aren't ideal for long, slow cooking. St. Louis ribs hit a happy medium. These ribs are cut from the same section as the whole spareribs, but they are sold with the brisket bone and surrounding meat already trimmed. They offer all of the flavor of whole spareribs, but without the extra trouble and bulk. We were easily able to find svelte 2½- to 3-pound racks of ribs—a substantial but not unreasonable size for two.

Knowing that rib meat takes quite a while to turn from tough to fall-off-the-bone tender, we decided to use a two-step cooking method for our two-person rack. We'd first braise the ribs in a simple sauce in the oven until the meat was tender, then brush the cooked ribs with a simple barbecue sauce and return them to the oven uncovered, continuing to baste the ribs with sauce as they cooked, to get a crusty exterior that approximated real barbecue "bark."

SMOKY INDOOR RIBS

Our cooking method worked perfectly for getting tender, meaty ribs, but we still needed to figure out how to get smoke flavor into the meat. Traditional barbecue relies on long exposure to wood smoke. In our initial testing, the wood chips we placed on the floor of the oven never got hot enough to start smoking. Perhaps we needed to crank up the heat? We increased the oven temperature as high as it would go and tested the chips on everything from preheated baking sheets to pizza stones, but none of the tests produced smoke. Even worse, the high oven temperature destroyed our ribs, turning them to stringy pork charcoal in less time than it took to cook up a barbecue sauce. Time to give up on the chips.

We'd already discovered that brushing a smoky sauce onto cooked ribs added only superficial smokiness. But what if we braised the ribs in a smoky liquid? We tested every smoky ingredient we could think of: chipotle powder, smoked paprika, liquid smoke, instant espresso powder, and Lapsang souchong tea. Except for a faint whiff in the liquid smoke batch, tasters detected no smoke, even after a full 1½ hours of simmering in the braising liquid. So we stuck with what (barely) worked and upped the liquid smoke from 1 teaspoon to 1 tablespoon. Now we were on to something. The ribs suddenly began to take on the flavor of the grill.

To up the smoke flavor even further, we mixed in some espresso powder; it hadn't done much on its own, but working in tandem with the liquid smoke, it helped deepen the smoky flavor. Next, we added both liquid smoke and espresso powder to our barbecue sauce to up the ante even further. Replacing the paprika in the sauce with smoked paprika contributed even more smoky depth.

These small-scale ribs now had such authentic smoky flavor that they could have fooled anyone into thinking they came straight off the grill.

NOTES FROM THE TEST KITCHEN

BRINGING THE SMOKER INSIDE

We halve the rib rack to fit it in a baking dish, then braise the ribs in a mixture of water, espresso powder, and liquid smoke. After 1½ hours, the ribs are ready to be slowly roasted with barbecue sauce for a caramelized "bark."

ALL ABOUT LIQUID SMOKE

We were among the many people who had always assumed that there must be some kind of synthetic chemical chicanery going on in the making of "liquid smoke" flavoring, but that's not the case. Liquid smoke is made by channeling smoke from smoldering chips through a condenser, which quickly cools the vapors, causing them to liquefy (just like the drops that form when you breathe on a piece of cold glass). The water-soluble flavor compounds in the smoke are trapped within this liquid, while the nonsoluble, carcinogenic tars and resins are removed by a series of filters, resulting in a clean, smoke-flavored liquid. When buying liquid smoke, be sure to avoid brands with additives such as salt, vinegar, and molasses. Our top-rated brand, **Wright's Liquid Smoke**, contains nothing but smoke and water.

Smoky Indoor Ribs

SERVES 2

Use liquid smoke that contains no salt or additional flavorings. Wright's All Natural Liquid Smoke is our favorite brand. Slicing the rack of ribs in half ensures that it fits perfectly in the baking dish.

RIBS

- 1 cup water
- 1 tablespoon instant espresso powder
- 1 tablespoon liquid smoke
- 1½ teaspoons salt
- 1 (2½- to 3-pound) rack pork spareribs, preferably St. Louis cut, trimmed, membrane removed, and rack cut in half

BARBECUE SAUCE

- 2 teaspoons vegetable oil
- 1 small onion, chopped fine
  Salt and pepper
- 1½ teaspoons smoked paprika
- ¾ cup low-sodium chicken broth
- ⅓ cup cider vinegar
- ⅓ cup dark corn syrup
- ⅓ cup ketchup
- ¼ cup molasses
- 1 tablespoon brown mustard
- 1½ teaspoons hot sauce
- 1½ teaspoons instant espresso powder
- ¼ teaspoon liquid smoke

1. FOR THE RIBS: Adjust oven rack to middle position and heat oven to 300 degrees. Bring water, espresso powder, liquid smoke, and salt to boil in small saucepan. Pour mixture into 13 by 9-inch baking dish. Place rib halves, meat side down, in liquid. Cover pan tightly with aluminum foil and bake for 1½ hours.

2. FOR THE BARBECUE SAUCE: Meanwhile, heat oil in medium saucepan over medium heat until shimmering. Add onion and ⅛ teaspoon salt and cook until softened, about 5 minutes. Stir in paprika and cook until fragrant, about 30 seconds. Add chicken broth, vinegar, corn syrup, ketchup, molasses, mustard, hot sauce, and espresso powder and simmer, stirring occasionally, until thickened and reduced to 1 cup, 20 to 25 minutes. Stir in liquid smoke and season with salt and pepper to taste. Let cool for 20 minutes. (Sauce can be refrigerated for up to 1 week.)

3. Reserve ¼ cup sauce for serving. Line rimmed baking sheet with foil and set wire rack inside. Remove ribs from baking dish and transfer, meat side up, to prepared wire rack; discard braising liquid. Brush both sides of ribs with sauce. Bake until tender and fork inserted into meat meets no resistance, about 1½ hours, brushing meat with sauce after 30 and 60 minutes of cooking. Tent ribs loosely with foil and let rest for 30 minutes. Slice meat between bones and serve with reserved sauce.

PRIME RIB FOR TWO

✔ **WHY THIS RECIPE WORKS:** When it comes to roast beef, prime rib is supreme. But even the smallest prime rib roast is too big for two, so we used bone-in rib steak. It's from the same juicy, tender rib section of the cow but is the perfect size for two. To get both the crusty, browned exterior and juicy, rosy interior of perfect prime rib, we seared the meat in a skillet, then moved it to a wire rack set in a rimmed baking sheet to cook through in a low oven. While the meat roasted, we used the skillet to make a quick jus with shallot, thyme, beef broth, and red wine. Finally, to approximate the big, rosy slices of prime rib, we sliced our rib steak on the bias.

JUICY, ULTRATENDER PRIME RIB IS THE ULTIMATE roast beef. Unfortunately, its steep price tag means that it's usually saved for large, festive dinners. But we think a dinner for two can be as special an occasion as any, so we set out to convert this lavish cut of beef into a luxurious but easy dinner for two.

We knew that even the smallest prime rib roast (this term refers to any roast that contains only the highly prized rib section of the cow) would be far too big for just two people. But we also knew that this cut could be divided into bone-in rib steaks (usually called rib-eye steaks) that are about 1½ inches thick and weigh around 1½ pounds each—perfect for two. You can sometimes find these thick-cut steaks in the meat case, but if not, you can request them at the supermarket meat counter.

But what's the best way to cook a cut of meat that looks like a steak but demands to be treated like a roast? Clearly, we needed to combine the two cooking techniques. After a few false starts, we got it right: We first seared the meat on the stovetop, then moved it to a low oven to gently cook through. The hybrid technique gave us just what we wanted: a roast with a crusty brown exterior and an interior that was juicy and rosy red from one edge to the other.

While the roast rested, we made the accompanying jus. We started with a little of the fat from the meat, then sautéed some shallot and added fragrant thyme. We wanted to include tomato paste for its rich, meaty tomato flavor, but we didn't want to have to open a whole can for a single teaspoon of paste. We scoured the pantry for a substitute that would give us similar tomato flavor—and hit upon ketchup. Sautéing the shallot and ketchup gave us plenty of flavorful fond; we just deglazed the pan with beef broth and red wine and our sauce was done.

Everything was ready, but when we plated it up, something was wrong. The cut is essentially a steak, so when you remove the bone, cut it in half, and serve it, each person gets just that—half a steak. The plate lacked that big, rosy slice of meat that distinguishes prime rib from other "lesser" cuts. The solution? Creative carving. We experimented with butterflying the steak, but this was tricky and the results weren't stellar. Next we tried cutting the meat in half on the bias; that didn't look right either. We finally succeeded by slicing the roast on the bias into four pieces. This technique gave us beautiful pieces of meat that showed off more of the rosy interior and presented like honest-to-goodness prime rib. We'd finally done it: We'd produced a delicious "prime rib" dinner fit for two.

Prime Rib for Two

SERVES 2

Be sure to brown the edges of the steak to render the fat. You can do this easily by using tongs to hold the steak on its side in the hot pan.

1 (1½-pound) bone-in rib-eye steak, 1½ inches thick
  Salt and pepper
1 tablespoon vegetable oil
2 tablespoons minced shallot
1 teaspoon ketchup
¼ teaspoon dried thyme
½ cup beef broth
¼ cup red wine

1. Adjust oven rack to lowest position and heat oven to 200 degrees. Pat steak dry with paper towels and season with salt and pepper.

2. Heat oil in 12-inch skillet over medium-high heat until just smoking. Brown steak all over, 10 to 12 minutes. Transfer steak to wire rack set in rimmed baking sheet. Roast until meat registers 120 to 125 degrees (for medium-rare), 25 to 30 minutes. Transfer steak to cutting board, tent loosely with aluminum foil, and let rest for 5 to 10 minutes.

3. Meanwhile, pour off all but 2 teaspoons fat from now-empty skillet. Add shallot and cook over medium heat until softened, about 1 minute. Stir in ketchup and thyme and cook until fragrant, about 30 seconds. Add broth and wine and simmer, scraping up any browned bits, until reduced to ⅓ cup, about 10 minutes. Carve bone from steak and cut steak on bias into four ½-inch-thick slices. Serve with jus.

MINUTE STEAKS WITH GARLIC-PARSLEY BUTTER

✔ **WHY THIS RECIPE WORKS:** Cubed steaks can be a delicious, easy, and inexpensive dinner, but they can also be tough, chewy, and bland if you don't cook them right. To eliminate any lingering toughness, we pounded the steaks to an even ¼-inch thickness. For an exceptionally crisp, browned crust, we dredged the steaks in flour and seared them in a hot skillet with plenty of oil. A simple herb butter flavored with garlic, parsley, and Worcestershire mixed with the steaks' juices to make a rich and flavorful sauce that belied their inexpensive price tag.

WANT A QUICK, INEXPENSIVE STEAK DINNER FOR TWO? Then minute steak is for you. Minute steaks, aka cube(d) steaks, are tough cuts from the rump or shoulder that usually require long, slow cooking to become palatable. To tenderize the steaks, butchers run them through the spiked rollers of cubing machines twice (at 90-degree angles) to produce ½-inch-thick steaks. Because of their thinness and reduced mass, they do cook quickly. But the recipes for minute steak that we tried gave us pale, rubbery, liver-y-tasting steaks that only Rin Tin Tin could love. Our goal was to produce well-browned, relatively tender minute steaks with great beefy flavor.

Working on flavor first, we started by marinating the steaks in a mixture the test kitchen has often used to boost beefy flavor: soy sauce, oil, and tomato paste. We've found that a marinade rich in sodium is necessary to season the meat—traditional marinades, which often rely on an acidic ingredient, typically flavor just the exterior of the meat. Our soy sauce marinade gave the steaks great flavor, but the moisture was a problem: Minute steaks cook so quickly (in about 5 minutes total) that in order to brown they needed to be absolutely dry when they hit the skillet. Even when we patted them dry after marinating, the textured surface of the steaks held on to the marinade for dear life, inhibiting browning and the flavor that comes with it. We decided to ditch the marinade and focus on browning for now.

Knowing that dry steaks, a hot pan, and plenty of oil were key, we carefully patted both sides of the steaks dry and seasoned them liberally while we heated a generous 2 tablespoons of vegetable oil in the skillet. To absorb even more moisture, we tried dredging a steak in flour, another in cornstarch, and a third in a combination of the two. The best crust formed on the steak that was dredged in plain flour. A few minutes in the skillet finally created the nicely browned, flavorful crust we were after, with meat that was cooked to a perfect medium-well (minute steak has a squishy texture if it's still pink).

We now had well-browned steaks, but they were bland. We knew we couldn't use a marinade without losing our crust, but these steaks needed a flavor boost. One taster suggested adding flavor by way of a steakhouse favorite: compound butter. This seemed like a step in the right direction. All we needed to do was mix softened butter with potent aromatics (parsley, garlic, and Worcestershire sauce were a great combo) and add the mixture to the steaks while they took their requisite 5-minute rest. The meat juices mixed with the melting butter to make a sauce that tasters greedily spooned up. No doubt about it: These steaks tasted good.

But they were still a tad tough. Perhaps meat tenderizer, another old-school butchery favorite, would help. We gave it a shot, hoping the steaks' textured surface would facilitate its tenderizing power. It did—to a fault. Our steaks had turned into a mushy mess.

Maybe we just needed to augment the cubing and vent our frustration with a meat pounder. We pounded the ½-inch steaks down to an even ¼-inch thickness, dredged and seared them, topped them with the herb butter, and then tasted the steaks side by side against unpounded steaks. Thanks to the pounding, which had broken up some of their tough muscle fibers, the thinner steaks were decidedly more tender than our earlier batches. Coated with garlic-parsley butter, these inexpensive steaks were tender and tasty enough to make tasters forget their tough beginnings. They may take a bit longer than a minute to cook, but they're a super-fast and easy option for a weeknight steak dinner for two.

NOTES FROM THE TEST KITCHEN

MAKING A BAD STEAK GOOD

1. Pound steaks to even ¼-inch thickness to tenderize and ensure even cooking.

2. For substantial crust, dredge steaks in flour. Cook in generous amount of oil for good browning.

3. Top steaks with assertively flavored compound butter to give them quick shot of flavor.

Minute Steaks with Garlic-Parsley Butter

SERVES 2

We like to serve these steaks with mashed potatoes.

- 1 tablespoon unsalted butter, softened
- 2 teaspoons minced fresh parsley
- 1 small garlic clove, minced
- ½ teaspoon Worcestershire sauce
  Salt and pepper
- ½ cup all-purpose flour
- 2 (6-ounce) beef cubed steaks
- 2 tablespoons vegetable oil

1. Combine butter, parsley, garlic, Worcestershire, and ⅛ teaspoon pepper in bowl; set aside. Place flour in shallow dish. Place steaks between 2 pieces of plastic wrap and pound to even ¼-inch thickness. Pat steaks dry with paper towels and season with salt and pepper.

2. Heat oil in 12-inch nonstick skillet over medium-high heat until just smoking. Coat steaks with flour, shaking to remove excess, and transfer to skillet. Cook until well browned on first side, about 3 minutes. Flip steaks and cook until browned on second side, 1 to 2 minutes longer. Transfer steaks to platter, top with seasoned butter, and serve.

ALL-AMERICAN MINI MEATLOAVES

✔ **WHY THIS RECIPE WORKS:** For a scaled-down but full-flavored take on this comfort-food classic, we started with tender meatloaf mix. Panko bread crumbs, milk, and an egg yolk helped to bind the mixture and added richness and moisture. Sautéed onion, garlic, Worcestershire sauce, mustard, and herbs mixed in with the meat gave us a flavorful loaf, and a classic sweet and tangy ketchup glaze pulled the flavors together. To keep things simple, we pressed the mixture into two free-form loaves by hand, browned them in a skillet, and cooked them through in the oven. Our mini loaves cooked through in no time and came out of the oven with nicely browned crusts.

A GREAT MEATLOAF IS ABOUT AS CLOSE AS YOU CAN get to the definition of down-home comfort food. But not all meatloaves are created equal, and the problems only multiply when the recipes are scaled down to serve two. Forget dry, crumbly meatloaves with gloppy, cloyingly sweet glazes and offbeat additions, such as canned pineapple, cranberry sauce, raisins, prepared taco mix, and even goat cheese. We wanted to make a classic meatloaf like the ones our mothers used to serve—without having leftovers for days.

For the recipe's ingredients, we were set on sticking with the tried and true. To determine which ground meat or mix of meats makes the best loaf, we followed a very basic meatloaf recipe and made loaves using ground beef chuck, pork, veal, bacon, and ham in numerous proportions and combinations. It turned out that premixed meatloaf mix (beef, pork, and veal, usually in equal proportions) worked best; meat markets haven't been selling it all these years for nothing. Not only did buying the mix keep things simple, but the loaves made with it were well balanced, tender, and nicely textured. If you can't get your hands on meatloaf mix, a combination of equal amounts of 90 percent lean ground beef and ground pork also worked well.

When it came to the filling, we again went through the gamut of options, including bread crumbs, oatmeal, and an array of cereals. In the end, we preferred panko bread crumbs for their mild flavor; they melted into the background of our loaves, whereas the oatmeal and cereals added odd flavors. For the binding, just 3 tablespoons of milk and a single egg yolk were enough to help bind together the meat and add richness, moisture, and tenderness. We also tried adding tomato sauce to the mixture, but it just made the loaves taste like meatballs with sauce. While we liked the tangy-sweet flavor ketchup added to the meat, we ultimately decided to save it for our glaze. After trying out numerous other classic additions, we settled on sautéed onion, garlic, Worcestershire sauce, Dijon mustard, thyme, and fresh parsley as the best combination.

Once we had cooked the onion, garlic, and thyme in our skillet, we combined all the ingredients in a bowl and set out to shape the loaf. Instead of making a single meatloaf, we thought individual loaves would be a nice twist for our classic components. In addition, smaller loaves would cook faster, allowing us to get dinner on the table in less time. To avoid the need for an odd size of loaf pan, we simply pressed the mixture into two free-form loaves with our hands. The binders worked well to keep the loaves from falling apart while cooking.

We first tried cooking our mini meatloaves on a baking sheet, but the meatloaf drippings burned on the large sheet. Our mini meatloaves would need a mini cooking vessel. An 8-inch baking dish fit the loaves comfortably, but the excess moisture retained by the high sides turned our loaves soggy. Instead, we found our answer in a low-sided but cozy 10-inch nonstick skillet. Using a skillet also made it easy to sear the loaves before moving them to the oven, significantly shortening the cooking time (to just 20 to 30 minutes total) while also developing the nicely browned crust that is the hallmark of any respectable meatloaf.

To get the familiar sweet and tangy glazed top crust, we made a ketchup–brown sugar mixture and added a few teaspoons of cider vinegar for tang and to keep the glaze from becoming overly sweet. After searing, we brushed the glaze on our loaves and slipped them into the oven to roast at 350 degrees. These meatloaves had great flavor and were made in short order; tasters were surprised by how much they tasted like the down-home classic.

ALL-AMERICAN MINI MEATLOAVES

With a flawless traditional version nailed down, we felt compelled to come up with a variation that offered a little kick. We settled on meatloaves with Southwestern flavors, adding smoky chipotle chiles in adobo sauce and canned green chiles and swapping fresh cilantro for the parsley. Whether you're looking for classic meatloaf or something with a little more spice, these mini meatloaves are sure to satisfy.

All-American Mini Meatloaves

SERVES 2

Meatloaf mix is a combination of equal parts ground beef, pork, and veal and is available in most grocery stores. If you can't find meatloaf mix, substitute 8 ounces each of ground pork and 90 percent lean ground beef.

GLAZE

- ¼ **cup ketchup**
- 2 **tablespoons packed light brown sugar**
- 2 **teaspoons cider vinegar**

MEATLOAVES

- 4 **teaspoons vegetable oil**
- ⅓ **cup finely chopped onion**
- 1 **small garlic clove, minced**
- ¼ **teaspoon dried thyme**
- ½ **cup panko bread crumbs**
- ¼ **cup minced fresh parsley**
- 3 **tablespoons whole milk**
- 2 **tablespoons Worcestershire sauce**
- 1 **egg yolk**
- 1 **tablespoon Dijon mustard**
- ¼ **teaspoon salt**
- ¼ **teaspoon pepper**
- 1 **pound meatloaf mix**

1. FOR THE GLAZE: Whisk all ingredients together in bowl.

2. FOR THE MEATLOAVES: Adjust oven rack to middle position and heat oven to 350 degrees. Heat 2 teaspoons oil in 10-inch ovensafe nonstick skillet over medium heat until shimmering. Add onion and cook until softened, about 5 minutes. Stir in garlic and thyme and cook

until fragrant, about 30 seconds. Transfer mixture to large bowl. Wipe out skillet with wad of paper towels.

3. Stir panko, parsley, milk, Worcestershire, egg yolk, mustard, salt, and pepper into cooked onion mixture. Using hands, gently mix in meatloaf mix until thoroughly combined. Divide mixture into 2 equal portions and press each portion into small oval loaf.

4. Heat remaining 2 teaspoons oil in now-empty skillet over medium-high heat until just smoking. Carefully brown meatloaves well on first side, 2 to 3 minutes. Carefully flip meatloaves, neaten edges with spatula, and cook until lightly browned on second side, about 2 minutes.

5. Brush meatloaves with glaze and transfer skillet to oven. Bake until meatloaves register 160 degrees, 20 to 30 minutes. Transfer meatloaves to serving platter and let rest for 5 minutes before serving.

VARIATION

Southwestern Mini Meatloaves

Substitute ¼ cup minced fresh cilantro for parsley. Add 1 (4.5-ounce) can chopped green chiles, drained, to skillet along with garlic and thyme in step 2. Add 2 teaspoons minced chipotle chile in adobo sauce to meatloaf mixture in step 3.

NOTES FROM THE TEST KITCHEN

MAKING MINI MEATLOAVES

1. Divide meatloaf mixture into 2 portions. Cup each portion with your hands to form 2 oval loaves.

2. While browning second side of loaves in skillet, use spatula to tidy up edges so they maintain their oval shape.

OKLAHOMA FRIED ONION BURGERS

✔ **WHY THIS RECIPE WORKS:** This Oklahoma specialty features a thin patty of ground beef with a crispy crust of caramelized onion, cooked on a griddle until well-done. Topped with a buttery grilled bun, yellow mustard, and dill pickles, this burger is well worth a road trip. To re-create it for two, we used a mandoline to make quick work of slicing the onion very thin. To rid the onion of excess moisture, we salted it like cabbage for coleslaw, then squeezed it dry. We cooked the burgers' onion sides over medium heat until the onion was golden brown, then flipped the patties and turned up the heat until the burgers cooked through.

IF YOU SHOULD HAPPEN TO DRIVE TO EL RENO, a small Oklahoma town about 25 miles west of Oklahoma City, you'll find an unusual burger that's the object of much local adoration. The fried onion burger (or FOB, to locals) was born in the 1920s out of Depression-era necessity at the Hamburger Inn out on Route 66. By adding thinly sliced onions to beef patties, cooks could use less meat without reducing the portion size. But the onions don't just sit on top of this burger: They are pressed into the meat patty to become an integral part of it. And because the onions are pressed into the outside of the patty rather than mixed into the meat, they get nicely caramelized by the direct contact with the hot griddle, infusing the meat with their flavor.

Every May, thousands attend the Fried Onion Burger Day festival to view the assembly of an 800-pound FOB. Our quest was for something more modest: fried onion burgers with all the oomph of the oversize original, scaled down to serve two. We wanted to be able to make two well-browned fried onion burgers in a skillet with the proper integration of beef and onion.

We knew that slicing the onion very thin was key, so we used a mandoline set to about ⅛ inch. On a restaurant's heavy-duty griddle, the slices get hit instantly with intense, even heat that dries them out and browns them

in minutes. Not so on a home stove. Our thin slices oozed moisture and refused to adhere to the burgers— they practically repelled the meat. So we borrowed a trick that we've used to remove moisture from cabbage for coleslaw: salting. We sprinkled the onions with half a teaspoon of salt and let them sit for 30 minutes. The slices gave off lots of moisture, and squeezing them in a clean dish towel dried them further.

In El Reno, a patty is slapped onto the hot griddle, a heap of sliced onions is set on top, and the mashing process begins. But our attempts to replicate this in a skillet, even with just two burgers, proved futile: It was far too awkward to maneuver a spatula on top of the burgers around the sides of the skillet. To get around the smashing issue, we decided to assemble our burgers before they hit the pan. We divided our onion slices into two piles on a large plate. Next we topped the onion with ground beef, mashed the beef into the onion right on the plate, then formed the beef into 4-inch patties with the onion slices firmly embedded in one side.

Despite what you'd think from a town that cooks up an 800-pound celebration burger, fried onion burgers in El Reno are quite thin. We tried replicating their super-slim patties, but with just 2 ounces of beef per burger, tasters thought the burgers were too small for the effort they took. Instead, we went up to 3 ounces of beef per burger—just a little bit thicker than in Oklahoma. These burgers were still thin but were big enough to feel like a substantial meal. But when we tried cooking them in our super-hot skillet, the onions burned before the burgers could finish cooking.

We had better luck starting the burgers onion side down over medium heat so the onions could gently brown, then flipping the burgers and cranking the heat to get a good sear on the other side. As they do in El Reno, we cooked the burgers until well-done. A nonstick skillet prevented the onions from sticking, and using butter (plus a little oil so the butter wouldn't burn) for searing added extra succulence.

Served on a buttered, griddled bun with mustard, pickles, and American cheese (on the bottom, to keep the onion crust crisp), these moist burgers were delicious—and very hard to stop eating.

OKLAHOMA FRIED ONION BURGERS

SERVES 2

A mandoline makes quick work of slicing the onion thinly. It's crucial to squeeze the salted onion slices until they're as dry as possible, or they won't adhere to the patties. Make sure to season the burgers lightly with salt. These burgers are traditionally served with yellow mustard and slices of dill pickle.

- 1 onion, halved and sliced ⅛ inch thick (2 cups)
  Salt and pepper
- 6 ounces 85 percent lean ground beef
- 1 tablespoon unsalted butter, cut into 2 pieces and softened
- ½ teaspoon vegetable oil
- 2 slices American cheese
- 2 hamburger buns, toasted

1. Combine onion and ½ teaspoon salt in bowl and toss to combine. Transfer to colander and let sit for 30 minutes, tossing occasionally. Using tongs, transfer onion to clean dish towel, gather edges, and squeeze onion dry. Sprinkle with ¼ teaspoon pepper.

2. Divide onion mixture into 2 separate mounds on baking sheet. Form beef into 2 lightly packed balls and season lightly with salt and pepper. Place beef balls on top of onion mounds and flatten beef firmly so onion adheres and patties measure 4 inches in diameter.

3. Melt 1 piece butter and oil in 10-inch nonstick skillet over medium heat. Using spatula, transfer patties to skillet, onion side down, and cook until onion is deep golden brown and beginning to crisp around edges, 6 to 8 minutes. Flip burgers, increase heat to high, and cook until well browned on second side, about 2 minutes. Spread remaining butter on toasted bun tops and place 1 slice cheese on each bottom bun. Place burgers on buns and serve.

NOTES FROM THE TEST KITCHEN

KEYS TO FRIED ONION BURGERS
A few tricks helped the onion adhere to the burgers and caramelize rather than burn.

1. After salting and squeezing onion dry, divide into 2 piles, place beef rounds on top, and press.

2. Brown onion side down over gentler medium heat. Then flip burgers and turn up heat to sear beef side.

GREEK MEATBALLS

✔ **WHY THIS RECIPE WORKS:** To make delicious, savory meatballs the star of the show, we livened up their flavor with a Greek twist. Using yogurt in the binder added a nice tang, then we mixed in shallot, garlic, and mint and sprinkled rich, salty feta over the top. To help bind the meat and ensure the meatballs would stay moist, we added an egg yolk and a panade (a paste of dairy and bread). Since all of the meatballs easily fit in a skillet, pan frying was the simplest cooking method. In less than 10 minutes our easy meatballs were cooked through with a crunchy browned crust.

WHY DO MEATBALLS NEED TO BE SERVED WITH spaghetti and tomato sauce? Short answer: They don't. Well-prepared meatballs are a blank canvas for flavor. And since they're made from common pantry ingredients and ground beef (easy to buy in small amounts), they're a great option when cooking for two. For our two-person meatball recipe, we decided to explore Greek flavors, envisioning ground beef enlivened by bright fresh mint and briny feta cheese: a fresh-flavored simple main course to partner with orzo or rice. But first we'd need to suss out the proper method for our meatballs.

The problem with most meatballs is that they can turn out too dense and heavy. Often cooks think of meatballs as seasoned hamburgers formed into a smaller round shape. However, unlike most hamburgers, which are best cooked rare or medium-rare, meatballs are cooked through until well-done. At this point, the ground beef and seasoning will form dry, tough hockey pucks. If the meatballs are just compact, overcooked little hamburgers, the dish will be leaden. Meatballs require additional ingredients to keep them moist and lighten their texture.

We started out with a simple recipe for pan-fried meatballs using ground beef (we knew we wanted to use just one type of meat for our meatballs in order to keep things simple) and tested the various binders—egg, dried bread crumbs, fresh bread crumbs, ground crackers, and bread soaked in milk (panade)—that are common in meatball recipes. Off the bat, we knew we liked the presence of egg. Meatballs made without the egg were heavier and drier. But the meatball mixture was sticky and hard to handle. Since the fats and emulsifiers in the yolk were all that we needed, we tried using the yolk only. Problem solved. These meatballs were much less sticky and easier to handle.

As far as the bread element was concerned, we found that crumbs and crackers soaked up any available moisture and compounded the problems caused by cooking meatballs to the well-done stage. In comparison, the meatballs made with the soaked bread panade were moister, creamier, richer, and even more pâtélike in consistency. Two tablespoons of milk was plenty to soften one slice of sandwich bread; we simply had to make sure that the bread and milk mixture was smooth before incorporating it into the meatballs in order to avoid errant chunks of bread in the final product.

Our meatballs were now moist and luscious, but we wondered if we were missing out on an opportunity by using plain milk. Could we infuse a bit of Greek flavor right into our panade? We've seen meatloaf recipes in which plain yogurt is used as a binding ingredient in lieu of milk. Perhaps this could add a pleasant tang to our dish. Not only was the yogurt batch more flavorful than the batches made with milk, but due to the thickened consistency of the yogurt, these meatballs were even richer and creamier than those made with plain milk. Out of curiosity, we also tested the panade made with Greek-style yogurt, but we found that this yogurt was too thick to mix properly with the bread.

With the dairy and bread portion of the binder settled, we could focus on building up Greek flavor. Some shallot and a clove of garlic were givens, adding pleasant savory notes. For a bit of brightness, we added some minced fresh mint (we liked dill as well). For a last bit of richness, we knew we wanted to add cheese

and reached for feta. We tried incorporating the feta into the meatballs themselves, but the cheese took on a rubbery quality that seemed to undo all of the hard work we had done to keep our meatballs moist and creamy. We didn't want to toss the feta out completely, so we decided to sprinkle a generous ¼ cup over the meatballs upon serving.

With our ingredients in order, we then tested three cooking techniques: roasting, broiling, and traditional pan frying. We had high hopes for the oven method, as it seemed cleanest and the most hands-off. After 25 minutes at 450 degrees, the meatballs emerged from the oven nicely browned. But one bite revealed the problem with this method—the meatballs were dry and crumbly. Broiling proved messier than pan frying as the excess fat splattered in the heat of the oven, covering the oven with grease. Pan searing would be our method of choice.

We made the meatballs relatively small (1½ inches) so that they would cook through in the same amount of time it took to get a thorough browning on their exterior. A relatively quick sear in 3 tablespoons of oil proved perfect. The meatballs needed just a final sprinkling of mint and feta and they were ready to serve. With a silky smooth texture and bright, vibrant flavor, our Greek-style meatballs were now anything but boring and heavy.

Greek Meatballs with Herbs and Feta
SERVES 2

Do not use Greek-style yogurt here—it is too thick. Serve with orzo or rice and a fresh green salad.

- 1 slice hearty white sandwich bread, torn into pieces
- 2 tablespoons plain yogurt
- 1 egg yolk
- 1 shallot, minced
- 1 small garlic clove, minced
- 2 tablespoons minced fresh mint and/or dill
- ½ teaspoon salt
- ¼ teaspoon pepper
- 12 ounces 85 percent lean ground beef
- 3 tablespoons olive oil
- 1 ounce feta cheese, crumbled (¼ cup)

1. Mash bread with yogurt in large bowl until smooth. Stir egg yolk, shallot, garlic, 1 tablespoon mint, salt, and

KEEPING HERBS FRESH LONGER

We use a lot of fresh herbs in the test kitchen, so we know firsthand that their shelf life is short—a particular problem when you're cooking for two and using small quantities. To get the most life out of your herbs, gently rinse and dry them (a salad spinner works perfectly), and then loosely roll them in a few sheets of paper towels. Put the roll of herbs in a zipper-lock bag and place it in the crisper drawer of your refrigerator. Stored in this manner, your herbs will be fresh, washed, and ready to use for a week or longer. (Note that this method does not work with basil, which should be washed only when you're ready to use it.)

pepper into yogurt mixture. Using hands, gently mix in beef until thoroughly combined. Form mixture into twelve 1½-inch meatballs.

2. Heat oil in 10-inch nonstick skillet over medium-high heat until just smoking. Add meatballs and cook gently, shaking pan and turning meatballs with tongs, until browned on all sides and cooked through, about 7 minutes. Transfer meatballs to paper towel–lined plate to drain briefly, then transfer to serving platter. Sprinkle with feta and remaining 1 tablespoon mint and serve.

BRAISED BRISKET WITH MUSHROOMS

✓ WHY THIS RECIPE WORKS: Hearty braised brisket is perfect winter-weather fare, but most recipes make enough for an army. For tender, juicy brisket for just two, we started with 1½ pounds of flat-cut brisket. Piercing holes in the fat cap allowed the melting fat to baste the meat as it cooked. We seasoned the meat and browned it on just one side to avoid overcooking). Then we used the fond from the meat to build a flavorful braising liquid in the pot with onion, garlic, thyme, chicken broth, and red wine. To round out the dish and complement the brisket, we sautéed white mushrooms and added a little minced dried porcini for deep, earthy flavor. A splash of balsamic vinegar cut the richness of the beef and mushrooms for a perfectly balanced dish.

FOR MANY OF US IN THE TEST KITCHEN, BRAISED brisket is one of the best traditional cold-weather comfort foods. This homey dish is warm and hearty enough to satisfy even the biggest appetites on a snowy winter day. But when faced with the prospect of eating left-over brisket for days on end, those of us with small households balk at this massive cut of beef. When cooking for just two, a whole brisket simply does not make sense. Could we find a way to get a tender, juicy braised brisket in a petite package? We figured it was high time to find out.

First we needed to decide what size brisket would work best for our two-person recipe. Normally, we allow 6 to 8 ounces of boneless meat per person (working out to 12 ounces to 1 pound total for two), but we had a hunch that brisket would be a little different. Because brisket cooks for a few hours, it loses quite a bit of its weight by the time it's ready to eat. Knowing this, we asked the butcher to cut a fairly generous 1½-pound piece of flat-cut brisket (our preferred choice for braising), and we got to testing.

We started out with a trick we've discovered when working with larger briskets—piercing holes in the brisket's fat cap so that the rendering fat will drip down and moisten the meat. We proceeded with our standard braising method. We seasoned and browned the meat on all sides, set it aside, and started to build our braising liquid. We added chopped onion (with a little brown sugar for added caramelization), garlic, thyme, and a little flour for thickening. Then we whisked in ½ cup each of chicken broth and red wine and let the sauce simmer a bit to thicken. We cooked the meat and sauce in a tightly covered baking dish in a 300-degree oven until the brisket was tender (about 4 hours).

Once we pulled the brisket out of the oven, we knew that our decision to cook a slightly larger roast was right on. The meat had shrunk considerably, and we were left with two generous but not overwhelming servings. Unfortunately, the serving size was about the only success we had with this test. Not only was the bottom of the brisket hard and crusty, but the sauce had evaporated to an overreduced, salty paste. Our smaller brisket wasn't giving off nearly enough juice to keep the sauce saucy.

For our next test, we held off on browning the bottom of the brisket in hopes of keeping the meat tender and went up on both wine and chicken broth to a full cup of each. This time the brisket was tender and the consistency of the sauce was spot-on, but the flavor was still salty and harsh. The excess chicken broth and tannic wine were not helping the cause. We knew we wanted to keep some of both for flavor and depth but decided we needed to cut them with water. After tinkering with proportions, we landed on equal parts (⅓ cup) wine and broth as well as 2 cups of water. Now our sauce was in balance, but the dish itself still needed some improvement.

Tasters wanted a complementary earthy vegetable to accompany the brisket, and we knew we'd need to choose something that would hold up to long cooking. Mushrooms seemed like the perfect solution. Eight ounces of quartered white mushrooms bulked up the dish, but they didn't add remarkable mushroom flavor. Adding more fresh mushrooms made the dish unwieldy, so we turned to dried porcini for deeper flavor. We rinsed them to rehydrate them enough to mince, then stirred them into the sauce along with the garlic and thyme. That did it: We had deep, full, balanced mushroom flavor. A little balsamic vinegar was the perfect foil to the rich beef and mushrooms.

Last, but far from least, we addressed the serving issue. Brisket is always dry if you eat it right away. In our standard recipe, we cool the brisket in the pan juices for several hours to allow it to reabsorb them until the brisket is juicy and tender. But we weren't willing to wait that long for our two-person brisket. Happily, by flipping the roast over halfway through its resting period, we were able to cut this time down to only 30 minutes. To reheat the meat, we quickly warmed the sauce in the microwave, then we simply added the sliced meat to the warm sauce, and our brisket was ready for serving. Now we had a tender brisket packed with mushroom flavor that made for a comforting cold-weather meal perfect for two.

Braised Brisket with Mushrooms

SERVES 2

This might seem like a lot of meat for two servings, but it will cook down substantially in the oven. Flat-cut brisket is easier to find and more uniform in texture than point-cut. Try to find a brisket with an even fat cap. Small briskets can be cut to order at the butcher counter. Serve with mashed potatoes or buttered egg noodles.

1   (1½-pound) brisket roast, fat trimmed to ¼ inch
    Salt and pepper
2   teaspoons vegetable oil
1   onion, chopped fine
8   ounces white mushrooms, trimmed and quartered
1   teaspoon brown sugar
1   tablespoon all-purpose flour
⅛   ounce dried porcini mushrooms, rinsed
    and minced
1   garlic clove, minced
1   teaspoon minced fresh thyme or ⅛ teaspoon dried
⅓   cup dry red wine
2   cups water
⅓   cup low-sodium chicken broth
1   bay leaf
½   teaspoon balsamic vinegar

1. Adjust oven rack to middle position and heat oven to 300 degrees. Pat brisket dry with paper towels, then prick fat side of roast all over with fork. Season with salt and pepper.

2. Heat oil in 10-inch skillet over medium-high heat until just smoking. Place brisket fat side down in pan and cook until well browned on one side, 3 to 5 minutes. Transfer, fat side up, to 8-inch square baking dish.

3. Add onion, white mushrooms, and sugar to fat left in skillet, cover, and cook over medium-high heat until mushrooms have released their liquid, about 5 minutes. Uncover and continue to cook until dry and brown fond has formed on bottom of pan, 5 to 10 minutes longer. Stir in flour, porcini, garlic, and thyme and cook for 1 minute. Slowly whisk in wine, scraping up any browned bits and smoothing out any lumps.

4. Gradually whisk in water, chicken broth, and bay leaf and bring to brief boil over high heat. Pour sauce over roast and cover dish tightly with aluminum foil. Bake brisket until tender and fork inserted into meat meets no resistance, about 4 hours. Carefully skim any fat off surface of braising liquid and remove bay leaf. Let brisket rest in dish, uncovered, for 30 minutes, flipping it halfway through.

5. Transfer roast to carving board. Stir vinegar into sauce, cover, and microwave until hot, 1 to 2 minutes. Slice roast in half crosswise, then slice each half against grain into ¼-inch-thick slices. Return sliced beef to dish with mushrooms and sauce to warm through. Season with salt and pepper to taste and serve.

POACHED FISH FILLETS WITH CRISPY ARTICHOKES AND TOMATO-SHERRY VINAIGRETTE

POACHED FISH FILLETS WITH TOMATO-SHERRY VINAIGRETTE

✔ **WHY THIS RECIPE WORKS:** This restaurant-style dish promises super-moist, delicately cooked fish fillets poached in flavorful olive oil. To make this technique work for two, we used a small skillet and flipped the fish halfway through cooking to minimize the amount of olive oil needed. The oil also pulled triple duty: We used it to crisp artichokes and garlic for a garnish, poached the fish in it, and then blended the oil into a creamy vinaigrette for serving. To get the oil temperature just right, we first fried the garnish, then added more room-temperature oil to quickly cool the oil. After adding the fish, we moved the skillet to the even heat of the oven to keep the temperature steady. A final garnish of cherry tomatoes and parsley brightened up this elegant dish.

IF YOUR EXPERIENCE WITH POACHED FISH IS limited to the lean, bland preparation you might be served at a wedding or a weight-loss spa, a technique popular at high-end restaurants will permanently change your perception. At its most basic, poaching entails submerging fish in liquid and gently cooking it at below-simmer temperatures to render the delicate flesh silky and supple. But instead of using the usual water or broth, this restaurant technique uses olive oil as the poaching liquid.

We had to admit: On paper, cooking delicate fish fillets in a pot of fat sounds like a recipe for a greasy disaster, but when we tasted the results, we were stunned—the fish was lighter, moister, and more fragrant than any traditionally poached fish we'd ever tasted, explaining why this technique has become so popular in top restaurants. Another plus: The flavor-infused poaching oil can be whirled into a rich, glossy emulsion and drizzled over the fish as a sauce. The dish, we realized, would make an elegant two-person dinner.

Our first decision was to go with skinless fillets since the oil would never get hot enough to crisp the skin. We settled on cod for its firm, meaty flesh and clean flavor. As for the amount of oil, we reasoned that the smaller the surface area of the cooking vessel, the deeper the liquid would pool, so we reached past our trusty 12- and 10-inch nonstick skillets for their petite 8-inch sibling. Unfortunately, this setup demanded over 1½ cups of oil to cover the two 6-ounce fillets, which seemed like a waste of olive oil for a dinner for two. Clearly, we needed to find a more creative solution.

That's when we started to wonder if completely immersing the fillets in oil was necessary. The alternative—pouring enough oil into the pan to come roughly halfway up the sides of the fish (about ½ cup)—would mean flipping the fish partway through poaching to ensure that it cooked through. But that seemed a small price to pay for significantly cutting our oil dependence. We gave it a shot, basting the exposed half of each fillet with a few spoonfuls of oil to prevent evaporation, popping a lid on the pan, and placing the skillet over low heat.

This method gave us fillets that were supremely moist and tender. Unfortunately, the method was fussy. With relatively little oil in the pan, the temperature spiked quickly and required that we constantly fiddle with the burner knob to keep the oil in the right range (140 to 150 degrees) to slowly bring the fish to an internal temperature of 130 degrees. What we needed was a steadier, less direct heat source, and for that we turned to the oven.

We figured that we could simply bring the oil to 140 degrees on the stovetop, slip in the fish, and then transfer the skillet into a low oven. But it wasn't quite that easy; the oil temperature immediately plummeted when we added the cold fillets, and the temperature was slow to recover in the oven. But we had another idea: We'd heat the oil on the stovetop to well above our target temperature so that when we added the fillets, it would end up closer to the right temperature. Then we could rely on the oven's even heat to keep it in the poaching sweet spot.

After a slew of tests, we hit upon a winning combination: Heat the oil to 180 degrees, nestle in the seasoned fillets, and set the pan in a 250-degree oven. The oil temperature recovered within 15 minutes, by which point the lower half of the fish was cooked. We removed the fish from the oven, flipped the fillets, replaced the lid, and popped the skillet back into the oven. This batch emerged incredibly moist and velvety, and, thanks to the oven method, the process was now largely hands-off. What we had was good—but we wanted to make it even better.

Restaurants often garnish their oil-poached fillets with lightly fried vegetables and fresh herbs, and we reasoned that we could do the same by crisping a topping in the oil before cooking the fish. Artichoke hearts have always been a favorite of ours, so we defrosted a couple of ounces, patted them dry, and halved them lengthwise before tossing them with cornstarch (for extra crispness) and dropping them into the shimmering oil with some minced garlic.

Tasters loved the crisp garnish, but after cranking up the heat to fry them, we had to wait more than 10 minutes for the oil to cool to our target of 180 degrees. The solution proved easy: Rather than dump in all the oil at once, we fried the garnishes in ¼ cup of oil, strained it, and added the remaining ¼ cup of room-temperature oil to the pan to speed the cooling. This tweak made all the difference; about 3 minutes after frying, the oil was cool enough for poaching.

Frying up a garnish had also left us with an added bonus: flavor-infused oil to use in our sauce. We poured some into the blender and whirled it with whole cherry tomatoes (for bright sweetness), sherry vinegar, and salt and pepper. After a quick spin on high speed and a pass through a fine-mesh strainer, we had a silky-smooth, flavorful vinaigrette.

Dressed up with the sauce, the crispy artichoke garnish, a few slices of fresh cherry tomato, and a fistful of minced parsley, our elegant meal was complete—not to mention plenty simple to pull off at home.

NOTES FROM THE TEST KITCHEN

WHY POACH IN OIL?

Poaching in oil allows fish to retain more of its juices than poaching in wine or broth, leading to remarkably moist, velvety results. This is because cooking in oil is inherently more gentle than cooking in water. And while you might expect that fish poached in fat would be greasy, it actually absorbs very little oil. Why? In order for oil to penetrate the fish, moisture must exit first. But because oil and water repel each other, it's very difficult for moisture inside the fish to readily enter the oil. Hence, more of the juices stay in the fish. In fact, in our tests, oil-poached fish lost just 14 percent of its weight during cooking, while water-poached fillets lost 24 percent.

Poached Fish Fillets with Crispy Artichokes and Tomato-Sherry Vinaigrette

SERVES 2

Fillets of meaty white fish like cod, halibut, sea bass, or snapper work best in this recipe. Just make sure the fillets are at least 1 inch thick. A neutral oil such as canola can be substituted for the pure olive oil. Serve with couscous or steamed white rice.

FISH

- 2 (6-ounce) skinless white fish fillets, 1 inch thick
  Kosher salt
- 2 ounces frozen artichoke hearts, thawed, patted dry, and sliced in half lengthwise
- 2 teaspoons cornstarch
- ½ cup olive oil
- 2 garlic cloves, minced

VINAIGRETTE

- 3 ounces cherry tomatoes
- 1 tablespoon sherry vinegar
  Kosher salt and pepper

- 1 ounce cherry tomatoes, cut into ⅛-inch-thick rounds
- 1 teaspoon minced fresh parsley

1. FOR THE FISH: Adjust oven racks to middle and lower-middle positions and heat oven to 250 degrees. Pat fish dry with paper towels and season each fillet with ¼ teaspoon salt. Let sit at room temperature for 20 minutes.

2. Meanwhile, toss artichokes with cornstarch in bowl to coat. Heat ¼ cup oil in 8-inch nonstick oven-safe skillet over medium heat until shimmering. Shake excess cornstarch from artichokes and add to skillet; cook, stirring occasionally, until crisp and golden, 2 to 4 minutes. Add garlic and continue to cook until garlic is golden, 30 to 60 seconds. Strain oil through fine-mesh strainer into bowl. Transfer artichokes and garlic to paper towel–lined ovenproof plate and season with salt. Do not wash strainer.

3. Return strained oil to skillet and add remaining ¼ cup oil. Let oil cool until it registers about 180 degrees, about 3 minutes. Place fish fillets, skinned side up, in skillet (oil should come roughly halfway up sides of fillets). Spoon some oil over each fillet, cover skillet, transfer to middle oven rack, and cook for 15 minutes.

4. Remove skillet from oven. Using 2 spatulas, carefully flip fillets. Cover skillet, return to middle rack, and place plate with artichokes and garlic on lower-middle rack. Continue to cook fish until it registers 130 to 135 degrees, 9 to 14 minutes longer. Gently transfer fish to serving platter, reserving ⅓ cup cooking oil, and tent fish loosely with aluminum foil. Turn off oven, leaving plate of artichokes in oven.

5. FOR THE VINAIGRETTE: Process cherry tomatoes, vinegar, ¼ teaspoon salt, and ¼ teaspoon pepper with reserved ⅓ cup fish cooking oil in blender until smooth, 1 to 2 minutes. Add any accumulated fish juices from platter, season with salt to taste, and blend for 10 seconds. Strain sauce through fine-mesh strainer, discarding solids.

6. To serve, pour vinaigrette around fish. Garnish each fillet with warmed crisped artichokes and garlic, tomato rounds, and parsley. Serve immediately.

VARIATIONS

Poached Fish Fillets with Crispy Scallions and Miso-Ginger Vinaigrette

For fish, substitute 6 scallion whites, sliced ¼ inch thick, for artichoke hearts; omit garlic; and reduce amount of cornstarch to 1 teaspoon. For vinaigrette, omit tomatoes, sherry vinegar, and parsley. Process 4 scallion greens, 4 teaspoons lime juice, 1½ tablespoons mirin, 1 tablespoon white miso paste, 1½ teaspoons minced fresh ginger, and ¼ teaspoon sugar with reserved ⅓ cup fish cooking oil in blender as directed in step 5. Garnish fish with 2 thinly sliced scallion greens and 1 halved and thinly sliced radish.

Poached Fish Fillets with Crispy Jalapeños and Spicy Vinaigrette

For fish, substitute 1 jalapeño chile, stemmed, seeded, and cut into ⅛-inch-thick rings, for artichoke hearts; reduce amount of cornstarch to 1 teaspoon. For vinaigrette, omit tomatoes, sherry vinegar, and parsley. Process 3 stemmed, halved, and seeded jalapeños, 4 sprigs fresh cilantro, 2 tablespoons lime juice, and ½ teaspoon salt with reserved ⅓ cup fish cooking oil in blender as directed in step 5. Garnish fish with 1 tablespoon fresh cilantro leaves.

BAKED FISH WITH CRISP BREAD CRUMBS

✔ **WHY THIS RECIPE WORKS:** Baked fish sounds like a great option for two: healthy and easy to prepare, with a crunchy, buttery crumb topping to complement the moist fish. To ensure that this easy weeknight meal lived up to its potential, we gently baked the fish in a low oven so there would be no chance of it overcooking. Elevating it on a wire rack allowed the air to circulate around it for even cooking and a crisp crust. To avoid bland bread crumbs, we sautéed them in butter with garlic, shallot, and thyme until golden brown. To keep the crumbs from falling off the fish, we used mayonnaise (flavored with lemon zest and pepper) to adhere them securely.

BAKED FISH HAS MANY VIRTUES: IT'S HEALTHY, quick-cooking, and easy to prepare for two. Add a crunchy, flavorful crumb topping and there's a lot to like. In the real world, though, baked fish is often dry and overcooked yet sitting in a pool of liquid. We've also eaten more than our share of soggy, boring crumb toppings—assuming they haven't fallen off the fillet. Surely moist, flavorful fish with a crisp crown of crumbs is a reasonable goal.

We know that as fish cooks, its proteins denature and its natural juices are squeezed out, which explains why overcooked fish is dry yet sits in a puddle of its own juices. Most recipes use relatively hot ovens (375 to 450 degrees) to evaporate excess juices, but when the window for perfect doneness is small, as it is for fish fillets, isn't this asking for trouble? Our strategy was to slow down the cooking so we could easily get the fish out of the oven before it overcooked. As extra insurance, we'd use fillets at least 1 inch thick, which are less likely to overcook. Finally, we wanted a recipe that would work with a variety of white fish, so we could cook this dish no matter which fish was fresh at the market. With these goals in mind, we jumped in.

We put our naked fish fillets in a baking dish, set it in a 300-degree oven, and waited, thermometer at the ready. We checked the temperature of the fillets at 5-minute intervals until they reached the optimum temperature (135 degrees). The fish wasn't bad, but it was slightly tough and soggy on the underside. A fellow test cook suggested elevating the fish on a wire rack, which would allow gentle heat to circulate all around the fillets and keep the fish from sitting in its juices. So we switched from a baking dish to a rack (greased so the fish wouldn't stick) set in a rimmed baking sheet. After about 35 minutes, the fish was perfectly cooked.

We moved on to the crumbs. We often waffle back and forth between using freshly prepared bread crumbs and store-bought Japanese panko crumbs for encrusting poultry and fish. Depending on the cooking method, one of these usually works better than the other. For this dish, we had a hunch that the crunch of the panko would be a boon to our fish, but we decided to test both options to be sure. As expected, the fresh bread crumbs, even when pretoasted, turned soggy in the oven. The super-crunchy panko, on the other hand, remained crisp all the way from the oven to the serving plate. Panko it would be.

To get the crumbs to stick, we tested a variety of options. First, we tried our standard breading procedure: We coated the fish in flour, then an egg wash, and then finally the panko. While this method works fine for foods like fried pork chops, it was a disaster for our baked fish. The entire coating turned to mush and slid off the fish before it could even begin to cook. We'd need to get more creative.

We racked our brains for alternative panko "glue," testing everything from egg white to a cornstarch slurry. None were successful, and we were thinking of changing course entirely when a taster suggested mayonnaise. Sure, the sandwich spread may seem out of place on baked fish, but it worked like a dream, enriching the lean fish while keeping the panko firmly in place. A little pepper and lemon zest mixed in with the mayonnaise rounded out the flavors.

But now that our mayonnaise mixture was taking center stage, tasters thought the panko, while still crunchy, was pale and bland. The oven temperature was simply too low to brown the crumbs in the 35 minutes it took to cook the fish. Obviously, we'd have to brown the panko before baking the fish. For the next test, we sautéed the panko in melted butter (fortified with garlic, thyme, salt, and shallot) until it was deep golden. We let it cool and then "glued" it onto the fillets with the seasoned mayonnaise. Now the crumbs not only stayed put but also tasted delicious. Flavorful, satisfying, and simple—this baked fish just earned a place in our weekly repertoire.

Baked Fish with Crisp Bread Crumbs
SERVES 2

Haddock or halibut fillets are good alternatives to cod.

- 2 tablespoons unsalted butter
- 1 small shallot, minced
  Salt and pepper
- 1 small garlic clove, minced
- ¾ teaspoon minced fresh thyme or ¼ teaspoon dried
- ½ cup panko bread crumbs
- 1½ tablespoons minced fresh parsley
- 2 tablespoons mayonnaise
- ¼ teaspoon grated lemon zest
- 2 (6-ounce) skinless cod fillets, 1 to 1½ inches thick

1. Adjust oven rack to middle position and heat oven to 300 degrees. Set wire rack inside rimmed baking sheet and spray with vegetable oil spray. Melt butter in 10-inch skillet over medium heat. Add shallot and ⅛ teaspoon salt and cook until softened, about 3 minutes. Add garlic and thyme and cook until fragrant, about 30 seconds. Add panko and ⅛ teaspoon pepper and cook, stirring constantly, until evenly browned,

---

BAKED FISH WITH CRISP BREAD CRUMBS

5 to 7 minutes. Remove from heat and stir in parsley. Transfer panko mixture to shallow dish and let cool for 10 minutes.

2. Whisk mayonnaise, lemon zest, and ⅛ teaspoon pepper together in bowl. Pat fish dry with paper towels and season with salt and pepper. Coat tops of fillets evenly with mayonnaise mixture. Working with 1 fillet at a time, dredge coated side in panko mixture, pressing gently to adhere, and place fish crumb side up on prepared wire rack. Bake until centers are just opaque and fish registers 135 degrees, 30 to 35 minutes, rotating pan halfway through baking. Serve.

MARYLAND CRAB CAKES

✔ WHY THIS RECIPE WORKS: When it comes to crab cakes, Maryland is king. We wanted Maryland-style crab cakes for two. We kept the ingredients simple— just a little hot sauce, scallion, and Old Bay seasoning gave us plenty of flavor without overwhelming the crab. We liked the flavor of saltines for our binder, but our crab cakes fell apart in the pan. Patting the crabmeat dry with paper towels and broiling, rather than pan-frying, the cakes were easy fixes. Pasteurized crabmeat from the supermarket was easier and more readily available than fresh crab, but we thought that it was lacking a little succulence. Adding a tablespoon of butter to the cakes gave them plenty of richness, and greasing the baking sheet with butter helped the bottoms of the cakes crisp to a perfect golden brown.

CITIZENS OF MARYLAND HOLD THIS TRUTH TO BE self-evident: The best crab cakes are all about the crab. That's why Marylanders typically serve their famous crab cakes with nothing but a squeeze of lemon. Not to be crabby, but that's easy for them: Fresh and fabulous crabmeat at a reasonable price is as common in Maryland as ants at a picnic. Where does that leave the rest of us? Refusing to be discouraged, we took as our model one of Maryland's best-loved versions: the jumbo-size, award-winning crab cakes from J. W. Faidley Seafood, made with meat handpicked from blue crabs,

bound with minimal mayonnaise and crushed saltines, and seasoned with Dijon mustard. This simple style seemed especially suitable for two, as we didn't want any extra ingredients weighing down our cakes or taking up space in our fridge. The bar was high, but our goal was to make something really meaty, succulent, and sweet.

Nine recipes and a day of picking, chopping, binding, shaping, and frying later, we pecked at pasty crab cakes full of cracker crumbs and greasy cakes containing an entire stick of butter. We despaired over crab cakes overpowered by Old Bay seasoning, mustard, and raw onion or tasting of nothing but lackluster crab and mayonnaise. Crab cakes that dialed back on binder to bring the crab flavor to the fore had problems of their own. They were so soggy they were hard to form, and even the ones we could get to hold together at first fell apart in the skillet.

Clearly we had to start from scratch. We put together a working recipe using 8 ounces of lump crabmeat, a whole egg, ¼ cup of saltines, 2 tablespoons of mayonnaise, and a dollop of Dijon mustard. As we were picking over the crabmeat to make a batch, we happened to notice how much liquid was pooling in the mixing bowl. Not a single recipe had suggested we begin by pressing the crabmeat dry. Obviously, we'd need less binder if the crab was drier from the start. Step 1 of our recipe would be drying the crabmeat with paper towels.

Next we gradually cut back on the cracker crumbs until we landed at 2 tablespoons. But while we liked the flavor of these lightly bound cakes, they just weren't sturdy enough to withstand pan frying in oil. We tried substituting both fresh and toasted bread crumbs in place of the saltines, but neither of these absorbed more moisture or tasted better than the saltines, so we stuck with the crackers. Next, we lost the egg white—and gained a slightly firmer crab cake. Unfortunately, the cakes still weren't holding together in the pan.

We tried exploring other more creative binders like pureed crabmeat and reduced cream, but they all added undesirable flavors or textures. Quickly running out of ideas, we looked back at some of our initial recipe research and realized that Marylanders often broil crab cakes. Perhaps this would be an easy solution. We mounded two cakes on a greased baking sheet and broiled them just long enough for them to warm and brown (about 15 minutes). Since we no longer had to flip the cakes, they held together just fine. We had even better results when we chilled the cakes for at least an hour to firm them up before broiling.

Satisfied with our cooking method, we turned our attention to the flavor. Most supermarket crabmeat has been pressure-steamed, canned in brine, and pasteurized. This process prolongs shelf life but diminishes flavor. To compensate for the crabmeat's shortcomings, we gently mixed in hot sauce, minced scallions, and just a pinch of Old Bay. Since we weren't planning on serving tartar sauce, we wondered if a richer crab cake was in order. Butter and shellfish are a time-tested pairing. Although we didn't want to replicate the earlier recipe we'd rejected that used a veritable bucket of melted butter, we wondered if a more modest amount would add richness. We found that replacing just 1 tablespoon of mayonnaise in the recipe with the same amount of melted butter added tremendous flavor. We also greased the baking sheet with butter instead of the nonstick spray we'd been using.

One nagging concern remained: The undersides of the crab cakes, which were exposed to less heat under the broiler, were soggy. For our final test, we dunked one side of each crab cake in extra saltine crumbs before refrigerating. Later, as the crab cakes broiled, the bottoms lightly fried in the butter, crisping, browning, and providing the perfect base for our crab cakes for two.

Maryland Crab Cakes

SERVES 2

Jumbo lump crabmeat is available at the fish counter of most grocery stores. If you can't find it, you can use pasteurized lump crabmeat.

- 7 **saltine crackers**
- 8 **ounces lump crabmeat, picked over for shells**
- 2 **scallions, minced**
- 1 **tablespoon unsalted butter, melted, plus**
  1 tablespoon softened
- 1 **tablespoon mayonnaise**
- 1 **egg yolk**
- 1½ **teaspoons Dijon mustard**
- 1 **teaspoon hot sauce**
- ½ **teaspoon Old Bay seasoning**
  Lemon wedges, for serving

1. Process crackers in food processor until finely ground, about 25 seconds. Dry crabmeat well with paper towels. Using rubber spatula, gently combine crabmeat, 2 tablespoons cracker crumbs, scallions, melted butter, mayonnaise, egg yolk, mustard, hot sauce, and Old Bay in large bowl.

2. Divide mixture into 2 equal portions and shape into tight, mounded cakes. Press 1 side of each cake in remaining crumbs. Transfer cakes crumb side down to large plate and refrigerate, covered, for at least 1 hour or up to 8 hours.

3. Adjust oven rack 8 inches from broiler element and heat broiler. Grease 8 by 4-inch rectangle in center of rimmed baking sheet with softened butter. Transfer crab cakes to greased portion of prepared baking sheet, crumb side down. Broil until crab cakes are golden brown, 12 to 15 minutes. Serve with lemon wedges.

NOTES FROM THE TEST KITCHEN

HOLDING IT ALL TOGETHER
Here's how we got our Maryland Crab Cakes to hold together without too much binder.

1. To cut down on amount of saltines needed to bind cakes, thoroughly dry crabmeat with paper towels before mixing.

2. Place shaped crab cakes on plate and refrigerate for at least 1 hour (or up to 8 hours) before broiling to firm up.

3. Transfer chilled cakes to butter-lined baking sheet and broil until golden brown—no tricky flipping required.

SKILLET CHICKEN FAJITAS

CHAPTER 2

ONE-DISH SUPPERS

SKILLET CHICKEN FAJITAS

✔ WHY THIS RECIPE WORKS: Fajitas are a convenient meal to make for two, but often the fillings fall flat. We wanted full-of-flavor chicken fajitas with classic peppers and onions. We used a combination brine and marinade to flavor and season easy chicken breasts, seared them until lightly charred on just one side, and finished them in the oven to keep the meat juicy. We charred fruity poblano peppers under the broiler, then sautéed onions with heavy cream to re-create Mexican *rajas con crema*. Simple garnishes of cilantro and lime juice let the flavorful meat and vegetables take center stage.

FAJITAS ORIGINATED AS A GRILLED COWBOY STEAK dinner in the 1930s, but these days the one-dish Tex-Mex specialty is made with everything from steak to shrimp to chicken. Fajitas are often viewed as an easy meal—throw your meat, vegetables, and a little seasoning into a skillet; fry everything up; and serve it all in a warm tortilla. This method is easy enough for two and makes a fine dinner, but it's nothing to get excited about. The meat is often lackluster, and it's usually buried under flavor-dulling gobs of sour cream and shredded cheese. We wanted to reinvigorate fajitas, using convenient boneless, skinless chicken breasts and cooking them indoors for year-round appeal. Our lighter, contemporary twist would abandon the stodgy Tex-Mex garnishes and put the spotlight where it belongs: on the chicken, peppers, and onions.

We decided on boneless, skinless chicken breasts because they require little prep work, slice easily into tortilla-friendly strips after cooking, and, best of all, are easily portioned for two. The only downside is that chicken breasts are also lean and somewhat bland. To make up for these shortcomings, our first inclination was to flavor the chicken with a "brinerade"—a concentrated liquid with the salt content of a brine plus the acid and seasonings of a marinade. The salt seasons the meat and helps keep it moist during cooking, while the herbs, spices, and acid lend the surface of the meat robust flavor.

We gave it a try, mixing up a punchy concoction of salt, lime juice, garlic, cumin, and cayenne pepper—some of the classic flavors of Mexican cuisine. We also added oil to help the fat-soluble flavor compounds in the garlic and cumin penetrate the meat. We pounded the breasts to a ½-inch thickness so they would cook evenly and fit tidily into tortillas, then transferred them to the brinerade. After 30 minutes, we removed the chicken, wiped off the excess brinerade, and seared the breasts in a hot skillet. The chicken was well seasoned and had good flavor from the brinerade. Unfortunately, by the time the meat was adequately charred, it was also dry as a bone.

We wanted chicken that was well browned, even charred in spots, as though it had come off the grill. We needed a way to get the chicken to brown faster. Would sugar do the trick? In a word, yes. Just ½ teaspoon of sugar added to our brinerade helped the chicken to char rapidly without contributing a noticeable sweetness. To further imitate the smoky heat of the grill, we stirred heady smoked paprika into the brinerade. Cooking the chicken in a nonstick skillet kept the char on the chicken instead of on the pan.

We now had some seriously flavorful chicken, but in spite of the brinerade it was difficult to keep it moist in the blazing-hot skillet. What if we compromised by searing just one side of the chicken over high heat and finishing the other side over low heat?

Sure enough, the chicken that we'd charred on only one side was indeed juicier. We had to wonder, though: If the low heat of a stove was good, would the indirect heat of the oven be even better? To find out, we seared a batch on one side over high heat, then flipped the breasts and transferred the skillet to a 200-degree oven for 10 minutes. After letting it rest, we sliced up the chicken, then tossed it back into the skillet to soak up the flavorful pan juices. Tasters agreed that this was the moistest chicken yet. Next up: veggies.

The ubiquitous peppers and onions of fajitas have a firm footing in Mexican cuisine, where they are known as *rajas*, or strips. While most rajas we eat stateside seem like an afterthought, they frequently take center stage in Mexico. In fact, rajas con crema—strips of roasted pepper and onion cooked down with tangy Mexican cultured cream—are often served alone in a tortilla. Providing a rich counterpoint to the lean chicken, rajas con crema seemed an ideal way to breathe new life into our fajitas.

We threw a final batch of chicken into its brinerade and then followed a promising-looking rajas recipe. The recipe called for poblano chiles, which have a fruitier, more complex flavor than the bell peppers usually found in Tex-Mex versions. We first broiled the chiles to blister the skins. After the broiled chiles had steamed in a covered bowl for about 10 minutes, most of the skins slipped right off (though we did leave some charred bits behind for flavor). We sliced the chiles and sautéed them along with onion strips. Mexican crema is hard to find, but we thought tangy sour cream would make a good substitute. But when we stirred the sour cream into the skillet, things started to fall apart—literally. First, the sour cream curdled as it made contact with the hot pan. Then, as we stubbornly persevered, the roasted poblanos overcooked into green mush.

Our first move was to swap heavy cream for the sour cream. Sour cream's high level of acidity and relatively low fat content make it a prime candidate for curdling, whereas fattier heavy cream is remarkably stable. To make up for the cream's lack of tang, we added a splash of lime juice toward the end of cooking. And to preserve the perfectly roasted poblanos, we added them at the last minute to rewarm with the onions and cream. Final touches of garlic and oregano tied everything together. These revamped rajas were tender-crisp yet luscious and flavorful. The best part? Since we already had the oven on to finish the chicken, we could cook the rajas in our nonstick skillet, transfer them to a serving bowl, and keep them warm in the oven while we reused the skillet to cook the chicken.

We proudly laid out the modern fajita feast with charred flour tortillas and just crumbled *queso fresco*, chopped cilantro, and lime wedges for garnishing. These skillet fajitas offer all of the easy-to-love flavor of their grilled forebears—no shredded cheddar or salsa required.

Skillet Chicken Fajitas

SERVES 2

We like to serve these fajitas with crumbled queso fresco or feta in addition to the cilantro and lime.

3½ tablespoons vegetable oil

2 tablespoons lime juice

4 garlic cloves (3 smashed, 1 minced)

1 teaspoon smoked paprika

½ teaspoon sugar

½ teaspoon ground cumin

Salt and pepper

¼ teaspoon cayenne pepper

2 (6-ounce) boneless, skinless chicken breasts, trimmed and pounded to even ½-inch thickness

8 ounces poblano chiles, stemmed, halved, and seeded

1 small onion, halved and sliced through root end into ¼-inch-thick pieces

¼ teaspoon dried oregano

¼ cup heavy cream

6 (6-inch) flour tortillas, warmed

2 tablespoons minced fresh cilantro

Lime wedges

NOTES FROM THE TEST KITCHEN

THE BEST FLOUR TORTILLAS

Tortillas are big business in the United States, second only to white sandwich bread in bread sales. We gathered four national brands of the 6-inch size to taste plain and with Skillet Chicken Fajitas. The thinner the tortilla, the more we liked it. The top-ranking brand was "delicate enough to let the flavor of the filling shine through." Also important: flaky texture. Our favorite tortilla earned accolades for featuring three distinct layers. And as is often the case, fat and salt were key: Our winner contains almost three times as much fat as our loser and nearly double the salt. The winning **Old El Paso 6-Inch Flour Tortillas** also boast mild, wheaty flavor. The brand's 8-inch "burrito-style" tortillas use the same recipe, so whatever our tortilla needs may be, Old El Paso has us covered.

1. Whisk 1½ tablespoons oil, 1 tablespoon lime juice, smashed garlic, paprika, sugar, cumin, ½ teaspoon salt, ¼ teaspoon pepper, and cayenne together in bowl. Add chicken and toss to coat. Cover and let stand at room temperature for at least 30 minutes or up to 1 hour.

2. Meanwhile, adjust oven rack to highest position and heat broiler. Arrange poblanos, skin side up, on aluminum foil–lined baking sheet and press to flatten. Broil until skin is charred and puffed, about 5 minutes, rotating baking sheet halfway through cooking. Transfer poblanos to bowl, cover, and let steam for 10 minutes. Rub skin from poblanos and discard majority (preserve some skin for flavor); slice into ¼-inch-thick strips. Adjust oven racks to middle and lowest positions and reduce heat to 200 degrees.

3. Heat 1 tablespoon oil in 10-inch ovensafe non-stick skillet over high heat until just smoking. Add onion and cook until charred and just softened, about 3 minutes. Add minced garlic and oregano and cook until fragrant, about 15 seconds. Add cream and cook, stirring frequently, until reduced and cream lightly coats onion, about 1 minute. Add poblano strips, remaining 1 tablespoon lime juice, ¼ teaspoon salt, and ⅛ teaspoon pepper and toss to coat. Transfer vegetables to bowl, cover, and place on middle oven rack. Wipe out skillet with paper towels.

4. Remove chicken from marinade and wipe off excess marinade. Heat remaining 1 tablespoon oil in now-empty skillet over high heat until just smoking. Add chicken and cook without moving until bottom side is well charred, 3 to 4 minutes. Flip chicken; transfer skillet to lower oven rack. Bake until chicken registers 160 degrees, 5 to 7 minutes. Transfer chicken to cutting board and let rest for 5 minutes; do not wash out skillet.

5. Slice chicken crosswise into ¼-inch-thick strips. Return chicken strips to skillet and toss to coat with pan juices. To serve, spoon slices of chicken into center of warmed tortilla and top with spoonful of vegetable mixture and cilantro. Serve with lime wedges.

PAN-ROASTED CHICKEN BREASTS WITH ROOT VEGETABLES

✔ WHY THIS RECIPE WORKS: For the ultimate easy roast chicken and vegetable dinner, we used bone-in, skin-on chicken breasts for roasted chicken flavor in less time. We tossed red potatoes, carrots, and Brussels sprouts with garlic and thyme and brushed the chicken with melted thyme butter. We spread the vegetables on a sheet pan and topped them with the chicken breasts so that they basted in the chicken's drippings as it roasted. A hot 475-degree oven gave us crisp, well-browned chicken skin by the time the breast meat was cooked to perfection.

ROAST CHICKEN AND VEGETABLES HOLDS THE promise of a satisfying, uncomplicated supper for two that's so easy you hardly need a recipe. But if you casually scatter a few potatoes, onions, and carrots around a couple of chicken pieces, the vegetables are usually still hard and crunchy by the time the chicken is done. We wanted chicken and vegetables that could go into the oven at the same time and still be perfectly cooked—without a lot of fuss.

Most of the recipes we found used whole birds and included steps like flipping the chicken and pouring off the fat partway through cooking. We wanted this dish to be quick and simple, so we decided to roast bone-in, skin-on chicken breasts. The bone and skin would give us the rich flavor of a whole roasted chicken and help keep the lean breast meat moist during roasting. To accompany our chicken, we'd need sturdy vegetables that could absorb the flavorful juices without falling apart when roasted. We settled on skin-on red potatoes, carrots, and Brussels sprouts. We also added halved shallots and whole garlic cloves, both of which would soften and mellow in the oven, as well as fresh thyme for herbaceous bite.

We cut the vegetables into rustic chunks; tossed them with salt, pepper, rosemary, thyme, and oil; laid them out on a sheet pan; and placed the chicken pieces on top, skin side up, so the fat could render and baste both the meat and the vegetables. Since we pictured this as a weeknight dinner, we knew we'd want it to be fast, so we set the pan in a hot 475-degree oven. When the chicken was finished cooking, we pulled the pan out of the oven and let the chicken rest before taking a taste.

The results of this first test were mixed. First the vegetables: They were plenty flavorful thanks to the drippings from the chicken, but they were charred around the edges and still hard in the center. The Brussels sprouts, especially, were problematic: They were simultaneously undercooked and dried out. We knew from previous test kitchen recipes that Brussels sprouts benefit from a combination of steaming and roasting. Could we arrange the vegetables in such a way as to give the sprouts a little extra steam? For our next test, we prepared the vegetables as before but arranged them with the sprouts in the center and the potatoes and carrots spread out around them. The strategy worked for the Brussels, but now we had a similar problem with the vegetables around the edges of the pan.

Since we weren't cooking enough vegetables to fill up the entire sheet pan, too much extra heat was getting to the thinly spread spuds and carrots. So instead of spreading the vegetables out across the pan, we crowded them together, leaving about a 2-inch border between the vegetables and the sides of the pan. This time, everything emerged from the oven tender, with no dried edges in sight. The only remaining problem? Our well-clustered vegetables were now lacking in color. A sprinkling of sugar helped, but it gave us only occasional light brown spots. We got the best results when we returned the vegetables to the oven for a few minutes while the chicken rested. Now the vegetables were perfectly cooked, tender, and browned.

As for the chicken, it was cooking through so quickly in the hot oven that the skin didn't have enough time to get crisp and well browned. To get the skin to brown faster, we raised the oven rack to get the pan into the hottest part of the oven (because heat rises). Brushing the raw chicken pieces with melted butter helped the skin crisp more thoroughly and added more savory flavor. As we were testing another batch of chicken, we spied the chopped thyme on the cutting board waiting to get tossed with the vegetables, and we got the idea to mix some of it into the butter for extra flavor.

Just 35 minutes later, the chicken skin was golden brown and fragrant with herbs, and the meat was cooked to perfection.

After several weeks of testing, we'd created a deliciously satisfying one-pan meal. In fact, we liked it so well, we developed an easy variation with fennel and parsnips to add even more variety to our chicken repertoire. Now we could get protein, starch, and vegetable on the dinner table in one easy recipe—with few dishes to clean later.

Pan-Roasted Chicken Breasts with Root Vegetables

SERVES 2

Use Brussels sprouts no bigger than golf balls, as larger ones are often tough and woody. Be sure to use a light-colored baking sheet; nonstick or other dark pans will cause the vegetables to burn.

- 6 ounces Brussels sprouts, trimmed and halved if small or quartered if large
- 6 ounces red potatoes, cut into 1-inch pieces
- 2 carrots, peeled and cut into 2-inch lengths, thick ends halved lengthwise
- 4 shallots, peeled and halved
- 3 garlic cloves, peeled
- 1 tablespoon vegetable oil
- 2 teaspoons minced fresh thyme
- ½ teaspoon sugar
-   Salt and pepper
- 1 tablespoon unsalted butter, melted
- 2 (12-ounce) bone-in split chicken breasts, trimmed

1. Adjust oven rack to upper-middle position and heat oven to 475 degrees. Toss Brussels sprouts, potatoes, carrots, shallots, garlic, oil, 1 teaspoon thyme, sugar, ¼ teaspoon salt, and ⅛ teaspoon pepper together in medium bowl. Combine melted butter, remaining 1 teaspoon thyme, ¼ teaspoon salt, and pinch pepper in small bowl; set aside.

2. Pat chicken dry with paper towels and season with salt and pepper. Place vegetables in single layer on rimmed baking sheet, arranging Brussels sprouts in center and leaving 2-inch border between vegetables and sides of baking sheet. Place chicken, skin side up, on top of Brussels sprouts.

3. Brush chicken with herb butter and roast until chicken registers 160 degrees, about 35 minutes, rotating sheet halfway through cooking. Transfer chicken to serving platter, tent loosely with aluminum foil, and let rest for 5 to 10 minutes. If necessary, return vegetables to oven until well browned and tender, 5 to 10 minutes. Toss vegetables with pan juices and transfer to platter with chicken. Serve.

VARIATION

Pan-Roasted Chicken Breasts with Fennel and Parsnips

Substitute ½ fennel bulb, stalks discarded, bulb halved, cored, and sliced into ½-inch wedges, for Brussels sprouts, and 4 ounces parsnips, peeled and cut into 2-inch pieces, thick ends halved lengthwise, for carrots.

NOTES FROM THE TEST KITCHEN

THE BEST RIMMED BAKING SHEET

Here in the test kitchen, we use rimmed baking sheets quite often. We're not talking about your grandmother's jelly roll pan, though, a flimsy 15 by 10-inch flat pan with 1-inch-high edges. When our recipes ask for a "rimmed baking sheet," we're referring to what chefs call a half sheet pan. Our favorite, the **Wear-Ever Half Size Heavy Duty Sheet Pan by Vollrath**, $21.79, is a roomy 17¾ by 12⅞ inches and can comfortably accommodate a cooling rack. Because it's made of heavy-duty (13-gauge) aluminum alloy, it can handle high heat with scant chance of warping. We use it to bake cookies, roast potatoes, and for one-pan meals like our Pan-Roasted Chicken Breasts with Root Vegetables. With a cooling rack set inside, it's twice as handy—keeping fried foods warm but not soggy, elevating broiled meats so they won't steam, and keeping our kitchen clean when we're glazing cookies.

CHICKEN AND RICE

✔ WHY THIS RECIPE WORKS: For the ultimate easy weeknight dinner, we wanted to get classic chicken and rice perfectly cooked in one pot. We chose bone-in, skin-on chicken thighs for rich flavor and seared them to get nicely browned skin. For aromatics, we sautéed onion, garlic, and a little fresh thyme. To get perfectly al dente rice without overcooking the chicken, we microwaved the rice to parcook it, then added it to the pot with the chicken to cook through gently in the even heat of the oven. A sprinkling of parsley finished the dish with bright freshness.

WHEN IT COMES TO SIMPLE, SATISFYING MEALS, FEW dishes surpass chicken and rice. Almost every culture has a version, from Indian *biryani* to Latin American *arroz con pollo*. As long as the chicken is moist and the rice is well cooked, it's usually a winner. But achieving that is harder than it sounds, and many versions yield dry poultry, mushy rice, and scant flavor. We wanted a foolproof recipe for two that would get chicken and rice on the table with minimum fuss and maximum flavor.

Our ingredient list would be straightforward, so we'd have to choose wisely. We opted for dark meat to get rich flavor throughout the dish; four bone-in, skin-on thighs fed two nicely. Long-grain white rice is the traditional choice—not to mention a pantry staple for most folks—so it would stay. After a few tests of our basic working recipe, we settled on some classic flavorings: onion, garlic, thyme, and white wine. Now for the cooking.

To start, we seared the chicken in a skillet and set it aside. We then sautéed onion and garlic in the rendered fat and added rice, a splash of wine, and chicken broth—a more flavorful cooking liquid than water. We returned the browned chicken to the skillet, covered it, and let everything simmer. Though clear-cut and easy, this method didn't work all that well. By the time the rice was tender, the chicken was dry and overcooked. As we saw it, we could either speed up the rice or slow down the chicken. We decided we'd parcook the rice.

CHICKEN AND RICE

First, we tried boiling it in a lot of water for a few minutes, as though we were making pasta. We then drained the rice, added it to the skillet, and proceeded with the recipe. Unfortunately, if we boiled the rice a moment too long, it turned mushy and waterlogged, and if we failed to boil it long enough, we had crunchy rice. In both cases, it was difficult to gauge exactly how much liquid we needed to finish cooking the parboiled rice. In the past, we've sometimes used the microwave to cook rice faster. We microwaved the rice with some of the broth and added this parcooked rice, plus the remaining broth, to the skillet with the chicken. Once the chicken was cooked through, the rice was mostly fluffy and tender.

But some of the rice was crunchy and dry. To further even out the cooking, we moved the skillet to the oven to finish cooking the rice in the oven's more even heat. Nonetheless, the dish was still ruined by the occasional crunch of rice. We realized that the skillet lid was letting some steam escape, drying out the top layer of rice. The skillet's wide surface area also meant that more rice was exposed to these drying conditions. Why not switch to a saucepan? We gave it a try, browning the chicken and sautéing the onion in a saucepan, then adding the broth, parcooked rice, and chicken and moving the saucepan to the oven to finish. We also let the rice sit, covered, to steam gently while the chicken rested. The problem disappeared—and when we called over the tasters, so did dinner.

While we loved the simplicity of this homey dish, we wanted to spice things up with a couple of variations. First, we added Chinese five-spice powder for multilayered flavor and sliced scallions for bite and freshness. For our second variation, we used complex smoked paprika and herbaceous cilantro for a warm, bright version.

Chicken and Rice

SERVES 2

Lundberg Organic Long-Grain White Rice is the test kitchen's winning brand.

- 1¼ cups low-sodium chicken broth
- ½ cup long-grain white rice
  Salt and pepper
- 4 (5- to 7-ounce) bone-in chicken thighs, trimmed
- 1 teaspoon vegetable oil
- 1 small onion, chopped fine
- 2 garlic cloves, minced
- ¾ teaspoon minced fresh thyme
- ¼ cup dry white wine
- 2 tablespoons chopped fresh parsley

1. Adjust oven rack to lower-middle position and heat oven to 350 degrees. Combine ¾ cup broth, rice, and ¼ teaspoon salt in medium bowl and microwave, covered, until liquid is absorbed, 6 to 8 minutes.

2. Meanwhile, pat chicken dry with paper towels and season with salt and pepper. Heat oil in medium ovensafe saucepan over medium-high heat until just smoking. Cook chicken until browned all over, about 10 minutes; transfer to plate.

3. Pour off all but 1 teaspoon fat from saucepan, add onion and ¼ teaspoon salt, and cook over medium-low heat until softened and lightly browned, about 5 minutes. Add garlic and thyme and cook until fragrant, about 30 seconds. Add remaining ½ cup broth and wine, scraping up any browned bits. Stir in parcooked rice, breaking up any large clumps, and bring

to simmer. Place chicken skin side up on rice, cover, and bake until rice is cooked through and chicken registers 175 degrees, about 25 minutes.

4. Remove saucepan from oven, transfer chicken to platter, and tent loosely with aluminum foil. Fluff rice with fork, cover, and let sit for 10 minutes. Stir parsley into rice and season with salt and pepper to taste. Serve rice with chicken.

VARIATIONS

Chicken and Rice with Five-Spice and Scallions

Substitute ¼ teaspoon five-spice powder for thyme and 2 thinly sliced scallions for parsley.

Chicken and Rice with Smoked Paprika and Cilantro

Substitute ¼ teaspoon smoked paprika for thyme and 2 tablespoons chopped fresh cilantro for parsley.

CHICKEN AND CHORIZO PAELLA

✔ **WHY THIS RECIPE WORKS:** Paella is a fragrant Spanish rice dish usually loaded with meat, seafood, and vegetables. While delicious, it's rarely worth the hassle, especially when cooking for two. We wanted to translate this classic into a streamlined weeknight version with all the flavor of the original. A combination of chorizo sausage and chicken breasts was hearty enough that we could forgo the seafood altogether. A rich *sofrito* of onion, garlic, and tomato gave our dish a deep flavor, and bright peas and briny olives added color and dimension. Just a pinch of pricey saffron was enough to give our paella authentic Spanish flavor.

SPAIN'S SAFFRON-INFUSED PAELLA IS A FESTIVE, flavorful rice dish made with an array of meats and vegetables. It is traditionally a complicated production with a commanding list of ingredients from artichokes, broad beans, bell peppers, and peas to chorizo, pork, chicken, and numerous types of seafood, all prepared in a special flat-bottomed, two-handled paella pan. We loved the flavors of classic paella, but we wanted to streamline it to make it a weeknight option for two.

We set out to create a less daunting recipe that could be made in a reasonable amount of time, with a manageable number of ingredients, and without a special paella pan.

We found that there are five key steps in most paella recipes: browning the sturdier proteins, sautéing the aromatics, toasting the rice, adding liquid to cook the rice, then adding the more delicate ingredients last and heating everything through. For the proteins, we quickly ruled out lobster and other shellfish (too much bother), diced pork (we preferred sausage), and fish (it flakes too easily and gets lost in the rice). We settled on chorizo for heat and spice and chicken for convenience.

We began by browning the chicken and chorizo to give the meat a head start and develop some fond to lend flavor to the dish. Tasters preferred Spanish chorizo for having more bite than Mexican-style chorizo. Slicing the sausage into half-moons increased the surface area for browning and made rendering the fat easier. We browned the sausage for about 2 minutes, then set it aside and turned our attention to the chicken.

While many recipes call for bone-in, skin-on chicken pieces, to avoid extra prep and save time we opted for one boneless, skinless chicken breast, which, along with the chorizo, would be just the right amount for two. We sliced the breast and browned it in the rendered sausage fat, then set it aside with the chorizo.

Now it was time to add some flavoring and aromatics. Paella traditionally includes a sofrito—a trio of onions, garlic, and tomatoes—as the building block for flavor. We began by sautéing one finely diced onion until softened along with a couple of teaspoons of minced garlic and ⅛ teaspoon of crumbled saffron. For the tomato component, we used half a can of drained diced tomatoes, leaving the pieces whole for added texture. We cooked this mixture until thick and slightly darkened.

We moved on to the rice. Light and fluffy long-grain rice seemed out of place, and most varieties of medium-grain rice had a one-dimensional, blown-out texture in this dish, though medium-grain Italian Arborio was acceptable. The traditional paella rice, Bomba rice from the Calasparra region of Spain, is prized for its ability to absorb liquid while retaining separate, distinct grains, but tasters disliked its chewy texture. Short-grained Valencia was preferred for its creamy but still distinct grains. To feed two, ½ cup of rice was just right. Once the rice was sautéed just long enough to become lightly toasted and coated with the flavorful sofrito, it was time to add the liquid.

Most recipes use a liquid-to-rice ratio of 2 to 1, but we found we needed to use up to 1½ cups of liquid to cook our ½ cup of rice through. The rich sofrito was so flavorful that tasters preferred the rice cooked in water rather than chicken broth or wine, as the water didn't compete with the other elements in the dish. We tried to prepare our rice in the classic manner, cooking it uncovered on the stovetop, but the rice wasn't consistently cooked. Some grains would inevitably overcook while others would remain stubbornly crunchy. We decided to try the microwave method from our Chicken and Rice recipe (page 52), jump-starting the rice in the microwave with a cup of water, then adding it to the pan with the rest of the

water plus the juice from the diced tomatoes to cook through to the perfect consistency.

Now our rice was deeply flavored and perfectly cooked, but the paella lacked a little green. Frozen peas were an easy addition. Adding them to the pan too soon resulted in shriveled, gray, cafeteria-style pebbles, but stirring them into the rice toward the end of cooking enabled them to warm through and still retain their bright green hue. We also added a quarter cup of quartered green olives to contribute a briny saltiness reminiscent of traditional seafood paella.

At this point we could easily have called it a day, but one thing was still missing: *soccarat*, the crusty brown layer of rice that develops on the bottom of a perfectly cooked batch of paella. To give our paella a crisp bottom layer, once we had stirred in the meat, olives, and peas, we removed the lid and put the skillet back on the stove. After about five minutes, the dish had a layer of crisp, nicely caramelized grains. Paella perfection.

NOTES FROM THE TEST KITCHEN

SAFFRON

Sometimes known as "red gold," saffron is the world's most expensive spice. Luckily, a little saffron goes a long way, and we have found that brand isn't important, as long as the recipe has other bold flavors, as this paella does.

THE BEST SHORT-GRAIN RICE

When it comes down to it, a good paella is all about the rice. Unfortunately, the rice you probably have in your pantry—the long-grain variety—just won't cut it. Long-grain rice is great for recipes in which light and fluffy grains are desirable (pilafs, for instance, or our Chicken and Rice, page 52), but not for paella. We like short-grain rice, which retains distinct individual grains while keeping the creamy-chewy texture that is so important in this dish. We tested three kinds of rice in our paella. Here's what we found.

Bomba rice, grown in the Calasparra region of Spain, is the traditional choice for paella. Its short, round grains are prized for their ability to absorb up to three times their volume in liquid while retaining a separate, distinct texture. Tasters liked the "nutty" flavor of this rice but didn't like its chewy texture.

Spanish Valencia rice has grains that are short and round like Bomba, though they are a bit larger. Tasters liked this rice best, praising its balance of textures: separate and chewy, but with a bit of creaminess. Use this rice if you can find it.

Italian Arborio rice (which is actually medium-grain rice) has larger, longer, and more opaque grains than Bomba and Valencia. Creamier, more tender, and a bit stickier than either of the two Spanish grains, it is an acceptable choice for paella.

Chicken and Chorizo Paella

SERVES 2

We like to use short-grain Valencia rice for this dish, but you can substitute Arborio rice if you cannot find Valencia. Do not substitute long-grain rice. See page 55 for a recipe to use up the leftover diced tomatoes.

- 1½ cups water
- ½ cup Valencia or Arborio rice
  Salt and pepper
- 4 teaspoons vegetable oil
- 4 ounces chorizo sausage, halved lengthwise and sliced ¼ inch thick
- 1 (8-ounce) boneless, skinless chicken breast, trimmed and sliced crosswise ¼ inch thick
- 1 small onion, chopped fine
- ¾ cup diced tomatoes, drained with juice reserved
- 2 garlic cloves, minced
- ⅛ teaspoon saffron threads, crumbled
- ¼ cup pitted green olives, quartered
- ¼ cup frozen peas

1. Combine 1 cup water, rice, and ⅛ teaspoon salt in bowl. Cover and microwave until rice is softened and most of liquid is absorbed, 6 to 8 minutes.

2. Meanwhile, heat 2 teaspoons oil in 10-inch non-stick skillet over medium-high heat until just smoking.

Add chorizo and cook until lightly browned, about 2 minutes. Using slotted spoon, transfer chorizo to plate. Pat chicken dry with paper towels and season with salt and pepper. Add chicken to fat left in skillet and cook until lightly browned, about 4 minutes. Transfer to plate with chorizo.

3. Add remaining 2 teaspoons oil and onion to now-empty skillet and cook over medium heat until softened, about 5 minutes. Add drained tomatoes and cook until beginning to soften and darken, 3 to 5 minutes. Stir in garlic and saffron and cook until fragrant, about 30 seconds. Add remaining ½ cup water and reserved tomato juice, scraping up any browned bits. Stir in parcooked rice, breaking up any large clumps, and bring to boil. Reduce heat to medium-low, cover, and simmer until rice is tender and liquid is absorbed, 8 to 12 minutes.

4. Stir in browned chorizo and chicken and any accumulated juices, olives, and peas and increase heat to medium-high. Cook, uncovered, until bottom layer of rice is golden and crisp, about 5 minutes, rotating skillet halfway through cooking to ensure even browning. Season with salt and pepper to taste and serve.

USE IT UP: DICED TOMATOES

Easy Tomato Chutney
SERVES 2

Serve with crackers and a soft cheese, such as cream cheese or goat cheese.

- ¾ **cup canned diced tomatoes**
- ¾ **cup water**
- 1 **shallot, minced**
- ½ **teaspoon grated lemon zest**
- 2 **tablespoons sugar**
- 2 **tablespoons cider vinegar**
- 1 **tablespoon golden raisins**
- ⅛ **teaspoon salt**
  Pinch cayenne

Combine all ingredients in medium saucepan. Bring to boil over medium-high heat. Reduce heat to medium-low and simmer, stirring occasionally, until thickened and reduced to 1 cup, about 45 minutes. Using potato masher, mash any large pieces of tomato. Let cool to room temperature before serving.

SKILLET CHICKEN AND ORZO

✔ WHY THIS RECIPE WORKS: To make this simple skillet chicken supper memorable, we wanted the side to be the star of the show. We chose orzo, a small pasta that's quick and easy to cook. To give it deep, complex flavor, we toasted it until golden brown, then simmered it in just the right amount of chicken broth until perfectly tender. To give the dish Mediterranean flair and vibrant flavor, we added garlic, oregano, and red pepper flakes and stirred in baby spinach, briny feta, and a squeeze of bright lemon juice at the end.

NOTHING GETS DINNER ON THE TABLE FASTER THAN boneless chicken breasts and a speedy stovetop cooking method. But while there are endless possibilities for simple stovetop chicken, there are also a lot of possible pitfalls, from blandness to dryness to being just plain forgettable. To revive this method for a great meal for two, we wanted to come up with a delicious (but still simple) side dish that would make our chicken dinner truly memorable. We'd need to do a little thinking and a lot of testing.

One easy solution was to use a quick-cooking starch to round out the meal. Orzo, a small pasta that is often treated as a grain, seemed like a great fit. Lots of ingredients pair nicely with its compact, even shape, but we especially like matching it with bright, bold Mediterranean flavors. We only needed to figure out how to cook it using a one-dish method. We decided the basic concept of our side dish would be similar to a bulked-up rice pilaf—we'd toast the orzo, brown the chicken, sauté the aromatics, add back the orzo and chicken, and simmer it all in a flavorful liquid until everything was cooked through. We'd start by fine-tuning the cooking of the orzo and chicken and then consider additional vegetables to round out our dish.

After toasting orzo to shades varying from pale yellow to golden brown, we found that the darker the orzo, the richer the flavor (short of burning it, of course). Well-browned orzo possessed a full, nutty flavor that tasters favored over that of more lightly toasted orzo. The key was timing—we opted for medium-high heat, which produced golden brown orzo in about five minutes, though it did require diligent stirring and a watchful eye to prevent scorching.

White rice requires around 1½ times its volume in liquid to cook, but we didn't know if this ratio would work for orzo. We figured we'd aim high with the volume of liquid and then reduce it if needed. First, we tried cooking ¾ cup of orzo (an ideal amount for two) with various amounts of water in a medium saucepan. Two cups of liquid gave us soup, and with just ¾ cup of water the orzo was chalky and undercooked. The perfect amount proved to be 1¼ cups; the orzo plumped to a tender yet firm consistency somewhere between that of pasta and rice. To bump up the flavor, we swapped the water for chicken broth.

With our orzo toasted and the liquid-to-pasta ratio settled, we focused on our cooking method. We had been cooking the orzo as we might a traditional risotto, by adding the liquid a little at a time until it was absorbed, but this technique was time-consuming and made it hard to incorporate additional vegetables. We tried simply covering the orzo and simmering it gently; this method was simple and worked well every time. A mere 10 to 15 minutes later, our orzo was finished.

But when we went to add back the chicken, our saucepan was nearly overflowing. We swapped the saucepan for a 10-inch nonstick skillet to accommodate the bulk of the meat. Once we had toasted the orzo, we lightly browned the breasts, then we set them aside and began building flavor in the skillet. Taking a cue from our initial Mediterranean inspiration, we toasted garlic, oregano, and red pepper flakes in olive oil before adding the toasted orzo and chicken broth. For a quick-cooking

vegetable and added color, we settled on baby spinach. We knew the delicate leaves would cook in no time, so we waited until the orzo was tender and the chicken cooked through before stirring in the greens.

Finally, a generous sprinkle of feta cheese and a squeeze of fresh lemon juice rounded out the dish with richness and bright flavor. Now we had a vibrant one-dish chicken dinner ready to eat in only 30 minutes.

Skillet Chicken and Orzo with Spinach and Feta

SERVES 2

Be careful not to overcook the chicken in step 4 or it will taste dry.

    ¾   cup orzo
    2   (6- to 8-ounce) boneless, skinless chicken breasts, trimmed
        Salt and pepper
    1   tablespoon olive oil
    2   garlic cloves, minced
    1   teaspoon minced fresh oregano or
    ¼   teaspoon dried
        Pinch red pepper flakes
    1¼ cups low-sodium chicken broth, plus extra as needed
    4   ounces (4 cups) baby spinach
    2   ounces feta cheese, crumbled (½ cup)
    1½ teaspoons lemon juice

1. Toast orzo in 10-inch nonstick skillet over medium-high heat until golden brown, 3 to 5 minutes; transfer to bowl.

2. Pat chicken dry with paper towels and season with salt and pepper. Heat 1 teaspoon oil in now-empty skillet over medium-high heat until just smoking. Brown chicken lightly on both sides, 3 to 5 minutes; transfer to plate.

3. Add remaining 2 teaspoons oil, garlic, oregano, and pepper flakes to now-empty skillet and cook until fragrant, about 30 seconds. Stir in broth and toasted orzo.

4. Nestle browned chicken into orzo with any accumulated juices, cover, and simmer gently until chicken registers 160 degrees, 10 to 12 minutes. Transfer chicken

---

NOTES FROM THE TEST KITCHEN

TOASTING ORZO

Toast orzo in a dry skillet over medium-high heat until deeply golden brown, 3 to 5 minutes, to develop deep nutty flavor in this dish.

to platter, brushing any orzo that sticks to chicken back into skillet; tent chicken loosely with aluminum foil.

5. Continue to cook orzo until al dente and creamy, 2 to 5 minutes longer, stirring in additional broth 1 tablespoon at a time as needed to loosen consistency. Stir in spinach, 1 handful at a time, until wilted, about 2 minutes. Stir in feta and lemon juice and season with salt and pepper to taste. Serve with chicken.

CAJUN-STYLE EGGS IN PURGATORY

✔ WHY THIS RECIPE WORKS: For a hearty but simple egg dish, we loved the idea of eggs in purgatory, where eggs are poached directly in a tomato sauce. We started with a simple sauce made with just canned tomatoes, green pepper, sautéed onion, garlic, and a little tomato paste. Chile-laced, spiced Ro-tel tomatoes gave the sauce punch and dimension without extra effort. A little bacon lent the sauce smoky meatiness. We cracked the eggs into the sauce then covered the skillet so the tops of the eggs would gently steam. A side of simple quick grits with plenty of cheddar rounded out our Cajun-inspired meal.

GIVEN ITS DEVILISH NAME, YOU'D THINK THAT EGGS in purgatory would be a challenging dish to make, full of sneaky details or tricky techniques. At the very least, the eggs would need to be carefully coddled or basted with steamy liquid, right? Fortunately, no; at its simplest, eggs in purgatory is a dish of eggs poached directly in tomato sauce. In Italy, the dish is often started with leftover Sunday gravy and served for breakfast, brunch, lunch, or dinner. But tomato sauce is a blank canvas for experimentation, so we figured this mischievous-sounding dish was ripe for a cooking-for-two makeover.

First up, the sauce itself. The tomato sauce can run the gamut from a smooth, souplike broth to a thick, meaty ragu. We weren't sure which version we'd like best, so we whipped up a few, simmering a sauce made with pureed tomatoes, another slightly thicker version made with diced tomatoes, as well as a thick, hearty meat sauce. Tasters found the thin, pureed sauce to be a little boring and the meat sauce far too rich and labor-intensive for our purposes. But they approved of the lightly chunky, simple sauce made with diced tomatoes. One 14.5-ounce can of tomatoes was the perfect amount for our two-person sauce. To bolster this sauce, we added a sautéed onion, a minced clove of garlic, and a tablespoon of tomato paste.

Next up, our egg-poaching technique. Knowing that we would need enough space to cook four eggs in our sauce, we chose a 10-inch nonstick skillet for our cooking vessel. For ease, we wanted to stick with tradition and cook the eggs directly in the sauce. But we weren't sure if the eggs should be submerged or cooked on top of the mixture, or if the whole dish should be simmered covered or uncovered. After cracking a couple of dozen eggs into tomato sauce every which way, we landed on the following technique: We built our tomato sauce, simmering it until it reached our desired thickness, and then used a spoon to create four 2-inch divots in the sauce. We cracked each egg into its own nest, covered the saucepan, and let the whole mixture simmer gently until the eggs were just cooked through. The sauce helped to insulate the bottoms of the eggs, keeping the whites supple and the yolks runny. By covering the skillet, we created steam that would gently cook the tops of the eggs so no bit of white would go uncooked.

Now we had a solid technique, but our dish was lacking a bit of oomph. One taster suggested adding flavor by swapping a can of Ro-tel tomatoes for our plain diced tomatoes. These moderately spicy tomatoes contain chopped chiles as well as additional spices, offering a no-fuss flavor boost. This was a big improvement, but there was one problem: Ro-tel tomatoes come in smaller cans than regular diced. To make up the difference, we added half a chopped green bell pepper to the sauce for extra color and volume.

Our sauce was good, but we thought we could do even more to improve it. We turned to one of our favorite ingredients for adding flavor: bacon. A couple of slices chopped and crisped in the skillet provided all of the cooking fat needed to sauté the onion and pepper and added a considerable rich, smoky backbone to the sauce.

CAJUN-STYLE EGGS IN PURGATORY WITH CHEESY GRITS

With bacon, green pepper, onion, and spice, our sauce was beginning to take on a Cajun feel. We figured we might as well embrace this direction by adding Southern flair to our side dish. While eggs in purgatory is typically served with just a slice of hearty bread or focaccia, we thought that grits might be a more fitting accompaniment for our version. We didn't want to break out a new saucepan to simmer the grits, but we guessed we could use the microwave to our advantage. About a 4:1 ratio of water to quick grits microwaved for 6 to 8 minutes gave us a thick, creamy side dish with minimal effort. To add even more richness and flavor, we stirred in half a cup of grated cheddar.

Finally, our eggs in purgatory were perfected. This simple meal came together in a snap, and whether we were making it for an easy weeknight dinner or a hearty Sunday brunch, it was heaven.

Cajun-Style Eggs in Purgatory with Cheesy Grits

SERVES 2

Do not substitute regular grits for the quick grits here.

- 2 cups water
- ½ cup quick grits
- Salt and pepper
- 2 ounces sharp cheddar cheese, shredded (½ cup)
- 2 slices bacon, cut into ½-inch pieces
- 1 small onion, chopped fine
- ½ green bell pepper, stemmed, seeded, and cut into ¼-inch pieces
- 1 tablespoon tomato paste
- 1 garlic clove, minced
- 1 (10-ounce) can Ro-tel tomatoes
- 4 large eggs

1. Combine 1¾ cups water, grits, and ⅛ teaspoon salt in medium bowl, cover, and microwave until grits are tender and water is absorbed, 6 to 8 minutes. Stir in cheddar and season with salt and pepper to taste. Cover to keep warm.

2. Meanwhile, cook bacon in 10-inch nonstick skillet over medium heat until crisp, 5 to 7 minutes; transfer to paper towel–lined plate. Add onion and bell pepper

to fat left in skillet and cook over medium-high heat until softened, about 5 minutes. Stir in tomato paste and garlic and cook until fragrant, about 30 seconds. Stir in tomatoes and remaining ¼ cup water and simmer until sauce is thickened, 8 to 10 minutes.

3. Make 4 shallow indentations (about 2 inches wide) in surface of sauce. Crack 1 egg into each indentation and season with salt and pepper. Cover, reduce heat to medium-low, and cook until eggs are just set, about 5 minutes. Remove skillet from heat, sprinkle with bacon, and serve with grits.

U.S. SENATE NAVY BEAN SOUP

✔ **WHY THIS RECIPE WORKS:** Navy bean soup is an American classic that combines hearty beans and rich ham in a thick, creamy broth. We wanted to both bulk up the soup and scale it down for two. Smoky bacon and ham steak gave the soup meaty flavor and substantial bites of ham; we sautéed the bacon until crisp, then caramelized the diced ham in the bacon fat. Canned beans kept the recipe simple; after just 15 minutes of simmering in our rich broth, they were tender and full of flavor. To thicken the broth, we simply mashed some of the beans right in the pot.

A CLASSIC AMERICAN BEAN SOUP, U.S. SENATE NAVY bean soup has supposedly been on the menu in the Senate restaurant since 1901. Legend has it that Senator Fred Dubois of Idaho, who served from 1901 to 1907, demanded that navy bean soup be on the restaurant menu in perpetuity. The mandate has been attributed to other epicurean senators as well, but it's certain that it has been on the menu for a very long time.

The authentic Senate version contains nothing more than dried beans and ham hocks simmered in water until the beans are tender and the ham has transformed the water into a smoky broth. A stray carrot or onion provides a bit more flavor, but that's about it. While we appreciate the government-sanctioned thrift behind this recipe, we were in the mood for not only a heartier, meatier navy bean soup, but also a soup scaled down and sped up for an easy weeknight meal for two.

We knew that we wanted smoky flavor and bites of meat in our soup, but we weren't up for simmering a ham hock all day. So we started by swapping the ham hock for a double dose of pork: smoky bacon and hearty ham steak. We minced the bacon and diced the ham and added them to the pot. While the bacon gave the soup well-rounded smoky flavor and the steak provided nice chunks of meat, after simmering in the soup for an hour, the ham was lacking in flavor and the soup was overly salty.

To improve the flavor of the ham, we tried first sautéing it before simmering it in the soup to give it a deeper, caramelized flavor. The flavor was even better when we sautéed the pieces in the rendered bacon fat. But while the flavor problem was fixed, the soup was still too salty. Patting the ham steak dry before dicing it helped but was not enough. We were using low-sodium chicken broth for the liquid, so we tried switching to water. Unfortunately, the resulting soup tasted flat. We tested the liquids in various combinations and ultimately landed on using slightly more water than broth (1 cup and ¾ cup, respectively). This combination provided good flavor while keeping the saltiness in check.

Now we could focus on the beans. Since we were after an easy weeknight soup, we knew that dried beans were out of the question. But could canned beans hold their own amid the bacon and ham? We were surprised to find that just a 15-minute simmer was enough to tenderize and fully flavor a can of rinsed navy beans. The short cooking time kept the beans from getting too soft and blown out.

For the vegetables, we sautéed onion, celery, and garlic with the ham, which gave them the same deep, caramelized flavor. Fresh thyme added a welcome herbal note, and ground black pepper added a touch of bite. Tasters also liked chunks of carrots, which we cut into hearty ½-inch pieces to preserve their texture. At this point the soup needed something to brighten and balance the robust flavors. A dash of red wine vinegar along with a good shake of hot sauce provided the acidity and heat the soup needed.

Our soup was almost there, but it was a bit thin. To thicken it, we opted for the simplest method—mashing some of the beans right in the soup pot using the back of a spoon—which gave our Senate soup a rustic look and texture. Now the broth was thick and creamy—a perfect base for the tender beans, ham, and carrots.

U.S. Senate Navy Bean Soup
SERVES 2

This soup can easily turn overly salty because of the ham; be sure to use low-sodium broth and taste the soup carefully before seasoning with any salt. You can get small ham steaks sliced to order at the deli counter.

- 1 slice bacon, chopped fine
- 4 ounces ham steak, patted dry and cut into ½-inch pieces
- 1 small onion, chopped fine
- 1 carrot, peeled and cut into ½-inch pieces
- 1 small celery rib, chopped fine
- 2 garlic cloves, minced
- ½ teaspoon minced fresh thyme or ⅛ teaspoon dried
  Salt and pepper
- 1 cup water
- ¾ cup low-sodium chicken broth
- 1 (15-ounce) can navy beans, rinsed
- 1 bay leaf
- ¼ teaspoon red wine vinegar
  Hot sauce

1. Cook bacon in large saucepan over medium heat until crisp, 6 to 8 minutes. Using slotted spoon, transfer bacon to paper towel–lined plate. Add ham to rendered fat and brown on all sides, 3 to 5 minutes. Stir in onion, carrot, and celery and cook until softened, 5 to 7 minutes.

2. Stir in garlic, thyme, and ⅛ teaspoon pepper and cook until fragrant, about 30 seconds. Stir in water, broth, beans, bay leaf, and vinegar and bring to simmer. Reduce heat to medium-low, partially cover, and continue to simmer until carrot is tender and beans are fully flavored, about 15 minutes.

3. Off heat, discard bay leaf. Use back of spoon to press about one-quarter of beans against side of pot to thicken soup. Season with salt and pepper to taste and serve with hot sauce.

NOTES FROM THE TEST KITCHEN

SLICING HAM STEAK
In order to get even browning on the ham steak, it is important to slice the steak into even pieces.

First slice steak into ½-inch-wide strips. Then line up strips and slice crosswise into ½-inch squares.

SESAME PORK WITH NAPA CABBAGE SALAD

✔ **WHY THIS RECIPE WORKS:** Crispy pork cutlets are an easy meal for two, but they often turn out bland and soggy. For perfect crispy pork cutlets for two, we pounded cutlets to ½-inch thickness so they would cook evenly. Using Japanese panko bread crumbs was easier than making fresh bread crumbs, and they tasted just as good. Sesame seeds added nutty flavor and even more crunch to the coating. Using a generous ⅓ cup of oil to fry the cutlets ensured that the coating came out crisp and golden brown. To round out the meal, we tossed together an easy gingery cabbage slaw.

CRISP FRIED PORK CUTLETS CAN MAKE A GREAT centerpiece to a weeknight meal for two—they cook through in minutes, and, if done right, the pork is tender and the breading crisp, golden, and substantial. Most of the time, however, the breading is at best bland and boring, or worse, soggy and falling apart. We wanted a foolproof version of fried pork cutlets with no soggy coating in sight, a vibrant side dish to round out the meal—and we wanted to make it all in one skillet.

We started testing with the basics: the pork. The two most suitable cuts of pork we found in the supermarket were boneless loin cutlets and tenderloin. These were also the two cuts used most often in the recipes we researched. We tested both, and tasters favored the cutlets for their mild flavor and ease of preparation (the tenderloin would need extra slicing and pounding).

Next, we needed to pound the cutlets to the ideal thickness. When the cutlets were too thick, the breading was too dark by the time the interior cooked through; when too thin, the meat was done long before the breading had taken on enough color. We ended up preferring cutlets pounded to a thickness of ½ inch. They were thick enough to offer some chew and a cushion against overcooking as the crust developed to a deep, even, golden brown. To make sure the pork was flavorful, we seasoned the cutlets liberally with salt and pepper.

Pork settled, we moved on to the breading. We tested a wide range of ingredients, including cornmeal and flour, dried bread crumbs, fresh bread crumbs, crushed crackers, and Japanese panko. Tasters were split between freshly ground bread crumbs and crisp Japanese panko. Both offered light, crisp, and flavorful coatings, but since the panko came ready to use, we decided to keep it simple and skip grinding fresh crumbs. We used our standard method for breading, first dredging the pork in flour, then dipping it in a beaten egg to help the crumbs adhere to the meat. We tried skipping the dip in flour to simplify the process, but the egg would not adhere to the meat on its own, leaving us with a meager, spotty coating of bread crumbs. With the flour, our coating was thick and firmly glued to the pork.

So far we had a sturdy coating, but its flavor left much to be desired. To complement the panko crumbs, one taster suggested adding sesame seeds to the coating. A 2:1 ratio of panko to sesame seeds proved to be just what the pork needed, adding nutty depth and a satisfying crunch. And since we would be frying our cutlets to golden brown, we didn't need to toast the seeds ahead of time.

Next, we tackled the cooking procedure. With just four cutlets in the pan, it was tempting to skimp on the frying oil, but when we tried cooking a batch of cutlets in just 4 tablespoons of oil, the spotty browning confirmed our hunch that using enough oil was critical. To develop a nicely golden, crunchy crust, it took enough oil to reach roughly halfway up the cutlets' sides, about ⅓ cup in a 12-inch skillet.

Heat, or lack thereof, is another potential problem when pan-frying. When we failed to heat the oil enough before adding the cutlets to the skillet, several problems arose. First, the breading absorbed too much oil, so the cutlets ended up greasy. Second, the breading took too long to brown properly, so that by the time the coating was browned, the meat was tough and overcooked. We found that the pan must be preheated over medium-high heat until the oil starts to shimmer and that 2½ minutes per side browned the breading to a gorgeous golden hue without overcooking the meat within. Now we had beautifully browned pork cutlets that were crisp on the outside and tender and juicy on the inside.

Now that we had perfectly fried cutlets, we needed a vibrant side dish to accompany them. Enter an easy-to-make bright, gingery slaw. We shredded some napa cabbage along with a carrot for color and sweetness. Simply tossed with a sesame oil, ginger, and garlic dressing, the slaw was good, but its raw crunch competed with the crisp pork. Before frying the pork, we bloomed the garlic and ginger in sesame oil, then tossed in the vegetables to soften slightly. With a splash of rice vinegar to brighten its flavor, our slaw was now worthy of our perfect crisp pork cutlets.

Crispy Sesame Pork Cutlets with Wilted Napa Cabbage Salad

SERVES 2

Don't let the pork cutlets drain on the paper towels for longer than 30 seconds, or the heat will steam the crust and make it soggy.

- ⅔ cup panko bread crumbs
- ⅓ cup sesame seeds
- ⅓ cup all-purpose flour
- 1 large egg
- 4 (3- to 4-ounce) boneless pork cutlets, trimmed and pounded to ½-inch thickness
  Salt and pepper
- 1½ tablespoons plus ⅓ cup vegetable oil
- 1½ teaspoons toasted sesame oil
- 1 garlic clove, minced
- ½ teaspoon grated fresh ginger
- ½ small head napa cabbage, cored and shredded (4 cups)
- 1 carrot, peeled and grated
- 1 tablespoon rice vinegar, plus extra to taste

1. Combine panko and sesame seeds in shallow dish. Spread flour in second shallow dish. Beat egg in third shallow dish. Line rimmed sheet pan with wire rack and large plate with paper towels.

2. Pat pork dry with paper towels and season with salt and pepper. Working with 1 cutlet at a time, dredge cutlets in flour, dip in egg, then coat with sesame bread crumbs, pressing gently to adhere. Transfer to prepared rack.

3. Heat 1½ tablespoons vegetable oil and sesame oil in 12-inch nonstick skillet over medium heat until shimmering. Add garlic and ginger and cook until fragrant, about 30 seconds. Stir in cabbage and carrot and cook until just wilted, about 1 minute. Off heat, add rice vinegar and toss to combine. Transfer to serving bowl and season with salt, pepper, and additional vinegar to taste. Wipe out skillet with paper towels.

4. Heat remaining ⅓ cup vegetable oil in now-empty skillet over medium-high heat until shimmering. Carefully place cutlets in skillet and cook until golden brown and crisp on first side, 2 to 3 minutes. Flip cutlets and cook until second side is golden brown and crisp and pork registers 145 degrees, 2 to 3 minutes longer. Transfer to prepared plate and let pork drain for 30 seconds on each side. Serve with cabbage salad.

USE IT UP: NAPA CABBAGE

Hot and Sour Napa Cabbage
SERVES 2

Don't leave the cabbage leaves in the skillet longer than 30 seconds or they will exude too much liquid and create a watery sauce.

- 2 teaspoons soy sauce
- 1 teaspoon Asian chili-garlic sauce
- ½ teaspoon sugar
- ½ teaspoon cornstarch
- 1 tablespoon vegetable oil
- ½ small head napa cabbage, stems and leaves separated, stems trimmed and cut diagonally into 2-inch pieces, and leaves shredded
  Salt

1. Whisk together soy sauce, chili-garlic sauce, sugar, and cornstarch in small bowl until smooth.

2. Heat oil in 12-inch nonstick skillet over high heat until just smoking. Add cabbage stems and cook, stirring frequently until browned and slightly softened, about 1 minute. Whisk sauce mixture to recombine and add to skillet. Continue to cook, stirring constantly, until sauce coats cabbage stems and is fragrant, about 1 minute. Off heat, add cabbage leaves and stir until leaves are warmed through and wilted, about 30 seconds. Transfer cabbage to platter, season with salt to taste, and serve.

SICHUAN STIR-FRIED PORK IN GARLIC SAUCE

✔ **WHY THIS RECIPE WORKS:** Stir-fried pork in garlic sauce is a staple at Chinese restaurants—but it rarely deserves to be. To fix this dish, we took a cue from the Sichuan classic *yu xiang* pork, which boasts tender pork, a well-balanced, flavorful brown sauce, and plenty of garlic. We kept the meat moist and tender by soaking it in a baking soda solution to raise its pH, then velveting it in a cornstarch slurry. For a sauce that tasted bold but balanced, we added sugar for sweetness and some fish sauce for meatiness. Just two cloves of minced garlic gave the dish its distinct garlicky flavor.

MOST PEOPLE PROBABLY THINK OF STIR-FRIED pork in garlic sauce as a vaguely Chinese dish of mealy pork strips swimming in a generic "brown sauce" that our parents ordered as kid-friendly (read: not spicy) fare to follow up the egg rolls. That's what we thought of, too—until our introduction to yu xiang pork. With thin-cut strips of pork, a soy-based sauce, and plenty of garlic, this Sichuan staple looks similar to the Cantonese version, but its punched-up flavors are anything but related. It's a mix of salty, sweet, hot, and—thanks to a healthy splash of Chinese black vinegar—sour flavors that, when prepared well, balance out into a bold-tasting, silky sauce that coats the super-tender meat and accompanying crisp vegetables. And since it's still essentially a stir-fry, we knew that it would make a perfect dinner for two.

But our attempts to re-create this dish were all disappointments. None achieved the requisite balance of yu xiang; one tasted cloyingly sweet, while another overdid it on the vinegar and left tasters puckering. Some were thin and watery, others slick and greasy. The pork itself was dry, chewy, and stringy, and the sauce wasn't sufficiently camouflaging those flaws. But the biggest problem was that the dish was full of hard-to-find ingredients and complex, wasteful steps (such as par-frying the pork in tons of oil) that were totally out of place when cooking for two.

We decided we'd tackle the meat first. We spread the test recipes out on the table and discovered a common

SICHUAN STIR-FRIED PORK IN GARLIC SAUCE

problem: Almost all of them called for pork loin, a lean, notoriously unforgiving cut that tends to cook up dry and fibrous. Switching to fattier pork shoulder or country-style pork ribs was an obvious move. Both cuts tasted markedly richer and juicier, but shoulder meat came with its own set of challenges. Not only was it hard to find in quantities small enough for a two-person stir-fry (we needed only half a pound), but it also required quite a bit of knife work to trim the excess fat and pare it down to strips. Country-style ribs, cut from the shoulder end of the loin, were a lot easier to prepare, so we went with them.

Now that we were using a fattier cut, we wondered if the par-frying step was still necessary. It seemed that the only purpose of that step was to ensure that the lean loin emerged moist and silky. But when we tried to eliminate the step, even the fattier ribs cooked up chewy. If we wanted supremely tender, juicy pork without the mess of all that oil, we'd have to look for another way to keep the meat moist.

Fortunately, there's a far simpler technique from Chinese cookery that tackles the problem of meat drying out in a stir-fry: velveting. This approach involves coating the meat in a cornstarch slurry to provide an insulating barrier that shields the meat from the pan's high heat. We gave it a whirl, mixing 1 teaspoon of cornstarch with an equal amount of rice wine and tossing it with the pork before proceeding with the recipe. Though a definite improvement, the meat still wasn't as tender and juicy as we wanted. For the results that we were after, we needed a technique that offered more than just a starch overcoat; it would have to actually tenderize the meat, too.

As it happens, tenderness, especially in pork, is highly dependent on the pH of the meat; the higher the pH, the more tender it will be. If we could find a way to artificially boost the pH of the meat, it might soften up a bit. And we had just the right ingredient in our pantry: alkaline baking soda.

Our plan was to soak the pork in a solution of baking soda and water for an hour or so and then proceed with velveting. The results were promising; even the leaner strips of meat were considerably more tender—too tender, in fact, and also soapy tasting. We'd overcompensated a bit, so for the next batch we cut the baking soda in half and soaked the meat for just 15 minutes. We also rinsed the pork afterward to remove any residual soda. This time the pork was perfectly juicy and supple. Even better, we needed only a couple of tablespoons of oil to cook the meat.

Meanwhile, the other half of the equation—the sauce—still needed adjusting to achieve just the right balance of salty, sour, sweet, and spicy flavors. Starting with a base of rice wine, 2 teaspoons of tangy Chinese black vinegar, and half a tablespoon of sesame oil, we diluted the mixture with enough chicken broth (⅓ cup) to amply coat the meat and vegetables and stirred in 1 teaspoon of cornstarch for thickening. Then we sautéed some minced garlic and scallion whites and a few teaspoons of broad-bean chili paste in a nonstick skillet, poured in the sauce mixture, and simmered it until it turned glossy. Not bad, tasters said, but they wanted more—particularly more sweetness and more savory depth.

The first problem was easily fixed with a bit of sugar. It was boosting the savoriness of the dish that was more challenging. After we had tinkered with the proportions of existing ingredients, our dish still lacked a certain full-bodied depth that comes from the use of homemade chicken stock. We started rooting through the pantry for something that could bulk up the dish's savory flavors. We came away with one successful (albeit untraditional) addition: fish sauce, which is naturally packed with flavor-enhancing glutamates. Just 1½ teaspoons rounded out the savory flavor we were looking for.

Now our pork was tender and moist and our sauce rich and balanced. We just needed a few last additions. Instead of traditional but hard-to-find wood ear mushrooms, we used shiitakes. We also settled on readily available celery for a contrasting crunch. Though Chinese black vinegar and Asian broad-bean chili paste are popping up in more and more supermarkets, we found that equal parts balsamic and rice vinegars provided a fine alternative to the former, and either Asian chili-garlic paste or Sriracha sauce made a good sub for the latter. At last, we had a version of yu xiang pork full of Sichuan flavor, but easily made for two.

Sichuan Stir-Fried Pork in Garlic Sauce

SERVES 2

If Chinese black vinegar is unavailable, substitute 1 teaspoon of balsamic vinegar and 1 teaspoon of rice vinegar. If Asian broad-bean chili paste is unavailable, substitute 1 teaspoon of Asian chili-garlic paste or Sriracha sauce. Serve with steamed white rice.

SAUCE

- ⅓ cup low-sodium chicken broth
- 2 teaspoons Chinese black vinegar
- 1½ teaspoons sugar
- 1½ teaspoons toasted sesame oil
- 1½ teaspoons Chinese rice wine or dry sherry
- 1½ teaspoons fish sauce
- 1 teaspoon cornstarch

PORK

- ¼ cup cold water
- ½ teaspoon baking soda
- 8 ounces boneless country-style pork ribs, trimmed and cut into 2 by ¼-inch strips
- 1 teaspoon Chinese rice wine or dry sherry
- 1 teaspoon cornstarch

STIR-FRY

- 2 tablespoons vegetable oil
- 3 ounces shiitake mushrooms, stemmed and sliced thin
- 1 celery rib, cut on bias into ¼-inch-thick slices
- 1 tablespoon Asian broad-bean chili paste
- 1 scallion, white part minced, green part sliced thin
- 2 garlic cloves, minced

1. FOR THE SAUCE: Whisk all ingredients together in bowl.

2. FOR THE PORK: Combine water and baking soda in bowl. Add pork, toss to combine, and let sit at room temperature for 15 minutes. Rinse pork in cold water. Drain well and pat dry with paper towels. Whisk rice wine and cornstarch together in bowl. Add pork and toss to coat.

3. FOR THE STIR-FRY: Heat 1½ teaspoons oil in 10-inch nonstick skillet over high heat until just smoking. Add mushrooms and cook, stirring frequently, until tender, about 3 minutes. Add celery and continue to cook until celery is crisp-tender, about 3 minutes. Transfer vegetables to bowl.

4. Add remaining 1½ tablespoons oil to now-empty skillet and place over medium-low heat. Add chili paste, scallion whites, and garlic and cook, stirring frequently, until fragrant, about 30 seconds. Add pork to skillet and cook, stirring frequently, until no longer pink, 3 to 5 minutes. Whisk sauce mixture to recombine and add to skillet. Increase heat to high and cook, stirring constantly, until sauce is thickened and pork is cooked through, 30 to 60 seconds. Return vegetables to skillet and toss to combine. Transfer to serving platter, sprinkle with scallion greens, and serve.

STRIP STEAKS WITH POTATO-ARTICHOKE RAGOUT

✔ **WHY THIS RECIPE WORKS:** To breathe new life into a basic steak-and-potatoes supper, we skipped the usual roasted or sautéed potato side in favor of a fresh tomato, artichoke, and potato ragout. For the main event, we chose beefy strip steak, patted dry and seasoned, and quickly seared in a hot skillet. While the steaks rested, we tossed sliced potatoes (parcooked in the microwave to save time) with fresh tomato and thawed frozen artichokes; a dash of rosemary added flavor. To bring the meal together, we made a quick tomato vinaigrette to drizzle over the steak and vegetable ragout.

STEAK AND POTATOES IS A CLASSIC COMBINATION for a reason: When the steak is seared properly, its contrasting crisp crust and tender interior are the perfect foils to a fluffy potato, no matter if the spud is mashed, fried, or baked. Still, no matter how perfectly prepared, the duo can grow dull. We wanted to rethink steak and potatoes into something new, portioned just right for two.

Luckily, we've already nailed down our favorite technique for cooking perfect steaks for two. We like to start with a 12-ounce strip steak and cut it into two

6-ounce individual steaks. Strip steaks offer great beefy flavor, plenty of exterior fat for moistness, and a thick cut that makes it easy to get a great seared crust with a rosy medium-rare interior. To cook the steaks, we pat them dry and season them generously with salt and pepper while heating vegetable oil in a 10-inch non-stick skillet over medium-high heat until it just starts to smoke. (The smoke lets us know that the pan is hot enough to deliver a solid sear.) A 10-inch skillet is just big enough for the steaks to fit without crowding, yet small enough that there isn't too much empty space in which oil can scorch. We cook the steaks until well browned on the first side, about 5 minutes, flip them, and then continue to cook them over medium heat until they hit 125 degrees in the centers.

We set the cooked steaks aside and got to work on our potatoes while the meat rested. We knew we didn't want to simply sauté potatoes, but we also didn't want to devote too much cooking time to the dish. One taster suggested adding tomatoes and artichoke hearts to our potatoes to make a simple vegetable ragout. This idea held promise, so we started testing.

To get the most flavor out of the potatoes, we chose Yukon Golds with the skins on. These potatoes not only added mild sweetness, but they also held together and were less likely to stick to the pan when they were sautéed. We knew that even thinly sliced potatoes would take longer to cook than the 10-minute resting time for the steak, so we tried giving them a jump start in the microwave. Once they were just tender, we added them to the skillet along with 5 ounces of thawed frozen artichoke hearts and a fresh chopped tomato. This mixture browned nicely and tasted OK, but it felt haphazard and was no match for our juicy, beefy steak.

To boost flavor, we added a bit of dried rosemary. To make the ragout more cohesive, we also added small amounts of both white wine and chicken broth. The added liquid also allowed us to cook the vegetables a bit longer, softening their edges. These were noted improvements, but when served alongside the steak, the two elements felt disjointed.

Perhaps we could bring the steak and vegetables together with a tasty sauce. Since we already had plenty of rich, earthy flavor from the steak and potatoes, we thought that a bright vinaigrette would work better than a buttery pan sauce. We were already including tomato in our ragout; what about a fresh tomato vinaigrette? We saved some of the chopped tomato from our ragout prep and added it to the food processor with a little oil, vinegar, and garlic. We processed the mixture until it was smooth; seasoned it with salt, pepper, and a little sugar to taste; then poured it over both the steak and the ragout.

The flavor of the vinaigrette was spot-on, adding freshness as well as a pop of color to the plate. Unfortunately, the food processor turned the tomato foamy and thin. So we swapped out the processor for our knife, simply chopping the tomato into fine pieces before mixing it with the oil, vinegar, and garlic.

A sprinkle of chopped parsley was all the plate needed. Now our steak and potatoes for two was anything but dull.

NOTES FROM THE TEST KITCHEN

THE BEST INEXPENSIVE NONSTICK SKILLET

You can easily spend as much on a quality nonstick skillet as you would on a traditional skillet—our longtime favorite, the All-Clad Stainless 12-inch Nonstick Fry Pan, costs $129.99. But no matter how much you spend, with regular use the nonstick coating inevitably scratches, chips off, or becomes ineffective. So why spend big bucks on a pan that will last only a year or two? To find the best nonstick pan under $50 on the market, we tested seven contenders against our favorite All-Clad pan and the Best Buy from our previous testing, the Calphalon Simply Calphalon Nonstick Omelette Pan, $55. We tested the nonstick effectiveness of each pan by frying eggs and stir-frying beef and vegetables. To see which pans cooked food evenly and had good size and heft but were comfortable to maneuver, we made crêpes in each. We also ran them through a number of durability tests. We'd like to say our new favorite pan, the **T-Fal Professional Total Non-Stick Fry Pan**, aced every test, but a loose handle that resulted from the durability testing was a sign that it's not high-end cookware. Still, at $34 for the 12.5-inch pan ($29.95 for the 10.25-inch pan and $25 for the 8-inch pan), it's a bargain, and it was the only pan in the lineup to give us the best of both worlds: an exceptionally slick, durable nonstick coating and top performance in cooking. As for the All-Clad, it is a solidly built pan, but its coating became slightly worn by the end of our tests (the T-Fal remained perfectly slick). Because the All-Clad boasts a lifetime warranty, we still recommend it, but we'll be buying the T-Fal from now on for our own kitchens.

Strip Steaks with Potato-Artichoke Ragout

SERVES 2

Be sure to thoroughly dry the artichokes before sautéing or else they will not brown properly. We prefer these steaks cooked medium-rare, but if you prefer them more or less done, see our guidelines on page 156.

- 1 tomato, cored, seeded, and chopped fine
- 3½ tablespoons olive oil
- 1½ teaspoons red wine vinegar
- 2 garlic cloves, minced
  - Salt and pepper
  - Sugar
- 8 ounces Yukon Gold potatoes, halved lengthwise and sliced crosswise ½ inch thick
- 1 (12-ounce) boneless strip steak, 1½–1¾ inches thick, trimmed and cut in half crosswise
- 5 ounces frozen artichoke hearts, thawed and patted dry
- ⅛ teaspoon dried rosemary
- ¼ cup white wine
- ¼ cup low-sodium chicken broth
- 1 tablespoon chopped fresh parsley

1. Measure out ¼ cup chopped tomato and set aside. Combine remaining tomato, 1 ½ tablespoons oil, vinegar, and ½ teaspoon garlic in small bowl. Season with salt, pepper, and sugar to taste.

2. Combine potatoes and 1 tablespoon oil in bowl and season with salt and pepper. Cover and microwave until potatoes are just softened, 3 to 5 minutes.

3. Meanwhile, pat steaks dry with paper towels and season with salt and pepper. Heat remaining 1 tablespoon oil in 10-inch nonstick skillet over medium-high heat until just smoking. Cook steaks until well browned on first side, 3 to 5 minutes. Flip steaks, reduce heat to medium, and continue to cook until steaks register 125 degrees (for medium-rare), 5 to 7 minutes longer. Transfer steaks to cutting board, tent loosely with aluminum foil, and let rest for 10 minutes.

4. Return skillet with remaining fat to medium heat until shimmering. Add potatoes and artichokes and cook until vegetables are starting to brown, about 2 minutes. Add remaining garlic and rosemary and cook until fragrant, about 30 seconds. Add reserved chopped tomato, wine, and broth and cook until potatoes are tender and liquid has evaporated, about 5 minutes. Stir in parsley and season with salt and pepper to taste. Slice steaks thin, transfer to platter, and drizzle with tomato vinaigrette. Serve with potato-artichoke ragout.

CATALAN-STYLE BEEF STEW WITH MUSHROOMS

✓ **WHY THIS RECIPE WORKS:** For complexly flavored Spanish-style beef stew, we started with a *sofrito,* a slow-cooked mixture of onions, spices, and herbs. A little salt and sugar helped the onions to caramelize, then we added a grated plum tomato and cooked it until the mixture was thick and jamlike. Boneless beef short ribs were easy to buy in small amounts and became ultratender after a slow simmer. A broth of water and white wine allowed the rich flavors of the meat and the sofrito to shine. A traditional *picada,* a mixture of toasted bread, almonds, garlic, and parsley, brightened the stew's flavor and thickened the broth.

FEW CUISINES CAN RIVAL THE COMPLEXITY OF Spanish food with its influences from ancient Greece and Rome, North Africa, and even the Americas. This multilayering of flavors and textures from different cuisines is particularly apparent in the meat stews from the country's easternmost region of Catalonia. Almost all begin with a slow-cooked jam of onions and tomatoes known as sofrito and end with the stirring in of picada, a pestolike paste that includes fried bread, herbs, and ground nuts and gives the stew body and even more dimension. Could we capture all of the rich and intricate flavors of Catalonia in a one-dish beef stew for two? This dish had too much potential not to try.

While most American beef stews are made with chuck roast, Spanish cooks employ a variety of cuts, including flank or skirt steak, blade steak, and short ribs. We tested all of these, comparing each one to chuck. The long, fibrous muscles of flank and skirt steak led to stringy results, and blade steak was flavorful but tended to dry out due to its lower fat content. In the end, we

CATALAN-STYLE BEEF STEW WITH MUSHROOMS

settled on boneless beef short ribs. Short ribs can be bought by the pound in small amounts, so they were a great choice for a two-person stew, and they boasted outstanding beef flavor and became supremely tender and moist after a long, slow simmer. We seared chunks of short ribs in batches in a medium saucepan and then transferred them to a plate so we could prepare the foundation of our stew: the sofrito.

This flavor base is the cornerstone of not only Catalan cooking but also much of Spanish cuisine, lending remarkable depth to countless recipes. A traditional sofrito consists of finely chopped onions browned slowly over low heat and brightened with tomatoes and sometimes herbs, spices, and aromatics. We've discovered that a small amount of salt and sugar added to the onion helps to draw out its moisture, both hastening and deepening the level of caramelization. We sprinkled some of each onto one minced onion as it cooked over very low heat in olive oil. Once the onion was soft and dark brown, 25 to 30 minutes later, we added the tomatoes.

We experimented with canned and fresh tomatoes, preferring a single fresh plum tomato for its brightness and convenient size. Instead of peeling the tomato (too fussy), we decided to try a simpler method we'd seen in a Spanish cookbook: scraping the pulpy flesh of the tomato over the large holes of a box grater and discarding the leathery skin. This worked beautifully. Along with the tomato, we stirred a bay leaf and half a teaspoon of heady smoked paprika into the onion. After 10 more minutes of cooking, the sweet and savory flavors of the sofrito had melded, and its texture was sticky and jamlike.

We nestled several batches of seared short rib chunks atop the slow-cooked sofrito and poured in cooking liquids, experimenting with various combinations of chicken broth, beef broth, water, and wine. Surprisingly, the broths actually detracted from the flavor of the beef and sofrito. Tasters preferred the clean flavor of a stew made with a mixture of water and white wine, which allowed the beef, onion, and tomato flavors to come through. To capture the warm spice typical of Catalan stew, we also stirred a pinch of cinnamon along with a sprig of fresh thyme into the pot.

The stew was coming along nicely, but after searing the short ribs and cooking the sofrito, we were an hour into the recipe, and we hadn't even started simmering the beef. We tried cutting back on the time we spent cooking the sofrito, testing sofritos cooked for 15 and 30 minutes alongside a 45-minute flavor base, but the long-cooked sample had a significantly richer, more developed taste that we weren't willing to sacrifice. We wondered whether spending 15 minutes searing the meat was absolutely necessary.

In tests of past test kitchen beef stew recipes, we found that we could do away with searing the meat by cooking the stew uncovered in a low oven. Arranged so that most of the meat sat above the cooking liquid, the meat was exposed to the heat of the oven, browning nearly as well as if it were seared. After running a seared versus unseared test, cooking each stew in a moderate 300-degree oven, we found they tasted remarkably similar.

Having achieved tender, intensely flavored beef, it was time for the critical final component: the picada. Some experts wager that this bracing mixture of fried bread, nuts (most often almonds or hazelnuts), garlic, olive oil, and herbs (typically parsley) has been used in Catalan cooking since the 13th and 14th centuries. In stews, the ground nuts and bread bulk up the braising liquid, and the garlic and parsley add flavor and freshness.

Not wanting to bring out an extra skillet for toasting, we decided to see if we could utilize the microwave. We combined 2 tablespoons of blanched almonds with small pieces of bread and a few teaspoons of olive oil and gave it all a quick zap. The bread toasted more quickly than the other elements, so we held off on adding it until the last 60 seconds or so. Then we processed the mixture with a clove of raw garlic in a food processor. Stirred into the finished stew along with minced fresh parsley, the picada gave the dish a jolt of bright, pungent flavor.

Thus far, the stew contained no vegetables, and although we didn't plan on loading it up with carrots, peas, and potatoes like a typical American stew, some additional element seemed appropriate. We chose easy-to-find white mushrooms. Added directly to the stew with the beef, the mushrooms soaked up the flavorful broth and added a much-needed textural element. Finally, we finished the stew with a dash of sherry vinegar. Here was a beef stew rich and fragrant with the flavors of Catalonia—perfect for an exotic meal for two.

Catalan-Style Beef Stew with Mushrooms

SERVES 2

Serve the stew with potatoes or rice.

STEW

1	tablespoon olive oil
1	onion, chopped fine
¼	teaspoon sugar
	Salt and pepper
1	plum tomato, halved lengthwise, pulp grated on large holes of box grater, and skin discarded
½	teaspoon smoked paprika
1	bay leaf
8	ounces white mushrooms, trimmed and quartered
¾	cup water
½	cup dry white wine
1	sprig fresh thyme
	Pinch ground cinnamon
1½	pounds boneless beef short ribs, trimmed and cut into 2-inch cubes

PICADA

2	tablespoons whole blanched almonds
2	teaspoons olive oil
½	slice hearty white sandwich bread, crust removed, torn into 1-inch pieces
1	garlic clove, peeled
1½	tablespoons minced fresh parsley
¼	teaspoon sherry vinegar

1. FOR THE STEW: Adjust oven rack to middle position and heat oven to 300 degrees. Heat oil in medium ovensafe saucepan over medium-low heat until shimmering. Add onion, sugar, and ¼ teaspoon salt; cook, stirring often, until onion is deeply caramelized, 25 to 30 minutes. Add tomato, smoked paprika, and bay leaf; cook, stirring often, until darkened and thick, 5 to 10 minutes.

2. Add mushrooms, water, wine, thyme, and cinnamon to pot, scraping up any browned bits. Season beef with salt and pepper and add to stew mixture. Increase heat to high and bring to simmer. Transfer saucepan to oven and cook, uncovered, for 1 hour. Stir stew to redistribute meat, return to oven, and continue to cook, uncovered, until meat is tender, 1½ to 2 hours.

3. FOR THE PICADA: While stew is in oven, combine almonds and oil in bowl and microwave until nuts are light golden, 45 to 60 seconds. Stir in bread and continue to microwave until bread is golden, 60 to 90 seconds. Transfer to food processor. Add garlic and process until mixture is finely ground, about 20 seconds, scraping bowl as needed. Transfer mixture to bowl, stir in parsley, and set aside.

4. Remove bay leaf from stew. Stir in picada and vinegar and season with salt and pepper to taste. Serve.

FIVE-ALARM CHILI

✔ **WHY THIS RECIPE WORKS:** For a seriously hot five-alarm chili, we combined fresh jalapeños, canned chipotle chiles, dried ancho chiles, cayenne, and chili pepper for complex, multilayered flavor. Ground beef and creamy pinto beans bulked up the chili, and fresh tomatoes added brightness. To round out the chili and give it some body, we turned to a few unusual additions: A splash of light-bodied beer gave our chili malty depth and a little bitterness, and crushed corn tortilla chips thickened it and added a subtle background of corn flavor.

GROUND BEEF AND BEAN CHILI IS A GREAT CHOICE when looking for a hearty wintertime dinner for two. It usually comes together quickly with just beef and a few pantry staples. The only problem? Chili gets boring quickly. To enliven our chili repertoire, we decided to turn to hot and spicy "five-alarm"-style chili for a twist on the old standby.

Not knowing how spicy we'd want our chili, or from which sources to bring the heat, we tested several different recipes. But despite their claims to the "five-alarm" name, these chilis were all harsh disappointments or, as one taster put it, "one-note firebombs." On the plus side, one thing was clear: Simply loading up on chili powder and cayenne was a dead end. For multilayered heat, we'd need to combine different types of chiles.

First, the basic chili mechanics: Brown and drain ground beef, cook chopped onion until softened, then add garlic and spices. Return the browned beef to the pot along with tomatoes, water, and beans. We preferred creamy pintos over starchier kidneys and stuck with canned beans for ease.

Next we looked at chile options, limiting ourselves to what we could find at an average supermarket. Cayenne gave an initial blast of heat. Chili powder—typically made from ground chiles plus cumin and oregano—was a strong supporting player, but we knew we needed more heat and more complex flavor. We tested jalapeños two ways: chopped jalapeños and canned chipotle chiles in adobo sauce. Chipotles in adobo are ripe jalapeños that have been dried, smoked, and canned in vinegar-tomato sauce. We liked both the freshness of the chopped jalapeños and the smokiness of the canned chipotles, so both went into the recipe. We were almost there, but we wanted a little more depth and a touch of sweetness.

USE IT UP: PINTO BEANS

Mexican-Style Pinto Bean Salad
SERVES 2

Serve with tortilla chips.

- 1 **tablespoon red wine vinegar**
- 1½ **teaspoons lime juice**
- ¼ **teaspoon ground cumin**
-   **Salt and pepper**
-   **Pinch sugar**
- 2 **tablespoons canola oil**
- ¾ **cup canned pinto beans, rinsed and patted dry**
- 2 **tablespoons chopped fresh cilantro**
- 1 **small shallot, minced**
- 1 **small clove garlic, minced**

Combine vinegar, lime juice, cumin, ¼ teaspoon salt, and sugar in medium bowl. Slowly whisk oil into vinegar mixture until emulsified. Stir in beans, cilantro, shallot, and garlic and toss well to coat. Cover and refrigerate for at least 30 minutes. Season with salt and pepper to taste and serve.

Sweet, fruity dried ancho chiles (known as poblanos when fresh) seemed like they might be the answer. Since they are tough and papery, these chiles require rehydrating, which was a snap to do in the microwave. To break them down and incorporate them into the chili, we also needed to puree them in a blender. Since we already had the blender out, we tossed in the canned chipotle chiles as well to save some time.

We now had our five alarms and, more importantly, deep, complex heat and flavor. Chiles selected, we moved on to the tomatoes. Most quick chilis call for canned tomatoes (either diced or whole), to save prep work, but since we were cooking only enough for two, we wondered if we could substitute fresh tomatoes without adding too much work. We cored a few plum tomatoes and added them to the blender with the chiles. They pureed like a dream and integrated perfectly into our chili, adding a burst of fresh brightness and acidity.

With the tomatoes settled, we thought we might be finished. But when we made the next batch, we were forced to admit that although the chili had multiple levels of flavor and heat, it tasted a little flat. How could that be? We studied the recipe, looking for places to cram in more flavor. We tried substituting chicken broth for some of the water, but it seemed out of place in our beefy chili. Then we thought of an unusual ingredient that we sometimes see in chili recipes: beer. Just a third of a cup of a light-bodied lager introduced malty, mellow depth and a hint of bitterness.

All our chili needed now was a little more body. Serious chiliheads' recipes often rely on masa (ground dried corn) to add a subtle background of corn flavor. Few of us keep masa on hand, but we loved the concept of a flavorful, corny thickener. One taster suggested substituting more convenient corn tortilla chips for the masa. We tried adding them to the blender with the tomatoes, chiles, and water, and they blended into a smooth paste that contributed body along with a slight taste of corn.

As the chili simmered, the flavors melded, the broth thickened, and complex flavor met raw heat. After 30 minutes, we cautiously dipped in our spoons. Our eyes teared, our faces flushed, and we had to mop our brows. Yes, this chili was five-alarm hot, but the other flavors came through loud and clear as well.

Five-Alarm Chili

Dried ancho chiles can be found in the international aisle of most supermarkets. Light-bodied American lagers, such as Budweiser, work best in this recipe. Serve with shredded cheddar cheese, sour cream, fresh cilantro, and tortilla chips. See page 72 for a recipe to use up the leftover pinto beans.

- ½ ounce dried ancho chiles, stems and seeds removed and flesh torn into 1-inch pieces
- 1⅓ cups water
- 4 plum tomatoes, cored and halved lengthwise
- 3 tablespoons crushed corn tortilla chips
- 1 tablespoon minced canned chipotle chile in adobo sauce
- 4 teaspoons vegetable oil
- 8 ounces 85 percent lean ground beef
  Salt and pepper
- 1 onion, chopped fine
- ½ jalapeño chile, stemmed, seeds reserved, and minced
- 2 garlic cloves, minced
- 1½ teaspoons ground cumin
- 1½ teaspoons chili powder
- ½ teaspoon sugar
- ⅛ teaspoon cayenne pepper
- ⅓ cup beer
- ¾ cup canned pinto beans, rinsed

1. Combine anchos and ⅓ cup water in bowl and microwave until softened, about 2 minutes. Drain and discard liquid. Process anchos, remaining 1 cup water, tomatoes, tortilla chips, and chipotle chile in blender until smooth, about 1 minute; set aside.

2. Heat 2 teaspoons oil in medium saucepan over medium-high heat until just smoking. Add beef, ¼ teaspoon salt, and ⅛ teaspoon pepper and cook, breaking up pieces with spoon, until all liquid has evaporated and beef begins to sizzle, 5 to 7 minutes. Drain in colander; set aside.

3. Heat remaining 2 teaspoons oil in now-empty saucepan over medium-high heat until shimmering. Add onion, jalapeño, and seeds and cook until onion is lightly browned, about 5 minutes. Stir in garlic, cumin, chili powder, sugar, and cayenne and cook until fragrant, about 30 seconds. Pour in beer and bring to simmer. Stir in reserved ancho-tomato mixture, reserved cooked beef, and pinto beans and bring to simmer. Cover, reduce heat to low, and cook, stirring occasionally, until thickened, about 30 minutes. Season with salt to taste and serve.

MOROCCAN FISH AND COUSCOUS PACKETS

☑ **WHY THIS RECIPE WORKS:** Cooking fish *en papillote* is a technique where fish and a side are artfully folded into a parchment paper packet to cook together in the oven. The technique has a lot going for it, but we would have to do away with the fussy folded paper. We replaced the parchment with easy aluminum foil. White fish fillets worked best; oilier fishes like salmon or tuna ended up greasy and overwhelmingly pungent. For a simple side, we liked quick-cooking couscous, and we dressed it up with a zesty chermoula sauce, a flavorful Moroccan condiment of cilantro, ginger, garlic, lemon, and spices.

WE LOVE COOKING FISH EN PAPILLOTE (IN A PACKET) since it's an easy, mess-free way to obtain perfectly moist, flaky, and flavorful fish. There are countless combinations of fish, vegetables, and grains you can cook en papillote, and, best of all, since each serving is self-contained, the method is easily adaptable for two.

Most classic recipes we found for fish en papillote called for cutting parchment paper into attractive shapes such as teardrops, hearts, or even butterflies, then creasing the seams into painstakingly precise little folds to secure the food inside. Sure, it makes for an impressive presentation, but we wanted to translate the technique into an easy weeknight meal for two, so we would choose a simpler route. We immediately swapped the fussy parchment paper for aluminum foil; simply folding the foil over the fish, then crimping the edges created an airtight seal that would lock in steam.

Next, we needed to decide what to cook for the main event. After trying a variety of fish, we found that fillets of flaky, mild white fish, such as halibut and cod, worked better than more assertively flavored fish such as salmon or tuna. In the moist, contained atmosphere of the foil pouches, the flavors of the oilier fish were concentrated and overpowered whatever else we added to the packets. In addition, their extra oils made the packets' contents greasy and overly pungent. White fish, on the other hand, stayed moist and flaky and came out lightly flavored and fragrant.

Determining when the fish was done proved more challenging: The old rule of thumb for fish—10 minutes of cooking time per inch of thickness—failed in this case, as the resulting fish was barely opaque. After experimenting with a range of oven temperatures and cooking times, we found that ¾- to 1-inch-thick fillets cooked best at 400 degrees for 14 to 18 minutes. While this was an unusually long cooking time at such high heat, the fish was well insulated within the sealed packets and emerged flaky and moist. To avoid unwrapping the packets when we wanted to test the fish for doneness, we simply stuck our instant-read thermometer directly through the foil into the fish; once the fillets hit 140 degrees, they were ready.

With our fish perfected, we moved on to an accompanying side. Rice or other grains would take too long to cook through, so they were out of contention. Instead we thought of quick-cooking couscous. This tiny pasta needs only a five- to 10-minute soak in boiling water to turn from dry to tender. Perhaps this was the solution?

We tried adding the dry couscous to the packets with water, but once the fish was cooked through, we still had a puddle of water and a pile of dry couscous in our packets. For our next test, we soaked the couscous ahead of time and then added the rehydrated pasta to the packets. This time, both the fish and the couscous emerged from the oven tender and moist. Now all our dish needed was a little sprucing up.

Couscous has its roots in North African cuisine, so we thought we would add a zesty chermoula sauce to the packets to complement it. Chermoula is a Moroccan condiment combining cilantro, smoky paprika, garlic, lemon, cumin, hot pepper flakes, and olive oil. Although not traditional, a little ginger added a welcome hint of warm spice. A tablespoon spread on top of the fish before wrapping it in the packets added not only flavor but also extra protection against drying out. We made a generous amount of sauce so that we could also serve it alongside the fish once it was cooked.

While the presentation was simple, the flavors of our dish were anything but. Fragrant Moroccan flavors mixed with the mild fish for a light but satisfying meal that was on the table in just 30 minutes.

Moroccan Fish and Couscous Packets

SERVES 2

Be sure to choose fillets of the same thickness so they will cook through at the same time.

¼ cup minced fresh cilantro
2 tablespoons extra-virgin olive oil
1 tablespoon grated fresh ginger
2 teaspoons smoked paprika
2 garlic cloves, minced
2 teaspoons grated lemon zest plus 1 tablespoon juice
1 teaspoon ground cumin
⅛ teaspoon red pepper flakes
    Salt and pepper
    Brown sugar
¾ cup couscous
1 cup boiling water
2 (6- to 8-ounce) skinless white fish fillets, ¾ to 1 inch thick
    Lemon wedges

1. Adjust oven rack to middle position and heat oven to 400 degrees. Combine 3 tablespoons cilantro, oil, ginger, paprika, garlic, 1 ½ teaspoons lemon zest, lemon juice, cumin, and pepper flakes in small bowl. Season with salt, pepper, and sugar to taste.

2. Place couscous in medium bowl. Pour boiling water over couscous. Immediately cover with plastic wrap and let sit until liquid is absorbed and couscous is tender, about 5 minutes. Fluff couscous with fork, stir in remaining ½ teaspoon lemon zest, and season with salt and pepper to taste.

MOROCCAN FISH AND COUSCOUS PACKETS

MAKING EASY MOROCCAN FISH PACKETS

1. Place mound of prepared couscous in center of each piece of foil, then place fish on top and spread prepared sauce over fish.

2. Crimp edges of foil to seal packet. Place on rimmed baking sheet and bake at 400 degrees for 14 to 18 minutes, until fish is just cooked through. Open packets, sprinkle fish with remaining cilantro, and serve with remaining sauce.

ALL ABOUT COUSCOUS

Although couscous looks like a grain, it is technically a pasta. This starch is made from durum semolina, a high-protein wheat flour that is also used to make Italian pasta. Traditional Moroccan couscous is made by rubbing coarse-ground durum semolina and water between the hands to form small, coarse granules. The couscous is then dried and cooked in a steamer called a *couscoussière* set over a simmering stew. The couscous plumps in the steam produced by the stew. The boxed couscous found in most supermarkets is a precooked version of traditional couscous. About the size of bread crumbs, the precooked couscous needs only a few minutes of steeping in hot liquid to be fully cooked.

3. Pat fish dry with paper towels and season with salt and pepper. Lay two 14-inch lengths of aluminum foil on counter. Divide couscous in half evenly, mound in center of each foil piece, then place fish fillets on top. Spread 1 tablespoon sauce over top of each piece of fish. Fold foil over fish and couscous, crimping edges to seal.

4. Arrange packets in single layer on rimmed baking sheet. Bake until fish registers 140 degrees and flakes apart when gently prodded with paring knife, 14 to 18 minutes. Sprinkle fish with remaining 1 tablespoon cilantro. Serve with remaining sauce and lemon wedges.

CHILI-GLAZED SALMON WITH BOK CHOY

✔ **WHY THIS RECIPE WORKS:** To bring glazed salmon home for two, we wanted a foolproof way to get perfectly cooked fish with a crisp, well-browned crust. Cooking the fillets in a nonstick skillet kept the browned crust on the fish, not stuck to the pan. Relying on an instant-read thermometer to test for doneness rather than visual cues took out the guesswork. We started our Asian-inspired glaze with sweet chili sauce; a little savory fish sauce and fresh ginger were all we needed to turn it into a boldly flavored glaze. Baby bok choy sautéed until lightly browned paired perfectly with the rich salmon.

GLAZED, PAN-SEARED SALMON IS A COMMON restaurant specialty—its crisp, browned crust and rich, unctuous flavor are pretty irresistible. But making this favorite at home can be a challenge. All too often, recipes for pan-seared salmon make fillets with little crust and a lot of overcooked, dry flesh. We wanted to find an easy, foolproof method for searing and glazing salmon for two with flavors inspired by Southeast Asia.

To prevent the fish from sticking and to promote browning, salmon is typically sautéed in a traditional skillet with a generous amount of oil. Most of the time, however, the oil ends up splattering all over the stovetop and does little to keep the fish from fusing to the skillet. Here in the test kitchen, we prefer to cook most fish fillets in a nonstick skillet, which helps keep them intact and allows us to cut back a bit on the oil. We knew that salmon also contains a moderate amount of fat itself, which would render in the skillet, allowing us to cut back even further on oil. After testing smaller and smaller amounts of oil, we found we needed only a single tablespoon to get the fish crisp and brown on both sides.

The crusts were perfect, but we still had to prevent the flesh from drying out. Most recipes for fish rely on visual cues, but we wanted our recipe to be foolproof, so we would use an instant-read thermometer to determine exact doneness. After several tests, we found that the fillets had the best texture when we removed them from the pan as their internal temperatures reached 125 degrees.

Next, we shifted our attention to the glaze. Tasters wanted bold flavors, so we began building the glaze with vibrant sweet chili sauce. The chili sauce added not only sweet and sour flavors but also viscosity and texture to the resulting glaze. To the chili sauce we added a full tablespoon of fish sauce for salty savoriness. A bit of ginger added some spicy warmth, and a quarter teaspoon of cornstarch thickened the glaze just enough to cling lightly to the fillets.

Our plan was to sear the salmon, then coat the fish with the glaze off the heat. The only problem with this plan was that the salmon, especially when we were working with farmed salmon, gave off far too much fat to make an edible glaze. When we added the glaze to the pan, the excess fat made the whole dish greasy and unappealing. Luckily, it was a quick fix. Before adding the glaze, we carefully held the salmon in place with a spatula and poured off the excess fat. Problem solved.

With our salmon seared and glazed, we turned to our side dish. We knew we wanted a quick-cooking vegetable that would pair well with our Asian-style glaze. Baby bok choy seemed like a perfect choice. The leafy cruciferous vegetable comes in single-serving-size 4-ounce heads, well suited for our two-person meal. We tried simply adding the bok choy to the skillet and

sautéing it in the leftover glaze after cooking the salmon, but this method was a flop.

While there was still plenty of glaze left in the skillet to coat the greens, the bok choy tasted watery and bland and never achieved any browning. Instead of adding it at the end, we thought a two-step cooking process might work better. We decided to sear the bok choy in a bit of vegetable oil before starting the salmon. We then set the browned bok choy aside while we cooked the salmon and returned it to the skillet at the very end for a quick toss in the glaze. The resulting side boasted an unbeatable combination of sweet vegetal flavors and crisp texture—the perfect match for our tender, golden-crusted salmon.

Chili-Glazed Salmon with Bok Choy
SERVES 2

Be sure to use sweet chili sauce here; hot chili sauce (such as chili-garlic sauce) will make the glaze far too spicy and thin.

- 2 tablespoons Asian sweet chili sauce
- 1 tablespoon fish sauce
- 1½ teaspoons grated fresh ginger
- ¼ teaspoon cornstarch
- 2 tablespoons vegetable oil
- 2 heads baby bok choy (4 ounces each), halved lengthwise
- 2 (6- to 8-ounce) skinless salmon fillets, 1½ inches thick
  Salt and pepper
  Lime wedges

1. Whisk chili sauce, fish sauce, ginger, and cornstarch together in small bowl; set aside. Heat 1 tablespoon oil in 10-inch nonstick skillet over high heat until shimmering. Cook bok choy, cut side down, until lightly browned, 1 to 2 minutes. Turn bok choy over and continue to cook until lightly browned on second side, about 1 minute. Transfer to platter.

2. Pat salmon dry with paper towels and season with salt and pepper. Add remaining 1 tablespoon oil to now-empty skillet and heat over medium-high heat until just smoking. Cook salmon until browned on first side, about 4 minutes. Flip salmon and continue to cook

---

NOTES FROM THE TEST KITCHEN

CLEANING BOK CHOY

Submerge halved baby bok choy in cold water and then swish heads to remove any dirt and grit.

ALL ABOUT SWEET CHILI SAUCE

Unlike the spicy Asian chili sauces, which add heat, sweet chili sauce lies at the other end of the flavor spectrum. This sweet, thick sauce is made primarily from palm sugar, pickled chiles, vinegar, and garlic. It makes a good dipping sauce for egg rolls and dumplings, it is often served in Thailand with barbecued chicken, and we also use it as a glaze.

until center is still translucent when checked with tip of paring knife and registers 125 degrees (for medium-rare), about 4 minutes longer. Holding fish in place with spatula, carefully pour off any rendered fat in skillet. Off heat, add chili sauce mixture to skillet with salmon and flip fish once or twice to coat. Transfer fish to platter.

3. Add bok choy to skillet with glaze and toss until coated. Serve with salmon and lime wedges.

SEARED SCALLOPS WITH BUTTERNUT SQUASH

✔ **WHY THIS RECIPE WORKS:** For an elegant seared scallop supper for two, we set out to re-create the blazing heat of a professional stovetop. To keep the scallops' liquid from preventing browning, we carefully patted them dry and cooked them in a roomy 12-inch skillet. Waiting until the oil was just smoking ensured that the pan was hot enough to give the scallops golden-brown crusts and juicy medium-rare centers. To complement the scallops we made a quick and easy butternut squash puree in the same skillet, then we finished the dish with a rich browned butter sauce to drizzle over the plate.

FOR A RESTAURANT CHEF, PAN-SEARED SCALLOPS are as easy as it gets: Slick a super-hot pan with oil, sear the shellfish on one side, flip them once, and serve. The whole process takes no more than a couple of minutes and produces golden-crusted beauties with tender, medium-rare interiors. But try the same technique at home and you're likely to run into trouble. The problem is that most home stovetops don't get nearly as hot as professional ranges, so it's difficult to properly brown the scallops without overcooking them. But since scallops are so easy to buy and cook in small quantities, they are tailor-made for two. We were determined to achieve superior pan-seared scallops—we just had to find a solution to the browning conundrum. We also wanted to create a rich, luscious side dish to pair with the scallops, but we didn't want to dirty an extra pan.

Our first stop was the supermarket fish counter. Scallops are available in a wide range of sizes, from the hard-to-find large sea variety, which contains eight to 10 scallops per pound, to the petite bay variety, which can contain as many as 100 scallops per pound. Since small scallops are more prone to overcooking than large, we opted for the biggest commonly available size: 10 to 20 scallops per pound. Twelve ounces of scallops seemed like the right amount for two; at this size, each serving would be about four scallops per person.

We started by seasoning the scallops simply with salt and pepper. We heated 1 tablespoon of vegetable oil in a 10-inch stainless steel skillet, in which the scallops would fit comfortably, then added the scallops in a single layer and waited for them to brown. After three minutes, they were steaming away in a ¼-inch-deep pool of liquid. At the five-minute mark, the moisture in the skillet evaporated and the flesh finally began to turn golden. But at this point it was too late: The scallops were already overcooked and tough, and we hadn't even flipped them yet.

To reduce the amount of liquid they exuded, we tried thoroughly drying the scallops before cooking. We also switched to a roomier 12-inch skillet to allow the liquid to spread out and cook off faster. But it became clear that to get serious browning on our scallops, we'd need to get the pan as hot as possible. Without a high-output professional range, it was important to pay careful attention to technique. We started by waiting to add the scallops to the skillet until the oil was beginning to smoke, a clear indication of high heat. Switching to a nonstick skillet ensured that as the scallops cooked, the browned bits formed a crust on the meat instead of sticking to the skillet. These scallops rivaled those made on a powerful restaurant range, with golden-brown crusts and juicy and tender interiors.

Now it was on to our side dish. We decided on creamy pureed butternut squash, which would pair perfectly with our favorite topping for scallops: browned butter. Keeping in mind our one-dish mission, we steamed a pound of peeled and cubed squash in our skillet before cooking the scallops. Half a cup of water and 10 minutes on the stovetop was all it took to render the squash tender. We drained the cooked squash, then transferred it to a food processor with a bit of butter, cream, and cayenne and processed it into a beautifully smooth, creamy puree.

Finally we made the browned butter sauce. After searing the scallops, we melted a couple of tablespoons

NOTES FROM THE TEST KITCHEN

PREPARING SCALLOPS

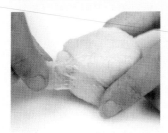

The small, crescent-shaped tendon that is sometimes attached to the scallop will be inedibly tough when cooked. Use your fingers to peel it away from the side of each scallop before cooking.

of butter in the hot skillet; it took only about 30 seconds for the butter to turn nutty brown. We added a minced shallot and a teaspoon of minced sage for an herbal note. All this rich sauce needed was a squeeze of bright lemon for balance.

Drizzled over the top of the scallops and squash, the browned butter sauce made our simple seafood dinner into a meal elegant enough to rival any restaurant special.

Seared Scallops with Butternut Squash
SERVES 2

We recommend buying "dry" scallops, which don't have chemical additives and taste better than "wet." Dry scallops will look ivory or pinkish; wet scallops are bright white. Cream or whole milk can be substituted for the half-and-half if necessary.

- 1 pound butternut squash, peeled, seeded, and cut into 1-inch pieces (2½ cups)
- ½ cup water
- 2 tablespoons unsalted butter, cut into 4 equal pieces
- 1½ teaspoons half-and-half
-    Salt and pepper
-    Pinch cayenne pepper
- 12 ounces large sea scallops, tendons removed
- 1 tablespoon vegetable oil
- 1 small shallot, minced
- 1 teaspoon minced fresh sage
- 1½ teaspoons lemon juice

1. Add squash and water to 12-inch nonstick skillet. Cover and cook over medium heat until squash is tender, about 10 minutes. Drain squash and transfer to food processor. Add 1 piece butter, half-and-half, ¼ teaspoon salt, and cayenne and process until smooth, about 30 seconds. Season with salt and pepper to taste, transfer to serving bowl, and cover to keep warm.

2. Pat scallops dry with paper towels and season with salt and pepper. Heat oil in now-empty skillet over medium-high heat until just smoking. Lay scallops in skillet and cook, without moving, until well browned, 1½ to 2 minutes. Flip scallops and continue to cook until sides are firm and centers are opaque, 30 to 90 seconds longer. Transfer to platter and cover.

3. Add remaining pieces butter to now-empty skillet and cook over medium heat until melted and just starting to brown, about 30 seconds. Add shallot and sage and cook until fragrant, about 1 minute. Off heat, stir in lemon juice and season with salt and pepper to taste. Pour sauce over scallops and serve with pureed squash.

USE IT UP: BUTTERNUT SQUASH

Sautéed Butternut Squash
SERVES 2

Be sure to add the shallot toward the end of cooking so that it does not burn.

- 1 tablespoon olive oil
- 1 pound butternut squash, peeled, seeded, and cut into ½-inch pieces (1¾ cups)
-    Salt and pepper
- 1 shallot, sliced thin
- 1 tablespoon butter
- 1 tablespoon chopped fresh parsley

Heat oil in 10-inch nonstick skillet over medium heat until shimmering. Add squash and ⅛ teaspoon salt and cook, without stirring, until beginning to caramelize, 4 to 5 minutes. Continue cooking, stirring occasionally, until spotty brown, 3 to 4 minutes longer. Add shallot and butter and continue to cook until squash and shallot are tender, 1 to 3 minutes. Off heat, stir in parsley and season with salt and pepper to taste. Serve.

VEGETABLE LASAGNA

SKILLET PASTA WITH FRESH TOMATO SAUCE

✔ WHY THIS RECIPE WORKS: For an effortless but flavorful pasta dinner featuring fresh tomatoes, we simmered the tomatoes briefly so they'd break down and release their juice, then added the pasta right to the pan to cook through. Not only did the released pasta starch help to thicken the sauce, making it nicely clingy, but the pasta picked up deep flavor from cooking in the sauce.

PICKED AT THE PEAK OF RIPENESS, CANNED tomatoes offer better tomato flavor than their fresh counterparts do—most of the year, that is. When you can get your hands on fully ripe, juicy in-season tomatoes, it's time to go with the real deal. In the test kitchen, we've developed a foolproof recipe for fresh tomato sauce to serve a crowd or store for winter, but now we wanted a super-fresh, low-fuss tomato sauce that was just enough for two, so we set out to whittle down our recipe.

Ripe height-of-season tomatoes boast not only an ultrajuicy texture, but also subtly contrasting sweet and tart flavors. The best fresh tomato sauces capture this complexity. But many fresh tomato sauces we've had are watery or mealy and have little tomato flavor. To eke out maximum flavor, our standard recipe calls for simmering a few pounds of chopped tomatoes with sautéed onion and garlic for a short amount of time, until the sauce is nicely thickened and the excess liquid has been cooked off. For our simple sauce, we decided to follow suit. After sautéing our aromatics, we cored and chopped 1 pound of tomatoes, then simmered them briefly, just until they started to break down and exude their juice.

Since we needed to give the tomatoes time to cook down and thicken to the proper consistency, we wondered if we could combine this step with cooking the pasta to make an easy one-pot supper. Once the tomatoes had a head start on the stovetop, we added 2 cups of water to the pan, plus our pasta, and let it simmer away. Unfortunately, the resulting pasta dish was far from richly flavored and saucy—all the liquid had evaporated, leaving us with dry pasta in an overly thickened sauce. The next time around, we covered the pan after adding the water and pasta to keep it from drying out. This worked perfectly: The starch from the pasta helped thicken the sauce, making it nicely clingy, and the pasta absorbed the rich flavor of the tomatoes as it simmered in the pan.

Since adding water to cook the pasta diluted the flavor of the sauce slightly, we had to figure out how to bump it up. The test kitchen often turns to tomato paste to amp up the savory complexity of dishes, and here it worked like a charm. Just 1½ teaspoons added much-needed depth and savory notes. Looking for something else to enhance the sauce's brightness, we hit on white wine; although not traditional for tomato sauce, it rounded out the flavor of our sauce nicely.

In less than 30 minutes, we had a bright, bold tomato sauce that clung to every piece of pasta perfectly. A few tablespoons of chopped basil stirred in at the end of cooking sent the freshness quotient soaring, and some grated Parmesan cheese added a savory, salty touch. With a recipe this easy and delicious, we knew we'd be making this dish all summer long.

Skillet Pasta with Fresh Tomato Sauce
SERVES 2

Other pasta shapes can be substituted for the campanelle; however, their cup measurements may vary (see page 88).

- 1 tablespoon extra-virgin olive oil
- 1 small onion, chopped fine
- 2 garlic cloves, minced
- 1½ teaspoons tomato paste
- 1 pound tomatoes, cored and cut into ½-inch pieces
  Salt and pepper
- ¼ cup dry white wine
- 2 cups water, plus extra as needed
- 6 ounces (2 cups) campanelle
- 2 tablespoons chopped fresh basil
  Grated Parmesan cheese

1. Heat oil in 12-inch nonstick skillet over medium heat until shimmering. Add onion and cook until softened, about 5 minutes. Stir in garlic and tomato paste and cook until fragrant, about 1 minute. Stir in tomatoes, ½ teaspoon salt, and ¼ teaspoon pepper and cook until tomato pieces lose their shape, 5 to 7 minutes. Stir in wine and simmer for 2 minutes.

2. Stir in water and pasta. Cover, increase heat to medium-high, and cook at vigorous simmer, stirring often, until pasta is nearly tender, 10 to 12 minutes.

3. Uncover and continue to simmer, tossing pasta gently, until pasta is tender and sauce has thickened, 3 to 5 minutes; if sauce becomes too thick, add extra water as needed. Off heat, stir in basil and season with salt and pepper to taste. Serve with Parmesan.

SPAGHETTI AL VINO BIANCO

✔ WHY THIS RECIPE WORKS: Spaghetti *al vino rosso*—a legendary dish in which the pasta cooks in an entire bottle of red wine—was the inspiration for this dish, but it needed some modifications to make it a satisfying weeknight dinner for two. Switching from red to white wine gave the dish bright acidity (and kept it from turning purple), and simmering a portion of the wine to a syrupy glaze ensured optimal flavor. Pancetta, arugula, and pine nuts ensured that this simple dish was hearty and filling.

A PLATE OF PASTA AND A GLASS OF WINE ARE A natural pairing. But we'd long heard references to a dish called spaghetti al vino rosso that exploits their affinity: The pasta itself is cooked in wine instead of water and then topped off with olive oil, a bit of butter, and a sprinkling of cheese. This sounded like an easy, yet flavorful and exciting, addition to our pasta-for-two roster.

But once we started our research, we learned that recipes are hard to track down, and the ones we found were all over the map. One called for boiling the spaghetti in a 50-50 mix of water and red wine that was then (wastefully) poured down the drain. In another, a whole bottle of wine was reduced to a glaze (eliminating all of its pleasant booziness) and used to coat spaghetti cooked separately in water. A third approach resembled risotto making and seemed the most promising: parcooking the pasta in water and then transferring it to a skillet where about 2 cups of wine were added in increments so that the pasta could absorb the wine as it finished cooking.

But even when prepared using the last approach, the dish wasn't perfect. While tasters liked the pasta's lively wine kick, they also found that the dish tasted tannic. The deal breaker, though, was its unappetizing purple-gray color.

Our research indicated that this dish is almost always made with red wine. Nevertheless, we couldn't help but wonder what would happen if we swapped the red wine for white, which would at least get rid of the unappealing mauve color. We tried it and found that the switch also solved the tannin problem, since such flavors come from the grape skins, which are removed early in the process of making white wine. But now we had a new issue: The spaghetti wasn't as robustly flavored when made with white wine.

We thought back to the method of reducing a full bottle of wine in a skillet. After scaling down the amounts proportionately, we experimented with reducing ¾ cup of white wine to a glaze while the spaghetti parcooked in water. Then we introduced the partially cooked spaghetti to the glaze and added another ¾ cup of wine gradually, stirring as the spaghetti finished cooking. The glaze provided a subtle complexity that the dish had previously lacked, but we agreed that this spaghetti was going to need more than just olive oil, butter, and grated Pecorino Romano to be anything other than an Italian *primo*, or first course.

Garlic and red pepper flakes were natural additions, and they were easily incorporated into the glaze. Crisp, salty pancetta sprinkled over the pasta before serving was also a shoo-in. Casting about for a green that wouldn't require parcooking, we landed on arugula. Its peppery notes complemented the other flavors perfectly. Pine nuts added textural dimension.

Our spaghetti was almost complete, but it seemed a tad dry. We had been stirring in some butter along with reserved pasta water at the end, but the resulting sauce was too insubstantial. A little bit of cream was just the thing to bulk it up. Admittedly, we'd taken liberties by using white wine, but we were willing to bet that no one who tasted our dish would complain.

Spaghetti al Vino Bianco

SERVES 2

For this dish, you should use a good-quality dry white wine but avoid a heavily oaked white such as Chardonnay. If the wine reduction is too sharp in step 2, season to taste with up to 1½ teaspoons of sugar, adding it in ½-teaspoon increments. See page 88 for a tip on how to measure out long strands of pasta without using a scale.

- 1½ teaspoons extra-virgin olive oil
- 2 ounces pancetta, cut into ¼-inch pieces
- 1 garlic clove, minced
   Pinch red pepper flakes
- 1½ cups dry white wine
   Salt and pepper
   Sugar
- 6 ounces spaghetti
- 3 ounces (3 cups) baby arugula
- 3 tablespoons heavy cream
- ¼ cup grated Pecorino Romano cheese,
   plus extra for serving
- 2 tablespoons pine nuts, toasted and chopped coarse

1. Heat oil and pancetta in 12-inch skillet over medium-high heat; cook until pancetta is browned and crisp, 4 to 5 minutes. Using slotted spoon, transfer pancetta to paper towel–lined plate. Pour off and discard all but 1 tablespoon rendered fat from skillet.

2. Return skillet to medium-low heat and add garlic and pepper flakes. Cook, stirring frequently, until garlic begins to turn golden, 1 to 2 minutes. Carefully add ¾ cup wine and increase heat to medium-high. Cook until wine is reduced to ⅓ cup, 8 to 10 minutes. Add ⅛ teaspoon salt. Taste and season with up to 1½ teaspoons sugar if needed.

3. Bring 4 quarts water to boil in large pot. Add pasta and 1 tablespoon salt and cook, stirring often, until pasta is flexible but not fully cooked, about 4 minutes. Reserve 1 cup pasta water, then drain pasta.

4. Transfer pasta to skillet with reduced white wine. Place skillet over medium heat; add ¼ cup unreduced wine and cook, tossing constantly, until wine is fully absorbed. Continue to add remaining ½ cup wine, ¼ cup at a time, tossing constantly, until pasta is al dente, 6 to 8 minutes. (If wine is absorbed before spaghetti is fully cooked, add reserved pasta water to skillet ¼ cup at a time and continue to cook.)

5. Remove skillet from heat. Place arugula on top of spaghetti; pour ¼ cup reserved pasta water over arugula, cover, and let stand for 1 minute. Add cream and 2 tablespoons Pecorino; toss until sauce lightly coats pasta and arugula is evenly distributed. Season with salt and pepper to taste. Transfer to serving platter and sprinkle with pancetta, remaining 2 tablespoons Pecorino, and pine nuts. Serve immediately, passing extra Pecorino separately.

PENNE WITH PANCETTA AND WHITE BEANS

✓ **WHY THIS RECIPE WORKS:** For an easy, Tuscan-inspired supper, we combined pasta with crispy pancetta, creamy cannellini beans, and woodsy rosemary. Canned beans made this dish weeknight-friendly, and simmering them with chicken broth and white wine gave them slow-cooked depth in minutes.

A HEARTY PASTA DISH FEATURING CREAMY, TENDER beans and cured pork is a staple in Tuscany. In the home of the slow-food movement, cooking white beans from scratch makes perfect sense, but for a quick-cooking meal for two, it seemed like a nonstarter. After all, dried beans must be soaked overnight before being simmered for hours. But while we wanted an easy weeknight meal, we didn't want to sacrifice the clean flavor and delicate texture of the slow-cooked version. Was there a way to have both?

To speed up our supper, our first move was to opt for canned beans instead of dried. But we'd have to find a way to give our can of mild-flavored beans a more slow-cooked taste, and to do so we would need to incorporate some additional flavors.

Cured pork and beans have a natural affinity for each other, and we wanted the pork to support, but not overwhelm, the flavor of the beans. While bacon is the go-to version of cured pork in the United States, its smokiness can easily overpower the milder flavors in a dish, so we decided to use pancetta instead. Pancetta is cured with salt and spices, not smoked like bacon, so it has a more subtle, complex flavor. To infuse the whole dish with its richness, we browned the pancetta in the skillet first, then set it aside and saved it for a crunchy garnish while we sautéed the aromatics in the fat left behind.

As far as the aromatics were concerned, we focused on a few well-chosen additions that would really bring our dish to the next level. Onion gave us a savory base of flavor for the beans. Garlic was a must, and though we didn't want it to dominate our dish, we didn't want to be shy with it either. In the end, three cloves did the trick. A small amount of rosemary added woodsy, herbal notes, and some red pepper flakes lent a much-needed punch of heat.

Chicken broth and white wine gave us the makings of a simple yet flavorful pan sauce, but this brothy base gave us an idea: What if we simmered the beans in this enhanced broth long enough to infuse them with flavor, instead of simply adding them to the sauce before serving? For our next test, we sautéed our aromatics, then added the broth, wine, and beans to the pan and let it all cook long enough for the sauce to thicken.

We were amazed at the difference in the beans. Still intact, they had softened slightly and were deeply flavored. The chicken broth added a savory richness, and the wine contributed a bracing acidity that kept the beans from tasting flat. Penne was the perfect pasta to add to our bean "broth"—its short length complemented the size and shape of the beans, and its ridges held on tightly to the thickened sauce.

To finish the dish, we stirred in a good amount of grated Parmesan cheese, which added richness and a nutty, savory flavor, and the crisped pancetta, which delivered a satisfying crunch. Sure, we took a few shortcuts to keep our cooking time to a minimum, but our pasta dish tasted so good, you'd never know it.

Penne with Pancetta, White Beans, and Rosemary

SERVES 2

Though we prefer pancetta here, you can substitute prosciutto or bacon. Other pasta shapes can be substituted for the penne; however, their cup measurements may vary (see page 88).

- 1½ teaspoons olive oil
- 2 ounces thinly sliced pancetta, cut into ¼-inch-wide strips
- 1 small onion, chopped fine
- 3 garlic cloves, minced
- ½ teaspoon minced fresh rosemary
  Pinch red pepper flakes
- ¾ cup low-sodium chicken broth
- ½ cup dry white wine
- 1 (15-ounce) can cannellini beans, rinsed
- 6 ounces (2 cups) penne
  Salt and pepper
- 1 ounce Parmesan cheese, grated (½ cup), plus extra for serving
- 2 tablespoons chopped fresh parsley

1. Cook oil and pancetta in 10-inch skillet over medium heat until pancetta is well browned and crisp, about 8 minutes. Using slotted spoon, transfer pancetta to paper towel–lined plate.

NOTES FROM THE TEST KITCHEN

THE BEST PENNE
Curious if there was any difference among the various brands of penne you find at the supermarket—from fancy imported brands to inexpensive domestic brands—we pitted eight brands against each other in a taste-off. Though the fancier brands from Italy boasted traditional techniques and ingredients (such as slow kneading, mixing cold mountain spring water with hard durum semolina, and extruding the dough through traditional bronze cast dies for a coarse texture), we found they didn't necessarily translate into better-tasting pasta. In fact, the three most expensive imports landed at the bottom of our rankings. Though none were so bad that they were deemed unacceptable, there were significant differences among the brands we tasted. In the end, tasters rated **Mueller's Penne Rigate** the highest for "hearty," "wheaty" flavor.

SUMMER PASTA WITH CORN, CHERRY TOMATOES, AND RICOTTA SALATA

2. Add onion to fat left in skillet and cook over medium heat until softened and golden brown, 8 to 10 minutes. Stir in garlic, rosemary, and pepper flakes and cook until fragrant, about 1 minute. Stir in broth, wine, and beans, bring to simmer, and cook until sauce is slightly thickened, about 10 minutes.

3. Meanwhile, bring 4 quarts water to boil in large pot. Add pasta and 1 tablespoon salt and cook, stirring often, until al dente. Reserve ½ cup cooking water, then drain pasta and return it to pot. Add sauce, crisped pancetta, Parmesan, and parsley and toss to combine. Season with salt and pepper to taste and add reserved cooking water as needed to adjust consistency. Serve with extra Parmesan.

SUMMER PASTA WITH CORN AND TOMATOES

✔ WHY THIS RECIPE WORKS: To enjoy the best of summer, we paired al dente pasta with crisp-tender corn and ripe, plump cherry tomatoes. The key to this dish's success was cooking everything briefly to keep it fresh tasting. Sweet corn and juicy cherry tomatoes needed a brief sauté to bring out their flavors and soften them slightly. Tossing the pasta with extra-virgin olive oil and chopped basil and mint kept everything light and bright, and toasted pine nuts and shaved salty ricotta salata added savory richness.

NOWADAYS, MOST VEGETABLES ARE AVAILABLE year-round, thanks to international shipping and greenhouse agriculture. Yet there's nothing quite like fresh, ripe veggies at the height of the summer season, especially tomatoes and corn. We wanted to create a pasta dish that showcased their sweet, bright flavors and was prepared with minimal fuss.

While we wanted to keep the dish fresh-tasting, we knew the corn required at least a little heat to enhance its natural sweetness and soften it slightly. Grilled corn is always a favorite at the test kitchen, but firing up the grill to sear a single ear of corn seemed downright silly. Instead, we cut the kernels from the cob and sautéed them briefly in some extra-virgin olive oil. The sugars in the corn caramelized to golden-brown perfection.

For substantial bites of tomato, we selected cherry tomatoes and halved them. The skin-to-flesh ratio of cherry tomatoes ensured that they would maintain their shape during a quick sear and not turn to mush. Adding them toward the end of cooking helped keep them intact; a few minutes was enough to soften them slightly and heat them through.

To keep this dish out of pasta salad territory, we bypassed the usual vinaigrettes and dressings and simply tossed the pasta with extra-virgin olive oil. While most pasta dishes call for just a sprinkling of herbs, we wanted to amp up the fresh herbal flavor in our summer pasta. Rather than reserve the herbs for a garnish, we used a generous amount of both chopped basil and chopped mint; a full 3 tablespoons of each contributed major flavor. Given the fresh herbs' prominent role in the dish, we found it important to treat them with extra care. Both basil and mint have a tendency to discolor once chopped, so we waited until just before serving to chop them and stir them in. A pinch of red pepper flakes and some garlic punched up the background notes.

Our simple pasta dish was coming together nicely, but it called out for some textural contrast. A few spoonfuls of nuts did the trick. Tasters preferred toasted pine nuts for their mild flavor and subtle crunch.

Finally, we looked to incorporate a creamy, cheesy element and considered our alternatives. Fresh mozzarella, a natural partner for fresh tomatoes, melted into the pasta, while tangy goat cheese overpowered the more understated flavors of the tomatoes and corn. In the end, we settled on salty ricotta salata, a firm, tangy Italian sheep's-milk cheese, to round out the dish. The saltiness of the cheese provided the perfect contrast to the sweetness of the tomatoes and caramelized corn. For a nice presentation, we shaved the cheese with a vegetable peeler and served the shavings atop the finished pasta.

With its bright, fresh notes and focus on ripe, in-season vegetables, this pasta dish delivered summer on a plate—make that two plates.

HOW TO COOK PASTA

If you ask 10 cooks how they cook pasta, you're likely to get 10 different answers. In an effort to standardize pasta cookery, we've come up with these guidelines that will guarantee perfect pasta every time.

USE 4 QUARTS OF WATER IN A LARGE POT: This may sound like a lot of water for just two servings, but it will ensure that the pasta cooks evenly and doesn't clump.

SKIP THE OIL AND USE PLENTY OF SALT: Many people dump oil into boiling pasta water, thinking it will keep the pasta from sticking together, but this is a myth. Adding oil does not prevent sticking; frequent stirring does. Skip the oil but make sure to add salt—roughly 1 tablespoon for 4 quarts of water—or the pasta will taste bland.

TASTE PASTA OFTEN FOR DONENESS: Reading the instructions on the box is a good place to start, but for al dente pasta, you may need to shave a few minutes off the recommended time. When you are a minute or two shy of the recommended cooking time, begin tasting for doneness.

SAVE SOME COOKING WATER: Wait! Before you drain that pasta, measure about ½ cup of the cooking water from the pasta pot with a liquid measuring cup. Then drain the pasta and immediately toss it with the sauce. (Don't let the pasta sit in the colander too long; it will get very dry very quickly.) When you toss your sauce with the pasta, add some (or all) of the reserved pasta cooking water to thin the sauce as needed.

MEASURING PASTA SHAPES

The best method for measuring pasta is to weigh it using a scale. However, if you do not own a scale, we have provided the equivalent cup measurements for various shapes. Use dry measuring cups for the most accurate measurements, and pack them full.

PASTA TYPE	4 OUNCES	6 OUNCES
Farfalle	1⅔ cups	2½ cups
Rigatoni, Rotini	1½ cups	2⅓ cups
Penne, Ziti	1¼ cups	2 cups
Campanelle	1¼ cups	2 cups
Orecchiette	1 cup	1¾ cups

When 6 ounces of uncooked spaghetti, thin spaghetti, spaghettini, fettuccine, linguine, or vermicelli are bunched together into a tight circle, the diameter measures about 1⅛ inches.

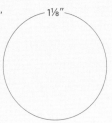
1⅛"

Summer Pasta with Corn, Cherry Tomatoes, and Ricotta Salata

SERVES 2

Both basil and mint have a tendency to discolor once chopped, so don't chop them too far ahead of time, and wait until just before serving to stir them into the pasta. We like the flavor of ricotta salata in this dish, but Pecorino Romano cheese can be substituted. Do not substitute frozen corn for the fresh corn here. Other pasta shapes can be substituted for the farfalle; however, their cup measurements may vary (see box at left).

- 2 tablespoons extra-virgin olive oil
- 1 shallot, minced
- 1 ear corn, kernels cut from cob
   Salt and pepper
- 2 garlic cloves, minced
   Pinch red pepper flakes
- 6 ounces cherry tomatoes, halved
- 6 ounces (2½ cups) farfalle
- 2 tablespoons pine nuts, toasted
- 3 tablespoons chopped fresh basil
- 3 tablespoons chopped fresh mint
- 1 ounce ricotta salata, shaved

1. Heat 1 tablespoon oil in 10-inch nonstick skillet over medium-high heat until shimmering. Add shallot and cook until softened, about 2 minutes. Add 1 teaspoon oil, corn, and ⅛ teaspoon salt and cook until corn is tender and spotty brown, 8 to 10 minutes. Stir in garlic and pepper flakes and cook until fragrant, about 30 seconds. Stir in tomatoes and cook until they just begin to soften, about 3 minutes.

2. Meanwhile, bring 4 quarts water to boil in large pot. Add pasta and 1 tablespoon salt and cook, stirring often, until al dente. Reserve ½ cup cooking water, then drain pasta and return it to pot. Add sauce, pine nuts, and remaining 2 teaspoons oil and toss gently to combine. Before serving, add reserved cooking water as needed to adjust consistency. Stir in basil and mint and season with salt and pepper to taste. Sprinkle with ricotta salata and serve immediately.

CAMPANELLE WITH ROASTED GARLIC, SHRIMP, AND FETA

✔ WHY THIS RECIPE WORKS: Roasted garlic adds sweet, intense flavor to this simple pasta dinner. To speed up the time required to deliver richly flavored, perfectly tender garlic, we turned out a few new tricks. First we separated the cloves and removed the skins, then we combined the peeled garlic cloves with oil and seasonings and roasted the mixture in a super-hot oven. Mashed with a fork, the soft, caramelized garlic made a savory sauce for the pasta. Adding shrimp right to the garlic and oil mixture to cook through instilled the briny shellfish with big flavor quickly.

PASTA WITH GARLIC AND OLIVE OIL MAKES THE ultimate easy weeknight supper—especially when cooking for two. Just bring a pot of water to a boil for your noodles, whip up a simple garlic and oil sauce, marry the two, and you're done. But sometimes we want a garlicky olive oil sauce with more oomph, and while the combination of garlic and olive oil is indeed simple, the standard preparation of standing over a skillet while slowly sautéing the garlic can be downright fussy. We wanted an easier way, and we wanted to add a little more heft to the dish in the form of quick-cooking shrimp.

We started with the sauce. There's a fine line between perfectly softened, mellowed garlic and garlic that's burnt and bitter—just a few extra seconds can push it over the edge. Roasting, on the other hand, doesn't run the same risk (or require as much attention), because the gentle, ambient heat of the oven allows the cloves to soften slowly and become nicely caramelized. But getting to this point can take up to an hour, which seemed silly when prepping a two-person supper; we needed a way to speed up the process.

Standard test kitchen protocol calls for roasting the garlic head whole with the top quarter sliced off; the head is drizzled with olive oil, wrapped in aluminum foil, and roasted on a baking sheet in a 350-degree oven.

To cut the hour-long roasting time in half, we made a few changes to our established roasting procedure. Our first move was to separate the cloves, which we hoped would allow them to cook through more quickly than when bunched together in a compact head. Then, since we weren't trying to ward off vampires with this dish, we whittled the number of cloves down to six, a number much more appropriate for two servings. We also cranked up the oven to 475 degrees. Finally, we swapped the baking sheet for a small baking dish, which would keep the cloves, plus a generous pour of olive oil, in close quarters and ideally prevent burning.

After half an hour, we checked the oven only to encounter tough, dark brown garlic cloves that were worlds away from the tender, richly caramelized garlic we'd hoped for. Thinking back to the traditional roasting method, we realized that the separated cloves of garlic still needed some protection from the direct heat of the oven. For the next test, we covered the baking dish with aluminum foil and lowered the oven temperature to 425 degrees.

In just 20 minutes, the garlic had become nicely caramelized and taken on a rich, sweet flavor. But although the flavor and texture of the garlic were spot-on, dealing with the scorching-hot, papery skins was a hassle; removing them prior to roasting solved the problem. Now we could mash the tender cloves right in the baking dish into a simple garlic and oil paste that would ensure that the rich garlicky flavor was evenly distributed throughout the dish. With a bit of salt and pepper, we had a flavorful start to our sauce.

As for the shrimp, we added them to the garlic and oil paste and returned the baking dish (which easily accommodated 8 ounces of shrimp) to the oven, uncovered, for about 10 minutes. Then we tossed the shrimp, garlic paste, pasta water, and campanelle together. A bit of salty crumbled feta complemented the sweet shrimp and garlic, and chopped basil added freshness.

After just a few forkfuls of this effortless, flavorful pasta dish, we had to pause to congratulate ourselves. We had successfully cut the time it takes to roast garlic in half—but we'd kept all the sweet roasted-garlic flavor intact. Weeknight cooking was never so easy.

Campanelle with Roasted Garlic, Shrimp, and Feta

SERVES 2

If your shrimp are larger or smaller, alter the cooking time in step 1 accordingly. Other pasta shapes can be substituted for the campanelle; however, their cup measurements may vary (see page 88).

2½	tablespoons olive oil
6	garlic cloves, peeled
	Salt and pepper
8	ounces medium-large shrimp (31 to 40 per pound), peeled, deveined, and tails removed
6	ounces (2 cups) campanelle
1½	ounces feta cheese, crumbled (⅓ cup)
⅓	cup chopped fresh basil

1. Adjust oven rack to upper-middle position; heat oven to 425 degrees. Combine oil, garlic, ⅛ teaspoon salt, and ¼ teaspoon pepper in small baking dish; cover with aluminum foil. Bake, stirring occasionally, until garlic is caramelized and soft, about 20 minutes. Let cool slightly, then mash garlic and oil into paste with fork. Stir in shrimp and continue to bake, uncovered, until shrimp are cooked through, about 10 minutes longer.

2. Meanwhile, bring 4 quarts water to boil in large pot. Add pasta and 1 tablespoon salt and cook, stirring often, until al dente. Reserve ½ cup cooking water, then drain pasta and return it to pot. Add shrimp mixture, feta, and basil and toss to combine. Season with salt and pepper to taste and add reserved cooking water as needed to adjust consistency. Serve.

NOTES FROM THE TEST KITCHEN

PREPEELED VERSUS FRESH GARLIC

Many supermarkets carry jars or deli containers of peeled garlic cloves, but how do they compare to fresh garlic bought by the head? We tasted both kinds in various recipes, both raw and cooked; in all cases the results were mixed. However, we did notice a difference in shelf life: A head of garlic stored in a cool, dry place will last for at least a few weeks, while peeled garlic in a jar (which must be kept refrigerated) lasts for only about two weeks before turning yellowish and developing an overly pungent aroma, even if kept unopened in its original packaging. But if you go through a lot of garlic, prepeeled cloves make a fine alternative. Just make sure they look firm and white and have a matte finish when you purchase them.

WHOLE-WHEAT ROTINI WITH BRUSSELS SPROUTS, BACON, AND PEAS

✔ **WHY THIS RECIPE WORKS:** The hearty flavor of whole-wheat pasta often requires a more robust sauce than tomato sauce. Enter earthy Brussels sprouts in this incredibly satisfying dish. Sautéing our sliced Brussels sprouts in rendered bacon fat ensured that our dish was intensely flavored, and simmering the sprouts in a combination of chicken broth and cream gave our sauce savory depth.

WHOLE-WHEAT PASTA HAS BECOME INCREASINGLY popular in recent years. But although it brings something different to the table on pasta night, whole-wheat pasta can be a challenge to dress. It has a robust, hearty flavor profile that doesn't take well to just any sauce—especially acidic, tomato-based sauces. Still, we wanted to find a way to bring this whole-grain product to the dinner table for two, and we thought we could find just the right combination of ingredients to make its flavor profile shine.

With its earthy, nutty flavors in mind, we set about finding appropriate matches for our whole-grain pasta. We tried an assortment of hearty vegetables, cooked into a simple sauce and tossed with our pasta. Though a few different options had their fans, one was the unanimous favorite. The firm texture and nutty flavor of Brussels sprouts won over our tasters; unlike other greens that wilt during cooking, Brussels sprouts soften but maintain their integrity and flavor. While we love the texture of Brussels sprouts when halved and roasted, we thought that thin slices of sprouts would meld into the dish better; using the food processor made short work of this task. To add more depth and flavor to our sauce, we decided to add a few slices of bacon. Once it was chopped and cooked, we set the bacon aside to be added to the dish later. Then we sautéed our thinly sliced sprouts in the rendered fat left behind in the skillet. The bacon fat infused our sprouts with wonderfully smoky flavor, and a sliced shallot added an earthy flavor base.

Though the Brussels sprouts browned and became deeply flavored, they cooked unevenly due to the different thicknesses of the leaves and cores. To make sure

WHOLE-WHEAT ROTINI WITH BRUSSELS SPROUTS, BACON, AND PEAS

the sprouts were evenly cooked, we added some chicken broth to the skillet and simmered the hearty vegetable until tender. In addition to cooking the sprouts, the broth was our first step toward making the sauce. But broth alone wouldn't be enough to form a substantial sauce that would cling to the pasta. We decided to add the same amount of heavy cream, which was just enough to enrich and thicken the sauce. A small amount of grated Parmesan cheese imparted a tangy note and added more richness.

At this point, we knew we were close; the sprouts were perfectly cooked and the sauce was clinging nicely to the pasta. But although the sliced sprouts melded into the pasta as we hoped, the dish begged for another vegetable for sweetness and brightness. A smattering of frozen peas fit the bill, adding color, texture, and a pleasant sweetness that played off the vegetal sprouts and smoky bacon nicely. Finally, toasted walnuts provided additional richness and an appealing crunch.

Miles away from ordinary, this satisfying melange of tender pasta and vegetables, coated in a rich, savory sauce, was so easy and flavorful, we knew we'd be making it again and again.

Whole-Wheat Rotini with Brussels Sprouts, Bacon, and Peas

SERVES 2

Small, firm Brussels sprouts (about 1 inch in diameter) work best here. Slicing the sprouts in a food processor cuts down on prep time and ensures that the sprouts integrate well with the pasta.

- 2 slices bacon, chopped
- 5 ounces Brussels sprouts, trimmed and sliced thin
- 1 shallot, sliced thin
- Salt and pepper
- ⅓ cup low-sodium chicken broth
- ⅓ cup heavy cream
- ¼ cup frozen peas, thawed
- 6 ounces (2⅓ cups) whole-wheat rotini
- ¼ cup grated Parmesan cheese, plus extra for serving
- 2 tablespoons walnuts, toasted and chopped

1. Cook bacon in 10-inch skillet over medium-high heat until crisp, about 5 minutes. Using slotted spoon, transfer to paper towel–lined plate.

SLICING BRUSSELS SPROUTS

While you could slice the Brussels sprouts for this recipe by hand, using a food processor fitted with the slicing disk makes quick work of the task and ensures even slices.

First, trim stem ends from Brussels sprouts. Then, working in batches, fill feed tube with sprouts and press them through with feed tube plunger.

2. Add Brussels sprouts, shallot, ¼ teaspoon salt, and ⅛ teaspoon pepper to fat left in skillet and cook over medium-high heat until sprouts begin to soften, about 5 minutes. Stir in broth and cream, cover, and simmer until sprouts are tender, about 3 minutes. Off heat, stir in peas, cover, and let sit until heated through, about 1 minute.

3. Meanwhile, bring 4 quarts water to boil in large pot. Add pasta and 1 tablespoon salt and cook, stirring often, until al dente. Reserve ½ cup cooking water, then drain pasta and return it to pot. Stir in crisped bacon, Brussels sprouts mixture, Parmesan, and walnuts and toss to combine. Season with salt and pepper to taste and add reserved cooking water as needed to adjust consistency. Serve with extra Parmesan.

CHEESE RAVIOLI WITH PESTOS

✔ **WHY THIS RECIPE WORKS:** Ravioli make for a convenient weeknight dinner, but because they trap so much water during cooking, they can wash out and dilute any sauce that is served with them. To solve this problem, we created a few thick, concentrated pestos that when mixed with the cooked ravioli loosened to the proper consistency. Pairing an assertive central ingredient with complementary herbs, toasted nuts or seeds, and citrus gave us four pestos with very different, and very delicious, flavor profiles.

PACKAGED CHEESE RAVIOLI SEEM LIKE A NO-BRAINER for a weeknight dinner for two: Just top the ravioli with a quick-simmered red sauce (or even reach for a jarred one) and dinner is served. But this approach ignores an unfortunate reality of premade ravioli: Inevitably, excess water trapped inside the ravioli during boiling leaks out when you cut into them, waterlogging the dish. Tomato sauce often doesn't have enough body or concentrated flavor to stand up to the extra liquid—and honestly, we were tired of this pairing. Simple sauces based on browned butter, olive oil, or cream aren't a great choice either: Lacking the sharpness required to provide a contrast with the typical ricotta filling, they make for a heavy, cloying dish.

A thick, concentrated mixture, such as pesto, which could dilute to the proper consistency and flavor once tossed with hot ravioli, did make sense. In addition to boasting a robust flavor and substantial texture, it would just about match the convenience of store-bought ravioli since it takes mere minutes to whip up in the food processor.

We're big fans of the traditional basil and pine-nut pesto, but we wanted to branch out and liven up the weeknight dinner hour. Taking inspiration from a red pepper sauce we sampled recently, we tried replacing the basil in a traditional pesto recipe with jarred roasted red peppers. It was a good start, but the slightly bitter edge of the pine nuts clashed with the peppers' sharpness. Replacing the pine nuts with sweeter pistachios improved matters, but the resulting dish lacked complexity. The solution: adding some basil back into the mix. Then there was the garlic. We had been using a single clove, which seemed appropriate for our two-serving pesto, but tasters still thought it was too harsh and overwhelmed the other flavors. So we borrowed a test kitchen trick, blanching the garlic in the boiling pasta water to mellow its bite. Problem solved.

With our template in place, we moved on to variations, pairing an assertive central ingredient (in addition to roasted red peppers, we liked browned butter, green olives, and kale) with Parmesan cheese, blanched garlic, and complementary herbs and toasted nuts or seeds. Because the water content varied with each batch, we tailored the fat level in each to obtain the right consistency.

There was one last consideration: how best to cook store-bought ravioli. Because the texture and moisture level of the pastas differed widely from brand to brand,

and because the package instructions universally overestimated cooking time, we came up with our own indicator: Once the corners of the ravioli were slightly tender—but not mushy—we took the pasta off the heat.

We now had a repertoire of fresh, easy, intensely flavorful ravioli dinners that were perfect for any night—or every night—of the week.

Cheese Ravioli with Roasted Red Pepper and Pistachio Pesto

SERVES 2

Fresh or frozen ravioli may be used.

- 1 garlic clove, unpeeled
- ¾ cup jarred roasted red peppers, rinsed and patted dry
- ½ cup fresh basil leaves
- ⅓ cup grated Parmesan cheese
- ¼ cup shelled pistachios, toasted
- 2 tablespoons extra-virgin olive oil
  Salt and pepper
- 9 ounces cheese ravioli

1. Bring 4 quarts water to boil in large pot. Add garlic to water and cook for 1 minute. Using slotted spoon, transfer garlic to bowl and rinse under cold water to stop cooking. Peel and mince garlic.

2. Pulse garlic, red peppers, basil, Parmesan, and pistachios in food processor until finely ground, 20 to 30 pulses, scraping down bowl as needed. With processor running, slowly add oil until incorporated. Transfer to bowl and season with salt and pepper to taste.

3. Add ravioli and 1 tablespoon salt to boiling water and cook, stirring often, until al dente. Reserve ½ cup cooking water, then drain ravioli and return to pot.

4. Add ½ cup pesto to ravioli and gently toss to combine, adding cooking water 1 tablespoon at a time, as needed, to adjust consistency. Serve, passing remaining pesto separately.

VARIATIONS

Cheese Ravioli with Sage, Walnut, and Browned Butter Pesto

Heat 3 tablespoons butter in 8-inch skillet over medium-high heat, swirling constantly, until golden brown and butter has nutty aroma, 2 to 4 minutes. Remove skillet from heat and add ¼ cup chopped fresh sage to butter. Set aside to cool, about 10 minutes. Proceed with recipe, substituting butter mixture for roasted red peppers, fresh parsley for basil, and toasted walnuts for pistachios and omitting olive oil.

Cheese Ravioli with Green Olive, Almond, and Orange Pesto

Substitute ¼ cup pitted green olives for roasted red peppers, ¾ cup fresh parsley for basil, and toasted slivered almonds for pistachios. Add ¼ teaspoon grated orange zest and 1 tablespoon orange juice to food processor in step 2 and increase amount of olive oil to ¼ cup.

Cheese Ravioli with Kale and Sunflower Seed Pesto

Substitute 1 cup chopped kale leaves for roasted red peppers and toasted sunflower seeds for pistachios. Add ⅛ teaspoon red pepper flakes to food processor in step 2 and increase amount of olive oil to ¼ cup.

NOTES FROM THE TEST KITCHEN

THE BEST RAVIOLI
Looking for the best supermarket ravioli, we sampled five brands—four frozen and one refrigerated—cooked and tossed with neutral-tasting plain olive oil. The best ravioli had the most filling per pasta square or round (at least a gram of filling for every 2 grams of pasta), and its filling tasted really cheesy, with the favored brands including Parmesan or Romano cheese along with the usual ricotta. The better samples also used a light hand when it came to spices, herbs, and additional fillers (like cracker meal) but were more generous with the salt (though brands with too much salt were downgraded). Overall, our favorite was a frozen brand, **Rosetto Cheese Ravioli**, which boasted a "creamy, plush, rich" blend of ricotta, Romano, and Parmesan that provided "a burst of creamy cheese" in every bite. As for fresh ravioli, which are essential for recipes where the pasta cooks in the sauce, tasters praised **Buitoni Four Cheese Ravioli** for its "nutty cheese flavor" that came from a blend of mozzarella, Parmesan, Romano, and ricotta, and for "great" pasta texture that offered "good bite."

SKILLET RAVIOLI WITH MEAT SAUCE

✔ WHY THIS RECIPE WORKS: For an effortless take on the classic duo of cheese ravioli and meat sauce, we cooked fresh ravioli in a quick sauce made from processed canned tomatoes and sweet Italian sausage. Dried porcini mushrooms ramped up the savory depth of our speedy sauce in short order.

A STAPLE ON EVERY ITALIAN RESTAURANT MENU, cheese-stuffed ravioli covered in meaty tomato sauce is the ultimate in comfort food. But a deeply flavored sauce, with bold tomato presence and tender bites of meat, can require a good chunk of time on the stovetop. We wanted to bring this hearty, satisfying dish home for the for-two table, but we didn't want it to take all day. Could we find a speedy, yet still flavorful, alternative to the long-simmered meat sauce?

Looking for the right cut of meat, we quickly bypassed larger cuts that might require a longer cooking time and yield a bit too much for two diners. Meatloaf mix, a convenient combination of ground beef, pork, and veal, is commonly used to give meatloaf and meatballs rich, deep flavor and a tender texture. Indeed, we found it became incredibly tender and offered big flavor with just a short simmering time. To further bump up the flavor of our sauce, we called upon one of the test kitchen's secret weapons, dried porcini mushrooms; we use this glutamate-rich ingredient to enhance the savory depth of many dishes, including soups, stews, and braises. Just a small amount (⅛ ounce) made our meat sauce taste even meatier.

The only problem so far was the inconvenient amount of meatloaf mix we were using. Meatloaf mix is usually sold in larger quantities than the 8 ounces we needed, and trying to make our own meatloaf mix with such slight amounts of ground beef, pork, and veal was more trouble than it was worth. That's when a colleague suggested using fresh Italian sausage instead. Available in links in the meat case or in bulk at the supermarket meat counter, this was the perfect solution for our scaled-down sauce. What's more, since sausage is preseasoned, it contributed some herbal and aromatic notes to the dish.

Moving on to the tomatoes, we usually prefer the canned crushed variety in quick-cooking sauces, as they contribute deep flavor in short order and thicken to the perfect consistency. Unfortunately, crushed tomatoes come in bigger cans than we needed for our small batch. Instead, we opted for a 14.5-ounce can of diced tomatoes, which we processed to a smooth puree, then started building our sauce. To avoid overcooking the sausage, we sautéed our aromatics first. An onion and two cloves of garlic were just enough to give the sauce character. Next we added our dried porcini, which softened in the skillet with the aromatics. Then we stirred in the sausage so it could brown before we added the tomatoes. Now we just needed to let the sausage cook through in the sauce and instill it with big flavor as it thickened.

As we reached for a pot to cook the pasta, we wondered if there was enough moisture in the skillet to cook the ravioli, too—this would save us time both upfront (we wouldn't have to wait for the water to boil) and later on (it would cut back on dirty dishes). Plus, it would give the ravioli more time in the sauce, allowing it to take on all the rich, savory flavors. To cook the pasta with our sauce, we would have to add at least some water to the pan. To figure out how much we needed, we added 9 ounces of fresh ravioli (just enough for two diners) and varying amounts of water to our meat sauce. We then vigorously simmered the ravioli until tender. One and a half cups of water proved just the right amount, producing nicely cooked ravioli and a perfectly thickened sauce.

To enhance the fresh flavor of the sauce, we stirred in some chopped basil just before serving and topped our plates with a sprinkle of Parmesan. True, the dish didn't have quite the depth of flavor of a cooked-all-day sauce, but none of our tasters seemed to mind—or at least they were too busy eating to say so.

Skillet Ravioli with Meat Sauce

SERVES 2

Because the ravioli cooks right in the sauce, fresh ravioli should be used; do not substitute frozen ravioli. If necessary, add hot water, 1 tablespoon at a time, to adjust the consistency of the sauce before serving.

1 (14.5-ounce) can diced tomatoes

1 tablespoon olive oil

1 small onion, chopped fine

2 garlic cloves, minced

⅛ ounce dried porcini mushrooms, rinsed and minced

8 ounces sweet Italian sausage, casing removed
  Salt and pepper

1½ cups water

9 ounces fresh cheese ravioli

2 tablespoons chopped fresh basil
  Grated Parmesan cheese

1. Process tomatoes in food processor until smooth, about 10 seconds; set aside. Heat oil in 12-inch skillet over medium heat until shimmering. Add onion; cook until softened and lightly browned, 5 to 7 minutes. Stir in garlic and porcini; cook until fragrant, about 1 minute.

2. Stir in sausage, breaking up meat with wooden spoon, and cook for 1 minute. Stir in processed tomatoes and ⅛ teaspoon pepper and simmer until sauce is slightly thickened, 8 to 10 minutes.

3. Stir in water and ravioli. Increase heat to medium-high and cook at vigorous simmer, stirring often, until ravioli is tender and sauce is thickened, 6 to 9 minutes. Off heat, stir in basil and season with salt and pepper to taste. Serve with Parmesan.

NOTES FROM THE TEST KITCHEN

PREGRATING YOUR OWN PARMESAN

While some shortcuts are acceptable in the cooking-for-two kitchen (think prepackaged broccoli florets and store-bought pie dough), the tasteless powdered Parmesan that comes in a green can is not one of them. In tests, we've also found that the higher-grade pregrated cheese in the refrigerator section of the supermarket is uneven in quality. But what about pregrating your own Parmesan to always have it at the ready? Do you sacrifice any flavor for convenience? To find out, we divided a block of Parmigiano-Reggiano in two, reducing one half to a powder in a food processor and leaving the other whole. We stored both in the refrigerator for two weeks, then compared them side by side on their own, mixed into polenta, and added to breading for chicken. After two weeks of storage, tasters were hard-pressed to detect a difference between the cheeses, even in the side-by-side tasting. But after a full month of storage, tasters found a noticeable drop-off in flavor in the pregrated cheese. So to save time and make dinner prep easier, we think pregrating is fine, as long as you don't store the cheese longer than two to three weeks. To make quick work of grinding Parmesan, process 1-inch chunks in a food processor (no more than 1 pound at a time) until ground into coarse particles, about 20 seconds. Refrigerate in an airtight container until ready to use.

FRESH PASTA WITH WALNUT CREAM SAUCE

FRESH PASTA WITHOUT A MACHINE

✓ WHY THIS RECIPE WORKS: Most fresh pasta recipes yield way too much for two and require special equipment—not ours. For a scaled-down pasta dough that could be easily rolled out by hand but would still cook up into delicate, springy noodles, we added extra egg yolks and a little olive oil. In addition, we incorporated an extended resting period to allow the gluten network to relax and developed a simple, effective rolling technique. To dress up our homemade noodles, we created two simple yet flavorful sauces.

THE IDEA OF HOMEMADE PASTA IS CERTAINLY appealing; what's not to love about eggy-rich ribbons of fresh pasta that boast a springy yet delicate chew? But most fresh pasta recipes require either brute strength and years of practice or a pasta machine to roll the dough to a uniformly thin texture. Purchasing a pasta roller might seem worthwhile if you're making a good amount of pasta or plan to use it frequently, but it makes a little less sense if you're just making pasta for two. We wanted a recipe for pasta that didn't require any extra equipment (or a gym membership); the dough had to be supple enough to be rolled by hand and still cook up to incredibly tender, silky strands with a slight, springy chew. And it had to yield just enough for two.

We started by searching our Italian cookbooks for advice. In addition to centuries of experience rolling out pasta, Italian cooks have another advantage— the best kind of flour for the job: *doppio zero*, or 00. The name denotes the fine, talcumlike grind that gives pasta and baked goods made with this low-protein flour an almost creamy texture. We mail-ordered some doppio zero (the brand we used had around 9 percent protein) and mixed up a batch of dough following a typical approach: We put the usual ratio of 2 cups of flour to three whole eggs in a food processor and processed until the dough formed a cohesive ball. We then turned the dough out onto the counter, kneaded it for several minutes, and set it aside to relax for about 20 minutes. Sure enough, the 00 produced a malleable dough that was far easier to work with than dough made from all-purpose flour.

But mail-ordering an ingredient for our recipe seemed like a hassle. To achieve a similarly soft dough with supermarket staples, our first inclination was to dilute the protein content of all-purpose flour (which boasts 10 to 12 percent protein) by cutting it with cake flour (which has 6 to 8 percent protein). Indeed, our testing of various ratios led us to a dough that was much softer, less elastic, and easier to roll out; unfortunately, the cooked strands released a lot of starch into the cooking water and emerged with a pitted, pebbly surface. Clearly, we needed a different strategy for producing more malleable dough, so we turned our attention to the amount of liquid in the recipe.

Traditional pasta dough is about 30 percent water, all of which comes from the eggs. We figured that simply upping the hydration level would help us toward our goal, so we experimented with adding plain water to a batch of dough and an extra egg white (the white accounts for 80 percent of an egg's moisture) to another. Just as we'd hoped, these more hydrated doughs were softer—at least initially—but they required the heavy use of bench flour during rolling, and with too much gluten development the dough would snap back to its original shape once stretched out and cook up tough and chewy. We wondered if olive oil, a common addition to many fresh pasta recipes, might loosen the dough without the pitfalls of water.

We mixed up a few more batches of dough, adding increasing amounts of olive oil. As the oil amount increased, the dough became more supple and easier to roll out. But because fat coats the proteins, inhibiting gluten formation, too much oil once again weakened the dough's structure, leading to excess starch loss in the water and a compromised texture. We found the upper limit at 2 tablespoons of oil.

Up to this point we had tried adding water, protein (from egg whites), and fat to the dough, but we hadn't experimented with the one ingredient that contains all three: yolks. In many pasta doughs yolks are substituted for some of the whole eggs because in addition to being 50 percent liquid, yolks are loaded with fat and emulsifiers, both of which limit gluten development. Since our first pasta tests yielded too much for two people, we scaled our flour amount down to 1 cup and began hydrating that amount. To 1 cup of flour, one whole egg (we ditched an egg from the traditional formula), and 1 tablespoon of olive oil we kept adding yolks until we had a truly soft, easy-to-work dough that also boiled up nice and tender. The magic number was three extra yolks. This dough took on a beautiful yellow hue, yielded to gentle pressure with a rolling pin, and cooked up into delicate ribbons with a springy bite.

Now we turned our attention to finding the best way to rest, roll, and cut the pasta. After being mixed, pasta dough is often rested for 20 to 30 minutes to allow the flour to fully hydrate and the newly formed gluten to cross-link into a network and then relax. Given that 30 minutes makes for a friendlier dough, would longer be even better? We let our dough sit at room temperature for an extended period of time, cutting and rolling out pieces every 30 minutes. As we suspected, after an hour the dough was significantly more malleable—and it continued to soften over the next three hours.

At last, we were ready to roll. But though this dough was worlds away from the dense blocks we'd struggled with in the past, it still required a bit of technique. We first cut the dough into three manageable pieces. Working with one at a time, we dusted each piece lightly with flour and flattened it into a 3-inch square. From there we switched to a rolling pin and doubled it to a 6-inch square. After another light dusting of flour, we began working the dough. We started with the pin in the middle of the dough and first rolled away, returned to the middle, and then rolled toward the body. When the dough reached 6 by 12 inches, we gave it another dusting of flour and then repeated the rolling process until the dough measured roughly 6 by 20 inches. To cut the dough into strands, we allowed the sheets to dry on dish towels until firm around the edges (a step that enabled us to avoid dusting with more flour) before folding them up at 2-inch intervals and slicing crosswise to the desired thickness.

With our homemade pasta ready to go, we simply needed a couple of simple sauces that would add flavor without stealing the limelight. For an intense, ultrasavory option, we sautéed a minced anchovy with a garlic clove, then added lemon juice and parsley for brightness and freshness. For a more elegant take on pasta night, we paired walnuts with cream and white wine; minced chives contributed an herbal, grassy note. Without having to purchase any special equipment, we'd still found a way to put wonderfully springy, delicate homemade noodles on the dinner table for two—we'd call that a win-win.

Fresh Pasta without a Machine

MAKES 9 OUNCES; SERVES 2

If using a high-protein all-purpose flour such as King Arthur brand, increase the number of egg yolks to four. The longer the dough rests in step 2, the easier it will be to roll out. When rolling out the dough, avoid adding too much flour, which may result in excessive snapback.

- 1 cup (5 ounces) all-purpose flour
- 1 large egg plus 3 large yolks
- 1 tablespoon olive oil
- 1 tablespoon salt
- 1 recipe sauce (recipes follow)

1. Process flour, egg and yolks, and oil in food processor until mixture forms cohesive dough that feels soft and is barely tacky to touch, about 30 seconds. (If dough sticks to fingers, add up to 2 tablespoons flour, 1 teaspoon at a time, until barely tacky. If dough doesn't become cohesive, add up to 1½ teaspoons water, ½ teaspoon at a time, until it just comes together; process 30 seconds longer.)

2. Turn dough ball out onto dry surface and knead until smooth, 1 to 2 minutes. Shape dough into 3-inch-long cylinder. Wrap with plastic wrap and set aside at room temperature to rest for at least 1 hour or up to 4 hours.

3. Cut cylinder crosswise into 3 equal pieces. Working with 1 piece of dough (rewrap remaining dough), dust both sides with flour, place cut side down on clean counter, and press into 3-inch square. Using heavy rolling pin, roll into 6-inch square. Dust both sides of dough lightly with flour. Starting at center of square, roll dough away from you in 1 motion. Return rolling pin to center of dough and roll toward you in 1 motion. Repeat steps of rolling until dough sticks to counter and measures roughly 12 inches long. Lightly dust both sides of dough with flour and continue rolling dough until it measures roughly 20 inches long and 6 inches wide, frequently lifting dough to release it from counter. (You should be able to easily see outline of your fingers through dough.) If dough firmly sticks to counter and wrinkles when rolled out, dust dough lightly with flour.

4. Transfer pasta sheet to dish towel and let sit, uncovered, until firm around edges, about 15 minutes; meanwhile, roll out remaining dough. Starting with 1 short end, gently fold pasta sheet at 2-inch intervals until sheet has been folded into flat, rectangular roll. With sharp chef's knife, slice crosswise into 3/16-inch-thick noodles. Use fingers to unfurl pasta and transfer to baking sheet. Repeat folding and cutting remaining sheets of dough. Cook noodles within 1 hour.

5. Bring 4 quarts water to boil in Dutch oven. Add salt and pasta and cook until tender but still al dente, about 3 minutes. Reserve ½ cup pasta cooking water. Drain pasta and toss with sauce; serve immediately.

TO MAKE AHEAD: Follow recipe through step 4, transfer baking sheet of pasta to freezer, and freeze until pasta is firm. Transfer to zipper-lock bag and store for up to 2 weeks. Cook frozen pasta straight from freezer as directed in step 5.

Olive Oil Sauce with Anchovy and Parsley
MAKES ENOUGH FOR 9 OUNCES PASTA

Mincing the anchovy ensures that its flavor gets evenly distributed. Use a high-quality extra-virgin olive oil in this recipe; our preferred brand is Columela.

- 3 tablespoons extra-virgin olive oil
- 1 garlic clove, minced
- 1 anchovy fillet, rinsed, patted dry, and minced
  Salt and pepper
- 1 tablespoon lemon juice
- 1 tablespoon chopped fresh parsley

1. Heat oil in 12-inch skillet over medium-low heat until shimmering. Add garlic, anchovy, pinch salt, and ¼ teaspoon pepper and cook until fragrant, about 30 seconds. Remove pan from heat and cover to keep warm.

2. To serve, return pan to medium heat. Add pasta, ¼ cup reserved pasta cooking water, lemon juice, and parsley and toss to combine. Add remaining cooking water as needed to adjust consistency. Season with salt and pepper to taste and serve immediately.

Walnut Cream Sauce
MAKES ENOUGH FOR 9 OUNCES PASTA

- ¾ cup walnuts
- ⅓ cup dry white wine
- ¼ cup heavy cream

ROLLING AND CUTTING PASTA DOUGH BY HAND

1. Shape dough into 3-inch cylinder; wrap in plastic wrap and let rest for at least 1 hour. Divide into 3 equal pieces. Reserve 1 piece; rewrap remaining 2 pieces.

2. Working with reserved piece of dough, dust both sides with flour, then press cut side down into 3-inch square. With rolling pin, roll into 6-inch square, then dust both sides again with flour.

3. Roll dough to 12 by 6 inches, rolling from center 1 way at a time, then dust with flour. Roll to 20 by 6 inches, lifting frequently to release from counter. Transfer dough to dish towel and air-dry.

4. Starting with short end, gently fold dried sheet at 2-inch intervals to create flat, rectangular roll.

5. With sharp knife, cut into 3/16-inch-thick noodles.

6. Use fingers to unfurl pasta and transfer to baking sheet.

¼ **cup grated Parmesan cheese**

Salt and pepper

2 **tablespoons minced fresh chives**

1. Toast walnuts in 12-inch skillet over medium heat until golden and fragrant, 2 to 4 minutes. Process ½ cup walnuts in food processor until finely ground, about 10 seconds. Transfer to small bowl. Pulse remaining ¼ cup walnuts in food processor until coarsely chopped, 3 to 5 pulses. Bring wine to simmer in now-empty skillet over medium-high heat; cook until reduced to 3 tablespoons, about 3 minutes. Whisk in cream, walnuts, Parmesan, ⅛ teaspoon salt, and ¼ teaspoon pepper. Remove pan from heat and cover to keep warm.

2. To serve, return pan to medium heat. Add pasta, ¼ cup reserved pasta cooking water, and chives and toss to combine. Add remaining cooking water as needed to adjust consistency. Season with salt and pepper to taste and serve immediately.

POTATO GNOCCHI WITH BROWNED BUTTER AND SAGE

✔ WHY THIS RECIPE WORKS: For impossibly light gnocchi with unmistakable potato flavor, we started with russet potatoes. Baking them (a quick stint in the microwave helped to shorten the oven time) produced intensely flavored spuds—an excellent start to our gnocchi base. We used a ricer to give us a smooth, supple mash and an exact amount of flour based on the ratio of potato to flour so that our gnocchi dough yielded just enough for two and was mixed as little as possible. An egg tenderized our gnocchi further, delivering delicate, pillowlike dumplings.

WHEN DONE RIGHT, POTATO GNOCCHI BOAST A pillowy texture and an earthy flavor that needs nothing more than a gloss of browned butter sauce. Creating them always looks easy: Mash cooked potatoes, bind them with flour and knead into dough, shape into dumplings, and boil. And yet most of the time, these dumplings turn out dense, gluey, or rubbery—and sometimes all of the above.

The fact is that even in a seemingly simple recipe such as this, there's plenty of room for error. First, the moisture in the potato will affect how much flour the dough absorbs—and, in turn, will impact the density of the gnocchi. Second, mashing the potatoes (a necessary step) bursts their starch cells; the more they burst, the more gluey the gnocchi will become. Third, developing some gluten is what gives gnocchi their pleasantly faint chew, but mixing in too much flour or overkneading the dough will result in leaden sinkers. And since even the most perfectly textured gnocchi can lack distinct potato flavor, the challenge looms even larger.

So, our goal for this Italian favorite was twofold: Find a way to make this simple recipe foolproof so that light, delicate, and potato-y gnocchi were not a happy accident, and figure out how to deliver just enough for two so we weren't producing enough gnocchi to feed a small village.

After testing other varieties, we settled on russet potatoes, since their low-moisture flesh absorbs less flour than other spuds. The problem is that they're also somewhat bland tasting, but we figured that we'd find a way to amp up the potato flavor in the precooking step. We found that baking deepened the potatoes' flavor, while boiling them washed it out. Even better, the oven's dry heat evaporated some of the spuds' moisture, yielding fluffier results. To hasten the process, we microwaved the potatoes for 10 minutes before moving them into a 450-degree oven, where they needed just 20 minutes to finish cooking. (Microwaving them the whole time led to unevenly cooked, bland potatoes.) We then used an oven mitt and paring knife to quickly peel the hot-from-the-oven potatoes.

Next, it was time to mash our spuds, and for the gentlest method possible, we chose a ricer. We've found that this tool ruptures fewer starch cells than hand mashing, since it compresses the potatoes only once. After passing the potatoes through the ricer, we spread the strands on a baking sheet, where they continued to release steam.

Once the potatoes had cooled slightly, we could incorporate the flour. Most recipes offered a range of flour amounts in the ingredient list, the idea being to form the dough with the lesser amount of flour and boil a few test dumplings to see if it's enough to keep the gnocchi intact. The problem is that more flour is inevitably required, which means extra kneading—and more gluten development—as you work it in. To limit the dough manipulation, we resolved that we needed

POTATO GNOCCHI WITH BROWNED BUTTER AND SAGE

to weigh out an exact amount of cooked potato and then determine the precise amount of flour necessary. Not only would we avoid guesswork during mixing, but the dough would turn out the same way every time.

To determine the minimum amount of flour required to bind 16 ounces of potato (more than that made too much gnocchi for two people), we made several batches of dough, using a fork to gently stir different amounts into each and kneading them for just a minute. The magic number was 5 ounces; any less, and the gnocchi feathered apart in the water. But although these gnocchi were relatively light and airy, they still weren't the delicate puffs we had envisioned.

Reasoning that we could do no more than we already had with the potatoes and flour, we turned to baking soda and baking powder, chemical leaveners that give baked goods their rise. Unfortunately, while both caused the gnocchi to puff up, they also encouraged absorption and caused the gnocchi to turn mushy. With so little gluten, the dough couldn't hold the gases created by leavening, and it blew apart, allowing water to seep in.

Almost out of ideas, we tried incorporating an egg, a relatively common addition that we'd avoided because we thought its proteins would coagulate during cooking and bind the dough together too firmly. With nothing to lose, we whipped up another batch of dough, this time stirring in a beaten egg before adding the flour. Predictably, the dough was a little wetter than usual, making us skeptical about the gnocchi holding together when they hit the boiling water. Amazingly, these gnocchi not only held their shape but also emerged from the water puffed and tender. We pressed our luck even further and made another batch, dropping the flour to a mere 4 ounces. Finally, the gnocchi had the impossibly light texture and rich potato flavor we'd been aiming for.

For shaping our gnocchi, we kept the method traditional: We cut the dough into eight pieces, rolled each into a ½-inch-thick rope, and then cut ¾-inch lengths. From there, we simply pressed each dumpling against the back of a fork to create an indentation and then rolled it down the tines to create ridges. This classic technique serves two purposes: The ridges trap sauce, and the indentation helps the gnocchi cook more evenly.

These potato-y puffs were good enough to eat straight from the pot, drizzled with a little extra-virgin olive oil, but we also wanted to whip up a simple sauce. The traditional nutty browned butter with shallot and fresh sage fit the bill perfectly—and took just 3 minutes to make.

Potato Gnocchi with Browned Butter and Sage

SERVES 2

For the most accurate measurements, weigh the potatoes and flour. After processing, you may have slightly more than the 3 cups (16 ounces) of potatoes required for this recipe. Discard any extra or set it aside for another use. This recipe makes two hearty portions. For lighter portions, freeze up to one-third of the gnocchi according to the directions below.

GNOCCHI

- 2 **pounds russet potatoes**
- 1 **large egg, lightly beaten**
- ¾ **cup plus 1 tablespoon (4 ounces) all-purpose flour, plus extra for counter**
- 1 **teaspoon plus 1 tablespoon salt**

SAUCE

- 4 **tablespoons unsalted butter, cut into 4 pieces**
- 1 **small shallot, minced**
- 1 **teaspoon minced fresh sage**
- 1½ **teaspoons lemon juice**
- ¼ **teaspoon salt**

1. FOR THE GNOCCHI: Adjust oven rack to middle position and heat oven to 450 degrees. Poke each potato 8 times with paring knife over entire surface. Microwave potatoes until slightly softened at ends, about 10 minutes, flipping potatoes halfway through cooking. Transfer potatoes directly to oven rack and bake until skewer glides easily through flesh and potatoes yield to gentle pressure, 18 to 20 minutes.

2. Holding each potato with potholder or dish towel, peel with paring knife. Process potatoes through ricer or food mill onto rimmed baking sheet. Gently spread potatoes into even layer and let cool for 5 minutes.

3. Transfer 3 cups (16 ounces) warm potatoes to bowl. Using fork, gently stir in egg until just combined. Sprinkle flour and 1 teaspoon salt over potato mixture. Using fork, gently combine until no pockets of dry flour remain. Press mixture into rough ball, transfer to lightly floured counter, and gently knead until smooth but slightly sticky, about 1 minute, lightly dusting counter with flour as needed to prevent sticking.

4. Line 2 rimmed baking sheets with parchment paper and dust liberally with flour. Cut dough into 8 pieces. Lightly dust counter with flour. Gently roll 1 piece of dough into ½-inch-thick rope, dusting with flour to prevent sticking. Cut rope into ¾-inch lengths. Holding fork with tines facing down in 1 hand, press each dough piece cut side down against tines with thumb of other hand to create indentation. Roll dough down tines to form ridges on sides. If dough sticks, dust thumb or fork with flour. Transfer formed gnocchi to sheets and repeat with remaining dough.

5. FOR THE SAUCE: Melt butter in 12-inch skillet over medium-high heat, swirling occasionally, until butter is browned and releases nutty aroma, about 1½ minutes. Off heat, add shallot and sage, stirring until shallot is fragrant, about 1 minute. Stir in lemon juice and salt; cover to keep warm.

6. Bring 4 quarts water to boil in large pot. Add remaining 1 tablespoon salt. Using parchment paper as sling, gently lower gnocchi from 1 sheet into water and cook until firm and just cooked through, about 90 seconds (gnocchi should float to surface after about 1 minute). Using slotted spoon, transfer cooked gnocchi to skillet with sauce. Repeat with remaining gnocchi. Gently toss gnocchi with sauce and serve.

NOTES FROM THE TEST KITCHEN

MAKING THE RIGHT IMPRESSION

To create ridges in gnocchi, hold fork with tines facing down. Press each dough piece, cut side down, against tines with thumb to make indentation. Roll dumpling down tines to create ridges on sides.

TO MAKE AHEAD: Follow recipe through step 4, then let gnocchi air-dry at room temperature for at least 1 hour or up to 4 hours. Transfer baking sheet to freezer and freeze until pasta is solid, about 45 minutes. Transfer to zipper-lock bag and store for up to 1 month. Cook frozen pasta straight from freezer as directed in step 6.

VEGETABLE LASAGNA

✔ **WHY THIS RECIPE WORKS:** For a petite lasagna better suited for a couple, we scaled down from the standard large baking dish to a loaf pan. Then we precooked our vegetables—eggplant, zucchini, and spinach—to concentrate their flavors and prevent a watery dish. Pairing two simple, no-cook sauces—a rich, creamy white sauce consisting of herbed Boursin cheese and whole milk, and a tangy tomato sauce—with no-boil noodles ensured that our lasagna for two was as easy as it was flavorful.

LASAGNA IS PERFECT WHEN YOU'RE COOKING FOR a group—most recipes make enough to feed the masses. But when you're cooking for two, spending all that time boiling noodles, making a sauce (or sauces), and carefully assembling the whole shebang doesn't make sense. We wanted a scaled-down take on this classic casserole that fed just two, not 10, and was easy to put together. Rather than the standard meat lasagna, we had a hearty, satisfying vegetable lasagna in mind, chock-full of fresh, tender eggplant, zucchini, and summer squash. But though a veggie-laden lasagna might look tempting enough, with a topcoat of bubbly cheese and thick tomato gravy, cutting out a square of it often reveals trouble at the core. Usually placed between the pasta sheets raw, the zucchini and squash tend to turn out steamy and limp, flooding the dish with their juices—or, in some instances, undercooked and crunchy. Then there's the eggplant, which is typically not only soggy, but also greasy from prefrying. Add to that the usual patches of dry, grainy ricotta and it was clear we had our work cut out for us. But we had a good idea of where to start: To make a full-flavored (but not full-size) lasagna with vegetables that could stand up to—not wash out—the cheese and sauce, we knew we'd have to rid the produce of some of its moisture and boost its flavor before adding it to the dish.

First, we focused our efforts on the most unruly element: the eggplant. Besides being full of water, eggplant is extremely porous and readily soaks up any available liquid (including oil). Previous test kitchen experience taught us that the best way to rid the eggplant of water and collapse its air pockets was to salt the eggplant and then heat it in the microwave. Salt pulls water out of it through osmosis at the same time the microwave causes it to steam. Microwaving also collapses the eggplant's air pockets, leaving the fruit shrunken, wrinkled, and less prone to absorbing oil or liquid. When we sautéed the pretreated eggplant to give it more flavor and color, it picked up hardly any oil at all.

Since we were trying to keep our ingredient list streamlined for this lasagna built for two, we opted to use just one type of squash (either zucchini or summer squash work just fine). We considered salting the squash to remove its excess water, but we were fairly certain that a turn in the skillet would drive off enough moisture and deepen its flavor. We combined cubed squash with the microwaved eggplant and sautéed the mixture with garlic and a sprinkling of salt and pepper. About seven minutes later, the vegetables had developed a lightly browned exterior and picked up some garlicky flavor, but we wondered if we could do better. We minced a couple more cloves of garlic and let the bits soak for a few minutes in a teaspoon of olive oil along with some minced fresh thyme. Added to the skillet as the vegetables finished cooking, this super-garlicky, herbal-infused mixture gave the eggplant and squash so much flavor that they were good enough to eat straight from the pan.

Now it was time to see how the vegetables would fare in the lasagna. We made a placeholder tomato sauce by briefly simmering canned tomato sauce with garlic, olive oil, basil, and a dash of pepper flakes. We then layered three no-boil noodles (our favorite alternative to fresh pasta) with the sauce, the sautéed eggplant and squash, and generous helpings of ricotta and mozzarella in an 8½ by 4½-inch loaf pan, which gave us just the right amount for two. Then we baked the casserole in a 375-degree oven until golden and bubbly.

The good news was that starting with precooked vegetables allowed us to cut the baking time to about 35 minutes. But improvements were still needed here and there. Instead of acting as a creamy binder, the ricotta had cooked up into grainy slicks, and some tasters wanted the dairy element to be even richer. What we really wanted, it seemed, was something more akin to a creamy béchamel to contrast with the earthiness of the vegetables. Plus, we needed only a small amount, since a little richness goes a long way, and we were making lasagna to serve only two. As we considered our cheese options, we hit on Boursin cheese, which is flavored with herbs and garlic. With a quick stint in the microwave, it was perfectly rich and creamy—and exactly what we were looking for. On a whim, we tried melting a few ounces with just enough milk to make it saucy. We found that 3 tablespoons of whole milk was the right amount to give 2½ ounces of Boursin the perfect sauciness. But would it work in the lasagna?

In a word: Yes. The creamy cheese produced a "sauce" that was considerably richer than the ricotta without a hint of graininess, and the herb flavors already at work in the cheese meant a shorter shopping list.

The cream sauce settled, we turned our attention to the underwhelming tomato sauce. We couldn't help but wonder if a similar no-cook approach might liven up its dull flavor—and save a few extra minutes at the stove. We prepared another batch, this time simply stirring together the ingredients and adding the sauce to the casserole without simmering it first. The results were better than ever. Even after baking and cooling, the sauce still tasted bright, livening up the filling with just enough acidity.

A few final touches punched up the flavor of our lasagna even more. A handful of minced kalamata olives added meaty texture and a briny, salty jolt of flavor. For freshness, we added a few handfuls of baby spinach, which took no time to sauté in a touch of olive oil until wilted and drain before layering into the filling. The final touch was a generous amount of chopped fresh basil, sprinkled on the casserole right before serving.

At last, our veggie lasagna had it all, with its rich flavors, creamy cheese, and substantial texture—along with a summery brightness that set it apart from the meat kind.

Vegetable Lasagna

SERVES 2

The test kitchen's preferred loaf pan measures 8½ by 4½ inches; if you use a 9 by 5-inch loaf pan, start checking for doneness five minutes earlier than advised in the recipe. We prefer the lasagna made with our favorite whole-milk, block-style mozzarella from Sorrento, but Kraft part-skim preshredded mozzarella is also fine.

- 1 **(8-ounce) can tomato sauce**
- ⅓ **cup chopped fresh basil**
- 3 **tablespoons extra-virgin olive oil**
- 4 **garlic cloves, minced**
- ⅛ **teaspoon red pepper flakes**
  Salt and pepper
- 2½ **ounces Boursin cheese, softened (5 tablespoons)**
- 3 **tablespoons whole milk**
- 8 **ounces eggplant, peeled and cut into ½-inch cubes (2 cups)**
- 12 **ounces zucchini or yellow summer squash, cut into ½-inch pieces (1½ cups)**
- ¾ **teaspoon minced fresh thyme**
- 4 **ounces (4 cups) baby spinach**
- 3 **no-boil lasagna noodles**
- 2 **tablespoons minced pitted kalamata olives**
- 4 **ounces low-moisture whole-milk mozzarella cheese, shredded (1 cup)**

1. Adjust oven rack to middle position and heat oven to 375 degrees. Whisk tomato sauce, ¼ cup basil, 1 tablespoon oil, 2 teaspoons garlic, and pepper flakes together in bowl; season with salt and pepper to taste and set aside. Combine Boursin and milk in bowl and microwave, covered, until cheese is melted, about 1 minute; set aside.

2. Toss eggplant with ¼ teaspoon salt in large bowl. Line surface of large plate with double layer of coffee filters and lightly spray with vegetable oil spray. Spread eggplant in even layer over filters. Wipe out and reserve now-empty bowl. Microwave eggplant, uncovered, until dry to touch and slightly shriveled, about 8 minutes, tossing once halfway through to ensure that eggplant cooks evenly. Let cool slightly. Return eggplant to bowl and toss with zucchini.

3. Combine 1 teaspoon oil, remaining 2 teaspoons garlic, and thyme in small bowl. Heat 4 teaspoons oil in 12-inch nonstick skillet over medium-high heat until shimmering. Add eggplant mixture and cook, stirring occasionally, until vegetables are lightly browned, about 7 minutes. Push vegetables to sides of skillet; add garlic mixture to clearing and cook, mashing with spatula, until fragrant, about 30 seconds. Stir to combine garlic mixture with vegetables and transfer to medium bowl.

4. Return now-empty skillet to medium-high heat, add remaining 1 teaspoon oil, and heat until shimmering. Add spinach and cook, stirring frequently, until wilted, about 2 minutes. Transfer spinach to paper towel–lined plate and let drain for 2 minutes. Stir into eggplant mixture.

5. Spray 8½ by 4½-inch loaf pan with vegetable oil spray. Layer ¼ cup tomato sauce, 1 noodle, half of vegetable mixture (1½ cups), followed by 1 tablespoon olives, ¼ cup cream sauce, and ¼ cup mozzarella into prepared loaf pan. Repeat layering process.

6. Add remaining 1 noodle and top with remaining ½ cup tomato sauce. Sprinkle evenly with remaining ½ cup mozzarella.

7. Cover pan tightly with aluminum foil that has been sprayed with vegetable oil spray. Bake until bubbling, about 35 minutes. Let cool for 20 minutes on wire rack. Sprinkle with remaining basil and serve.

NOTES FROM THE TEST KITCHEN

SHRINKING EGGPLANT DOWN TO SIZE

Eggplant is full of water that will wash out the flavors of lasagna as it bakes in the oven. It's also riddled with air pockets that act as a magnet for oil. Salting the cubed eggplant, then microwaving it, solves both problems: Microwaving not only speeds up salt's ability to pull moisture out of the eggplant but also collapses the eggplant's air pockets. (We set the eggplant on a double layer of coffee filters to absorb the excess moisture as it is released.) The result: low-moisture, meaty-tasting eggplant that doesn't soak up too much oil when sautéed.

RAW   **SALTED AND MICROWAVED**

SPANISH-STYLE TOASTED PASTA WITH SHRIMP

✔ **WHY THIS RECIPE WORKS:** A rich seafood paella made with noodles instead of rice, *fideuà* can take several hours to prepare. We wanted to streamline and scale down the recipe to serve two but keep the deep flavor intact. In place of the usual slow-cooked fish stock, we made a quick shrimp stock using shrimp shells, chicken broth, water, and a bay leaf. We also made a speedy *sofrito,* the aromatic base common in Spanish cooking, with a finely minced onion and finely chopped single tomato, which softened and browned quickly. To boost the flavor of our shrimp, we marinated them briefly in olive oil, garlic, salt, and pepper.

THE BIGGEST STAR OF TRADITIONAL SPANISH cooking is arguably paella, but there's another closely related dish equally deserving of raves: fideuà. This richly flavored dish swaps the rice for thin noodles that are typically toasted until nut-brown before being cooked in a garlicky, tomatoey stock loaded with seafood and sometimes chorizo sausage. While paella is moist but not soupy, fideuà is often a little brothy. The two dishes are plenty different, but there is one big thing that paella and fideuà have in common: a lengthy and involved cooking process. Most recipes we've seen call for the same series of steps: Fish and shellfish scraps are simmered to create stock, the *fideos* noodles are toasted, a flavorful base (the sofrito) is put together by slowly reducing fresh tomatoes with aromatics and seasonings, the sofrito and stock are combined and the noodles and seafood are added to the rich-tasting liquid to cook through, and finally the whole thing goes into the oven to create a crunchy layer of pasta on top. We knew from experience that the results were often well worth the effort. As with paella, tinkering with fideuà is part of the art. We decided that our tweaks would be aimed at streamlining a recipe for a weeknight meal for two but leaving it every bit as deeply flavorful as the more time-consuming versions.

Our first decision was to keep things simple in the seafood department and go with shrimp alone. Our next step was to make a stock without even dirtying a pot. We knew that shrimp shells can build a surprisingly flavorful broth without much help, so we combined the shells from 8 ounces of shrimp in a bowl with some water and a bay leaf and microwaved it all until the shells turned pink and the water was hot. The resulting broth wasn't bad for something that took such little effort, but its taste improved when we replaced a portion of the water with chicken broth and added a small measure of white wine for brightness.

Fideos come in varying thicknesses and shapes, including short, straight strands and coiled nests of thin, vermicelli-like noodles, but we wanted our recipe to be an easy weeknight dinner that didn't require seeking out specialty ingredients. We found that snapping spaghettini (more widely available than fideos) into pieces gave us a fine approximation of the first type of fideos. Not all fideuà recipes call for toasting the pasta, but skipping that step led to a dish that tasted weak and washed out. Toasting the pasta in the oven provided controlled heat but required repeatedly moving a baking sheet in and out in order to stir the noodles—and added another item to the dirty-dish pile. We opted to use the stovetop instead. Toasting the pasta in a skillet—the same skillet in which the dish would be cooked and served—also required stirring, but this was much easier to monitor. Since we were working in the tight space of a 10-inch skillet, we found that 1-inch pieces of spaghettini were easy to toss and guaranteed even toasting.

Next we examined the sofrito. This flavor base shows up in a variety of forms in Spanish dishes but always features some combination of aromatics—onion, garlic, celery, and bell pepper are common—slow-cooked in oil to soften and concentrate their flavors. In fideuà, onion and garlic are typical, along with tomato. In the interest of efficiency, we ruled out preparing the sofrito separately, in another skillet. We also finely chopped our onion so that it would cook quickly and added ⅛ teaspoon of salt to help draw out moisture so that the onion softened and browned even faster in the oil.

A single tomato gave us just enough of an acidic base for our dinner for two, and chopping the tomato finely meant it took a short amount of time to cook down and develop deep flavor. Added to the skillet with the softened onion, the tomato reduced to a thick paste in minutes. Then we introduced minced garlic and cooked the mixture for a minute to bloom the flavors.

Our next task: getting the right proportion of liquid to pasta. For 6 ounces of pasta, 2½ cups of liquid was the perfect amount. It allowed the pasta to soak up enough liquid to become tender while leaving just a little behind in the skillet.

Now it was time to fine-tune the flavors. A mixture of sweet and Spanish smoked paprikas won praise for its balance of smokiness and earthy sweetness, and while we liked the distinctly Spanish flavor of saffron, it wasn't worth the exorbitant cost, so we left it out. A small amount of anchovy paste, a go-to flavor booster in the test kitchen because of its high level of glutamates, added to the sofrito with the garlic and paprika offered depth, and its flavor blended seamlessly with the shrimp.

As for the shrimp, we found that simmering them in the stock with the pasta made them rubbery. Adding them during the last five minutes of cooking and covering the pan improved their texture. For more flavor, we soaked them briefly in olive oil, garlic, salt, and pepper.

In some recipes fideuà is finished in the oven, which turns the surface of the pasta crisp and brown—a nice contrast with the tender noodles and seafood underneath. The broiler seemed ideal for achieving such a crust, but when its intense heat toughened the shrimp, we decided to make a small change: After scattering the raw shrimp over the surface of the pasta, we gently stirred them into the noodles to partially submerge them and protect them from the heat. Finally, we accompanied our fideuà with two traditional condiments: lemon wedges and a spoonful of *aïoli*, a garlic mayonnaise that adds richness.

NOTES FROM THE TEST KITCHEN

BREAKING PASTA FOR FIDEUÁ

1. Loosely fold 3 ounces spaghettini in dish towel, keeping pasta flat, not bunched.

2. Break into 1-inch lengths by positioning bundle so 1 inch rests on counter and remainder hangs off edge. Press pasta against counter, pressing down on towel to break strands into pieces, sliding bundle back over edge after each break.

What had our tweaks accomplished? A recipe for Spanish-style fideuà that delivered terrific flavor in far less time and with far less effort, and it was perfectly scaled down for two.

Spanish-Style Toasted Pasta with Shrimp
SERVES 2

In step 5, if your skillet is not broiler-safe, once the pasta is tender transfer the mixture to a broiler-safe 8-inch baking dish lightly coated with olive oil; scatter the shrimp over the pasta and stir them in to partially submerge. Broil and serve as directed. Serve this dish with lemon wedges and Aïoli (recipe follows), stirring it into individual portions at the table. See page 88 for a tip on how to measure out long strands of pasta without using a scale.

- 2 tablespoons extra-virgin olive oil
- 2 garlic cloves, minced
  Salt and pepper
- 8 ounces extra-large shrimp (21 to 25 per pound), peeled and deveined, shells reserved
- 1¾ cups water
- ¾ cup low-sodium chicken broth
- 1 bay leaf
- 6 ounces spaghettini or thin spaghetti, broken into 1-inch lengths
- 1 small onion, chopped fine
- 1 tomato, cored and chopped fine
- ½ teaspoon paprika
- ½ teaspoon smoked paprika
- ¼ teaspoon anchovy paste
- 2 tablespoons dry white wine
- 2 teaspoons chopped fresh parsley
  Lemon wedges
- 1 recipe Aïoli (optional; recipe follows)

1. Combine 1 teaspoon oil, 1 teaspoon garlic, ⅛ teaspoon salt, and pinch pepper in medium bowl. Add shrimp, toss to coat, and refrigerate until ready to use.

2. Place reserved shrimp shells, water, broth, and bay leaf in medium bowl. Cover and microwave until liquid is hot and shells have turned pink, about 6 minutes. Set aside until ready to use.

3. Toss spaghettini and 2 teaspoons oil in broiler-safe 10-inch skillet until spaghettini is evenly coated. Toast spaghettini over medium-high heat, stirring frequently, until browned and nutty in aroma (spaghettini should be color of peanut butter), 6 to 8 minutes. Transfer spaghettini to bowl. Wipe out skillet with paper towels.

4. Heat remaining 1 tablespoon oil in now-empty skillet over medium-high heat until shimmering. Add onion and ⅛ teaspoon salt and cook, stirring frequently, until onion is softened and beginning to brown around edges, 4 to 6 minutes. Add tomato and cook, stirring occasionally, until mixture is thick, dry, and slightly darkened in color, 4 to 6 minutes. Reduce heat to medium and add remaining garlic, paprika, smoked paprika, and anchovy paste. Cook until fragrant, about 1½ minutes. Add spaghettini and stir to combine. Adjust oven rack 5 to 6 inches from broiler element and heat broiler.

5. Pour broth through fine-mesh strainer into skillet, discarding solids. Add wine, ⅛ teaspoon salt, and ¼ teaspoon pepper and stir well. Increase heat to medium-high and bring to simmer. Cook, uncovered, stirring occasionally, until liquid is slightly thickened and spaghettini is just tender, 8 to 10 minutes. Scatter shrimp over spaghettini and stir shrimp into spaghettini to partially submerge. Transfer skillet to oven and broil until shrimp are opaque and surface of spaghettini is dry with crisped, browned spots, 5 to 7 minutes. Remove from oven and let stand, uncovered, for 5 minutes. Sprinkle with parsley and serve immediately with lemon wedges and, if using, Aïoli.

Aïoli

MAKES ½ CUP

We prefer ground white pepper here because it's not as visible in the finished aïoli as black pepper, but either can be used.

1 small garlic clove, finely grated
1 large egg yolk
2 teaspoons lemon juice
⅛ teaspoon salt
Pinch sugar
Ground white pepper
⅓ cup olive oil

In large bowl, combine garlic, egg yolk, lemon juice, salt, sugar, and pepper to taste until combined. Whisking constantly, very slowly drizzle oil into egg mixture until thick and creamy. Season with salt and pepper to taste.

COCONUT RICE NOODLES WITH SHRIMP AND PINEAPPLE

WHY THIS RECIPE WORKS: For an exotic yet effortless Thai-style noodle dish, we turned to store-bought curry paste and ramped up its flavor with a fresh chile. Sweet, briny shrimp kept our dish quick-cooking, and pineapple reinforced the tropical notes of the coconut milk used in the sauce. Cooking everything in one pan kept dirty dishes to a minimum and made our recipe easy and streamlined.

IN A PERFECT WORLD, THAI NOODLE DISHES flavored with curry would be sweet, bright, and pungent—something to wake the senses and the palate. But while we have had memorable takeout versions, we've more often than not been disappointed by lackluster noodles. Even more frustrating are the numerous "authentic" recipes we've labored over, only to be let down by the results. The problems we encounter most are gummy noodles, overcooked seafood or meat, and unbalanced sauces. Our goal was to learn from others' mistakes and produce a consistently superlative coconut curry rice noodle dish that could be prepared for just two people using one pan; we wanted the ease of takeout without the mess or the leftovers.

First, we'd need to find the right noodle. Flat rice noodles, or rice sticks, the type of noodles used in Southeast Asian cuisine, come in a variety of thicknesses. For this dish, we bypassed the ½-inch-thick noodles and went straight for the vermicelli-style noodles; they have a delicate texture perfect for the light, bright-tasting supper we envisioned. We found three different methods for preparing them: soaking them in room-temperature water, soaking them in hot tap water, and boiling them. We quickly rejected both boiling and soaking in room-temperature water; boiling yielded gummy, sticky noodles, and room-temperature water was insufficient to soften the noodles. We finally tried soaking the noodles in very hot tap water. After about 20 minutes, the noodles softened and turned limp and pliant but were not fully tender. Drained, they were loose and separate and cooked through easily with stir-frying. The result? Noodles that were at once pleasantly tender and chewy.

COCONUT RICE NOODLES WITH SHRIMP AND PINEAPPLE

Although the cooking time for Thai noodle dishes is short, the ingredient lists generally aren't. The curry paste, which forms the basis of the sauce, can be quite involved and take a lot of time to prepare. Looking for a more accessible option for our for-two version, we reached for store-bought curry paste instead. The two most common types of Thai curries are green curry and red curry; in this application, we preferred the bright, grassy notes of the green variety. To amp up the flavor of the store-bought paste, we supplemented it with a fresh Thai chile. Coconut milk was a given in our curry; a full can offered ample volume. To round out the flavor of the sauce, we added a few teaspoons of fish sauce, which provided a salty pungency, and a small amount of dark brown sugar to balance the salty and spicy notes.

Moving on to the other ingredients, tasters preferred shrimp over chicken and beef; the shrimp contributed a sweet, briny flavor and kept with the light, fresh tone of the dish. To keep our shopping list on the shorter side, we narrowed the long list of possible vegetables to just snow peas, which offered some crunch and color.

While we'd successfully streamlined our shopping list, we now looked to keep the cooking method as effortless as possible. For our easy one-pan dinner, we started by building our coconut-curry sauce. We cooked the curry paste in a tablespoon of oil with the chile to bloom and deepen its flavor, then added the other sauce ingredients. Next, we stirred in the shrimp and snow peas so they would cook right in the sauce and take on some flavor before adding the noodles; in less than five minutes, the shrimp were perfectly cooked and tender. So far, so good, but tasters complained that something was missing. In an effort to add more substance and also enhance the tropical feel of our dish, we decided to add some pineapple. One cup, cut into ½-inch pieces and added to the pan with the shrimp, ramped up the sweet, tangy notes of the dish and made it heartier.

The flavor was spot-on, but tasters were now complaining that the sauce was too thick and weighed down the delicate rice noodles. We tried simmering it for a shorter period of time, but to no avail. Wondering if the problem might be the type of coconut milk we were using, we switched from the full-fat variety to the light kind. Bingo! This swap gave us the same amount of sauce and rich coconut flavor, without overwhelming the dish or making the sauce too heavy. A spritz of lime juice and cilantro provided the perfect finishing touches to our better-than-takeout Thai noodle dish.

Coconut Rice Noodles with Shrimp and Pineapple

SERVES 2

To make this dish spicier, add the reserved chile seeds to the oil in step 2. Do not substitute other types of noodles for the rice vermicelli here. Light coconut milk adds the perfect flavor and texture to the dish without making it too rich; do not substitute regular coconut milk.

- 4 ounces rice vermicelli
- 1 tablespoon vegetable oil
- 1 tablespoon green curry paste
- 1 Thai, serrano, or jalapeño chile, stemmed, seeds reserved, and minced
- 4 teaspoons fish sauce
- 1½ teaspoons packed dark brown sugar
- 1 (14-ounce) can light coconut milk
- 6 ounces medium-large shrimp (31 to 40 per pound), peeled, deveined, and tails removed
- 1 cup pineapple, cut into ½-inch pieces
- 3 ounces snow peas, strings removed, halved crosswise on bias
- 1½ teaspoons lime juice
- 2 tablespoons minced fresh cilantro

1. Cover noodles with very hot tap water in large bowl and stir to separate. Let noodles soak until softened, pliable, and limp but not fully tender, about 20 minutes; drain.

2. Cook oil, curry paste, and chile in 12-inch skillet over medium heat until paste begins to sizzle and no longer smells raw, about 2 minutes. Stir in fish sauce and sugar and cook for 1 minute. Stir in coconut milk and simmer until thickened, about 8 minutes.

NOTES FROM THE TEST KITCHEN

TRIMMING SNOW PEAS

Use paring knife and thumb to snip off tip of pea and pull along flat side of pod to remove string at same time.

3. Gently stir in shrimp, pineapple, and snow peas and cook until shrimp are just opaque, about 3 minutes. Stir in drained noodles and cook, tossing gently, until shrimp are cooked through and noodles are well coated, 2 to 3 minutes. Off heat, stir in lime juice. Sprinkle with cilantro and serve.

DRUNKEN NOODLES WITH CHICKEN

✓ WHY THIS RECIPE WORKS: For our version of this spicy, potent Thai noodle dish, we selected the widest noodles we could find and soaked them in hot water until they were pliable but not fully limp. Then we tossed the noodles over the heat with a combination of soy sauce, lime juice, dark brown sugar, and chili-garlic sauce (for heat and spicy flavor) to ensure that they would absorb the sauce's flavors and finish cooking. Baby bok choy provided textural interest, and thin slices of chicken, quickly stir-fried, made our noodle dish hearty and filling.

WHILE WE LOVE PAD THAI, WE PREFER TO BYPASS it in favor of another popular dish that offers bolder flavor: *pad kee mao*, also known as drunken noodles. Though you might suspect there's booze in this dish, the name reputedly refers to the fact that the spicy, potent sauce is a good cure for a serious hangover. In addition to the heat-packing fresh Thai chiles, drunken noodles are also defined by a good dose of holy basil, a sharper variety of basil that's popular in Thailand. All in all, the sauce delivers a mix of spicy, sweet, and salty flavors that's incredibly addictive. We wanted to develop our own recipe for this stir-fry using supermarket staples so that we could satisfy our craving any time it struck, without having to plan ahead or hunt down obscure ingredients.

We started with the foundation of the dish: the noodles. Like pad thai, drunken noodles are made with flat rice noodles, which are a mixture of rice flour and water; unlike pad thai, this recipe calls for very wide—almost ½-inch-wide—noodles. Although fresh rice noodles would be more traditional, seeking out an Asian market was not on our to-do list, so we opted for the easier-to-find dried noodles. Research we had done for our Coconut Rice Noodles with Shrimp and Pineapple (page 110) gave us insight into the best way to prepare the rice noodles. Forgoing boiling or soaking in room-temperature water, we soaked the noodles in hot water and removed them when they were pliable but not fully limp, knowing they'd continue to cook in the hot pan. The noodles cooked through easily with stir-frying, and they were pleasantly tender and resilient.

Next up: the sauce. Besides fresh Thai chiles and holy basil, most recipes include two types of soy sauce (black soy sauce and regular soy sauce), oyster sauce, garlic, and sugar. We began testing with the hope of shortening the shopping list and finding substitutes for the harder-to-find items. Right off the bat, we found that Thai basil—or cilantro in a pinch—stood in well for the holy basil; it provided a stronger, more assertive flavor than regular basil. Black soy sauce was also hard to find, but regular soy sauce wasn't a perfect substitute for the thicker, sweeter black variety; we would need to find another ingredient that would add the rich, molasses-like flavors we were missing. In the test kitchen, we often trade granulated sugar for light brown sugar in both baked goods and savory dishes to up the richness quotient. Here, this swap worked wonders, and switching to dark brown sugar proved even better, both adding rich caramel flavors and contributing some complexity. And the oyster sauce didn't add much to the final dish; we found we could skip it without sacrificing flavor.

At this point, the dish was still lacking in potent heat. Two fresh Thai chiles provided a good amount of heat, but we wanted more complexity. That's when a colleague suggested using the Asian chili-garlic sauce we keep as a staple in the pantry instead. Two tablespoons amped up the heat and spicy flavor of the sauce—and now we could cut the garlic (and a little prep time) from our recipe thanks to this two-for-one ingredient. The final tweak was adding a good amount of lime juice, which lent some sharpness and bright, sweet-tart notes that brought the sauce into balance. Tossing the softened noodles with the sauce over the heat for about five minutes allowed the noodles to release some starch and gave the sauce a chance to thicken nicely.

Finally, we looked to take this noodle dish from a carb lover's dream to a well-rounded, satisfying supper. In many recipes chicken, pork, or beef is added to the noodles, so we gave all three a try. In the end, we opted for skinless chicken breasts, which we sliced thin and stir-fried before adding the noodles and sauce to the pan. The mild-flavored meat added substance but didn't compete with the flavors of the dish. Napa cabbage often shows up in drunken noodles; we found that two heads of baby bok choy made the perfect stand-in and gave us just enough for two servings. Combined with a thinly sliced scallion, the bok choy contributed some crunch and color, and it needed just a few minutes in the pan to brown and soften slightly.

At last, we'd made this spicy, brightly flavored Thai noodle dish easy enough that we could make it any night of the week—no special shopping trip necessary.

NOTES FROM THE TEST KITCHEN

SLICING CHICKEN THINLY

1. To slice chicken breasts thinly, cut them across grain into ¼-inch-wide strips that are 1½ to 2 inches long. Cut center pieces in half so that they are approximately same length as end pieces and cook at same rate.

2. For tenderloins, cut them on diagonal to produce pieces of meat that are roughly same size.

ALL ABOUT RICE NOODLES

This delicate pasta, made from rice flour and water, is used in a variety of dishes in Southeast Asia and southern China. These noodles should be steeped in hot water to soften them; they overcook quickly, so boiling tends to make them mushy. Flat rice noodles (left) come in several widths; a medium-width noodle is traditionally used in pad thai, but we like a larger noodle for our Drunken Noodles with Chicken. Round rice noodles, also called vermicelli (right), come in a variety of sizes, but we prefer the thinner kind. These delicate noodles make the perfect match for the light, bright sauce in our Coconut Rice Noodles with Shrimp and Pineapple (page 110).

Drunken Noodles with Chicken
SERVES 2

Do not substitute other types of noodles for the rice noodles here. This dish is spicy; for sensitive palates, use 1 tablespoon of chili-garlic sauce. Freezing the chicken for 15 minutes makes it easier to slice.

- **6 ounces (⅜-inch-wide) rice noodles**
- **6 ounces boneless, skinless chicken breasts, trimmed and sliced thin**
- **1½ teaspoons plus ¼ cup soy sauce**
- **⅓ cup packed dark brown sugar**
- **2½ tablespoons lime juice (2 limes), plus lime wedges for serving**
- **1–2 tablespoons Asian chili-garlic sauce**
- **2 tablespoons vegetable oil**
- **2 heads baby bok choy (4 ounces each), stems and leaves divided, sliced ½ inch thick**
- **1 cup water**
- **½ cup coarsely chopped fresh Thai basil or cilantro**
- **1 scallion, sliced thin on bias**

1. Cover noodles with very hot tap water in large bowl and stir to separate. Let noodles soak until softened, pliable, and limp but not fully tender, 35 to 40 minutes; drain.

2. Meanwhile, toss chicken with 1½ teaspoons soy sauce in bowl, cover, and refrigerate for at least 10 minutes or up to 1 hour. In separate bowl, whisk remaining ¼ cup soy sauce, sugar, lime juice, and chili-garlic sauce together; set aside.

3. Heat 1 teaspoon oil in 12-inch nonstick skillet over high heat until just smoking. Add chicken in single layer and cook without stirring for 1 minute. Stir and continue to cook until nearly cooked through, about 2 minutes longer; transfer to bowl.

4. Add 1 teaspoon oil to now-empty skillet and heat over high heat until just smoking. Add bok choy stems and cook, stirring often, until spotty brown, about 2 minutes; stir in leaves and cook until wilted, about 1 minute. Transfer to bowl with chicken.

5. Wipe now-empty skillet clean with paper towels, add remaining 4 teaspoons oil, and heat over medium heat until shimmering. Add drained rice noodles, soy sauce mixture, and water and cook, tossing gently, until noodles are tender and well coated, 5 to 10 minutes. Stir in chicken-vegetable mixture and basil. Sprinkle with scallion and serve with lime wedges.

BEEF LO MEIN

✔ **WHY THIS RECIPE WORKS:** For a full-flavored, not bland, beef lo mein, we started with the sauce, looking for bold, complex flavor from a few key ingredients: soy sauce, hoisin sauce, and toasted sesame oil. Marinating thinly sliced flank steak in this mixture before stir-frying ensured that it was well seasoned. To guarantee crisp-tender broccoli, we steamed it first, then cooked it uncovered so it could brown. A generous amount of scallions added a sweet, grassy pungency.

BEEF LO MEIN IS A SIMPLE DISH—BASICALLY A BEEF stir-fry with boiled noodles. So why is this dish so often poorly executed? The lo mein served in many Chinese restaurants is frequently oily and uninteresting; the noodles are often a tasteless mass, and the sauce, a bland, muddy gravy. We wanted something different—flavorful strands of noodles mingled with thin slices of perfectly cooked beef coated in a light, tangy sauce.

Lo mein literally translates to "tossed noodles," referring to the way the strands, made from wheat and egg and resembling thick spaghetti, are tossed in sauce. Most lo mein recipes call for fresh Chinese noodles, which are more tender and chewier and absorb flavors more readily than fresh Italian pasta. Some fresh Chinese noodles contain eggs and some do not. We tried both styles and much preferred the noodles with eggs for their richer flavor. We cooked the noodles in 4 quarts of water, our usual method for cooking pasta, until just tender. Since we'd be using a soy-based sauce, we omitted the salt in the cooking water but reserved some of the starchy liquid to adjust the consistency of the finished dish. Now we needed to figure out the beef, vegetables, and sauce.

After trying a few cuts of beef, we opted for flank steak, which offered a meaty chew and nice beefy flavor, and 8 ounces proved just enough for a meal for two. Before cooking, we sliced it thinly across the grain; to make it easier to slice, we froze the steak for 15 minutes. Once cut into thin pieces, the steak needed only a quick two-minute sear, then we could set it aside while we stir-fried the vegetables. For vegetables, broccoli and red bell pepper give the lo mein freshness and crunch. To guarantee crisp-tender broccoli, we steamed it first, then cooked it uncovered so it could brown. Our red

bell pepper strips simply needed to be sautéed for a couple of minutes until they were the perfect texture.

Next, we moved on to the sauce. Our goal was to generate the greatest flavor with the fewest ingredients. We also wanted to keep the sauce lighter than the usual gloppy Chinese takeout sauces. We started with a simple but robust blend of hoisin sauce, soy sauce, and toasted sesame oil. We found, and tasters agreed, that the hoisin sauce gave the lo mein an appealing salty richness and lush texture, plus it contributed an interesting complexity. Some recipes call for the addition of oyster sauce, but we found that hoisin contributed much the same texture, making a second rich sauce unnecessary. Adding a little chicken broth to the sauce kept it from being too thick. To amp up the flavor of the beef, we reserved a portion of the sauce and used it to marinate the beef for an hour before stir-frying.

A generous amount of scallions added a sweet, grassy pungency, ginger and garlic contributed some punch, and sweet and spicy Asian chili-garlic sauce completed the dish. Almost as easy as takeout, but with a much bigger payoff, our beef lo mein for two really delivered.

Beef Lo Mein with Broccoli and Bell Pepper
SERVES 2

Freezing the flank steak for 15 minutes makes it easier to slice.

- 3 **tablespoons hoisin sauce**
- 2 **tablespoons soy sauce**
- 2 **teaspoons toasted sesame oil**
- 8 **ounces flank steak, trimmed and sliced thin across grain on bias**
- ⅓ **cup low-sodium chicken broth**
- ½ **teaspoon cornstarch**
- 1 **garlic clove, minced**
- 1 **teaspoon grated fresh ginger**
- 1 **tablespoon vegetable oil**
- 6 **ounces broccoli florets, cut into 1-inch pieces**
- 2½ **tablespoons water**
- ½ **red bell pepper, stemmed, seeded, sliced into ½-inch-wide strips, and halved crosswise**
- 1 **bunch scallions, white parts sliced thin, greens parts cut into 1-inch pieces**
- 6 **ounces fresh Chinese noodles or 4 ounces dried linguine**
- 1½ **teaspoons Asian chili-garlic sauce**

1. Whisk hoisin sauce, soy sauce, and sesame oil together in medium bowl. Measure 1½ tablespoons of mixture into separate bowl and stir in beef; cover and refrigerate for at least 15 minutes or up to 1 hour. Whisk broth and cornstarch into remaining mixture; set aside. In separate small bowl, combine garlic, ginger, and ½ teaspoon vegetable oil.

2. Heat 1 teaspoon vegetable oil in 10-inch nonstick skillet over high heat until just smoking. Add beef in single layer and cook without stirring for 1 minute. Stir beef and continue to cook until browned, about 1 minute; transfer to large bowl.

3. Wipe now-empty skillet clean with paper towels, add ½ teaspoon vegetable oil, and heat over high heat until just smoking. Add broccoli and cook for 30 seconds. Add water, cover, and steam until broccoli is bright green and begins to soften, about 2 minutes. Uncover and continue to cook until water has evaporated and broccoli begins to brown, about 2 minutes; transfer to bowl with beef.

4. Add remaining 1 teaspoon vegetable oil and bell pepper to now-empty skillet and cook over high heat until crisp-tender and spotty brown, about 2 minutes. Add scallions and continue to cook until wilted, 2 to 3 minutes. Clear center of skillet, add garlic-ginger mixture, and mash into pan until fragrant, about 30 seconds; stir into vegetables. Stir in cooked beef and broccoli with any accumulated juices. Stir in broth mixture and simmer until sauce has thickened, about 1 minute. Remove from heat and cover to keep warm.

5. Meanwhile, bring 4 quarts water to boil in large pot. Add noodles and cook, stirring often, until tender. Reserve ½ cup cooking water, then drain noodles and return them to pot. Add beef mixture and chili-garlic sauce and toss to combine. Add reserved cooking water as needed to adjust consistency. Serve.

SOBA NOODLES WITH EGGPLANT AND SESAME

✔ **WHY THIS RECIPE WORKS:** The creamy texture and mild flavor of cooked eggplant made the perfect foil to rich, nutty soba noodles in this recipe. Roasting proved an easy, hands-off way to cook the eggplant; tossing it with soy sauce beforehand helped to season the vegetable and draw out its moisture. For a richly flavored sauce, we started with soy sauce and added oyster sauce, Asian chili-garlic sauce, sake, and toasted sesame oil for a nice balance of sweet and spicy flavors.

JAPANESE SOBA NOODLES, WHICH ARE MADE WITH buckwheat flour, are typically served hot in a simple broth along with vegetables or meat, or cold with a simple dipping sauce. Because of their unique rich flavor and chewy texture, they need little adornment, so we thought these noodles could easily become a quick, substantial meal for two. We decided that the creamy texture and mild flavor of cooked eggplant would make the perfect foil to the rich, nutty noodles for a simple yet unexpected pasta dish.

From the outset, we wanted the eggplant to share the stage with the noodles, so we started with a full pound. We left the eggplant in large chunks—about 1-inch pieces—so they wouldn't cook down too much and

---

NOTES FROM THE TEST KITCHEN

THE BEST SOY SAUCE

At its most basic, soy sauce is a fermented liquid made from soybeans and wheat. Soybeans contribute a strong, pungent taste, and wheat lends sweetness. Soy sauce should add flavor and complexity to your recipes, not just make them salty. We use it not only in numerous Asian noodle recipes, but also to enhance meaty flavor in pasta sauces, soups, stews, and braises. To find the best brand, we sampled 12 soy sauces three different ways: plain, drizzled over warm rice, and cooked in a simple teriyaki glaze over chicken thighs. Our favorite was **Lee Kum Kee Tabletop Soy Sauce**, which has a robust flavor that tasters described as "salty, sweet, roasted, and pleasant" and holds up well throughout cooking.

ALL ABOUT FRESH CHINESE NOODLES

Fresh Chinese noodles are a bit more starchy and chewy than dried noodles. Though they are made from wheat flour, their flavor is less wheaty than that of Italian pasta, making them an excellent match for potent, highly seasoned sauces, as in our Beef Lo Mein with Broccoli and Bell Pepper. If you can't find them, you can substitute dried linguine.

disappear into the dish. But we had to figure out the best way to cook them. Roasting seemed promising—it would provide an effortless, hands-off way to ensure tender, evenly cooked bites of eggplant. Since eggplant is notoriously full of sauce-diluting moisture, we took a cue from our Vegetable Lasagna (page 105) and salted the eggplant to draw out its moisture before cooking. Although this method worked, we wondered if we could substitute soy sauce for the salt, essentially boosting the eggplant's flavor while also drawing out its moisture. Indeed, tossing the eggplant with soy sauce worked well and eliminated the need to separately salt the vegetable. To keep the eggplant from becoming dried out in the oven and to guarantee that it browned nicely, we added a small amount of vegetable oil to the soy sauce before tossing the eggplant in it. Then we roasted the eggplant on a sheet pan for about 30 minutes until it was tender; oiling the pan beforehand ensured that the vegetable didn't stick.

While we usually call for 6 ounces of dried pasta when cooking for two, we decided to dial back the amount in this dish. The hearty texture of soba noodles makes them much more filling than the standard dried pasta made with durum wheat. Four ounces of soba proved ample; coupled with our chunks of eggplant, this seemed just right and provided two sizable servings.

Moving on to the sauce, we started with a base of soy sauce for savory richness. Oyster sauce thickened the sauce with its *umami*-rich maltiness. A bit of sugar and Asian chili-garlic sauce provided a nice balance of sweet and spicy flavors, and a tablespoon of toasted sesame

oil grounded the sauce with its warm, earthy richness. For even more complexity, we added a splash of sake.

Once the noodles were cooked, we tossed them in the sauce, along with our tender roasted eggplant; a splash of pasta cooking water helped to loosen the sauce to just the right consistency. A quarter cup of cilantro added a fresh, grassy element to the earthy pasta, and a sprinkling of toasted sesame seeds provided texture and crunch and echoed the nutty flavor of the sesame oil.

Soba Noodles with Roasted Eggplant and Sesame

SERVES 2

Vermouth can be substituted for the sake if necessary. Do not substitute other types of noodles for the soba noodles here.

- 2 tablespoons vegetable oil
- 1 pound eggplant, cut into 1-inch pieces
- 2 tablespoons soy sauce
- 2 tablespoons sugar
- 1 tablespoon oyster sauce
- 1 tablespoon toasted sesame oil
- 1½ teaspoons Asian chili-garlic sauce
- 2 teaspoons sake or dry vermouth
- 4 ounces soba noodles
- ¼ cup fresh cilantro leaves
- 1 teaspoon sesame seeds, toasted

1. Adjust oven rack to middle position and heat oven to 450 degrees. Line rimmed baking sheet with aluminum foil and brush with 1½ teaspoons vegetable oil. Toss eggplant with remaining 1½ tablespoons vegetable oil and 1½ teaspoons soy sauce, then spread on prepared baking sheet. Roast until well browned and tender, 25 to 30 minutes, stirring halfway through roasting.

2. In small saucepan, whisk remaining 1½ tablespoons soy sauce, sugar, oyster sauce, sesame oil, chili-garlic sauce, and sake together. Cook over medium heat until sugar has dissolved, about 1 minute; cover and set aside.

3. Meanwhile, bring 4 quarts water to boil in large pot. Add noodles and cook, stirring often, until tender. Reserve ½ cup cooking water, then drain noodles and return them to pot. Add roasted eggplant, sauce, and cilantro and toss to combine. Add reserved cooking water as needed to adjust consistency. Sprinkle individual portions with sesame seeds and serve.

NOTES FROM THE TEST KITCHEN

ALL ABOUT SOBA NOODLES

Soba noodles possess a rich, nutty flavor and delicate texture. They get their unusual flavor from buckwheat flour, which contains no gluten, so a binder, usually wheat, is added to give the noodles structure and hold them together during cooking. The Japanese agricultural department requires that all noodles labeled as soba contain a minimum of 30 percent buckwheat flour, and the higher the percentage of buckwheat flour, the higher the price. Soba noodles are traditionally served chilled with a dipping sauce, but we also like them warm and accompanied by a simple sauce, as in our Soba Noodles with Roasted Eggplant and Sesame.

VEGETABLE POT PIE

FARMHOUSE VEGETABLE AND BARLEY SOUP

✔ **WHY THIS RECIPE WORKS:** Most recipes for hearty winter vegetable soups are neither quick nor easy. For a satisfying soup for two that wouldn't take the better part of a day to make, we started with canned vegetable broth. To boost its flavor, we added soy sauce and just one dried porcini mushroom. These ingredients gave the soup plenty of savory, meaty flavor. To make the soup seriously satisfying, we added barley to the hearty combination of carrot, parsnip, potato, leek, and cabbage. A pat of butter, some thyme, and lemon juice added richness and brightened the flavors.

WINTERTIME IS SOUP TIME, AND IT'S ALSO THE TIME of year when our crisper drawers are overflowing with cold-weather vegetables. These hearty vegetables seem perfect for a satisfying vegetable soup, but our attempts often turn out lackluster. The problem is time: The best soups—vegetable or otherwise—start with a rich, full-bodied broth that serves as the soup's main component and its flavor foundation, and we usually need the weekend to make a really good one. Rather than sideline a rustic vegetable soup as a lazy Sunday-afternoon project, we wanted to pack all the rich, earthy flavor and depth of a long-simmered stock into a recipe that took only about an hour's work.

We knew we wouldn't be able to make homemade broth in less than an hour, so we would have to start with store-bought broth and find ways to punch up its flavor. Some recipes rely on adding a little meat to the vegetable broth to beef up the flavor, but we were determined to keep this hearty soup strictly vegetarian. Curious to see how far we could get by simply doctoring commercial broth and tossing in vegetables, we threw together a test batch in which we sweated leek, carrot, and parsnip in a pat of butter, bundled up some aromatics—crushed garlic, a few sprigs of fresh thyme, and a bay leaf—in cheesecloth, and poured in about 3 cups of vegetable broth. We simmered this base for about 15 minutes, then stirred in small chunks of potato and chopped green cabbage and let everything cook until the vegetables were just tender. Tasters had

no complaints about the vegetables themselves: Their flavors worked well together, and the crinkly cabbage leaves offered a pleasing crisp-tender crunch. Nor could we gripe about the time or labor involved, both of which were minimal. But there was no denying that the soup felt thin, lacking both flavor and body.

The good news was that we'd been here before. A few years back the test kitchen developed a recipe for quick beef and vegetable soup, and we learned that the most effective way to get big flavor in a hurry is to bolster the broth with ingredients rich in flavor-enhancing *umami,* the fifth taste that describes savory, "meaty" flavor. Soy sauce and mushrooms were at the top of our list of umami-rich ingredients, so we started our testing there. We "seasoned" the pot with a dash of soy sauce and a single dried porcini for intense, earthy depth. The difference was significant; the soup suddenly took on a savory depth and complexity that had previously been missing.

The soup was now so good that we found that we could substitute water for some of the store-bought broth, which eliminated the slightly commercial flavor we got from using all broth. A little acidic white wine added along with the first batch of vegetables further improved things, as did the last-minute additions of frozen peas, a splash of fresh lemon juice, and a tablespoon of minced parsley.

Flavorwise, we were in great shape, but we still had to confront the soup's lack of body. The vegetables themselves were substantial, and roughly chopping them amped up their heartiness, but even the starchy potatoes weren't doing much to thicken the broth. We tried adding dairy, but the fat just dulled the flavor of the broth that we had worked so hard to build. Then a fellow test cook mentioned an interesting idea he had picked up on a trip to Ireland: adding oatmeal to the soup. We found this frugal trick for bulking up the broth charming in theory, but it didn't play out as we had hoped. Tasters complained that even though the dish took on a nice nuttiness, the chewy oats made it feel like a vegetable-heavy gruel.

Despite this failure, we liked the idea of bulking up the soup with a grain. After testing several different types, we settled on barley. We added a few tablespoons of the pearl variety to the pot just as we poured in the liquids. By the time we were ready to add the potato,

FARMHOUSE VEGETABLE AND BARLEY SOUP

turnip, and cabbage, the beads were partially plumped, and they were perfectly al dente about 15 minutes later, when the soup was ready to be served.

This change gave the soup exactly the heft and substance it needed. But a few of our tasters still wanted to get another dimension of flavor and richness into the pot. We had a holdout idea that we had come across in one of the Irish cookbooks we researched: finishing the soup with herbs and butter. It would be an unusual addition for sure. Still, we held out hope that stirring in a dollop of butter and some fresh thyme right before serving would contribute not only a burst of fresh flavor but also the plush body that only dairy can give without the cloying, flavor-dampening effect of milk or cream. When we caught sight of our tasters going back for seconds, we knew that we'd hit it right. At last, a rustic, full-bodied vegetable soup thrown together in under an hour that didn't need a speck of meat to taste hearty and satisfying.

Farmhouse Vegetable and Barley Soup

SERVES 2

We prefer an acidic, unoaked white wine such as Sauvignon Blanc for this recipe. Garnish the soup with crumbled cheddar cheese or herbed croutons, if desired.

- 2 parsley stems plus 1 tablespoon minced fresh parsley
- 2 sprigs fresh thyme plus ½ teaspoon chopped
- 1 dried porcini mushroom, rinsed
- 1 bay leaf
- 2 tablespoons unsalted butter
- 1 leek, white and light green parts only, halved lengthwise, sliced ½ inch thick, and washed thoroughly
- 1 small carrot, peeled and cut into ½-inch pieces
- 1 small parsnip, peeled and cut into ½-inch pieces
- 2 tablespoons dry white wine
- ¾ teaspoon soy sauce
- Salt and pepper
- 2 cups water
- 1½ cups vegetable broth
- 3 tablespoons pearl barley
- 1 small garlic clove, peeled and smashed
- 1 small Yukon Gold potato, peeled and cut into ½-inch pieces
- ½ cup chopped green cabbage
- ¼ cup frozen peas
- 1 teaspoon lemon juice

1. Bundle parsley stems, thyme sprigs, mushroom, and bay leaf in cheesecloth and tie with kitchen twine to secure. Melt 1 tablespoon butter in medium saucepan over medium heat. Add leek, carrot, parsnip, wine, soy sauce, and ½ teaspoon salt. Cook, stirring occasionally, until liquid has evaporated and leeks are softened, about 5 minutes.

2. Add herb and mushroom bundle, water, broth, barley, and garlic to saucepan; increase heat to high and bring to boil. Reduce heat to medium-low and simmer, partially covered, for 15 minutes.

3. Add potatoes and cabbage to saucepan and return to simmer. Cook, stirring occasionally, until barley, potatoes, and cabbage are tender, about 15 minutes.

4. Remove saucepan from heat and remove bundle. Stir in minced parsley and chopped thyme, remaining 1 tablespoon butter, peas, and lemon juice. Season with salt and pepper to taste. Serve.

NOTES FROM THE TEST KITCHEN

BUILDING SAVORY FLAVOR ON THE DOUBLE

To ramp up savory flavor in our Farmhouse Vegetable and Barley Soup, we added two umami boosters: soy sauce and a porcini mushroom. Soy sauce contains high levels of naturally occurring flavor-enhancing compounds called glutamates, while mushrooms are rich in flavor-amplifying compounds known as nucleotides. When used together, the two compounds can boost savory flavor exponentially.

GLUTAMATES + NUCLEOTIDES = BIG SAVORY FLAVOR

VEGETABLE POT PIE

✓ **WHY THIS RECIPE WORKS:** For a vegetable pot pie that would be both hearty and delicious, we chose a filling of rich sweet potatoes, grassy fennel, and earthy mushrooms. Sweating the vegetables before adding them to the filling ensured that they were tender when the pie came out of the oven. A little cheddar in the filling lent a nice tang and creaminess. We split the filling between two ramekins for perfectly portioned individual pot pies. And we switched out traditional pie crust for easy, tasty cheddar-scallion biscuits and baked them right on top of the filling.

A REALLY GOOD VEGETABLE POT PIE IS EASIER SAID than done. The biggest challenge: how to develop a full-flavored, satisfying filling without chunks of beef or chicken. We wanted to develop a vegetable pot pie that was more than just a vessel for bland starch. Our first task was to choose the best combination of vegetables. Thinking that potatoes would be an essential addition to our rustic pie, we started there. Red Bliss potatoes gave the pie bulk, but they didn't add much flavor. For a starch that would be both filling and flavorful, we tried sweet potato. Tasters loved the creaminess and sweetness that it lent, so it was a keeper. Looking for another vegetable to complement the sweet potato, we tried a battery of different kinds: parsnips (too sweet), turnips (too boring), and broccoli (the texture was all wrong). Then some fennel that had just been delivered to the test kitchen caught our attention; its bright anise flavor profile fit right in next to the sweet potato.

To add warmth, complexity, and flavor to our vegetarian dish, we looked to meaty mushrooms. We tested shiitake, portobello, and cremini, and tasters unanimously liked both the flavor and texture of the cremini, touting their tender chew and subtle sweetness.

With our main vegetables settled, we got to work figuring out the best cooking method for each. We tried simply mixing the raw vegetables into the sauce before the pie was topped and baked, but they failed to fully cook by the time the topping browned. Parboiling each vegetable separately until tender worked well, but it seemed too fussy for what should be a simple,

homey dish. A third option proved the best: We tossed the sweet potatoes, fennel, and mushrooms in butter in the pot and put the lid on so that the vegetables would "sweat" in their own moisture. After just 10 minutes, the vegetables were tender but still al dente at the core. We added the sauce, topped the pot pie, and moved it to the oven, and by the time the topping was nicely browned, the vegetables were cooked to perfection.

But as good as the vegetables were, the filling was still lacking. To bump up flavor, we sautéed a minced shallot in a little butter before adding the other vegetables. A bit of garlic and some fresh herbs were givens— parsley added color, but little flavor, and rosemary was simply too much, overwhelming the other flavors. Woodsy thyme won the most votes.

It was time to tackle the sauce. We wanted to use vegetable broth as our base to keep this pie vegetarian friendly, but broth alone proved too weak to stand up to our flavorful, hearty vegetables. We used a bit of cream to add richness, but the cream's high fat content muted the filling's flavor. We decided to try something a bit less conventional: cheddar cheese. It gave the sauce a slight tang and creamy cheese flavor that everyone loved. A splash of cider vinegar brightened the sauce, rounding out the flavors.

Finally, we considered the topping. We started by narrowing down what type of crust we wanted. We tried everything, from pie dough and puff pastry to biscuits. We found that pot pies prepared with a pie crust topping yielded a soupy, mushy mess. The topping was preventing steam from escaping, causing the filling to boil. When we pulled the pies from the oven and dug in, the filling was still boiling away. Puff pastry didn't feel like a homey enough partner to the filling. The option we liked best proved to be a traditional buttermilk biscuit; when we mounded the biscuit dough in the center of the filling, it allowed the steam to escape on the sides, solving our boiling problem, and the tender, buttery biscuits proved to be a perfect complement to our chunky vegetable filling.

We started with a basic drop biscuit dough, then bumped up the flavor with a little cheddar and sliced scallion greens. To keep the biscuit method simple, we melted butter and stirred it into cold buttermilk, then added it to a simple mixture of flour, leaveners, salt, cheese, and scallions. The hot butter hitting the cold buttermilk created lumps of butter that turned to steam in the oven, helping to create a nice rise and a tender crumb. This method mimicked the positive effects of making biscuits the old-fashioned way—cutting cold butter into the dough—but it was much easier and less messy. We hit on another shortcut when we saw the scrap pile of leftover whites from the scallions and realized that we could reduce waste and simplify our recipe by mincing them and using them in place of the shallot in the filling. Now the only hard part about these pot pies was having to wait for them to cool before devouring them.

Vegetable Pot Pie

SERVES 2

You will need two 12-ounce ramekins for this recipe (see page 3). If you don't have buttermilk on hand, you can substitute ⅓ cup of milk and 1½ teaspoons of lemon juice; stir together and let the mixture sit until it thickens, about five minutes.

½ cup plus 1½ tablespoons all-purpose flour

2 ounces sharp cheddar cheese, shredded (½ cup)

2 scallions, white parts minced, green parts sliced thin

½ teaspoon baking powder

¼ teaspoon baking soda

   Salt and pepper

⅓ cup buttermilk, chilled

2 tablespoons unsalted butter, melted

1 (8-ounce) sweet potato, peeled and cut into ½-inch pieces

½ small fennel bulb, stalks discarded, bulb halved, cored, and cut into ½-inch pieces (½ cup)

4 ounces cremini mushrooms, trimmed and quartered

1 garlic clove, minced

¼ teaspoon minced fresh thyme or ⅛ teaspoon dried

1⅓ cups vegetable broth

⅓ cup frozen peas

½ teaspoon cider vinegar

1. Adjust oven rack to middle position and heat oven to 425 degrees. Whisk ½ cup flour, 2 tablespoons cheddar, scallion greens, baking powder, baking soda, ⅛ teaspoon salt, and ⅛ teaspoon pepper together in medium bowl. Combine chilled buttermilk and 1 tablespoon butter in small bowl and stir until butter forms small clumps. Stir buttermilk mixture into flour mixture with rubber spatula until just incorporated. Refrigerate until ready to use.

2. Add remaining 1 tablespoon butter to medium saucepan over medium heat. Add scallion whites and ¼ teaspoon salt and cook, stirring occasionally, until softened and beginning to brown, about 1 minute. Stir in sweet potato, fennel, and mushrooms. Cover and cook, stirring occasionally, until sweet potato is softened around edges, 8 to 10 minutes.

3. Stir in garlic and thyme and cook until fragrant, about 30 seconds. Add remaining 1½ tablespoons flour and cook, stirring constantly, for 30 seconds. Slowly stir in broth. Bring to simmer, scraping up any browned bits, and cook until sauce thickens, 1 to 3 minutes. Off heat, stir in remaining 6 tablespoons cheddar, peas, and vinegar and season with salt and pepper to taste. Divide filling evenly between two 12-ounce ramekins.

4. Divide dough in half and place mound of dough in center of filling in each ramekin. Transfer ramekins to aluminum foil–lined rimmed baking sheet and bake until biscuits are golden brown and filling is bubbling, 20 to 25 minutes. Let cool for 5 to 10 minutes before serving.

NOTES FROM THE TEST KITCHEN

PREPARING FENNEL

1. Cut off tops and feathery fronds, then trim thin slice from base and remove any tough or blemished outer layers.

2. Cut bulb in half through base. Use small sharp knife to remove pyramid-shaped core. Cut bulb into ½-inch pieces.

SUMMER VEGETABLE TAMALE PIE

✔ **WHY THIS RECIPE WORKS:** Packed with summery zucchini, fresh corn, and poblano chile and bound in a cheesy Southwestern tomato sauce, this one-dish skillet supper was as filling as it was easy to make. The poblano chile plus pepper Jack cheese and chili powder perfected the Southwest flavor profile. We packed the vegetables into an 8-inch skillet and steamed them, rather than sautéing, to keep the generous filling from spilling over. To top it off, a simple buttermilk cornbread spread on top and baked until golden brown provided a delicious foil to the saucy, spicy vegetables.

THE TEX-MEX CLASSIC TAMALE PIE USUALLY contains a juicy, spicy mixture of meat and vegetables with a crisp, browned cornmeal crust. But bad tamale pies abound, dry and bland with too much or too little filling. We wanted to develop a really good tamale pie that had just the right proportion of filling to topping—and to up the ante, we were going to make it vegetarian.

We found that recipes for vegetarian tamale pies were few and far between, so we would have to start from scratch. We began our testing by making a traditional tamale pie and simply omitting the meat to see where it would get us. Cutting the meat left us with a filling of fresh corn, pepper Jack cheese, and diced tomatoes. It sounded great, but tasters demanded more substance. We would have to bulk up the filling with more vegetables.

To find vegetables that would feel at home in our simple skillet tamale pie, we had a few criteria: They had to be quick-cooking, and they had to pair well with our summery Southwest flavor profile. When we think about abundant summer vegetables, the first thing that comes to mind is zucchini. It fit in perfectly, and tasters were impressed with how much the zucchini bulked up the pie. Next, we tried adding a red pepper, but it made the pie a little too sweet, so we swapped the sweet pepper for a poblano, a fruity, only slightly spicy chile pepper. Tasters loved the mix of zucchini, corn, poblano, and diced tomatoes. To further boost the flavor of the filling, we added a sautéed shallot and a teaspoon of chili powder. Our filling was coming along.

But our hearty mix of vegetables was creating a new problem: An 8-inch skillet gave us just the right size pie for two, but the skillet was now bursting with fresh vegetables that were too cumbersome to sauté. We tried switching to a 10-inch skillet, but that made the filling too thin, more like a casserole than a pie. Then we thought of a method we often use in our low-fat recipes: To save on fat, we cover the vegetables and let them steam instead of sautéing them with lots of oil. With this method, we'd only need to stir the vegetables gently every so often, solving the problem of our packed skillet. We tried it out in our 8-inch skillet, first sautéing the poblano and shallot in a little oil until just softened, then adding the other vegetables, covering the skillet, and letting the vegetables steam until just tender. This method worked perfectly. Our pie was even easier, and thanks to our new method, it was spillover free.

Our last task was the topping. A traditional tamale pie boasts a cornmeal topping, but should it taste like an actual tamale (made from *masa*)? Or should it be more like cornbread? We tried both. Tasters rejected the tamale-style topping; it was a bit bland, and the masa was hard to find. The slightly sweet cornbread topping was the clear winner; made with equal amounts of cornmeal and flour, it had a nice texture and was just the right amount of topping to balance the spicy vegetable filling. We simply poured the cornbread batter over the filling in the skillet and spread it in an even layer to the edges. A moderately high oven temperature of 450 degrees for just 15 minutes gave us a light, golden crust. This fresh tamale pie packed with summery vegetables came together in a snap, and no one missed the meat.

NOTES FROM THE TEST KITCHEN

THE PERFECT PEPPER
The fruity, subtly spicy flavor of a poblano chile gives this dish bright, fresh flavor without overwhelming it with heat. Poblano chiles are dark green in color and about 4 to 5 inches long. Common in the Southwest and in Central America, they can be found in Latin markets and in many supermarkets. When dried, they are known as ancho chiles.

Skillet Summer Vegetable Tamale Pie

SERVES 2

If you don't have buttermilk on hand, you can substitute ⅓ cup of milk and 1½ teaspoons of lemon juice; stir together and let the mixture sit until it thickens, about 5 minutes. To make individual portions, divide the filling evenly between two 6-inch pie plates in step 4. Spread half of the cornbread topping evenly over the filling in each pie plate and bake on a rimmed baking sheet. Serve with sour cream, if desired.

FILLING

- 1 tablespoon olive oil
- 1 poblano chile, stemmed, seeded, and cut into ½-inch pieces
- 1 shallot, chopped
  Salt and pepper
- 1 ear corn, kernels cut from cob
- 1 (8-ounce) zucchini, quartered lengthwise and cut into ½-inch pieces
- 1 (14.5-ounce) can diced tomatoes, drained with juice reserved
- 1 teaspoon chili powder
- 2 ounces pepper Jack cheese, shredded (½ cup)
- 2 tablespoons chopped fresh cilantro

TOPPING

- ⅓ cup all-purpose flour
- ⅓ cup cornmeal
- 1 tablespoon sugar
- ¼ teaspoon baking powder
- ⅛ teaspoon baking soda
- ¼ teaspoon salt
- ⅓ cup buttermilk
- 1 large egg
- 1 tablespoon unsalted butter, melted and cooled

1. FOR THE FILLING: Adjust oven rack to middle position and heat oven to 450 degrees. Heat oil in 8-inch ovensafe skillet over medium heat until shimmering. Add poblano, shallot, and ¼ teaspoon salt and cook, stirring frequently, until softened, about 5 minutes. Add corn, zucchini, and tomatoes. Cover and cook, stirring occasionally, until just tender, 6 to 8 minutes. Stir in chili powder and cook until fragrant, about 30 seconds.

2. Off heat, stir in reserved tomato juice, pepper Jack, and cilantro. Season with salt and pepper to taste; set aside.

3. FOR THE TOPPING: Whisk flour, cornmeal, sugar, baking powder, baking soda, and salt together in medium bowl. Whisk buttermilk and egg together in small bowl. Stir buttermilk mixture into flour mixture until uniform, then stir in melted butter until just combined.

4. Dollop cornbread topping evenly over filling, then spread into even layer, covering filling completely. Bake until cornbread is golden and cooked through completely in center, 12 to 15 minutes. Serve.

FENNEL, OLIVE, AND GOAT CHEESE TARTS

✔ WHY THIS RECIPE WORKS: For an elegant savory tart easy enough for a weeknight dinner for two, we pulled store-bought puff pastry from the freezer to form the base. For the filling, fresh, anise-flavored fennel paired with cured olives was light but flavorful. Herbed goat cheese provided a tangy contrast with the rich, flaky pastry and helped bind everything together. To keep the pastry crispy and browned and the filling firmly in place, we first parbaked the puff pastry, then cut a border around the edges and pressed down the centers to make a neat bed for the cheese and vegetables.

PUFF PASTRY TARTS MAKE FOR AN ELEGANT MEAL that is surprisingly easy to put together, thanks to readily available frozen puff pastry that bakes up crisp and golden brown with plenty of delicate, flaky layers. We wanted to combine elegance and ease into a simple and delicious savory vegetable tart, using just a few well-chosen ingredients to deliver lots of flavor without a lot of work.

We started with our vegetable filling. We knew we wanted a light, fresh vegetable tart to complement the rich, buttery crust. We landed on fast-cooking, delicately flavored fennel as the perfect vegetable to showcase. Tasters loved its subtle anise flavor. To ensure that the fennel would cook through by the time the tart was baked, we first softened the fennel by cooking it, covered, in a sauté pan with a little bit of wine. To enhance the flavor, we added a minced garlic clove along with some fresh lemon juice. A handful of briny

FENNEL, OLIVE, AND GOAT CHEESE TARTS

olives was a quick and easy addition that provided contrast and sharp, salty flavor.

Next, we wanted to complement the fennel with a cheesy, creamy base that would help hold everything together. We tried spreading some goat cheese on each tart and were pleased to find that it provided a nice tangy contrast to the crisp, buttery puff pastry. However, tasters still thought that the goat cheese could use a little boost. The lemon juice had done so much to brighten the fennel flavor that we wondered what would happen if we mixed a little lemon zest into the goat cheese to add a fragrant, citrusy note. We also added some chopped basil for freshness, and a little olive oil made the goat cheese creamier and easier to spread on the delicate pastries without crumbling. Tasters loved the improved flavor of the goat cheese paired with the fresh fennel and olives.

With our filling perfected, we moved on to the crust. Since we were using store-bought pastry, we figured the crust of our tarts would be the easiest part. Half of a sheet of thawed puff pastry cut into two squares made tarts just the right size for two. But when we tried to bake the raw pastry dough with our fillings spread on top, the pastry was too weighed down to rise, and the

tarts came out soggy and flat. We decided we would have to parbake the pastry squares until they were puffed and browned before adding the filling. But when we spread the filling on top of the parbaked pastries, we were left with a mess. The weight of even our light filling was still squashing the delicate pastry layers, and bits of filling were falling off the sides and burning in the oven. We solved this problem by cutting a ½-inch border around the perimeter of the shells, then gently pressing the centers down with our fingertips to create a bed for the filling. The filling stayed put, and we were left with a lovely golden-brown crust around the edge that baked up tall and flaky. After we spooned the filling in, the tart needed to bake for only about 5 minutes until the filling was hot and bubbling. The empty plates confirmed one thing: We had developed a fast, easy tart worthy of a special occasion.

Fennel, Olive, and Goat Cheese Tarts
SERVES 2

To thaw frozen puff pastry, let it sit either in the refrigerator for 24 hours or on the counter for 30 to 60 minutes. See page 273 for a recipe to use up the leftover puff pastry.

½ (9½ by 9-inch) sheet frozen puff pastry, thawed and cut in half widthwise to make two 4½-inch squares

4 ounces goat cheese, softened

¼ cup chopped fresh basil

1½ tablespoons extra-virgin olive oil

½ teaspoon grated lemon zest plus 2 teaspoons juice
Salt and pepper

½ fennel bulb, stalks discarded, bulb cored and sliced thin

1 garlic clove, minced

¼ cup dry white wine

¼ cup pitted oil-cured black olives, chopped

1. Adjust oven rack to middle position and heat oven to 425 degrees. Lay pastry squares on parchment paper–lined baking sheet, poke all over with fork, and bake until puffed and golden brown, 12 to 15 minutes, rotating sheet halfway through baking. Using tip of paring knife, cut ½-inch-wide border into top of each pastry shell, then press centers down with fingertips.

NOTES FROM THE TEST KITCHEN

MAKING PUFF PASTRY TART SHELLS
Creating a bed for the filling within the tart shell ensures that none of the filling will escape when baked.

1. Lay pastry squares on parchment-lined baking sheet and poke them all over with fork. Bake pastry until puffed and golden, 12 to 15 minutes.

2. Using tip of paring knife, cut ½-inch border into top of each pastry shell and press centers down with your fingertips to create beds for filling.

2. Meanwhile, mix goat cheese with 2 tablespoons basil, 2 teaspoons oil, lemon zest, and ¼ teaspoon pepper in small bowl. Heat remaining 2½ teaspoons oil in 8-inch skillet over medium heat until shimmering. Add fennel and cook, stirring occasionally, until softened and brown in places, about 5 minutes. Add garlic and cook until fragrant, 30 seconds. Add wine, cover, and cook for 5 minutes. Uncover and continue to cook until liquid has evaporated and fennel is very soft, 3 to 5 minutes longer. Off heat, stir in lemon juice and olives.

3. Working with 1 tart at a time, spread goat cheese mixture evenly in center of shells, leaving raised edges clean, then spoon fennel mixture evenly over cheese layer. Transfer filled tarts to oven and bake until cheese is heated through and crust is deep golden brown, about 5 minutes. Sprinkle with remaining 2 tablespoons basil, season with salt and pepper to taste, and serve.

INDIVIDUAL RICOTTA AND EGG CASSEROLES

✔ **WHY THIS RECIPE WORKS:** Cooking these easy egg casseroles in individual ramekins not only added charm but also cut way down on oven time. Mixing ricotta with the eggs lent them a rich and decadent texture. Spinach made the dish hearty and satisfying, and tomato brightened the flavors. Shingling the tomato on top of the egg mixture exposed it to the oven's direct heat so the excess water baked off, keeping the filling from becoming watery. These egg casseroles were a snap to assemble, yet were perfect for a special brunch or light dinner.

WHETHER YOU WANT AN ELEGANT BRUNCH OR A creative supper, eggs can be a simple and easy solution for the two-person table. Scrambled, hard-cooked, and over easy are just fine for breakfast, but when eggs make the leap to the supper table, we yearn for a dish with a little more substance and style. We imagined an egg casserole, one with a refined, custardlike filling enriched with cheese and vegetables. It would have the elegance of a quiche but with a hearty, satisfying filling and

without a finicky crust. We'd just need to come up with the right cooking method and some bold, interesting flavors to make up the filling.

To make our dish easier to serve (and to assemble), we decided to use ramekins to make two individual casseroles. For the flavors, we looked to Italy for some inspiration. An Italian spinach pie is a specialty dish made primarily with chopped spinach, ricotta cheese, Parmesan, and eggs. The recipes we found were almost as time-consuming as making a quiche, but we did like the idea of a filling of flavorful spinach, creamy ricotta, and sharp Parmesan cheese. Starting with that idea, we combined two eggs, spinach, ricotta, and Parmesan and baked the mixture in the ramekins until just set. We were already getting somewhere with this test—tasters loved the spinach and egg combination, and the ricotta made the casseroles extra smooth and creamy. The Parmesan, however, was gritty and not well incorporated. We decided to switch it out for a better melting cheese. We tested fontina, mozzarella, and Monterey Jack. All of them melted well, but the fontina won hands down for having both melting power and a distinctive flavor to go with it.

Next, tasters wanted to round out the casserole and make it a little more substantial by adding another vegetable. Fresh tomato seemed like a perfect addition to complement the rich cheese and spinach. We chopped up a plum tomato and mixed it into the filling, but when we pulled the casseroles out of the oven, they were watery and bland. The juicy tomato was watering down the filling, making it taste thin. What if we pulled the tomato out of the filling and baked it on top of the casseroles? For our next test, we thinly sliced the tomato, patted the slices dry, and shingled them on top of each ramekin. This method paid off. With the tomato exposed to the heat of the oven, the extra water evaporated and the filling stayed creamy. As an added bonus, the beautiful slices of tomato not only added bright, balancing flavor but gave the casseroles a more elegant, colorful presentation.

We had our components nailed down, and the overall flavor was fresh and delicious, but tasters thought it was still lacking a little depth. We decided to add some aromatic heavy hitters to our egg casseroles. We sautéed a shallot until softened, then stirred in a minced clove of garlic until fragrant. Once they were mixed into the filling and baked, the change was subtle but significant; this batch had the most depth and sophisticated flavor yet. We had achieved our goal of elevating the humble egg casserole to fancy supper status, and the casseroles were a snap to assemble, too.

Ricotta and Egg Casseroles with Spinach and Tomato

SERVES 2

Removing the excess moisture from the spinach and tomato is important here. The tomato will release some juice while cooking; do not mistake it for the eggs being underdone. We found that 7-ounce ramekins worked best here, but 6-ounce or 8-ounce ramekins will also work.

- 2 teaspoons olive oil
- 1 shallot, minced
- ⅛ teaspoon salt
- 1 garlic clove, minced
- 4 ounces (½ cup) whole-milk ricotta cheese
- 3½ ounces frozen chopped spinach, thawed and squeezed dry
- 1½ ounces fontina cheese, shredded (⅓ cup)
- 2 large eggs, lightly beaten
- ⅛ teaspoon pepper
- 1 small plum tomato, cored, sliced into ⅛-inch-thick rounds, and patted dry

NOTES FROM THE TEST KITCHEN

RICOTTA CHEESE

Originally crafted from the whey byproduct of Romano cheese making, ricotta cheese has garnered fame as a delicious, cushiony filling for baked pasta dishes. But there are many other uses for ricotta; we put it to use to make a rich, creamy filling for our individual egg casseroles. Our favorite brand of ricotta cheese is **Calabro**, which boasts a certain freshness that many commercial brands lack.

It's made from fresh curds (drawn from nothing but Vermont farm whole milk), skim milk, a starter, and a sprinkle of salt. Granted, its shelf life spans only a matter of days, but one spoonful should be enough to guarantee its quick disappearance from your fridge. If you can't find Calabro, look for another fresh ricotta without gums or stabilizers.

1. Adjust oven rack to middle position and heat oven to 350 degrees. Grease two 7-ounce ramekins with baking spray with flour and place on rimmed baking sheet.

2. Heat oil in 8-inch skillet over medium heat until shimmering. Add shallot and salt and cook, stirring occasionally, until softened, 2 to 3 minutes. Add garlic and cook until fragrant, about 30 seconds. Transfer shallot mixture to bowl and stir in ricotta, spinach, fontina, eggs, and pepper until uniformly combined.

3. Divide mixture between prepared ramekins and shingle tomato slices evenly over top. Bake until filling is set, about 25 minutes. Let cool for 5 to 10 minutes before serving.

MOROCCAN-STYLE QUINOA WITH CHICKPEAS

✓ WHY THIS RECIPE WORKS: We combined two powerhouse vegetarian staples—quinoa and chickpeas—in one pot in this unique pilaf-style dish. Hearty kale helped tie our two proteins together, and golden raisins and carrot imparted a sweet, earthy flavor. To emphasize the Moroccan flavors, we spiced the dish with fragrant coriander and hot red pepper flakes and stirred in toasted pine nuts, salty feta, and a squirt of lemon juice. Packed with exotic flavors and a snap to pull together, our grain, bean, and greens trifecta made a great vegetarian dish for two.

QUINOA IS A NUTRITIOUS WHOLE GRAIN REGARDED as a staple by most vegetarians; notoriously healthy, it is a complete protein, is high in fiber, and has a mild, nutty flavor. We've enjoyed quinoa as a side dish many times, but we wanted to use it as a jumping-off point for a main dish by pairing it with greens and beans.

We started with the beans. Because the quinoa would need about 20 minutes to cook all the way through, we needed a canned bean (we wanted to keep this in weeknight territory so soaking dried beans was out) that would have a firm enough texture to hold up for longer cooking times. Hearty, buttery chickpeas were our first choice. We simply simmered them in vegetable broth with the quinoa until they were tender and plump.

Next, we turned to the greens. Hearty braised greens

would be the perfect addition; they would be able to stand up to the long simmer, keeping our pilaf an easy one-dish meal. We tried collard and mustard greens, but their intense peppery flavors overwhelmed the rest of the dish. The milder flavor of kale was a much better match. We chopped it coarsely and placed it on top of the quinoa, chickpea, and broth mixture. Once covered, we let everything simmer until the quinoa was tender. While the quinoa was cooking and absorbing the liquid, it created the perfect steamy environment for the greens. When perfectly cooked, both the quinoa and kale were tender with a pleasant little chew to them.

This was shaping up to be a great one-pot supper, but it still needed some bolder flavors to complement the earthy grains and greens. We sautéed a small onion in the pot before adding the rest of the ingredients. A taster suggested that chopped carrot would add a burst of color as well as sweetness. We sautéed the carrot along with the onion to give it a head start on cooking. Tasters loved the carrot, and they commented that our dish was starting to take on a Moroccan feel. To expand on the Moroccan flavors, we added garlic, red pepper flakes, and fragrant ground coriander to the onion and carrot mixture. Since tasters liked the subtle sweetness the carrot lent, we wondered if the dish could use even more. Golden raisins, a common ingredient in North African cuisine, gave each bite a sweet edge that kept tasters coming back for more.

A drizzle of extra-virgin olive oil and a squeeze of lemon balanced the sweetness with a nice tart quality, and tossing in some toasted pine nuts added richness and rounded out the sharper flavors. A sprinkle of crumbled feta was our final addition, providing a salty component that brought out the other flavors. Finally, our unique approach to quinoa was complete. This dish was bright and boldly flavored, and with our easy one-pot technique it was a great way to liven up our weeknight cooking routine.

Moroccan-Style Quinoa with Chickpeas and Kale

SERVES 2

Be sure to rinse the quinoa to remove its bitter coating (known as saponin). Don't dry the greens completely after washing; a little extra water clinging to the leaves will help them wilt when cooking. See page 135 for a recipe to use up the leftover chickpeas.

2 tablespoons olive oil

1 small onion, chopped fine

1 carrot, peeled and cut into ¼-inch pieces

2 garlic cloves, minced

¼ teaspoon ground coriander

⅛ teaspoon red pepper flakes

½ cup quinoa, rinsed

1½ cups vegetable broth

¾ cup canned chickpeas, rinsed

2 tablespoons golden raisins

Salt and pepper

6 ounces kale, stemmed and chopped into 1-inch pieces

2 tablespoons pine nuts, toasted

¼ teaspoon lemon zest plus 1 teaspoon juice

2 tablespoons crumbled feta cheese

1. Heat 1 tablespoon oil in medium saucepan over medium heat until shimmering. Add onion and carrot and cook until onion is softened, about 5 minutes. Stir in garlic, coriander, and pepper flakes and cook until fragrant, about 30 seconds. Add quinoa and cook, stirring often, until lightly toasted and aromatic, about 3 minutes.

2. Stir in broth, chickpeas, raisins, and ⅛ teaspoon salt. Place kale on top and bring to simmer. Cover, reduce heat to low, and simmer until quinoa is transparent and tender, 18 to 20 minutes. Off heat, gently stir in remaining 1 tablespoon oil, pine nuts, and lemon zest and juice. Sprinkle with feta and season with salt and pepper to taste. Serve.

NOTES FROM THE TEST KITCHEN

ALL ABOUT QUINOA

Quinoa originated in the Andes Mountains of South America, and while it is generally treated as a grain, it is actually the seed of the goosefoot plant. Quinoa has gained in popularity in recent years, in part because of its reputation as a "super-grain." This moniker refers to the fact that quinoa is high in protein, and its protein is complete—that is, quinoa possesses all of the amino acids in the balanced amounts that our bodies require. Beyond its nutritional qualities, we love quinoa for its addictive crunch, nutty taste, and ease of preparation. Note that unless it is labeled as "prewashed," quinoa should always be rinsed before cooking to remove its protective layer (called saponin), which is unpleasantly bitter.

RISOTTO PRIMAVERA

RISOTTO PRIMAVERA

✔ **WHY THIS RECIPE WORKS:** Most risotto recipes require constant stirring from start to finish, even when cooking for two. We wanted an easier way. To streamline the process, we cooked the risotto undisturbed for the first 12 minutes; we found that just six minutes of stirring at the end was enough to release the necessary starch to give us remarkably creamy risotto. For a risotto with the flavors of spring, we added mushrooms, asparagus, and peas and brightened the dish with lemon juice and fresh basil.

RISOTTO IS A CLASSIC ITALIAN RICE DISH THAT IS typically made with a starchy short-grain Italian rice called Arborio. After 30 minutes of constant stirring, the rice turns creamy and rich. Most risotto recipes feed a crowd, but with just two to feed, we weren't willing to spend all that time glued to the stove. However, in the past the test kitchen has developed a risotto recipe that cuts way back on the constant stirring. Could we adapt that technique to make just enough risotto for two?

Before working on the cooking method, we selected our ingredients and scaled them down for two. To avoid having leftover ingredients, we wanted to use a 14-ounce can of vegetable broth for the liquid. We just had to determine the right amount of rice for that much liquid. After testing several different proportions, we found the perfect amounts: ½ cup of rice, plus the broth and a little water, gave us 2½ cups of risotto—just right for two.

Next, we had to tackle the real work: adapting our almost-no-stir technique to our two-person portion. In traditional risotto recipes, the constant stirring causes the rice to release starch granules, which then absorb broth, expand, and thicken the dish to its hallmark creaminess. In the test kitchen's original almost-hands-free risotto, most of the liquid is added to the rice at the beginning of cooking, then the rice is allowed to cook, stirred just twice, until it absorbs the liquid. Then the rest of the liquid is added and the risotto is constantly stirred for just a few minutes.

Working with a total of 2¼ cups of liquid to our ½ cup of rice, we tested adding various amounts of liquid at the beginning. We tried ¾ cup of liquid, then 1 cup, and then 1½ cups. The more we added up front, the less stirring we had to do at the end, and there wasn't a marked difference in texture. So we settled on introducing 1½ cups at the beginning and cooking the rice until the liquid was absorbed, which took about 12 minutes, stirred just once halfway through. Then we added the remaining ¾ cup of liquid in two stages, stirring constantly for 3 minutes after each, for a total of just 6 minutes of stirring. This was enough time for the rice to release its starches, giving our risotto the classic creamy consistency we were aiming for with much less hands-on work.

Now we just needed to bump up the flavor. We knew we wanted the classic risotto flavors of sautéed onion, Parmesan cheese, and a bit of butter. We also needed an acidic component to brighten things. We tested wine, vinegar, and lemon juice and ultimately chose lemon juice for its clean, bright flavor. When we added the lemon at the beginning of cooking, its acidity faded, so we stirred it in at the end along with the butter.

Next, the risotto needed some vegetables to make it a meal. We opted for spring vegetables inspired by pasta primavera: mushrooms, asparagus, and peas. Timing the addition of each so they'd all be tender when the rice was done took some more testing. First, we sautéed the mushrooms to concentrate their flavor, then we set them aside to add back in at the end so they wouldn't turn soggy in the risotto. Steaming asparagus spears usually takes about 6 minutes, but we found that since we were cooking them right in the risotto, they took a couple of extra minutes to cook. We added them 8 minutes before the end of cooking, which conveniently coincided with the one quick stir we were giving the risotto during the hands-off phase. Peas went in at the end, just before the sautéed mushrooms, to warm through. Then we just stirred in the lemon juice, butter, and Parmesan along with a handful of fresh basil. Thanks to its bright flavors and inventive technique, our Risotto Primavera tasted like spring and was a breeze to make.

Risotto Primavera

SERVES 2

White button, shiitake, or portobello (caps only) mushrooms can be substituted for the cremini in this recipe. High-quality Parmesan makes a big difference here.

1¾   cups vegetable broth
½   cup water
4   teaspoons olive oil
3   ounces cremini mushrooms, trimmed and sliced thin
    Salt and pepper
1   small onion, chopped fine
½   cup Arborio rice
3   ounces asparagus, trimmed and cut into ½-inch pieces
¼   cup frozen peas
¼   cup grated Parmesan cheese, plus extra for serving
2   tablespoons chopped fresh basil
1   tablespoon unsalted butter
2   teaspoons lemon juice

1. Bring broth and water to simmer in small saucepan over medium heat. Remove from heat, cover, and keep warm.

2. Heat 2 teaspoons oil in medium saucepan over medium heat until shimmering. Add mushrooms and ¼ teaspoon salt and cook, covered, until just starting to brown, about 4 minutes. Transfer mushrooms to bowl and set aside. Return now-empty pot to medium heat, add remaining 2 teaspoons oil, and heat until shimmering. Add onion and ¼ teaspoon salt and cook until just beginning to soften, about 2 minutes. Add rice and cook, stirring constantly, until grains are translucent around edges, about 1 minute.

3. Stir in 1½ cups broth, cover, reduce heat to medium-low, and simmer until almost all liquid is absorbed, about 12 minutes. Stir in asparagus, cover, and cook 2 minutes longer. Add ½ cup broth and cook, stirring constantly, until broth is absorbed, about 3 minutes. Add remaining ¼ cup broth and peas and cook, stirring constantly, until rice is creamy and al dente, 3 minutes longer.

4. Off heat, stir in cooked mushrooms, cover, and let sit for 2 minutes. Stir in Parmesan, basil, butter, and lemon juice. Season with salt and pepper to taste. Serve, passing extra Parmesan separately.

NOTES FROM THE TEST KITCHEN

VEGETABLE BROTH

There are a slew of vegetable broth options available today, but how do they all taste? We sampled 10 broths, both plain and cooked into soups and risotto. Flavors ranged from bland to overpowering; some broths were astonishingly salty or sweet, others oddly sour, and many tasted nothing like vegetables. What we learned is that broths listing vegetable content (whether from fresh whole vegetables or extracts) first on the ingredient list fared best. Also important were generous amounts of flavor-enhancing additives (such as MSG) and salt. **Swanson Vegetarian Vegetable Broth** was the overall winner; tasters praised its "good balance of vegetable flavors."

OUR FAVORITE ARBORIO RICE

The stubby, milky grains of Arborio rice, once grown exclusively in Italy, are valued for their high starch content and the creaminess they bring to risotto. But does the best Arborio have to come from Italy? To find out, we cooked up batches of Parmesan risotto with two domestically grown brands of Arborio rice and four Italian imports. To our surprise, the winning rice, **RiceSelect Arborio Rice**, hailed not from Italy, but from the Lonestar State. Its "creamy, smooth" grains won over tasters with their "good bite." There really isn't a substitute for Arborio rice that will deliver the same results, but our tasters found that batches of risotto made with medium- and short-grain rice were acceptably creamy—however, they lacked the signature firmness of the Arborio grains.

THAI VEGETABLE GREEN CURRY

✔ **WHY THIS RECIPE WORKS:** For a full-flavored curry that we could pull together in a snap, we relied on a few spoonfuls of flavorful store-bought green curry paste. We sautéed it to bring out its rich flavors, then balanced the flavors with fresh lime juice and brown sugar and enriched the sauce with coconut milk. Cauliflower, zucchini, red bell pepper, and snap peas made our curry hearty, flavorful, and colorful. Rather than serving our curry over plain white rice, we formed precooked rice into patties and cooked them in a skillet until the outsides were browned and crisp. Our tasty rice cakes provided a nice textural contrast to the rich, saucy curry and made this weeknight meal something really special.

MAKING A DEEPLY FLAVORED AND SATISFYING curry typically involves a laundry list of ingredients (many of them exotic) as well as loads of steps. Making a curry that is flavorful, quick, and vegetarian is even more of a challenge. But the appeal of a hearty, aromatic stew with long, slow-simmered flavor on a weeknight was undeniable; we were determined to find a way to make a great vegetarian curry for two.

Thai curries blend a variety of tastes, textures, temperatures, and colors to work their magic. They almost always contain coconut milk, which not only blends with and carries the flavors but also forms the base of the sauce. The focus is on the aromatics, which are added in the form of a paste usually consisting of garlic, ginger, shallots, lemon grass, kaffir lime leaves, shrimp paste, and chiles. These curry pastes can be quite involved; fortunately, the curries themselves come together rather quickly and need to simmer for only a short amount of time.

Since our goal was a weeknight meal, we would have to skip the long preparation of making curry paste from scratch. Instead, we would start with a store-bought paste and balance the flavors with additional ingredients as needed. Thai chile pastes are available in green curry or red curry; green curry paste is made with fresh green chiles, while red curry paste is made with dried red chiles. We opted for green curry paste, thinking that its fresher, brighter flavor would be better

suited to a vegetarian dish. We started by sautéing the curry paste in hot oil to bloom and intensify its flavor, then whisked in the coconut milk. The thick gravy was delightfully unctuous (the word *curry* comes from the Tamil word *kari*, which means "sauce" or "gravy"), but the richness of the coconut milk muted the flavors of the jarred curry paste. The spicy flavors of garlic, ginger, and chiles came through, but the more delicate flavor of kaffir lime was lacking.

Since exotic kaffir lime would be difficult to find, we tried to mimic the flavor with fresh lime juice, adding it at the end of cooking to keep the flavor bright. Tasters were almost satisfied, but we were still missing a little sweetness. Many Thai recipes use palm sugar to balance the flavors. Since its rich, caramel-like sweetness is similar to that of brown sugar, we added a little to the curry. Finally, the flavors came into balance.

Next, we focused on the vegetables. We wanted this vegetarian dish to make no apologies; it needed to be rich and hearty. Our goal was to pack as many different textures and colors into the dish as possible. For a hearty vegetable to anchor the dish, we chose cauliflower, a substantial, almost meaty vegetable that would maintain its texture in the thick curry. Since it required the longest cooking time, we added the cauliflower to the skillet with the curry paste, giving it an extra hit of flavor with a sear in the hot oil before adding the coconut milk. For the rest of the vegetables, we settled on a trio of zucchini, red bell pepper, and snap peas, added near the end of cooking to preserve their more delicate textures. They added heft, sweetness, and crunch, respectively, as well as giving the curry a burst of color.

Our curry was really good, but now we needed something to soak up all that flavor. Fragrant jasmine or basmati rice seemed a perfect fit for the flavors of the dish, but we were loath to simply heap our delicious curry on a pile of rice. Just because it was a weeknight meal didn't mean it needed to be boring, after all. We also wanted to add a little more texture to the dish; with all that creaminess, it needed a little crunch. What if we fashioned cooked jasmine rice into cakes, then sautéed them to develop a browned, crispy crust?

We warmed the rice briefly in the microwave, then mixed in a beaten egg and some flour and formed the rice into patties. We added the patties to a hot skillet and sautéed them until they were browned. But when we went to flip the cakes, they broke into craggy pieces.

Clearly we needed a better binder. Adding another egg made them too wet, and adding flour was equally unsuccessful. Then we thought of our recipe for black bean burgers, where we pulse a portion of the beans to serve as a gluey binder to hold the burgers together. Would that work with our rice cakes? We pulsed half of the warm rice in the food processor until it was coarsely ground, then added it to the unprocessed rice, egg, and flour.

The starchy, sticky rice bits were just what the rice cakes needed. The next batch came out of the skillet browned and crisp on the outside, soft and tender on the inside. Served with a heaping ladle of our Thai vegetable green curry, they made an easy, elegant entrée for any night of the week.

NOTES FROM THE TEST KITCHEN

THAI GREEN CURRY PASTE

Curry paste, which can be either green or red depending on the type of chile peppers used, is key for adding deep flavor to Thai curries. It's a lot of work to make from scratch since it uses a number of hard-to-find ingredients such as lemon grass, kaffir lime leaves, and shrimp paste. We've found that store-bought curry paste does a fine job and saves significant shopping and prep time. It is usually sold in small jars next to the other Thai ingredients at the supermarket. Be aware that these pastes can vary in spiciness depending on the brand, so use more or less as desired.

THE BEST COCONUT MILK

Coconut milk is made by steeping shredded coconut meat in an equal amount of either warm milk or water. The meat is pressed or mashed to release as much liquid as possible, the mixture is strained, and the result is coconut milk. We tasted seven nationally available brands (five regular and two light) in coconut pudding, coconut rice, a Thai-style chicken soup, and green chicken curry. In the soup and curry, tasters preferred **Chaokoh** because of its particularly low sugar content. Of the two light brands tasted, we preferred the richer flavor of A Taste of Thai, though neither was nearly as creamy as the full-fat options. Ka-Me brand coconut milk is best suited for sweet recipes.

Thai Vegetable Green Curry with Jasmine Rice Cakes

SERVES 2

Though we like the flavor of jasmine rice here, regular long-grain rice can be substituted. We found that a package of Uncle Ben's Jasmine Ready Rice worked well in this recipe. Do not substitute light coconut milk here. See page 12 for a recipe to use up the leftover coconut milk.

- 2 cups cooked and cooled jasmine rice
- 1 large egg
- 2 tablespoons all-purpose flour
  Salt and pepper
- 2 tablespoons vegetable oil
- 6 ounces cauliflower florets, cut into 1-inch pieces
- 1½ tablespoons Thai green curry paste
- ¾ cup coconut milk
- 1 tablespoon fish sauce
- 1½ teaspoons brown sugar
- 1 zucchini, quartered lengthwise and cut into ¾-inch pieces
- 1 small red bell pepper, stemmed, seeded, and cut into 2-inch-long matchsticks
- 4 ounces snap peas, strings removed
- 1 tablespoon lime juice
- 1 tablespoon chopped fresh cilantro

1. Microwave rice in covered bowl until hot, about 90 seconds. Pulse half of rice in food processor until coarsely ground, about 10 pulses; return to bowl with unprocessed rice. Stir in egg, flour, ¼ teaspoon salt, and ½ teaspoon pepper. Using hands, form rice mixture into 2 patties.

2. Heat 1 tablespoon oil in 10-inch nonstick skillet over medium-high heat until shimmering. Add rice patties; cook until crisp and browned on both sides, about 3 minutes per side. Transfer rice cakes to plate; tent loosely with aluminum foil. Wipe skillet clean with paper towels.

3. Heat remaining 1 tablespoon oil in now-empty skillet over medium-high heat until shimmering. Add cauliflower and curry paste; cook until cauliflower begins to soften, about 5 minutes. Stir in coconut milk, fish sauce, and sugar and bring to simmer. Add zucchini, bell pepper, and snap peas. Cover and cook, stirring occasionally, until vegetables are just tender, about 5 minutes. Uncover and cook until sauce is slightly thickened, about 2 minutes. Off heat, stir in lime juice and season with salt and pepper to taste. Sprinkle with cilantro and serve over rice cakes.

GLAZED CARIBBEAN TOFU

✔ WHY THIS RECIPE WORKS: For a Caribbean-inspired tofu dish, we seared tofu and made a quick but flavor-packed glaze with pineapple preserves brightened with lime juice and seasoned with red pepper flakes. While the tofu drained, we made an easy rice dish to serve on the side. We added onion, jalapeño, and pigeon peas to the rice for flavor and textural contrast. Cooking the rice in coconut milk made it rich and creamy, a perfect counterpart to the sweet and spicy tofu.

WHETHER STIR-FRIED, STEAMED, OR GLAZED, TOFU is a common ingredient in Asian cuisines. But this versatile protein easily lends itself to any flavor profile, and since it's generally sold in small amounts, it's a great option when cooking for two. We wanted to expand our tofu repertoire, so we hit the books in search of other cuisines' takes on tofu.

Our research led us to the bold, fruity flavors of the Caribbean. In Caribbean cooking, tofu is often seared until well browned and finished with a tasty glaze. This seemed like a great technique for a quick weeknight dinner with a flavorful payoff. We thought that the sweetness of pineapple would be the perfect Caribbean complement for the tofu. But prepping fresh pineapple was a hassle (not to mention wasteful when we wanted just enough for two), and simply throwing chunks in the skillet didn't give us the cohesive sauce we were after. We wanted a thick, sweet pineapple glaze that would coat the tofu with bright, tropical flavor. We decided to scrap the fresh pineapple in favor of pineapple preserves. The thick, sweet preserves were packed with pineapple flavor. A few seconds in the microwave loosened it, then we brightened the flavor and balanced some of the sweetness by adding lime juice and red pepper flakes.

Tasters loved the mix of spicy and sweet flavors, so we decided to bump up the heat even more. Curry powder, a blend of several spices including coriander, cumin, and turmeric, added both heat and complexity. After draining the tofu to remove excess liquid, we sprinkled the pieces with the curry powder before searing. With this addition, our glazed tofu was well on its way to becoming a fan favorite with the tasters. Now all we needed to do was come up with just the right dish to serve it over.

To go along with our Caribbean theme we knew we wanted a rice dish, but plain white rice just wouldn't do our flavor-packed tofu justice. To flavor the rice itself, we sautéed diced onion and jalapeño in a little oil before adding the rice and water. The jalapeño gave a little heat to the rice but didn't knock us over with too much burn. To add some more textural contrast, we decided to add canned pigeon peas to the rice. Pigeon peas are small, creamy, and slightly sweet, and they livened up the rice perfectly.

Our side dish was starting to come together, but everyone agreed it was still missing something. To make it worthy of our glazed tofu, we decided to replace some of the rice cooking water with coconut milk. The coconut milk imparted a rich creaminess and distinctly tropical flavor to the rice that paired perfectly with the sweet glazed tofu. We started our testing with full-fat coconut milk but found that no matter how little we added to the rice, the rice came out too heavy and greasy. Light coconut milk worked much better, imparting the same richness and flavor while keeping our rice fluffy and light. The rice needed about 20 minutes to cook, so we started it while our tofu was draining, then seared the tofu and made the glaze while the rice steamed so that everything

---

USE IT UP: CHICKPEAS AND PIGEON PEAS

Crispy Spiced Chickpeas or Pigeon Peas
MAKES ¾ CUP

Make sure to dry the chickpeas or pigeon peas thoroughly with paper towels before placing them in the oil.

- ⅛ teaspoon smoked paprika
- ⅛ teaspoon sugar
- ⅛ teaspoon salt
  Pinch pepper
- ⅓ cup olive oil or vegetable oil
- ¾ cup canned chickpeas or pigeon peas, rinsed and patted dry

Combine paprika, sugar, salt, and pepper in medium bowl. Heat oil in 8-inch skillet over medium-high heat until shimmering. Add chickpeas and cook, stirring occasionally, until deep golden brown and crisp, 6 to 8 minutes. Using slotted spoon, transfer chickpeas to bowl with spices and toss to coat. Serve.

GLAZED CARIBBEAN TOFU WITH RICE AND PIGEON PEAS

ended up being done at the same time. Our quick and easy Caribbean take on tofu was so good, we almost felt like we were on vacation when we took our first bite.

Glazed Caribbean Tofu with Rice and Pigeon Peas

SERVES 2

Canned pigeon peas can be found in most supermarkets; however, black-eyed peas or kidney beans can be substituted if necessary. Light coconut milk works best here; do not substitute regular full-fat coconut milk, or your rice will turn out heavy and greasy. To make this dish spicier, add the reserved chile seeds in step 2. See page 135 for a recipe to use up the leftover pigeon peas. See page 12 for a recipe to use up the leftover coconut milk.

14	ounces firm tofu
	Salt and pepper
1½	teaspoons curry powder
4	teaspoons vegetable oil
1	small onion, diced
1	jalapeño chile, stemmed, seeds reserved, and minced
½	cup long-grain white rice
¾	cup canned pigeon peas, rinsed
¾	cup light coconut milk
⅓	cup plus 1½ tablespoons water
¼	cup pineapple preserves
1	tablespoon lime juice
⅛	teaspoon red pepper flakes

1. Cut tofu in half lengthwise, then cut each half crosswise into 6 slices. Spread tofu out on paper towel–lined baking sheet and let drain for 15 minutes. Gently pat tofu dry with paper towels. Season with salt and pepper and sprinkle with curry powder.

2. Meanwhile, heat 1 teaspoon oil in medium saucepan over medium-high heat until shimmering. Add onion and jalapeño and cook until softened, about 5 minutes. Stir in rice and cook until opaque, about 1 minute. Stir in peas, coconut milk, ⅓ cup water, and ¼ teaspoon salt and bring to boil. Cover, reduce heat to low, and cook until rice is tender, 20 to 25 minutes. Season with salt and pepper to taste.

3. While rice cooks, place preserves in medium bowl and microwave until bubbling, about 30 seconds. Whisk in remaining 1½ tablespoons water, lime juice, and pepper flakes.

4. Heat remaining 1 tablespoon oil in 12-inch nonstick skillet over medium-high heat until just smoking. Add tofu and cook until golden and crisp on all sides, about 5 minutes, turning as needed. Add pineapple mixture and simmer, turning tofu to coat, until glaze thickens, about 1 minute. Serve over rice.

SPICY ASIAN LETTUCE WRAPS

✓ WHY THIS RECIPE WORKS: Asian lettuce wraps are traditionally filled with seasoned ground meat. Our fast, flavor-packed vegetarian version swaps the meat for soy crumbles, which are made from seasoned, textured soy and have a satisfying texture similar to that of ground meat. We added some crisp, sweet red bell pepper and cooked rice to bulk up the filling. For a flavorful sauce, we started with chili-garlic sauce and punched it up with soy sauce, fresh ginger, and a little brown sugar. Piled into a crisp lettuce leaf, our meaty vegetarian filling kept tasters coming back for more.

ASIAN LETTUCE WRAPS ARE A GREAT IDEA FOR AN easy weeknight supper with an exotic flair. Typically it's a simple dish made with a tasty blend of ground meat, flavorful sauce, and chopped vegetables, so we thought we would have no problem adapting this delicious Cantonese specialty to a vegetarian version. Unfortunately, when we tried the few recipes we found, the bland finished products left us hungry. Developing a substantial vegetarian lettuce wrap that packed protein as well as flavor would be our challenge.

The standard meat-based recipes we found shared more or less the same technique: stir-fry the meat over high heat, add chopped vegetables, pour in the sauce, and spoon the mixture into Bibb lettuce leaves. First we would need to find the right substitute for the meat. We wanted something close to ground meat in texture, so we didn't bother trying soft tofu, which we knew would be too soft. Instead we started with extra-firm tofu, which we love in stir-fries. But even when we painstakingly drained and diced the extra-firm tofu before cooking, tasters were still disappointed with the too-soft and mushy texture. Tofu was definitely out.

Next, we tried tempeh, another soy product with a much firmer texture, but we found that its distinctive flavor was too strong and overwhelming in the finished dish. We wanted a delicate balance of flavors among the filling, sauce, and Bibb lettuce. We tried several types of mushrooms, but although tasters liked their flavor, none of them felt substantial enough to stand in for the meat.

Then a test cook suggested we try soy crumbles, a relative newcomer to the vegetarian aisle. Made of seasoned, textured soy protein, they had the look and texture of ground meat and a mild meaty, earthy flavor. We simply browned the soy crumbles in the skillet before tossing them in the sauce, then piled them in lettuce leaves to have a taste. We were surprised by their substantial, meaty flavor and texture; we definitely had a winner. To add freshness, sweetness, and a little crunch to the filling, we added a chopped red bell pepper. Lettuce cups are traditionally served with rice on the side, but we thought we could further bulk up our filling by adding the rice directly to the skillet with the crumbles and red pepper. We finally had a hearty filling that would satisfy the hungriest dinner guest.

USE IT UP: SOY CRUMBLES

Hearty Vegetarian Queso Dip
MAKES ABOUT 2 CUPS

Serve with tortilla chips.

- 6 ounces soy crumbles
- 1 tomato, seeded and chopped
- 1 teaspoon cornstarch
- ½ cup milk
- 4 ounces pepper Jack cheese, shredded (1 cup)
- 2 scallions, sliced thin

1. Combine soy crumbles and tomato in small saucepan and cook over medium heat until soy crumbles are heated through, about 2 minutes. In small bowl, stir cornstarch into 1 tablespoon milk and set aside.

2. Add remaining 7 tablespoons milk to saucepan and bring to simmer. Stir in cornstarch mixture and simmer until thickened, 2 to 3 minutes. Reduce heat to low, add pepper Jack and scallions, and cook, stirring constantly, until cheese melts and thickens, about 2 minutes. Serve warm.

But our sauce was still pretty wan. We definitely needed to give it more punch. We started with spicy, flavorful chili-garlic sauce, loosening it with a little vegetable broth. Soy sauce and grated fresh ginger added seasoning and gave it a more complex heat. A pinch of sweet brown sugar balanced the spiciness. This sauce was almost perfect, but it wasn't clinging to the crumbles and rice properly. We wanted just a little more body, so we added cornstarch as a thickener. The cornstarch worked like a charm, thickening the sauce just enough to coat the filling. We piled our flavorful filling into crisp lettuce leaves and topped them off with some scallions. Our vegetarian lettuce wraps were now as bold and complex as they were fresh and filling.

Spicy Asian Soy and Rice Lettuce Wraps
SERVES 2

To make a lettuce cup, put a spoonful of soy and rice mixture in the middle of a lettuce leaf, fold the leaf edges up to form a taco shape, and eat with your hands. You can use leftover or precooked rice here; our favorite precooked brand is Minute Ready to Serve White Rice.

- ¼ cup vegetable broth
- 1½ teaspoons Asian chili-garlic sauce
- 1½ teaspoons soy sauce
- 1½ teaspoons brown sugar
- ¼ teaspoon cornstarch
- 1 tablespoon vegetable oil
- 1 small red bell pepper, stemmed, seeded, and cut into ¼-inch pieces
- 6 ounces soy crumbles
- 1 cup cooked rice
- 1 teaspoon grated fresh ginger
- 2 scallions, sliced thin
- 1 tablespoon minced fresh cilantro
- 6 Bibb or Boston lettuce leaves (½ head)

Whisk broth, chili-garlic sauce, soy sauce, sugar, and cornstarch together in bowl. Heat oil in 10-inch nonstick skillet over medium-high heat until shimmering. Add bell pepper and cook, stirring occasionally, until softened, about 3 minutes. Add soy crumbles, rice, and ginger and cook until fragrant, about 30 seconds. Whisk sauce to recombine, then add to skillet and cook until thickened, about 30 seconds. Off heat, stir in scallions and cilantro. Serve in lettuce leaves.

SPICY ASIAN SOY AND RICE LETTUCE WRAPS

GRILLED PESTO CHICKEN WITH CORN ON THE COB

CHAPTER 5

DINNER OFF THE GRILL

GRILLED PESTO CHICKEN WITH CORN ON THE COB

✔ **WHY THIS RECIPE WORKS:** To instill our pesto chicken with pesto flavor throughout, we took a three-pronged approach. We started with a batch of homemade pesto, then thickened a portion with extra Parmesan cheese to make a stuffing for our bone-in, skin-on chicken breasts that would stay put and wouldn't leak out. A cheese-less portion of pesto acted as a marinade, flavoring the exterior of the meat. Finally, cheesy pesto, thinned out to a sauce and served with the chicken, provided one last hit of bright, rich flavor. Grilled corn on the cob, smeared with a little butter, made the perfect partner to our moist, tender chicken.

FRAGRANT BASIL PESTO ISN'T JUST FOR PASTA— it can enhance any number of dishes. One dish that we're big fans of in the test kitchen is grilled pesto chicken. But more often than not, the pesto flavor becomes weak and washed out by the time the chicken makes it to the table. The reason for this is that the heat is tough on basil's delicate flavor compounds. For our recipe, we'd have to find a way to imbue the chicken so deeply with the basil and garlic that the pesto flavor held up no matter how hot it got on the grill.

Initial recipe tests showed that pesto adhered poorly to boneless, skinless chicken breasts; bone-in breasts were more substantial, and the pesto adhered to them better. So, working with store-bought pesto for convenience, we explored ways to give our pair of skin-on, bone-in chicken breasts a powerful pesto punch. We slathered it on the chicken and used it to flavor brines, marinades, and vinaigrettes in which we soaked the meat. We even used it to flavor butter and mayonnaise, which we smeared under the skin and all over the meat. Unfortunately, we were disappointed time and again. Not even the pesto on its own conveyed basil flavor deep into the meat.

If the pesto flavor wasn't working its way in from the outside, we figured we should put some on the inside. We cut deep horizontal slits in the thick sides of the breasts, creating pockets that we stuffed with pesto. We tied the breasts with kitchen twine to prevent the pockets from opening up on the grill and for good measure smeared the exterior of the breasts with pesto. What came off the grill this time gave us a glimmer of hope. Though some of the pesto we'd put in the pockets had leaked out, its flavor was still evident in the meat.

Reasoning that if we thickened the pesto it might stay put in the pockets during grilling, we tried mixing it with both cream cheese and shredded mozzarella. These thicker pestos did indeed leak less than the standard pesto, but it wasn't the dish we wanted. The mild cheeses had diluted the pesto flavor.

Since using a thicker pesto showed promise, we turned our attention to its primary components: basil, Parmesan, pine nuts, and olive oil. Customizing the texture meant altering the ingredient amounts, so we ditched the store-bought stuff and started making our own. Though it meant more work, we didn't mind because homemade pesto tastes stronger and fresher, and even for-two kitchens tend to have most of these ingredients on hand. We found that the basil and Parmesan contributed more to the chicken than the pine nuts did, so we replaced them with extra Parmesan. Not wanting to use this thicker, cheesy mixture to coat the exterior for fear it might burn, we pureed the basil and garlic with some, but not all, of the oil in the food processor and reserved a portion of this cheese-less pesto for marinating. Then we stirred a generous quantity of cheese into the remaining basil mixture, turning it into an extra-stiff, cheesy pesto that worked well as a stuffing, leaking very little on the grill.

This was progress, but the pesto tasted a bit flat, and it turned a dark, unattractive color on the grill. Adding a small amount of acid, such as lemon juice, can help retain the bright color of foods, so we gave it a try. In this case, it gave the flavor a lift, too.

Next we turned to the grilling method. We followed the test kitchen's method for grilling bone-in breasts by building a half-grill fire. In this grill setup, all the coals are placed on one side of the grill, effectively creating a hot zone and a cool zone. We grilled the breasts skin side up using indirect heat on the cool side (over medium-low heat on the gas grill), then flipped them and moved them over the coals to crisp the skin near the end of cooking (we turned the burners up to medium-high on the gas grill).

At last we had grilled chicken that tasted distinctly of pesto, both inside and out. Pleased as we were, we decided to really drive home the point by serving the chicken with even more cheesy Parmesan pesto that hadn't been exposed to the heat of the grill. To do this, we simply made more of our pesto filling and loosened it up with some olive oil, so it was the perfect consistency for drizzling over the chicken. Now this was grilled pesto chicken that lived up to its billing.

With an entrée this flavorful, we wanted to complete the meal with a simple side dish. Summer-fresh sweet corn was the answer. We placed two large ears of corn on the grill while the chicken rested; the corn took on plenty of smoky flavor and char in less than 10 minutes. With a dab of softened butter and a drizzle of our pesto sauce, this easy side was ready for the plate.

Grilled Pesto Chicken with Corn on the Cob

SERVES 2

Note that the pesto base is divided into three separate mixtures for marinating, stuffing, and saucing the grilled chicken. Extra pesto sauce works well drizzled over the grilled corn.

- 2 **cups fresh basil leaves**
- 6 **tablespoons plus 1 teaspoon extra-virgin olive oil**
- 2 **garlic cloves, peeled**
- 2½ **teaspoons lemon juice**
- **Salt and pepper**
- 1 **ounce Parmesan cheese, grated (½ cup)**
- 2 **(12-ounce) bone-in split chicken breasts, trimmed**
- 2 **ears corn, husks and silk removed**
- 2 **tablespoons unsalted butter, softened**

1. Process basil, ¼ cup oil, garlic, lemon juice, and ¼ teaspoon salt in food processor until smooth, about 1 minute, scraping down bowl as needed. Remove 2 tablespoons pesto from processor and reserve for marinating chicken. Add Parmesan to pesto in processor and pulse until incorporated, about 3 pulses. Remove 2 tablespoons Parmesan pesto from processor and reserve for stuffing chicken. Add 2 tablespoons oil to Parmesan pesto in processor and pulse until combined, about 3 pulses; set aside for saucing cooked chicken.

2. Starting on thick side of breast, closest to breastbone, cut horizontal pocket in each breast, stopping ½ inch from edge so halves remain attached. Season chicken, inside and out, with salt and pepper. Place 1 tablespoon Parmesan pesto reserved for stuffing in pocket of each breast. Evenly space 2 pieces of kitchen

twine beneath each breast and tie to secure breast, trimming any excess twine. Place stuffed breasts in bowl and add pesto reserved for marinating. Rub pesto all over chicken, cover, and refrigerate for 1 hour.

3A. FOR A CHARCOAL GRILL: Open bottom vent completely. Light large chimney starter filled with charcoal briquettes (6 quarts). When top coals are partially covered with ash, pour evenly over half of grill. Set cooking grate in place, cover, and open lid vent completely. Heat grill until hot, about 5 minutes.

3B. FOR A GAS GRILL: Turn all burners to high, cover, and heat grill until hot, about 15 minutes. Turn all burners to medium-low. (Adjust burners as needed to maintain grill temperature of 350 degrees.)

4. Clean and oil cooking grate. Place chicken, skin side up, on grill (over cool side if using charcoal).

NOTES FROM THE TEST KITCHEN

MAKING A POCKET FOR PESTO CHICKEN

1. Starting on thick side closest to breastbone, cut horizontal pocket in each breast, stopping ½ inch from edge.

2. Stuff each breast with Parmesan-pesto mixture, then tie them with two pieces of kitchen twine at even intervals.

KEEPING CORN SWEET

Generally, it's best to eat corn on the cob the same day you buy it, as its sugars start converting to starches as soon as it is harvested, causing the corn to lose sweetness. But if you buy corn and don't plan to cook it the same day, it should be stored in the refrigerator until you're ready to use it. We recommend storing corn unshucked and wrapped in a wet paper bag to slow down the conversion from sugar to starch, then placing the wet paper bag in a plastic bag (any shopping bag will do). Because corn on the cob is sensitive to chill injury, it should be placed in the front of the fridge, where the temperatures tend to be higher.

Cover and cook until chicken registers 155 degrees, 25 to 35 minutes.

5. Flip chicken skin side down. Slide chicken to hot part of grill if using charcoal, or turn all burners to medium-high if using gas. Cover and cook until well browned and chicken registers 160 degrees, 5 to 10 minutes. Transfer chicken to cutting board, tent loosely with aluminum foil, and let rest for 5 to 10 minutes.

6. While chicken rests, brush corn with remaining 1 teaspoon oil and season with salt and pepper. Place corn on grill (over hot part if using charcoal) and cook until lightly charred on all sides, 6 to 10 minutes, turning as needed. Remove from grill and brush with butter.

7. Remove twine from chicken and carve meat from bone. Serve with corn, passing Parmesan pesto sauce separately.

GRILLED WINE-MARINATED CHICKEN WITH ASPARAGUS

WHY THIS RECIPE WORKS: For a grilled take on the classic pairing of wine and chicken, we started with two leg quarters, which gave us two perfect portions and lots of rich, moist meat. Combining dry white wine with garlic, herbs, and a little sugar in the blender produced a flavorful marinade, and poking the chicken with a skewer helped the flavors of the marinade penetrate the skin, so the meat was deeply flavored. Tender spears of asparagus proved an elegant match to our grilled chicken.

WINE IS A NATURAL FIT WITH CHICKEN. THE BOLD acidity and fruity, complex flavors of both red and white wines pair beautifully with the mild-tasting meat—think of the classic French braise coq au vin or a wine-based pan sauce spooned over roasted chicken. But while those are great cold-weather dishes, we wanted to develop a recipe for grilled chicken with a wine and herb flavor profile—one that we could enjoy in warmer weather. And since we had the grill fired up, we thought we'd add an easy side to make it a hearty meal for two.

The first step was selecting the chicken. Most recipes use a 4-pound bird, which is a nonstarter if you're cooking for two. Since breast meat is more likely to dry out on the grill, we opted for dark meat. Two chicken leg quarters gave us a thigh and drumstick for each person—perfect for a weeknight dinner with no leftovers.

Next, it was on to the wine. Disappointed with the wine flavor (or lack thereof) in many of the recipes we tried, we searched for a way to make the wine, and the herbs that would go with it, really shine. It took plenty of testing to choose the right wine. We quickly eliminated red wine because it gave the chicken an unattractive purple tint. Trying marinades with eight common white wine varieties revealed that dry wines, such as Sauvignon Blanc (as opposed to sweeter varieties such as Riesling or Gewürztraminer), instilled our chicken with more flavor. Opening bottle after bottle showed that neither the variety of dry white wine nor the price point—we tried wines from less than $10 to $35 per bottle—mattered much. In terms of quantity, many recipes we saw called for as little as ¼ cup, but we found that it took 1 cup of wine in the marinade to flavor our chicken pieces.

Moving on to the herbs, we tried all the major players and found that fresh parsley and thyme complemented the wine best (stronger herbs like rosemary and oregano overpowered it). A healthy dose of salt was essential to season the meat deeply; the salt facilitates an exchange between the meat's natural moisture and the marinade, allowing the flavorful liquid to penetrate more deeply. Garlic and lemon accented the marinade, and a little brown sugar balanced the wine and lemon.

Rather than simply stirring our marinade ingredients together, we whizzed them all together in the blender. In the machine, the herbs broke down for optimal flavor and distribution. In the test kitchen, we've found that puncturing the surface of chicken or meat can help marinades penetrate better, so we reached for a skewer and started poking the leg quarters. This noticeably bumped up the wine flavor with no appreciable loss of juices in the meat. As for marinating time, we discovered that the chicken had the best flavor if we marinated it for at least two hours.

When it came to grilling, we needed to minimize flare-ups from the rendering fat and marinade dripping on the coals. A half-grill fire was the answer; in this type of grill setup, a hot zone and a cool zone are created by placing all the coals on one side of the grill. We started the chicken over indirect heat (the cool side) with the skin side down so the fat would render and the skin would slowly crisp. Then we flipped the chicken and moved it to the hot side for the final few minutes of cooking to fully crisp the skin on the underside.

The chicken was well seasoned and evenly cooked and had impressive wine and herb flavor, but we still had one more card to play: the mop. In the barbecue world, a mop is a thin basting sauce used to add complexity and freshness to the meat being grilled. We had tried and rejected basting during cooking—it made our crisp skin soggy—but this time we set aside a bit of the marinade (minus the salt) before adding the chicken and brushed it on near the end of grilling, once the skin had already become crisp. It worked just as we'd hoped, adding a bright burst of flavor.

Now that we had flavorful, perfectly cooked chicken, we wanted a grilled vegetable to complement it and thought the fresh, grassy flavor of asparagus would be ideal. Since the chicken needed to rest after grilling, we had plenty of time to cook enough spears for two on the hot side of the grill. The duo of wine-and-herb-infused chicken and bright, crisp-tender asparagus made for one winning meal for two.

Grilled Wine-and-Herb-Marinated Chicken with Asparagus

SERVES 2

Use a dry white wine, such as Sauvignon Blanc, for this recipe.

- 1 cup dry white wine
- 2½ tablespoons extra-virgin olive oil
- 1½ tablespoons lemon juice
- 1 tablespoon chopped fresh parsley
- 1 tablespoon chopped fresh thyme
- 1 tablespoon packed light brown sugar
- 2 garlic cloves, minced
- ½ teaspoon pepper
- 2 teaspoons salt
- 2 (12-ounce) chicken leg quarters, trimmed
- 1 pound asparagus, trimmed

1. Process wine, 1½ tablespoons oil, lemon juice, parsley, thyme, sugar, garlic, and pepper in blender until emulsified, about 40 seconds. Reserve 2 tablespoons marinade. Add salt to remaining mixture in blender and process to dissolve, about 20 seconds.

2. Poke holes all over chicken with skewer. Place chicken in large zipper-lock bag, pour in salted marinade, seal bag, and turn to coat. Set bag in baking dish, skin side down, and refrigerate for 2 to 3 hours.

3A. FOR A CHARCOAL GRILL: Open bottom vent completely. Light large chimney starter filled with charcoal briquettes (6 quarts). When top coals are partially covered with ash, pour evenly over half of grill. Set cooking grate in place, cover, and open lid vent completely. Heat grill until hot, about 5 minutes.

3B. FOR A GAS GRILL: Turn all burners to high, cover, and heat grill until hot, about 15 minutes. Turn secondary burner(s) to low and primary burner to medium. (Adjust primary burner as needed to maintain grill temperature between 350 and 375 degrees.)

NOTES FROM THE TEST KITCHEN

TRIMMING ASPARAGUS

1. Remove one stalk of asparagus from bunch and bend it at thicker end until it snaps.

2. With broken asparagus as guide, trim tough ends from remaining asparagus bunch using chef's knife.

THE BEST GRILL TONGS

For the most part, we pass on the new models of grill tongs each grilling season and rely on a traditional and effective pair. But to make sure that we weren't missing anything, we picked up a few of the latest on the market. Unfortunately, most looked and performed like medieval torture devices, with sharp, serrated edges that nicked the surface of steaks and shredded fish into flakes. Our overall winner was a plain pair of **OXO Good Grips 16-Inch Locking Tongs**, $14.95. Not only do they grip, turn, and move food around the grill easily, but they are also long enough to keep hands a safe distance from the grill.

4. Remove chicken from marinade and pat dry with paper towels; discard used marinade. Clean and oil cooking grate. Place chicken, skin side down, over cooler part of grill (over secondary burner(s) if using gas), with legs closest to hotter side of grill. Cover and cook until chicken is well browned and thigh meat registers 150 degrees, 20 to 30 minutes. Brush chicken with 1 tablespoon reserved marinade. Flip chicken, slide to hot side of grill (over primary burner if using gas), and brush with remaining 1 tablespoon reserved marinade. Cook, covered, until thighs register 175 degrees, 10 to 15 minutes longer.

5. Transfer chicken to platter, tent loosely with aluminum foil, and let rest for 5 to 10 minutes.

6. While chicken rests, toss asparagus with remaining 1 tablespoon oil in large bowl. Place asparagus on hot side of grill (over primary burner if using gas) and cook until tender and spotty brown, 3 to 6 minutes, turning as needed. Transfer asparagus to platter with chicken. Serve.

BARBECUED PULLED CHICKEN WITH WARM CABBAGE SLAW

✔ WHY THIS RECIPE WORKS: Working with chicken parts, rather than a whole chicken, brought this barbecue classic into for-two territory. Using a leg quarter and split breast gave us bites of both tender white meat and rich dark meat, and brining kept the breast meat moist and juicy. Poking holes in the chicken skin allowed the meat to pick up serious smoke flavor. A sweet, tangy, and smoky barbecue sauce added even more flavor, and a warm cabbage slaw made the perfect partner to our pulled chicken sandwiches.

IT TAKES HOURS FOR DECENT SMOKE FLAVOR TO penetrate meat on the grill (think racks of ribs and pork butts), which might explain why most pulled chicken sandwiches we've tried are filled with disappointingly dry meat. Most recipes, no matter if they call for parts, whole birds, or something in between, share the common thread of overcooking the meat; some recipes have you leave the chicken on the grill for four hours—as long as it takes to tenderize ribs—which of course dries out the meat. We wanted a recipe with tender, moist (not overcooked) chicken with deep smoke flavor, and it couldn't feed a crowd—it had to make just enough for two. To complete our backyard barbecue, we looked to serve our pulled chicken with a tangy slaw.

Initial tests revealed that tasters had a preference for a combination of white and dark meat. Since we were cooking for two, a whole bird was a no-go. That meant working with a combination of parts, which would need different cooking times. We wanted enough meat for two substantial sandwiches, so we settled on a split chicken breast and a leg quarter and fired up the grill.

After almost an hour of indirect smoking, the dark meat was perfect but the white meat was getting chalky. How could we even out the cooking time? We tried putting the more resilient leg quarter closer to the fire and moving the breast farther away. Giving the more delicate white meat a little distance from the heat slowed down its cooking, which helped. What helped even more was brining the chicken to season it and protect it from overcooking. A 30-minute soak in salt water was all it took for white meat just as moist and tender as the dark. The white meat easily pulled into strands, but the dark meat, although tender, didn't have the right texture to do so. No problem: We chopped it and mixed it in with the pulled white meat.

Our texture problem was solved, but there just wasn't enough smoky flavor in this smoked chicken. Using more wood chips didn't make a difference, since we were discarding the skin after smoking the chicken. The skin was absorbing a lot of the smoke that should have been flavoring the meat, but smoking the breast without the skin didn't work, as the skin was also helping to keep the meat moist. If the skin had to stay, could we make it more permeable? Taking a cue from our Grilled Wine-and-Herb-Marinated Chicken (page 145), we poked the chicken skin all over with a skewer before grilling, hoping the perforated skin would still insulate the meat while allowing more smoke in. It worked. The chicken was much smokier, with no loss of moisture.

Now it was time to address the sauce. We prepared a variety of different barbecue sauce recipes and tried them with the chicken. Our favorite was the molasses-y, smoky, Kansas City–style barbecue sauce, but we made a couple of tweaks to the usual ingredient list while cutting down this ketchup-based condiment for two. For more depth, we added brewed coffee, which we

BARBECUED PULLED CHICKEN WITH WARM CABBAGE SLAW

had seen in some other sauce recipes; tasters found it boosted the smoky flavor of the dish. Also, we bumped up the amount of cider vinegar to make the flavor more pungent. After a half-hour simmer, our barbecue sauce was nicely thickened and ready to be tossed with our pulled chicken before it was piled atop two kaiser rolls.

Finally, we could focus on barbecue's best friend: the slaw. For the main ingredient, we chose napa cabbage; we liked its thin, crisp leaves and delicate, mild flavor, and half of a small head was just the right amount for two servings. Cutting our cabbage half lengthwise through the core kept the leaves together and gave us more surface area for grilling. After pulling the chicken from the grill, we brushed the cabbage pieces with oil and grilled them until the tips of the outer leaves were charred. We then sliced it thinly and tossed it, still warm, with raisins, a carrot, and a sweet-and-sour dressing of vinegar, mustard, and sugar. This bright and tangy slaw made the perfect match for our robustly flavored barbecued chicken.

At last, we had a dinner that offered plenty of smoke and big barbecue flavor—but it served only two.

Barbecued Pulled Chicken with Warm Cabbage Slaw

MAKES ABOUT 2 CUPS; ENOUGH FOR 2 SANDWICHES

Do not remove the core from the cabbage; it will help keep the leaves together on the grill. See page 63 for a recipe to use up the leftover napa cabbage.

CHICKEN

- ½ cup salt
- 1 (12-ounce) bone-in split chicken breast, trimmed
- 1 (12-ounce) chicken leg quarter, trimmed
  Pepper
- 2 cups wood chips, soaked in water for 15 minutes and drained
- 2 kaiser rolls

SAUCE

- 1 teaspoon vegetable oil
- 1 small onion, chopped fine
- 2 cups low-sodium chicken broth
- ⅔ cup cider vinegar
- ½ cup brewed coffee
- ⅓ cup molasses
- ¼ cup tomato paste

- ¼ cup ketchup
- 1 tablespoon brown mustard
- 1½ teaspoons hot sauce
- ¼ teaspoon garlic powder
- ¼ teaspoon liquid smoke

SLAW

- ½ small head napa cabbage, halved lengthwise through core
- 1½ tablespoons vegetable oil
  Pepper
- 1 carrot, peeled and shredded
- 2½ tablespoons cider vinegar
- 2 tablespoons raisins
- 1½ teaspoons sugar
- 1 teaspoon brown mustard

1. FOR THE CHICKEN: Dissolve salt in 2 quarts cold water in large container. Using metal skewer, poke holes all over each piece of chicken. Submerge chicken pieces in brine, cover, and refrigerate for 30 minutes to 1 hour. Remove chicken from brine, pat dry with paper towels, and season with pepper. Using large piece of heavy-duty aluminum foil, wrap soaked wood chips in foil packet and cut several vent holes in top.

2. FOR THE SAUCE: Meanwhile, heat oil in medium saucepan over medium-high heat until shimmering. Add onion and cook until softened, about 5 minutes. Whisk in broth, vinegar, coffee, molasses, tomato paste, ketchup, mustard, hot sauce, and garlic powder and bring to boil. Reduce heat to medium-low and simmer until mixture is thick and reduced to 2 cups, 30 to 35 minutes. Off heat, stir in liquid smoke. Reserve ½ cup sauce for serving. (Sauce can be made up to 2 days in advance.)

3A. FOR A CHARCOAL GRILL: Open bottom vent halfway. Light large chimney starter filled with charcoal briquettes (6 quarts). When top coals are partially covered with ash, pour into steeply banked pile against side of grill. Place wood chip packet on coals. Set cooking grate in place, cover, and open lid vent halfway. Heat grill until hot and wood chips are smoking, about 5 minutes.

3B. FOR A GAS GRILL: Place wood chip packet over primary burner. Turn all burners to high, cover, and heat grill until hot and wood chips are smoking, about 15 minutes. Leave primary burner on high and turn off other burner(s).

4. Clean and oil cooking grate. Place chicken pieces, skin side up, on cool side of grill with leg quarter closer to heat source and breast farther away. Cover and cook until breast registers 160 degrees and thigh registers 175 degrees, 30 to 45 minutes. Transfer chicken to cutting board, tent loosely with foil, and let rest until cool enough to handle, 5 to 10 minutes.

5. FOR THE SLAW: While chicken rests, brush cabbage with 1½ teaspoons oil and season with pepper. Place cabbage cut side down on hotter part of grill and cook (covered if using gas) until slightly wilted and browned on all sides, 6 to 10 minutes, turning as needed. Transfer cabbage to cutting board and cut crosswise into thin strips, discarding core. Transfer cabbage to bowl and stir in carrot. In small bowl, combine remaining 1 tablespoon oil, vinegar, raisins, sugar, and mustard and microwave, covered, until hot, about 1 minute. Pour dressing over cabbage mixture and toss to coat.

6. To serve, remove and discard chicken skin. Pull meat off bones, separating dark and light meat. Roughly chop dark meat into ½-inch pieces. Using 2 forks, shred white meat into thin strands. Add chicken to pot with sauce and cook over medium-low heat until chicken is warmed through, about 5 minutes. Serve pulled chicken on kaiser rolls with slaw, passing reserved ½ cup sauce separately.

CHINESE-STYLE GLAZED PORK TENDERLOIN WITH SESAME BOK CHOY

✔ **WHY THIS RECIPE WORKS:** For an easy take on Chinese-style glazed and charred pork, we turned to the grill and opted for pork tenderloin, which cooks quickly, stays moist, and offers just enough meat for two. Butterflying and pounding the tenderloin meant we had even more surface area to glaze. A number of pantry staples like ketchup and jelly, plus a few Asian ingredients, gave us a salty-sweet sauce that acted as both marinade and glaze. Continuously flipping and glazing the pork on the grill created a charred and caramelized—but not burnt—exterior. Grilled baby bok choy completed our takeout-at-home supper.

WHEN IT COMES TO CHINESE FOOD, BONELESS barbecue spareribs are a popular favorite. In the wrong hands, they can turn out flabby and greasy. But when they're done right—marinated, slowly roasted, brushed with a salty-sweet red glaze, and then broiled to a crispy, charred finish—they are perfection. We wanted to bring this dish outdoors and use the heat of the grill to deliver the same charred look and flavor, and also streamline the ingredient list so it would be easy to put this dish on the table for two (no specialty shopping required).

"Boneless barbecue spareribs" is a misnomer: They are neither spareribs (they're usually strips of pork shoulder) nor barbecue (there's no smoke involved). Right from the outset, we knew we'd need a replacement for the pork shoulder, which takes hours to cook and results in way too much food for two. We picked up some boneless pork chops, pork tenderloin, and boneless country-style ribs. We made a quick marinade and fired up the grill. The pork chops looked great but weren't quite tender enough; the same held true for the country-style ribs. Thankfully, the tenderloin cooked quickly and was very tender, just as the name advertises. We decided to butterfly and pound the tenderloin, turning the meat into a thin sheet, so we'd have faster, more even cooking as well as extra surface area for glazing once we hit the grill.

Some marinade recipes for Chinese pork call for exotic ingredients such as black vinegar, sweet soy sauce, and maltose (a malt sugar). For the home cook, however, supermarket ingredients were in order: Soy sauce, sherry, garlic, ginger, and five-spice powder all proved essential. Hoisin added depth, toasted sesame oil a nutty aroma, and black pepper just enough kick. For sweetness, we wondered if those little packets of duck sauce might do the trick. Before we scoured the office refrigerators for packets, we remembered that duck sauce is basically just apricot jelly, so we gave that a shot. The fruity, sweet-tart jelly was just what the pork needed.

Traditionally, the "glaze" used for barbecue spareribs is more of a "baste": The drippings are brushed onto the pork as it roasts. Since our new technique didn't produce any drippings, we set aside some of the marinade mixture to brush on the pork. It dripped right off. Thickening with more hoisin or jelly made the glaze too sweet. Reducing the sauce on the stove helped, but it still lacked body. What if we added ketchup? Although not traditional, many modern Chinese recipes use it. The ketchup thickened the glaze, its tanginess played nicely with the other ingredients, and its color guaranteed that familiar red hue. To finish, we added a little molasses, which tied everything together, from the smokiness imparted by the grill to the sweet, meaty taste of the pork.

At last, we were ready to grill. Although the test kitchen typically recommends glazing meats during the last minute or two of cooking to avoid burning or sticking, this method didn't give the pork a sticky, lacquered exterior. Instead, we found that by flipping and glazing the meat throughout grilling, we could produce a charred, caramelized exterior as good as the real deal, especially considering the time investment.

To complete the meal, we wanted a fresh vegetable to provide some contrast to the sweet and sticky glaze of the pork. Crisp-tender baby bok choy fit our Asian theme, and a light dressing of sesame oil and rice wine vinegar with a garnish of toasted sesame seeds added nutty flavor, brightness, and texture. Since the delicate bok choy began to burn on the grill before it had time to soften, we steamed it in the microwave for a few minutes before grilling.

From marinating to eating, we had richly flavored and nicely charred boneless "spareribs," plus a side of sesame bok choy, on the table in about an hour—and there was no need to tip for delivery.

Chinese-Style Glazed Pork Tenderloin with Sesame Bok Choy

SERVES 2

Do not remove the core from the bok choy; it will help keep the leaves together on the grill.

PORK

- 1 (12-ounce) pork tenderloin, trimmed
- ¼ cup soy sauce
- ¼ cup apricot jelly
- 2 tablespoons hoisin sauce
- 2 tablespoons dry sherry
- 1 tablespoon grated fresh ginger
- 1½ teaspoons toasted sesame oil
- 1 garlic clove, minced
- ½ teaspoon five-spice powder
- ½ teaspoon pepper
- 1 teaspoon vegetable oil
- 2 tablespoons ketchup
- 1½ teaspoons molasses

BOK CHOY

- 3 heads baby bok choy (4 ounces each), halved
- 1 tablespoon water
- 2 teaspoons vegetable oil
  Salt and pepper
- 1 tablespoon toasted sesame oil
- 2 teaspoons rice wine vinegar
- 1 teaspoon toasted sesame seeds

1. FOR THE PORK: Butterfly tenderloin by slicing lengthwise through side; do not cut through meat completely. Open up tenderloin like book and place between 2 pieces of plastic wrap. Gently pound to even ¾-inch thickness.

2. Combine soy sauce, jelly, hoisin, sherry, ginger, sesame oil, garlic, five-spice powder, and pepper in bowl. Reserve ⅓ cup marinade. Place pork in large zipper-lock bag and pour remaining marinade into bag with pork. Seal bag, turn to coat, and refrigerate for at least 30 minutes or up to 4 hours. Remove pork from marinade and pat dry with paper towels; discard used marinade. Rub pork all over with vegetable oil.

3. Meanwhile, combine reserved marinade, ketchup, and molasses in small saucepan. Cook over medium heat until syrupy and reduced to ⅓ cup, 2 to 4 minutes. Reserve 1 tablespoon glaze for glazing cooked tenderloin.

4. FOR THE BOK CHOY: Place bok choy in bowl and add water. Microwave, covered, until bok choy is slightly softened but still firm, 3 to 4 minutes. Transfer bok choy to paper towel–lined plate to cool and pat dry with paper towels. Brush bok choy with vegetable oil and season with salt and pepper.

5A. FOR A CHARCOAL GRILL: Open bottom vent completely. Light large chimney starter filled with charcoal briquettes (6 quarts). When top coals are partially covered with ash, pour evenly over grill. Set cooking grate in place, cover, and open lid vent completely. Heat grill until hot, about 5 minutes.

5B. FOR A GAS GRILL: Turn all burners to high, cover, and heat grill until hot, about 15 minutes. Turn all burners to medium-high.

6. Clean and oil cooking grate. Grill pork (covered if using gas) until lightly charred on first side, about 2 minutes. Flip and brush grilled side of pork evenly with 1 tablespoon glaze. Continue grilling until lightly charred on second side, about 2 minutes. Flip and brush evenly with 1 tablespoon glaze. Repeat flipping and glazing twice more, until pork registers 140 degrees and is thickly glazed, about 4 minutes longer. Transfer pork to cutting board and brush with reserved 1 tablespoon glaze. Tent loosely with aluminum foil and let rest for 5 to 10 minutes.

7. While pork is resting, place bok choy on grill and cook until slightly wilted and well browned on all sides, 3 to 5 minutes, turning as needed. Gently toss bok choy with sesame oil and vinegar and season with salt and pepper to taste. Sprinkle with sesame seeds. Slice pork ¼ inch thick and serve with bok choy.

NOTES FROM THE TEST KITCHEN

PREPARING PORK TENDERLOIN

1. Place tenderloin on cutting board and slice down side, leaving ½ inch of meat uncut, and open like a book. This provides extra surface area for grilling.

2. Place butterflied tenderloin between two sheets of plastic wrap. Using meat pounder, pound to ¾-inch thickness for quick and even cooking.

ENHANCED VERSUS UNENHANCED PORK?

Because modern pork is remarkably lean and therefore somewhat bland and prone to dryness if overcooked, a product called "enhanced" pork has overtaken the market. In fact, it can be hard to find unenhanced pork. Enhanced pork has been injected with a solution of water, salt, sodium phosphate, sodium lactate, potassium lactate, sodium diacetate, and varying flavor agents to bolster both flavor and juiciness; these enhancing ingredients add 7 to 15 percent extra weight. After several taste tests, we have concluded that although enhanced pork is indeed juicier and more tender than unenhanced pork, the latter has more genuine pork flavor. Some tasters also picked up artificial, salty flavors in enhanced pork. It can also leach juice that, once reduced, will result in overly salty sauces. We prefer natural pork, but the choice is up to you.

SPICY PORK TACOS (AL PASTOR)

✓ **WHY THIS RECIPE WORKS:** Traditional recipes for tacos *al pastor* call for roasting a pork butt on a vertical spit, but that wouldn't do for an easy, streamlined supper for two. Instead, we opted for boneless country-style ribs and fired up the grill. So the ribs would cook through evenly, we pounded them to an even ¾-inch thickness to break down the fattier dark meat, and we brined them to keep the white meat juicy. Then we basted the ribs during grilling with a potent sauce made from dried chiles, tomatoes, and spices. The meat stayed tender as it picked up the tangy flavors and a nice char.

TACOS AL PASTOR, OR "SHEPHERD-STYLE" TACOS, are a Mexican taqueria classic. The pork is marinated in a chile sauce before being packed onto a vertical spit with layers of pork fat, topped with a whole pineapple, and roasted. As the meat cooks, the tangy, sweet pineapple juices trickle down, encouraging the meat to caramelize as it turns. When the exterior is browned and crisp, thin shavings of the roasted pork and pineapple are carved off directly onto a warm tortilla and topped with garnishes that contrast with the rich meat: minced raw onion or scallion, cilantro, and a squeeze of fresh lime. Since preparing tacos al pastor in the traditional manner is neither quick nor sensible for the home cook (who owns a vertical spit?), the test kitchen recently developed a much easier recipe that still delivered all the rich flavors and textures. First, a pork butt is cut into ½-inch-thick pieces and braised in a potent chile-tomato sauce until tender, then brushed with more sauce and grilled until crisp and charred. Just before serving, the pork is tossed back into the braising liquid to absorb the flavor from the rendered fat. Since this approach is still quite involved, we looked to streamline it where we could so that even households of two could enjoy the incredibly tender and deeply flavored meat.

First off, we'd need to find an appropriate stand-in for the 4-pound pork shoulder. Looking for a smaller cut of meat that boasted some of the marbling and darker meat of pork butt, we turned to boneless country-style ribs. Country-style ribs aren't actually ribs at all; they're well-marbled pork chops cut from the blade end of the loin. After whipping up a batch of scaled-down chile-tomato sauce—a bold blend of fruity guajillos, tomatoes, lots of garlic, bay leaves, cumin, and sugar—we nestled a pound of the boneless ribs into the liquid and let it all simmer for about 40 minutes before we moved the meat to the grill to crisp.

Unfortunately, the resulting ribs weren't all that tender. One of the challenges of using boneless country-style ribs is the variance in the ratio of light to dark meat. If the ribs are cooked to optimize the white meat, the dark meat stays tough, and if they are cooked to optimize the dark meat, the white meat turns dry and chalky. Even at a low simmer, the lighter meat toughened before the dark meat had become tender. Since we would be finishing the ribs on the grill to develop the traditional charred exterior, we wondered if we could eliminate the braising step completely and do all of our cooking on the grill. In the test kitchen, we've had luck brining boneless country-style ribs to keep them juicy on the grill and protect the white meat, so we followed suit here. We also pounded them slightly to break down the dark meat and add more surface area to the ribs. Since we would be losing the opportunity for the ribs to pick up flavor from the sauce during braising, increased surface area meant more room to baste and develop char.

For our next test, we brushed the unctuous liquid over both sides of each pork rib before grilling and then flipped and basted the ribs every 2 minutes until the pork reached a temperature of 145 degrees. The layers of sauce became concentrated into a thick glaze that browned and crisped beautifully over the heat of the grill. Pineapple was a given to keep with the authenticity of the dish, so while the meat rested, we skewered a cup of pineapple chunks and grilled them until they were softened and caramelized. After a coarse chop, they were ready to garnish the tacos.

To replicate the appearance and texture of meat shaved from a spit, we sliced the crisped ribs crosswise into short ⅛-inch-thick strips. Then, just before serving, we tossed the meat with some warm reserved sauce spiked with a bit of lime juice for brightness.

Topped with thinly sliced scallions and chopped cilantro, our tacos al pastor, imbued with all of the complexity and rich flavor of the spit-roasted original, helped us bring the taste of an authentic taqueria home for two.

Spicy Pork Tacos (al Pastor)
SERVES 2

If you can't find guajillo chiles, New Mexican chiles may be substituted, although the dish may be spicier. To warm tortillas, place them on a plate, cover with a damp dish towel, and microwave for 60 to 90 seconds. Keep the tortillas covered and serve immediately.

    Salt and pepper
1   pound boneless country-style pork ribs, trimmed
3   large dried guajillo chiles, wiped clean
¾   cup water
8   ounces plum tomatoes, cored and quartered
2   garlic cloves, peeled
1   bay leaf
½   teaspoon sugar
¼   teaspoon ground cumin
1   lime, cut into 6 wedges
1   cup 1-inch pineapple pieces
1   teaspoon vegetable oil
6   (6-inch) corn tortillas, warmed
2   scallions, sliced thin
2   tablespoons coarsely chopped fresh cilantro

1. Dissolve 1 tablespoon salt in 2 cups cold water in large container. Place ribs, cut side down, between 2 sheets of plastic wrap and pound to ¾-inch thickness. Submerge pork in brine, cover, and refrigerate for 30 minutes to 1 hour. Remove pork from brine and pat dry with paper towels.

2. Meanwhile, toast guajillos in small saucepan over medium-high heat until softened and fragrant, 2 to 4 minutes. Transfer to large plate and, when cool enough to handle, remove stems.

3. Bring toasted guajillos, water, tomatoes, garlic, bay leaf, sugar, cumin, ½ teaspoon salt, and ⅛ teaspoon pepper to simmer in now-empty saucepan over medium-high heat. Cover, reduce heat to medium-low, and simmer, stirring occasionally, until guajillos are softened and tomatoes have broken down, about 30 minutes.

4. Transfer guajillo-tomato mixture to blender and process until smooth, about 1 minute. Strain puree through fine-mesh strainer, pressing on solids to extract as much liquid as possible. Transfer ¼ cup to bowl for grilling. Return remaining sauce to now-empty saucepan. Squeeze 1 lime wedge into sauce in pot and add spent wedge; season with salt to taste and set aside.

5A. FOR A CHARCOAL GRILL: Open bottom vent halfway. Light large chimney starter filled with charcoal briquettes (6 quarts). When top coals are partially covered with ash, pour evenly over half of grill. Set cooking grate in place, cover, and open lid vent halfway. Heat grill until hot, about 5 minutes.

5B. FOR A GAS GRILL: Turn all burners to high, cover, and heat grill until hot, about 15 minutes. Leave primary burner on high and turn off other burner(s).

6. Clean and oil cooking grate. Place pork on hot part of grill and brush uncooked side of pork with 1 tablespoon sauce. Grill until lightly charred on first side, about 2 minutes. Flip and brush grilled side of pork evenly with 1 tablespoon glaze. Continue grilling until lightly charred on second side, about 2 minutes. Repeat flipping and glazing twice more, until pork registers 145 degrees and is thickly glazed and charred, about 4 minutes longer. Transfer to cutting board, tent loosely with aluminum foil, and let rest for 5 to 10 minutes.

7. Meanwhile, thread pineapple chunks onto 12-inch metal skewer, brush with oil, and season with salt. Place skewer on hot part of grill and cook until pineapple is softened and caramelized, 5 to 7 minutes, turning skewer as needed; transfer pineapple to cutting board. Coarsely chop grilled pineapple and transfer to serving bowl.

8. Using tongs to steady hot pork, slice each piece crosswise into ⅛-inch pieces. Bring remaining sauce in pot to simmer, add sliced pork, remove pot from heat, and toss to coat pork well. Season with salt to taste. Spoon small amount of pork into each warm tortilla. Serve, passing chopped pineapple, remaining lime wedges, scallions, and cilantro separately.

NOTES FROM THE TEST KITCHEN

BUYING BONELESS COUNTRY-STYLE RIBS
These meaty, tender ribs are cut from the upper side of the rib cage from the fatty end of the loin. They contain mostly fattier meat and are a favorite for braising, smoking, and slow cooking. Butchers usually cut them into individual ribs and package several together. When shopping, be sure to choose ribs with plenty of fat and dark meat to ensure tenderness.

GRILLED MARINATED SKIRT STEAK WITH ZUCCHINI RIBBONS

✔ **WHY THIS RECIPE WORKS:** Skirt steak is a popular cut for grilling, and though a marinade might add flavor, it usually causes the meat to steam on the grill. To achieve a charred crust, we seasoned our steak with salt, pepper, and sugar before grilling and didn't marinate it until after it came off the grate. Since the marinade never touched raw meat, we could serve it as a sauce on the side. Thinly shaved slices of zucchini and Parmesan, tossed with mint and lemon juice, created a fresh, cool counterpoint to the grilled steak.

FIFTEEN YEARS AGO, THE ONLY PLACE MOST OF US could find skirt steak was in Latin American restaurants and markets; it is a common cut for fajitas and *carne asada*. But as American diners slowly grew to appreciate the appeal of this intensely beefy, pleasantly chewy cut, supermarkets caught on—especially during grilling season. Most recipes call for marinating before grilling, as skirt steak's loose, almost shaggy grain makes it ideal for soaking up flavor. In terms of an easy dinner for two, a robustly flavored steak meant we could keep our side dish simple. But all too often, "simple" is synonymous with "boring." Keeping the side dish's flavors bright and vibrant was just as important as developing a proper sear on our steak. And as we would come to realize, the latter proved more difficult to achieve than we expected.

While marinating works well with the texture of skirt steak, it doesn't exactly work well with grilling. In the half-dozen recipes we tried, even with the grill cranked up high, the marinated meat steamed and fizzled rather than seared and sizzled—not one produced rosy meat with a deeply charred exterior. The problem: Skirt steaks are thin, so they are apt to overcook by the time they get a nice sear. And the marinade was compounding this by making the meat wetter and slowing down the searing. Patting the meat dry before grilling helped, but even then the thin, still-moist meat didn't get the kind of crusty char we were after. This might not be a problem with red-hot restaurant grills, but it was for us on a regular backyard grill. What's a home cook to do?

GRILLED MARINATED SKIRT STEAK WITH ZUCCHINI RIBBONS AND SHAVED PARMESAN

Since we were determined to marinate our meat, we figured we'd work on the flavor first and get to the char later. The test kitchen has a lot of experience with beef marinades, so we weren't starting from scratch. We used soy sauce for seasoning and meaty flavor, garlic for depth, olive oil to help carry the flavors, and mustard for pop. Knowing that we'd need about half a cup of marinade for a 12-ounce skirt steak, which offered just the right amount of meat for two, we started fiddling with ratios and realized that we needed to bump up the flavor. Worcestershire sauce added complexity, and balsamic vinegar brought both sweetness and acidity. Scallions lent a mild onion flavor. Finally, to make sure the flavors were evenly distributed, we took a hint from vinaigrette recipes and emulsified the marinade by slowly whisking the oil into the base.

With the marinade squared away, it was time to work on getting a substantial char. A colleague thought a sprinkling of sugar might help the steak caramelize, and yes, the meat did get some char. Still, "some" char was a long way from a proper char. We were stumped. We were patting the meat dry, sugaring it, preheating the grill, and oiling the grill grates. And still the steaks weren't taking on a hard sear.

Then it hit us. In restaurant kitchens, chefs often rest cooked meat—steak, lobster, and more—in melted butter until it is ready to be served. The meat stays warm, and it absorbs some of the butter, giving it rich, buttery depth. Would this work with a marinade, too?

For the next test, we simply seasoned a skirt steak with salt, pepper, and sugar and threw it on a hot grill. After a few minutes of good, hard searing on both sides, we moved the steak to the marinade; it drank it up. To push the recipe over the top, we poked the steak a few times with a fork when it came off the grill to allow the marinade to penetrate even deeper. Tasters loved the thoroughly seasoned meat, and they were surprised when we served the marinade on the side as a sauce for drizzling over the steak. Since it never touched raw meat, it was good eating.

Finally, to complete this seriously low-fuss meal, we wanted an equally simple but flavorful salad—ideally something that could be assembled during the steak's short resting time in the marinade. Mild-tasting, subtly sweet zucchini seemed to fit the bill—and one was just enough to serve two. While we love grilled zucchini, we wanted to find a way to serve it without softening its crunchy texture or altering its fresh flavor, so we used a vegetable peeler to shave it into long, delicate ribbons. We liked the idea of adding some creamy, nutty Parmesan, but grated cheese muddied the clean look of the dish. Instead, we turned the peeler on the cheese, shaving thin slices to mimic the ribbons of zucchini. A quick toss with salt and pepper and a splash of olive oil and lemon juice balanced the flavors, and a sprinkling of chopped mint added a cool component to this super-fresh, and incredibly easy, side dish.

Grilled Marinated Skirt Steak with Zucchini Ribbons and Shaved Parmesan

SERVES 2

Keep the marinade at room temperature or it will cool down the steaks. Using in-season zucchini, good olive oil, and high-quality Parmesan is crucial in this simple side dish. Make sure to dress the zucchini just before serving.

¼ cup soy sauce
2 tablespoons Worcestershire sauce
4 teaspoons sugar
1 scallion, sliced thin
2 garlic cloves, minced
1½ teaspoons Dijon mustard
1 teaspoon balsamic vinegar
Salt and pepper
3 tablespoons olive oil
1 (12-ounce) skirt steak, cut crosswise into 4-inch pieces and trimmed
1 zucchini
2 teaspoons lemon juice
1 ounce Parmesan cheese, shaved
2 teaspoons minced fresh mint or basil

1. Combine soy sauce, Worcestershire, 1 tablespoon sugar, scallion, garlic, mustard, vinegar, and ¾ teaspoon pepper in bowl. Slowly whisk in 2 tablespoons oil until incorporated and sugar has dissolved. Pat steaks dry with paper towels and season with remaining 1 teaspoon sugar, ¼ teaspoon salt, and ¼ teaspoon pepper.

2A. FOR A CHARCOAL GRILL: Open bottom vent completely. Light large chimney starter mounded with charcoal briquettes (7 quarts). When top coals are partially covered with ash, pour evenly over half of grill. Set cooking grate in place, cover, and open lid vent completely. Heat grill until hot, about 5 minutes.

SHAVING PARMESAN

To make Parmesan shavings, run vegetable peeler over block of cheese, making sure to use light touch to ensure thin shavings.

ALL ABOUT SKIRT STEAK

Once reserved for fajitas and carne asada, skirt steak has become very popular in recent years—and for good reason. Cut from the underside of the animal, it's well marbled, which means it has great flavor. It's thin, which means it cooks quickly. And it has an open grain, which means it readily soaks up flavor from a marinade. When shopping for skirt steak, choose fattier cuts, as they will offer more flavor.

TESTING MEAT FOR DONENESS

An instant-read thermometer is the most reliable method for checking the doneness of poultry and meat. To use an instant-read thermometer, simply insert it through the side of a chicken breast, steak, or pork chop. The chart below lists temperatures at which the meat should be removed from the heat, as the temperature of the meat will continue to climb between 5 and 10 degrees as it rests. (Thin cutlets cook too quickly for an actual doneness test, and you will have to rely more on visual cues and cooking times.)

WHEN IS IT DONE?

MEAT	COOK UNTIL IT REGISTERS	SERVING TEMPERATURE
Chicken Breasts	160 degrees	160 degrees
Chicken Thighs	175 degrees	175 degrees
Pork Chops and Tenderloin	145 degrees	150 degrees
Pork Loin and Roasts	140 degrees	150 degrees
Beef and Lamb		
Rare	115 to 120 degrees	125 degrees
Medium-rare	120 to 125 degrees	130 degrees
Medium	130 to 135 degrees	140 degrees
Medium-well	140 to 145 degrees	150 degrees
Well-done	150 to 155 degrees	160 degrees

2B. FOR A GAS GRILL: Turn all burners to high, cover, and heat grill until hot, about 15 minutes. Leave all burners on high.

3. Clean and oil cooking grate. Grill steaks (uncovered and directly over coals if using charcoal; covered if using gas) until well browned and meat registers 125 degrees (for medium-rare), 2 to 4 minutes per side. Transfer steaks to 8-inch square baking pan and poke all over with fork. Pour marinade over steaks, tent with aluminum foil, and let rest for 5 to 10 minutes. Transfer meat to cutting board and slice thinly against grain. Pour marinade into serving vessel.

4. While meat is resting, use vegetable peeler or mandoline to slice zucchini lengthwise into very thin ribbons. Gently toss zucchini ribbons with salt and pepper in shallow platter. Drizzle with remaining 1 tablespoon oil and lemon juice, then sprinkle with Parmesan and mint. Serve immediately with steaks and reserved marinade.

GRILLED STEAK WITH NEW MEXICAN CHILE RUB AND RED POTATOES

✔ WHY THIS RECIPE WORKS: For an affordable steak night for two, we used a two-stage rub to make the most of a comparatively inexpensive cut, the shell sirloin. We started with a rub of salt, onion powder, garlic powder, fish sauce, and tomato paste for deep, savory flavor and enhanced juiciness. For the second stage, we made our own coarsely ground rub with toasted whole spices and dried chiles. Making shallow cuts in the steak increased its surface area and allowed the meat to absorb the flavors. Grilled halved red potatoes, flavored with chives and garlic, turned this into a steakhouse-worthy dinner.

WITH THEIR TENDER TEXTURE AND BIG-TIME BEEF flavor, pricey steaks like rib eyes and T-bones need little more than salt, pepper, and a few minutes over a hot fire to render them impressive. But try that minimalist technique on cheaper steaks and you'll get meat that's chewy and dry, with flavors that veer toward liver-y and gamy. And spice rubs don't help matters much; because cheap steaks exude little fat to bond with the spices, the rub tends to fall off in chunks. If by some stroke of luck the rub remains intact, it usually tastes dry and dusty, plus nuances of flavor can vaporize over the fire. Still, we're not ones to give up easily. We wanted a great grilled steak for two, and we didn't want to spend an arm and a leg on it. Surely there was a way to create a recipe for inexpensive grilled steak that was also tender and juicy, with a flavorful, crunchy crust that stayed in place. But first, we had to find a steak that provided the best taste and texture for the money.

After considering our options and sampling several rounds of steak, we settled on the shell sirloin steak, which is also sold as top butt, butt steak, top sirloin butt, top sirloin steak, and center-cut roast. Tasters described the shell steak as having a relatively beefy taste, with none of the liver-y flavor found in other cuts. A single shell steak provided just the right amount of meat for two diners.

Salting the steak before cooking was a given. Salt sprinkled liberally on the surface of the meat draws moisture from inside, which over time is then reabsorbed as the meat sits, seasoning it and changing the structure of the muscle fibers so that they hold on to more juices. But we'd have to do more than just salt our cheap cut to turn it into a steakhouse-worthy supper. We already knew that a spice rub might not deliver the results we wanted: Most flavor compounds in spices are fat-soluble rather than water-soluble, so they can't penetrate below the surface of the steak. Furthermore, in tests of marinades, we've found that other than salt, the only water-soluble flavor compounds that can travel deep into meat are glutamates, which are naturally occurring flavor compounds that enhance savory qualities.

So, maybe glutamate-rich ingredients were the way to go. Scanning the pantry, we singled out two of the most potent sources of these compounds: tomato paste and fish sauce, a condiment that is unusual in a steak recipe but one we've called upon in other unlikely applications to amp up savory taste. We made a rub with kosher salt and a teaspoon each of these two ingredients (to compensate for their extra sodium we cut back a little on the salt) and applied it to our steak an hour before grilling. The difference in the steak was remarkable: It boasted a much deeper flavor without any trace of our secret enhancements. Spurred by this success, we decided to add ¼ teaspoon each of garlic powder and onion powder to the rub. Though neither substance contains significant levels of glutamates, their water-soluble flavors are potent enough (especially in concentrated powdered form) that even if they penetrated only a little into the meat, they might make a difference in the overall flavor. Tasters confirmed that our hunch was correct: The steak from our next test had noticeably richer flavor. It was time to move on to the spice rub.

Our plan was to treat the steak with our savory salt paste first, wait an hour, and then apply a second, more conventional dry rub right before grilling. We tried a variety of rubs, but we found that those made mostly with dried herbs lost their flavor, while those based on spices, particularly those containing capsaicin—namely, peppers, chiles, and paprika—fared better. First we tried rubs made with preground spices, but these formed a coating that was more pasty than crunchy. Then we tried toasting some whole spices (cumin, coriander, red pepper flakes, and black peppercorns) in a skillet along with an earthy-tasting dried New Mexican chile, then we ground the mixture coarsely in a coffee grinder. To round out the flavors, we also incorporated sugar, paprika, and ground cloves before pressing the rub onto the surface of the steak.

Tasters pronounced the steak juicy, tender, and flavorful, and they greatly preferred the more robust texture of this home-ground rub. Still, there were two problems to be solved. First, despite the toasting step, the spices retained a slightly raw taste, the result of being cooked with very little fat, so the flavors couldn't bloom. Second, tasters requested a more substantial crust (there had been more rub when we started grilling, but half of it had been left on the cooking grate). Clearly, we needed to find a way to help the spices stick to the steak and not to the grate.

In the past, we've made shallow cuts in pork chops and other cuts of meat to help give breadings and coatings more purchase. Doing the same with our steak before adding the first rub seemed likely to be doubly advantageous: It would increase the surface area, which could give that first rub more opportunity to really get into the meat, plus it could help the spice rub stick to the meat.

As we liberally greased the cooking grate in preparation for grilling the newly crosshatched steak, we wished that there were some way to put a layer of oil on the steak itself without disturbing the spice crust (which—we were pleased to see—was sticking quite nicely). The easy solution: A light spritz of vegetable oil spray helped keep the rub intact through the grilling process. The steak was crusty and crunchy on the outside, with just enough heat and spice to complement the meat's rich flavor, and that little bit of added fat imparted by the spray gave the spices the deep flavor that tasters were after. The tender and juicy meat belied its $5.99-per-pound price tag.

Now we were ready to move on to the side dish and thought grilled potatoes would complete our steak dinner. We halved a few small red potatoes (which held their shape over the high heat of the grill better than other varieties) and skewered and grilled them once our steak came off the grill. However, by the time the steak had finished resting, our potatoes were still raw on the inside. We often give hardier vegetables a jump start in the microwave before grilling, so we decided to give it a go with our potatoes. After skewering our spuds, we brushed them with oil and sprinkled them with salt, then microwaved them until they were almost tender and placed them over the hot fire. This time, when the steak was ready for the plate, our spuds were tender and creamy on the inside and nicely charred on the outside. Tasters had only one complaint: The interiors of the potatoes didn't have much flavor. Piercing each potato prior to microwaving encouraged the salt on the skin to migrate to the inside. For a final boost of flavor, we tossed the grilled potatoes with olive oil, chives, and garlic just before serving.

Our grilled steak-and-potatoes dinner offered all the rich flavor and great texture we'd expect—but not the price tag.

Grilled Steak with New Mexican Chile Rub and Red Potatoes

SERVES 2

Shell sirloin steak is also known as top butt, butt steak, top sirloin butt, top sirloin steak, and center-cut roast. Spraying the rubbed steak with oil helps the spices bloom, preventing a raw flavor. Use small red potatoes, measuring 1 to 2 inches in diameter. You will need two 12-inch wooden skewers for this recipe.

STEAK AND POTATOES

- 1 teaspoon tomato paste
- 1 teaspoon fish sauce
- ¾ teaspoon kosher salt
- ¼ teaspoon onion powder
- ¼ teaspoon garlic powder
- 1 (12- to 16-ounce) boneless shell sirloin steak, ½ to 1 inch thick
- 2 tablespoons extra-virgin olive oil
- 2 tablespoons minced fresh chives
- 1 small garlic clove, minced
  Salt and pepper
- 12 ounces small red potatoes, halved and skewered

SPICE RUB

- 1 dried New Mexican chile, stemmed, seeded, and torn into ½-inch pieces
- 1½ teaspoons cumin seeds
- 1½ teaspoons coriander seeds
- ⅛ teaspoon red pepper flakes
- ⅛ teaspoon black peppercorns
- 1 teaspoon sugar
- 1 teaspoon paprika
  Pinch ground cloves
  Vegetable oil spray

1. FOR THE STEAK AND POTATOES: Combine tomato paste, fish sauce, salt, onion powder, and garlic powder in bowl. Pat steak dry with paper towels. With sharp knife, cut ¹⁄₁₆-inch-deep slits on both sides of steak, spaced ½ inch apart, in crosshatch pattern. Rub salt mixture evenly on both sides of steak. Place steak on wire rack set in rimmed baking sheet; let stand at room temperature for at least 1 hour. After 30 minutes, prepare grill.

2. Combine 1 tablespoon oil, chives, garlic, ¼ teaspoon salt, and ⅛ teaspoon pepper in medium bowl and set aside for serving. Place skewered potatoes on large plate and poke each potato several times with skewer. Brush potatoes with remaining 1 tablespoon oil and season with salt. Microwave until potatoes are softened but still hold their shape, 6 to 8 minutes, flipping them halfway through cooking.

3. FOR THE SPICE RUB: Toast chile, cumin seeds, coriander seeds, pepper flakes, and peppercorns in 8-inch skillet over medium-low heat, stirring frequently, until just beginning to smoke, 3 to 4 minutes. Transfer to plate to cool, about 5 minutes. Grind spices in spice grinder or in mortar with pestle until coarsely ground. Transfer spices to bowl and stir in sugar, paprika, and cloves.

4A. FOR A CHARCOAL GRILL: Open bottom vent completely. Light large chimney starter mounded with charcoal briquettes (7 quarts). When top coals are partially covered with ash, pour two-thirds evenly over half of grill, then pour remaining coals over other half of grill. Set cooking grate in place, cover, and open lid vent completely. Heat grill until hot, about 5 minutes.

4B. FOR A GAS GRILL: Turn all burners to high, cover, and heat grill until hot, about 15 minutes. Leave primary burner on high and turn other burner(s) to medium.

5. Clean and oil cooking grate. Sprinkle half of spice rub evenly over 1 side of steak and press to adhere until spice rub is fully moistened. Lightly spray rubbed side of steak with vegetable oil spray, about 3 seconds. Flip steak and repeat process of sprinkling with remaining spice rub and coating with vegetable oil spray on second side.

6. Place steak over hotter part of grill and cook until browned and charred on both sides and center registers 125 degrees for medium-rare or 130 degrees for medium, 2 to 4 minutes per side. If steak has not reached desired temperature, move to cooler side of grill and continue to cook. Transfer steak to clean wire rack set in rimmed baking sheet, tent loosely with aluminum foil, and let rest for 5 to 10 minutes.

7. While steak rests or cooks on cooler part of grill, place potatoes, cut side down, on hotter part of grill. Cover and cook until browned on both sides, 4 to 6 minutes, flipping them halfway through cooking. Slide potatoes to cooler part of grill, cover, and continue to cook until tip of paring knife slips in and out of potatoes easily, 4 to 6 minutes longer.

8. Remove skewers from grill, carefully slide potatoes off skewers into bowl with reserved oil mixture, and toss to combine. Slice meat thin against grain and serve with potatoes.

VARIATION

Grilled Steak with Spicy Chipotle Chile Rub and Red Potatoes

Substitute 1 dried chipotle chile for New Mexican chile, ¼ teaspoon dried oregano for paprika, and ⅛ teaspoon ground cinnamon for ground cloves.

GRILL-SMOKED SALMON WITH CUCUMBER SALAD

✓ WHY THIS RECIPE WORKS: For a new take on salmon for two, we grill-smoked our fillets. First, to prepare the salmon for smoking, we quick-cured our fillets with a mixture of salt and sugar to draw moisture from the flesh and firm it up and to season it inside and out. We then cooked the fish indirectly over a gentle fire with ample smoke to produce salmon that was sweet, smoky, and tender. A creamy sauce and bright-tasting cucumber and radish salad made the perfect complements to our silky, smoky fillets.

WHILE WE LOVE THE TEXTURE AND FLAVOR OF grilled salmon fillets, we wanted to up the ante when it came to our grilling repertoire. With its unique taste and texture, smoked salmon seemed to fit the bill, but both cold-smoking and hot-smoking require loads of time (the former calls for cooking the salmon for at least 24 hours). Though both approaches deliver terrific results, they're impractical for a home cook making just two servings. Sure, you can impart a touch of smokiness by tossing wood chips onto hot charcoal and quickly grilling the fish, but we had also heard of a lesser-known, more intriguing option that captures both the intense, smoky flavor of hot-smoked fish and the firm but silky texture of the cold-smoked type. It's easy because the fish is cooked via indirect heat on a grill—a familiar and uncomplicated technique. And although the resulting fillets have a distinctive taste, they are not overpoweringly salty or smoky, so they're suitable as an entrée either warm from the grill or at room temperature.

To try out these smoky, succulent fillets, we looked for recipes. The typical first step in smoking fish is to cure the flesh with salt; some recipes recommended brining, others salting. For a simple dinner for two, we steered away from recipes that cured the fish for longer than an hour. The other criteria, smoking temperature and length of exposure—both crucial to the final result—were all over the map. One recipe called for smoking the fish at 350 degrees for a modest 20 minutes; another let it go twice as long at only 275 degrees. We decided to start by nailing down the salting step.

Since most brining methods involved a soak of two hours, taking this recipe too far from weeknight-friendly, we turned to salting. We covered the salmon with a generous blanket of kosher salt—its coarse texture makes it cling to food better than table salt—and refrigerated it, uncovered, on a wire rack on a baking sheet. After an hour, a considerable amount of liquid had been drawn to the surface, so we promptly removed the fish from the refrigerator, blotted the moisture with a paper towel, and took it out to the grill for smoking. This sample was promising, but not perfect; most tasters found it too salty to be enjoyed as a main dish. We tried dialing down the amount of salt as well as salting for a shorter amount of time, but, alas, the fish didn't achieve the proper texture.

Searching for a different tack, we looked at recipes that we'd collected and came across a few that called for adding sugar to the cure. We knew that, like salt, sugar is hygroscopic, meaning it attracts water. Could sugar pull moisture from the salmon as effectively as salt? Not quite, we found out, but it was a workable option. Eventually, we determined that a ratio of 2 parts sugar to 1 part salt produced well-balanced taste and texture in the finished salmon. When we used these proportions, the fish firmed up nicely; plus, it was far less salty and the sugar counterbalanced its richness.

With a reliable curing method in hand, we could finally fine-tune our smoking technique. The current setup was far from ideal: By the time the fish was sufficiently smoky, it was dry and flaky. Conversely, when it was cooked perfectly—still silky and slightly pink in the interior, or about 125 degrees—the smoke flavor was faint. Adding more wood chunks only gave the fillet a sooty flavor. Instead, we tried to cool down the temperature of the grill by reducing the amount of charcoal. This helped somewhat, since the fish cooked more slowly and had more time to absorb the smoke.

But the smoke flavor still wasn't as bold as we wanted. Rather than manipulating the cooking time any further, we turned to the salmon itself, swapping our single 12-ounce fillet for two smaller 6-ounce portions. This seemingly minor tweak resulted in big payoffs: First, it ensured more thorough smoke exposure (in the same amount of time) by creating more surface area. Second, the smaller pieces were far easier to get off the grill in one piece than a single bulky fillet. (To that end, we also started placing the fillets on a piece of foil.) Finally, we found that we could now use an even cooler fire (produced with a mere 2 quarts of charcoal). The smaller fillets still reached their ideal serving temperature in the same amount of time that the single, larger

GRILL-SMOKED SALMON WITH CUCUMBER, RADISH, AND WATERCRESS SALAD

fillet had taken, and the gentler fire rendered the fillets incomparably tender.

With a smoky, rich taste and a silky, supple texture, our quick smoked salmon recipe was complete. To provide some contrasting flavors and textures, we devised a mayonnaise sauce that incorporates many of the garnishes commonly served on a smoked salmon platter—shallot, capers, and dill. Looking to turn this dish into a complete meal, we also created a refreshing salad that cut the richness of the salmon and complemented the creamy herb sauce. Cucumber, radishes, and watercress, tossed with a lemon-mustard vinaigrette, made for a light, bright partner to the rich, smoky salmon.

After just a few bites, all of our tasters agreed that smoked salmon wasn't just for bagels anymore—it had more than earned its place at the dinner table.

Grill-Smoked Salmon with Cucumber, Radish, and Watercress Salad

SERVES 2

Use center-cut salmon fillets of similar thickness so that they cook at the same rate. Avoid mesquite wood chunks for this recipe.

SALMON

- 3 tablespoons mayonnaise
- 2 teaspoons capers, rinsed, plus 1 teaspoon brine
- 1 small shallot, minced
- 1 tablespoon minced fresh dill
- 2 teaspoons sugar
- 1 teaspoon kosher salt
- 2 (6-ounce) center-cut, skin-on salmon fillets
- 2 wood chunks, soaked in water for 30 minutes and drained (if using charcoal), or 2 cups wood chips, half of chips soaked in water for 15 minutes and drained (if using gas)

SALAD

- 1 small cucumber, peeled, halved lengthwise, seeded, and cut on bias into ¼-inch pieces
  Kosher salt and pepper
- ¼ teaspoon lemon zest plus 2 teaspoons juice
- 1 teaspoon Dijon mustard
- ½ teaspoon sugar
- 1½ tablespoons extra-virgin olive oil
- 2 ounces watercress (2 cups)
- 2 radishes, trimmed and sliced thin

1. FOR THE SALMON: Gently combine mayonnaise, capers, brine, shallot, and dill in bowl. Chill until serving time. Combine sugar and salt in second bowl. Set salmon on wire rack set in rimmed baking sheet and sprinkle flesh side evenly with sugar mixture. Refrigerate, uncovered, for 1 hour. With paper towels, brush any excess salt and sugar from salmon and blot dry. Return fish on wire rack to refrigerator, uncovered, while preparing grill.

2A. FOR A CHARCOAL GRILL: Open bottom vent halfway. Light large chimney starter one-third filled with charcoal briquettes (2 quarts). When top coals are partially covered with ash, pour into steeply banked pile against side of grill. Place wood chunks on top of coals. Set cooking grate in place, cover, and open lid vent halfway. Heat grill until hot and wood chunks begin to smoke, about 5 minutes.

2B. FOR A GAS GRILL: Combine soaked and unsoaked chips. Use large piece of heavy-duty aluminum foil to wrap chips into foil packet and cut several vent holes in top. Place wood chip packet directly on primary burner. Turn primary burner to high (leave other burners off), cover, and heat grill until hot and wood chips begin to smoke, 15 to 25 minutes. Turn primary burner to medium. (Adjust primary burner as needed to maintain grill temperature of 275 to 300 degrees.)

3. Clean and oil cooking grate. Fold piece of heavy-duty foil into 6 by 6-inch square. Place foil rectangle over cool side of grill and place salmon pieces on foil, spaced at least ½ inch apart. Cover grill (positioning lid vent over fish if using charcoal) and cook until center of thickest part of fillet registers 125 degrees and is still translucent when cut into with paring knife, 30 to 40 minutes. Transfer to platter and tent with foil, or allow to cool to room temperature.

4. FOR THE SALAD: Meanwhile, toss cucumber with ¼ teaspoon salt and let drain in colander for 15 minutes. In small bowl, whisk lemon zest and juice, mustard, and sugar together. Whisking constantly, drizzle in oil.

5. Combine drained cucumber, watercress, and radishes in large bowl. Just before serving, whisk dressing to re-emulsify, then drizzle over salad and toss gently to coat. Season with salt and pepper to taste. Serve salad with salmon and sauce.

GRILLED BACON-WRAPPED SCALLOPS WITH RADICCHIO SALAD

✔ **WHY THIS RECIPE WORKS:** To bring this cocktail-party favorite to the dinner table for two, we moved it to the grill. To ensure that the sturdy, fatty bacon and lean, delicate scallops cooked through at the same rate, we parcooked the bacon in the microwave to render some of its fat and prevent flare-ups when it hit the grill. To prevent the bacon from taking over the dish, we didn't wrap each scallop individually in bacon; instead, we wrapped each bacon slice around two scallops, then skewered the bundles so everything was secure. Grilled radicchio and crumbled gorgonzola offered a boldly flavored side that paired well with the contrasting textures of our main dish.

ANYONE WHO'S EVER BEEN TO A WEDDING OR cocktail party knows a thing or two about bacon-wrapped scallops, and there's a reason this passed appetizer is a crowd favorite: The smoky, salty bacon beautifully accents the sweet, succulent scallops. Surely taking it to the grill for an exciting new dinner for two would make it even better. And because we weren't cooking scallops for a crowd, it would be easier to monitor them over the heat for a perfectly cooked supper.

Once we fired up the grill, we realized that the shellfish wouldn't be problematic at all. In fact, grilling scallops is a straightforward matter: Start with "dry" scallops, which have no chemical additives or excess moisture; toss them with oil or melted butter to keep them from sticking to the grate; skewer them; and sear them over high heat for a minute or two on each side until they're just cooked through. But you can't grill bacon like that. The fat will cause flare-ups, and the bacon needs longer, gentler cooking to render and crisp. We knew that parcooking the bacon before skewering and grilling was a must. We were hoping that we could make life easier by doing it in the microwave.

We started by microwaving the bacon on a plate between layers of paper towels (to absorb the grease). To make sure we could get a snug fit when wrapping the bacon around the scallops, we placed another plate on the bacon to prevent it from curling. After testing various durations, we landed on four minutes for bacon

that had given up a good bit of its fat and would finish crisping up after a few minutes on the grill.

Now we needed to find the best way to wrap and skewer the scallops. In the test kitchen, we've grilled scallops on a single skewer as well as on double skewers (two parallel skewers running through each scallop). Though the double skewers would make it easier to flip the scallops, it would take some effort to double-skewer them while keeping the bacon in position. (Once the bacon is cut to length and wrapped around the scallop, the skewer needs to go through the overlapped bacon ends to hold it in place.) For the sake of ease, we decided on a single skewer, taking care to firmly press each bacon-wrapped scallop into its neighbor on the skewer to minimize spinning. We found that tossing the scallops in a small amount of melted butter not only helped prevent sticking to the grill but also made the scallops a little tacky and thus easier to handle and skewer.

After several grilling attempts, though, we still had one problem: the fire. We'd been working over medium heat to reduce the risk of flare-ups, but with only two skewers on the grill and much of the bacon fat already rendered in the microwave, we seemed to be solving a problem that didn't exist. In fact, the result of our cautious cooking was flabby bacon. In order to achieve a crisp exterior on the bacon, we needed to turn up the heat. So we mounded two-thirds of the coals on one side of the grill, leaving the final third to make a cooler side to grill a side dish. We cooked the two bacon sides of the skewers over the hot side until browned and crispy, and then just one of the nonbacon sides to get a flavorful sear and finish cooking the scallops. (There was no need to cook the other nonbacon side, as the scallops were now cooked just right.)

Though a few scallops wrapped in bacon are perfect as an appetizer, six scallops wrapped in bacon means you're eating six slices of bacon for dinner—too much, even for a tasting panel of cured pork–loving cooks. We decided to double up the scallops and wrap a single slice of bacon around two of them. Three two-scallop bundles made for one perfect dinner portion. Plus, this meant we didn't have to cut the bacon into shorter lengths to comfortably fit around just one scallop—one slice of bacon fit almost perfectly around two scallops.

With the scallops ready to go, we decided to take advantage of the cooler side of the grill to cook an equally tempting side dish. We chose slightly bitter radicchio, which would make a flavorful partner to the rich scallops. We quartered a head of radicchio—a single head was plenty for two people—and brushed it with oil. Leaving the core intact kept the wedges together on the grill, as the leaves tend to separate as they cook. After 5 minutes, the radicchio was browned and lightly charred. We sliced the grilled radicchio into thin strips before tossing it with balsamic vinegar, olive oil, and crumbled Gorgonzola cheese. The interplay of sweet, creamy, and bitter won tasters over.

As final flourishes, we grilled lemon halves and squeezed the juice over the bacon and scallop skewers, then sprinkled them with chopped chives. In about 30 minutes we had created a complexly flavored dinner of perfectly cooked scallops, crispy bacon, and a balsamic-spiked radicchio and Gorgonzola salad—not too shabby for a simple dinner off the grill.

Grilled Bacon-Wrapped Scallops with Radicchio and Gorgonzola Salad

SERVES 2

Use ordinary bacon, as thick-cut bacon will take too long to crisp on the grill. When wrapping the scallops, the bacon slice should fit around both scallops, overlapping just enough to be skewered through both ends. We recommend buying "dry" scallops, which don't have chemical additives and taste better than "wet" scallops. Dry scallops will look ivory or pinkish; wet scallops are bright white. You will need two 12-inch metal skewers for this recipe.

- 6 slices bacon
- 12 large sea scallops, tendons removed
- 1½ tablespoons unsalted butter, melted
  Salt and pepper
- 1 small head radicchio (6 ounces), quartered lengthwise through core
- 2 tablespoons extra-virgin olive oil
- 1 lemon, halved
- 1 tablespoon chopped fresh chives
- 1 ounce Gorgonzola cheese, crumbled (¼ cup)
- 1 tablespoon balsamic vinegar

1. Place 4 layers of paper towels on large plate and arrange bacon over towels in single layer. Cover with 2 layers of paper towels; place second large plate on top and press gently to flatten. Microwave until fat begins to render but bacon is still pliable, about 4 minutes.

2. Toss scallops, butter, ¼ teaspoon salt, and pinch pepper together in bowl until scallops are thoroughly coated with butter. Press 2 scallops together, side to side, and wrap with 1 slice bacon, trimming excess as necessary. Thread onto skewer through bacon. Repeat with remaining scallops and bacon, threading 3 bundles onto each of two 12-inch metal skewers. Brush radicchio with 1 tablespoon oil and season with salt and pepper.

3A. FOR A CHARCOAL GRILL: Open bottom vent completely. Light large chimney starter filled with charcoal briquettes (6 quarts). When top coals are partially covered with ash, pour two-thirds evenly over half of grill, then pour remaining coals over other half of grill. Set cooking grate in place, cover, and open lid vent completely. Heat grill until hot, about 5 minutes.

3B. FOR A GAS GRILL: Turn all burners to high, cover, and heat grill until hot, about 15 minutes. Leave primary burner on high and turn other burner(s) to medium.

4. Clean and oil cooking grate. Place skewers, bacon side down, and lemon halves, cut side down, on hotter side of grill. Cook (covered if using gas) until bacon is crisp on first side, about 4 minutes. Flip skewers onto other bacon side and cook until crisp, about 4 minutes longer. Flip skewers scallop side down and grill until sides of scallops are firm and centers are opaque, about 4 minutes on 1 side only. Transfer skewers to platter, squeeze lemon over, and sprinkle with chives.

5. When scallops are flipped for final time, place radicchio, cut side down, on cooler part of grill and cook until slightly wilted and browned on all sides, about 5 minutes, turning as needed. Transfer to cutting board.

6. Slice radicchio into thin strips, discarding core. Toss sliced radicchio, remaining 1 tablespoon oil, Gorgonzola, and vinegar together in bowl. Season with salt and pepper to taste. Serve with scallops.

NOTES FROM THE TEST KITCHEN

SKEWERING SCALLOPS

To skewer scallops, wrap 1 strip of parcooked bacon around 2 scallops and run skewer through overlapped bacon. Place three 2-scallop bundles on each skewer.

GRILLED SHRIMP MASALA WITH COUSCOUS SALAD

✔ **WHY THIS RECIPE WORKS:** Grilled shrimp, rubbed with a potent paste made from garam masala, chili powder, sweet paprika, ginger, and garlic, delivered an exotic dinner for two that was ready in no time. To ensure that the shrimp cooked through evenly, we packed them tightly onto two skewers. An easy-to-make yogurt dipping sauce served as a cooling counterpoint to the boldly spiced shrimp, and grilled zucchini and couscous salad, flavored with lemon, feta, and mint, made for a bright, fresh-tasting side dish.

THE BRINY, SWEET TASTE OF SHRIMP, COUPLED WITH its sheer convenience and ease of cooking, make shrimp one of our favorite go-to proteins when cooking for two. Plus, a bag of frozen shrimp can be kept on hand in the freezer, making it ideal for a last-minute meal. But rather than simply grill our shrimp and spritz it with some lemon juice, we looked to elevate our entrée to an exotic dinner for two boasting all the rich, intense flavors and colors of Indian cuisine. We wanted a lively dish in the spirit of an Indian masala, featuring tender, juicy shrimp that tasted of warm, potent spices and was a showstopper on the plate, with its rich, red hue and lightly charred exterior. To complete our dinner, we looked to serve it with an effortless, yet brightly flavored, side dish.

To infuse our shrimp with big flavor, we planned to make a spice paste, which we'd apply prior to grilling. First things first; we started with the spice blend. *Masala* means spice mixture, and the ingredients in a masala blend depend largely on the whims of the cook. To keep things simple, we began with store-bought garam masala, which is a blend of warm spices such as cardamom, black pepper, cinnamon, and coriander. To make a paste that would stick to the shrimp, we stirred in a tablespoon of vegetable oil. The oil would pull double duty, simultaneously giving the paste the right texture while helping the fat-soluble spices bloom and develop in flavor over the heat of the grill.

We tossed the shrimp into the paste and then threaded them onto skewers. Our first test was promising, but the dish definitely needed some work. The spice blend alone was rather flat, and the paste was far too thick, giving the spices a raw flavor that tasters disliked. The paste

also lacked the characteristic red hue of many masalas, so we added a combination of paprika and chili powder to add complexity and color. To add freshness to the paste, we added minced garlic, ginger, lemon zest, and a bit of lemon juice. Finally, we increased the amount of oil to loosen the paste so it wouldn't clump on the shrimp. What a difference! The looser texture of the paste allowed the spices to bloom, alleviating the unpleasant rawness of the previous test, and the combination of fresh aromatics and dried spices gave the paste a bright complexity.

While the spice paste was now balanced, it was still intensely flavored with a touch of heat from the garlic and chili paste. Many of the masala recipes we researched included a dairy element—either heavy cream or yogurt—to mitigate the overwhelming spiciness. Serving the shrimp skewers with a yogurt sauce seemed like a great way to tame the heat. Though plain yogurt worked fine, we preferred the thicker, richer texture of Greek yogurt. To unite the dish, we stirred a small amount of our spice blend into the yogurt before we added the oil to turn it into a paste. This livened up our yogurt sauce, though it still needed some salt and acidity. A splash of lemon juice and a pinch of salt and pepper did the trick.

With our masala ready to go, we turned to the shrimp. Lean shrimp can easily become tough and dry, especially when cooked over a super-hot grill. A bit of trial and error taught us how to avoid these pitfalls. Packing the shrimp tightly on two skewers ensured that they cooked more slowly and kept them from spinning on the skewers when we flipped them, and building an ultrahot fire meant our shrimp picked up great grill marks in a short amount of time and didn't have to stay over the heat any longer than necessary. When a nice crust had formed on the first side, which took about 2 minutes, we flipped the skewers and gave the second side a few minutes to finish up. Our shrimp were not only perfectly tender with a good amount of char on the outside, but they also offered big flavor.

Having pulled off great-tasting grilled shrimp masala, we set our sights on a simple side dish. Tasters liked the idea of a salad starring grilled zucchini, so we sliced one in half lengthwise, brushed it with oil, and tossed it on our super-hot grill right before we placed our shrimp skewers on the grate. Once it was done, we cut it into ½-inch pieces. To keep our side dish as interesting and brightly flavored as our entrée, we bypassed

GRILLED SPICY SHRIMP MASALA WITH ZUCCHINI AND COUSCOUS SALAD

the usual salad lettuces and tossed our zucchini chunks with cooked couscous, crumbled feta, lemon juice, and minced mint. Our zucchini and couscous salad provided a fresh-tasting partner to our boldly seasoned grilled shrimp.

Grilled Spicy Shrimp Masala with Zucchini and Couscous Salad

SERVES 2

Feel free to substitute 0 percent Greek yogurt for a lighter version of this dish. You will need two 12-inch metal skewers for this recipe.

- ½ cup boiling water
- ½ cup couscous
- 1 zucchini, halved lengthwise
- 3 tablespoons vegetable oil
- Salt and pepper
- ½ teaspoon grated lemon zest plus 2½ tablespoons juice
- 2 teaspoons garam masala
- 1½ teaspoons grated fresh ginger
- 1 garlic clove, minced
- 1 teaspoon paprika
- ½ teaspoon chili powder
- ½ teaspoon sugar
- ¼ cup plain Greek yogurt
- 12 ounces extra-large shrimp (21 to 25 per pound), peeled and deveined
- 2 ounces feta cheese, crumbled (½ cup)
- 2 tablespoons minced fresh mint or basil

1. Combine boiling water and couscous in medium bowl, cover, and let sit until liquid is absorbed and couscous is tender, about 5 minutes. Fluff with fork and set aside. Brush zucchini with 1 teaspoon oil and season with salt and pepper.

2. In large bowl, combine lemon zest, 4 teaspoons lemon juice, garam masala, ginger, garlic, paprika, chili powder, sugar, and ¼ teaspoon salt to make paste. In separate bowl, stir together ¼ teaspoon spice paste, ½ teaspoon lemon juice, and yogurt until combined. Season with salt and pepper to taste; set aside.

3. Stir 2 tablespoons oil into remaining spice paste, breaking up any clumps. Add shrimp to bowl with spice paste and toss to coat. Thread shrimp tightly onto two 12-inch metal skewers, alternating direction of heads and tails.

4A. FOR A CHARCOAL GRILL: Open bottom vent completely. Light large chimney starter mounded with charcoal briquettes (7 quarts). When top coals are partially covered with ash, pour evenly over grill. Set cooking grate in place, cover, and open lid vent completely. Heat grill until hot, about 5 minutes.

4B. FOR A GAS GRILL: Turn all burners to high, cover, and heat grill until hot, about 15 minutes.

5. Clean and oil cooking grate. Place zucchini on grill and cook (covered if using gas) until spottily charred on both sides, 10 to 15 minutes, flipping zucchini halfway through grilling.

6. When zucchini is flipped, place shrimp on grill and cook until lightly charred and opaque throughout, 2 to 3 minutes per side. Transfer shrimp skewers to platter, tent loosely with aluminum foil, and let rest while making salad.

7. Cut zucchini into ½-inch pieces. Gently fold zucchini, remaining 2 teaspoons oil, remaining 1 tablespoon lemon juice, feta, and mint into couscous and season with salt and pepper to taste. Serve with shrimp and yogurt sauce.

NOTES FROM THE TEST KITCHEN

CROWDING SHRIMP ONTO A SKEWER

Pass skewer through center of each shrimp. As you add shrimp to skewer, alternate direction of heads and tails for compact arrangement of about 8 shrimp. Shrimp should be crowded and touching each other.

THE BEST GARAM MASALA

This spice blend is a key ingredient in our Grilled Spicy Shrimp Masala, but making it from scratch can add a great deal of time to recipe preparation. In search of a good-tasting commercial garam masala, we tested a handful of top brands. Tasters' favorite was **McCormick Gourmet Collection Garam Masala** for its ability to both blend into dishes and round out their acidic and sweet notes. Tasters also liked the subtle warmth of cardamom, cinnamon, and cloves. Widely available in supermarkets, McCormick won praise from tasters for adding a mellow, well-balanced aroma to most dishes.

BRAISED COD PEPERONATA

CHILLED FRESH TOMATO SOUP

✓ WHY THIS RECIPE WORKS: To create a chilled tomato soup for two that offered complex flavor, we used a combination of fresh and roasted tomatoes, which gave us a bright, tangy freshness as well as a deep, sweet flavor. We also used a small amount of tomato paste and lightly roasted garlic and shallot to boost the soup's flavor. Cream is a common inclusion, but to keep our chilled tomato soup light and bright-tasting, we opted for a mere drizzle of olive oil, which added body and richness without weighing the soup down.

ON A SWELTERING DAY, AN ICY BOWL OF CHILLED soup is one of summer's great pleasures. Vegetable-filled gazpacho has its place, but ripe, peak-season tomatoes deserve a soup in which they don't have to share the spotlight. An ideal cold tomato soup captures the essence of the fruit in silky-smooth liquid form: light yet satisfying, savory yet sweet, and deeply flavorful yet simple. At its best, tomato soup is the perfect light summer meal for two; after all, it contains just tomatoes, plus a few additional seasonings.

But the many failed attempts at attaining tomato soup perfection in the test kitchen proved that exemplary fruit alone doesn't guarantee success. Our results ranged from the thin, mealy mess that we got from blending raw tomatoes with a couple of ice cubes to an overthickened, ketchuplike sludge that was the result of simmering tomatoes with tomato juice for half an hour before chilling. Determined to get it right, we loaded up on tomatoes and headed back into the test kitchen.

Before we started cooking, we studied our past recipe flops. It occurred to us that in order to get the best of both worlds—fresh yet potent flavor—a hybrid half-raw, half-cooked approach might be in order. We knew that oven roasting is an effective way to concentrate flavor, so we halved 1 pound of fruit crosswise (to help excess moisture escape) and experimented until we determined that roasting the tomatoes for about 25 minutes at 375 degrees was enough to intensify their taste. We also found that this method required no additional oil (a bonus for our lightened soup) as the moisture in the tomatoes kept them from completely shriveling up, and

just a quick spritz of vegetable oil spray on the baking sheet prevented them from sticking. We pureed the roasted tomatoes with an equal amount of uncooked fruit and strained out the skins and seeds, happily finding that this approach produced both deep, sweet flavor and bright, tangy freshness.

Though our pureed tomatoes offered rich flavor, we still needed to round out the profile of our soup. Red bell pepper (a common addition) was nixed, as it overwhelmed the tomatoes. Garlic and mild shallot seemed like natural additions but only if we tamed their raw pungency. We roasted two garlic cloves and one sliced shallot together with the tomatoes for the first 15 minutes, removing them from the oven as soon as they had softened. When we pureed the raw and roasted tomatoes with the gently roasted aromatics, the soup's flavor improved, but it was still missing some backbone. It made sense to turn to a test kitchen secret weapon: tomato paste, which is high in glutamates and adds depth and savory richness to a variety of recipes. We blended some into our next batch, and sure enough, a small dose of the sweet paste dramatically upped the flavor quotient. Finally, smoked paprika and cayenne pepper added even more layers of complexity.

With the flavor profile complete, we now had to focus on texture. As it stood, our soup was dismally thin and runny. Cream is a common thickener in chilled soups, but we wanted to keep our soup on the lighter side. Blending some bread with the tomatoes thickened the mixture, but its starchiness seemed out of place in our cool, fresh soup.

Inspiration struck as we noticed another test cook making a batch of mayonnaise. We watched the slow drizzle of oil into eggs transform into creamy billows as the ingredients formed an emulsion. Lo and behold, just 1 tablespoon of olive oil added gradually to the blender as we pureed the tomatoes added rich thickness. The fruity, peppery notes of the oil were an ideal accent to the savory-sweet tomatoes, and even with its addition, each serving was still low in fat. Strained and chilled for at least two hours to let the flavors blend, the soup was velvety and delicious.

Finally, as is the case with many soups, this one benefited greatly from a touch of acid and a sprinkle of fresh herbs. Just a teaspoon of sherry vinegar and a scattering of basil (mint works well, too) perked up all of the flavors. This healthy chilled tomato soup was now summertime perfection in a bowl—make that two bowls.

Chilled Fresh Tomato Soup

SERVES 2

In-season, locally grown tomatoes and high-quality extra-virgin olive oil are ideal for this recipe.

- 2 pounds tomatoes, cored
- 1 shallot, sliced thin
- 2 garlic cloves, unpeeled
- 2 teaspoons tomato paste
- ⅛ teaspoon smoked paprika (optional)
  Pinch cayenne pepper
  Salt
- 1 tablespoon extra-virgin olive oil
- 1 teaspoon sherry vinegar, plus extra as needed
- 1 tablespoon chopped fresh basil or mint
  Pepper (optional)

1. Adjust oven rack to middle position and heat oven to 375 degrees. Line rimmed baking sheet with aluminum foil and lightly spray with vegetable oil spray.

2. Cut 1 pound tomatoes in half horizontally and arrange cut side up on prepared baking sheet. Arrange shallot and garlic in single layer over 1 area of baking sheet. Roast for 15 minutes, then remove shallot and garlic. Return baking sheet to oven and continue to roast tomatoes until softened but not browned, 10 to 15 minutes longer. Let cool to room temperature, about 30 minutes.

3. Peel garlic cloves and place in blender with roasted shallot and roasted tomatoes. Cut remaining 1 pound tomatoes into eighths and add to blender along with tomato paste; paprika, if using; cayenne; and ½ teaspoon salt. Puree until smooth, about 30 seconds. With motor running, drizzle in olive oil in slow, steady stream.

4. Pour puree through fine-mesh strainer into nonreactive bowl, pressing on solids in strainer to extract as much liquid as possible. Discard solids. Stir in vinegar. Cover and refrigerate until well chilled and flavors have blended, at least 2 hours or up to 24 hours.

5. To serve, stir soup to recombine (liquid separates on standing). Taste and adjust seasoning with salt and vinegar, as needed. Ladle soup into chilled bowls, sprinkle with basil, and grind pepper, if using, over each. Serve immediately.

PER SERVING: Cal 180; Fat 9 g; Sat fat 1.5 g; Chol 0 mg; Carb 22 g; Protein 5 g; Fiber 5 g; Sodium 610 mg

NOTES FROM THE TEST KITCHEN

THE BEST BLENDERS

A good blender needs to tackle a variety of tasks—from crushing ice and making frozen drinks, to blending lump-free soups, smoothies, and milkshakes, and even making hummus—quickly and easily. To find the best one, we gathered nine models and put them through their paces, using them not only on the aforementioned tasks, but also pressing them into service every day for a month to make thick smoothies with fibrous frozen pineapple and stringy raw kale. We identified three key features that can make or break a blender's performance: long blades, each set at a different position and angle; a jar with a bowl-shaped bottom; and a relatively powerful (at least 750-watt) motor. In the end, two blenders clearly outperformed the others. The **Vitamix 5200**, left, is the longtime test kitchen favorite thanks to its durability, long-armed, well-configured blades, and souped-up (1,300-watt) motor—but it costs $449. Fortunately, our co-winner, **The Hemisphere Control by Breville**, right, costs less than half the price at $200. It sports all three key blender features we identified, and it sailed through all of our tests.

THE BEST TOMATO PASTE

Tomato paste is basically tomato puree with most of the moisture cooked out. It adds body, color, and intensity to many dishes, including pastas, stews, and soups. To find out which brand is best, we gathered 10 brands for a tasting: nine in small cans and one in a toothpaste-like tube. We had tasters sample the paste straight from the container, cooked by itself, and cooked in marinara sauce.

When the brands were sampled uncooked, tasters downgraded some for "dried herb" notes, including oregano. Because tomato paste is usually cooked, we sautéed each brand in a skillet and tasted again. Some pastes became dull; others sprang to life. In the marinara sauce, tasters leaned toward those pastes that provided long-simmered flavor and depth. But ultimately, we found that while better tomato pastes improved the taste of the marinara, no brand ruined the dish.

Overall scores were relatively close, but one paste came in slightly ahead of the pack. **Goya** tomato paste was praised for its "bright, robust tomato flavor." Tasters liked its sweetness (this brand had one of the highest levels of natural sugars in the lineup) yet found it well balanced.

SPAGHETTI AL LIMONE

✓ **WHY THIS RECIPE WORKS:** Spaghetti *al limone* comes together with just a handful of ingredients, making it the perfect weeknight dinner for two. But classic recipes go heavy on the cream to mitigate the acidity of fresh lemon juice. For a lighter dish, we turned to a slurry of cornstarch and half-and-half, which gave us the slightly thickened sauce we were looking for, but with a lot less fat. Grated lemon zest added more lemony kick without the acidity. Letting the sauced pasta sit, covered, for a few minutes allowed the pasta to absorb the flavors and the sauce to thicken.

SPAGHETTI AL LIMONE, A STAPLE OF SOUTHERN Italy, is a simply flavored pasta dish that puts the emphasis on bright lemony flavor, with a few key background ingredients to support it. Sure, it sounds like the ideal light and healthy pasta dish. Yet traditional recipes, and the version we had recently developed in the test kitchen, rely on heavy cream, Parmesan cheese, and a generous amount of olive oil to create a sauce that clings to each strand of spaghetti. We wanted to slim down and scale back this recipe to make a truly light and fresh pasta dish for two.

We already knew from testing our original full-fat recipe that the right amount of dairy fat serves a dual purpose. First, it dampens the sourness of the lemon by neutralizing some of the acids in the juice. Second, it actually changes the part of the lemon's flavor profile (the oils) responsible for the fruity, floral notes by working in tandem with the olive oil to emulsify those flavors into a form that really coats the tastebuds. We wanted to cut the fat that went into this dish, but without the rich ingredients to tame the bracing acidity of the lemon, the flavor was thrown totally out of balance.

We started by looking at what kinds of low-fat dairy might work in place of the heavy cream. Fat-free evaporated milk came to mind first since it has a rich, silken texture, but tasters found it too sweet and overpowering. Regular low-fat milk was pretty unimpressive also. Weak in flavor, it was easily overpowered by the lemon, and its thin consistency meant it didn't coat the pasta but rather sat at the bottom of the pot in a puddle. Half-and-half certainly had the desired richness and

was our best bet, but it didn't quite cling to each strand of spaghetti the way we wanted. We needed to find another ingredient to work as a thickener.

A little bit of light cream cheese seemed like a logical choice since it would maintain the dairy profile. Combined with the half-and-half, it gave the sauce more body, but tasters found that the one-dimensional and "generic cheese flavor" competed with the purer ingredients in the dish like the lemon and Parmesan. Cornstarch or flour often helps thicken sauces in the test kitchen, so that angle seemed worth a try. We tried mixing just ⅛ teaspoon of cornstarch into our half-and-half. We added the mixture to the pot and brought it up to a simmer with some of the starchy water we used to cook our spaghetti to give a little more volume, and *voilà*, we had a clean, silky sauce that lightly coated our pasta and really allowed the lemon to shine. Tossing the pasta in the sauce, then letting it rest, covered, for a couple of minutes ensured that the strands absorbed the flavors and gave the sauce a chance to thicken nicely.

To finish our pasta, we added a little chopped basil for fresh herbal flavor and color and a minced shallot for depth. At this point, our numbers were so low we didn't need to change anything else about the original recipe. We happily kept the grated Parmesan cheese (just 2 tablespoons), as it lent a nutty, salty tang and really brought our dish to life.

NOTES FROM THE TEST KITCHEN

THE BEST EXTRA-VIRGIN OLIVE OIL
Extra-virgin olive oil has a uniquely fruity flavor that makes it a great choice for a vinaigrette or a pesto, but the available options can be overwhelming. We recently gathered 10 brands and sampled them plain and warmed and tossed with pasta, looking for the best one. Many things can impact the quality and flavor of olive oil, but the type of olives, the harvest (earlier means greener, more peppery; later, more golden and mild), and processing are the most important factors. The best-quality oil comes from olives picked at their peak and processed as soon as possible, without heat or chemicals (which can coax more oil from the olives but at the expense of flavor). Our favorite oils were produced from a blend of olives and, thus, were well rounded. Our favorite is **Columela Extra Virgin Olive Oil** from Spain; it took top honors for its fruity flavor and excellent balance.

SPAGHETTI AL LIMONE

Spaghetti al Limone

SERVES 2

Because this recipe is so simple, it is important to use high-quality extra-virgin olive oil, fresh-squeezed lemon juice, and fresh basil here. Let the pasta rest briefly before serving so the flavors develop and the sauce thickens. See page 88 for a tip on how to measure out long strands of pasta without using a scale.

6 ounces spaghetti

Salt and pepper

2 teaspoons extra-virgin olive oil

1 small shallot, minced

⅛ teaspoon cornstarch

2 tablespoons half-and-half

½ teaspoon finely grated lemon zest plus 1 tablespoon juice

2 tablespoons finely grated Parmesan cheese

2 teaspoons chopped fresh basil

1. Bring 4 quarts water to boil in large pot. Add pasta and 1 tablespoon salt and cook, stirring often, until al dente. Reserve ¾ cup cooking water, then drain pasta and set aside.

2. Combine ½ teaspoon oil, shallot, and ⅛ teaspoon salt in now-empty pot. Cover and cook over medium-low heat, stirring occasionally, until softened, 3 to 5 minutes.

3. Whisk cornstarch into half-and-half, then whisk into pot along with ½ cup reserved cooking water. Bring to simmer and cook until thickened slightly, about 2 minutes.

4. Off heat, add cooked pasta and toss until coated. Add remaining 1½ teaspoons oil, lemon zest and juice, Parmesan, and ⅛ teaspoon pepper and toss to combine. Cover and let stand for 2 minutes, tossing frequently. Before serving, add remaining ¼ cup cooking water as needed to adjust consistency. Stir in basil and season with salt and pepper to taste. Serve.

PER SERVING: **Cal** 390; **Fat** 8 g; **Sat fat** 2.5 g; **Chol** 10 mg; **Carb** 66 g; **Protein** 13 g; **Fiber** 3 g; **Sodium** 500 mg

CHINESE CHICKEN SALAD

✔ WHY THIS RECIPE WORKS: To keep our scaled-down salad on the lighter side, we cut back on the oil in the dressing and bumped up the flavor with rice vinegar, fresh ginger, soy sauce, and hoisin sauce. Using a hybrid cooking method (browning, then poaching) delivered moist, tender chicken and required a minimal amount of fat. Thinly sliced cabbage, shredded carrot, sliced red bell pepper, and bean sprouts provided a good mix of textures and flavors and rounded out our salad. Rather than finish the dish with nuts, we opted for a handful of chow mein noodles, which contributed a big crunch factor.

TYPICALLY COMPOSED OF A MIXTURE OF TENDER chicken and bright vegetables tossed in a toasted sesame oil vinaigrette, Chinese chicken salad is quick to prepare and offers an enticing variety of tastes, textures, and visual appeal. But a heavy hand with oil can obscure any hint of freshness. Plus, we've seen a number of versions topped with overly generous handfuls of high-calorie cashews, peanuts, or sesame seeds. This dish would need some serious work to become a healthier dinner option, so we headed into the test kitchen right away, set on creating a simple version for two that was light and flavorful, with a mixture of crisp, colorful vegetables and moist chicken, tossed in a bright, well-balanced vinaigrette.

Since the dressing was responsible for most of the problems, that's where we started. We began with a basic vinaigrette, scaled down to serve two, using ¼ cup of canola oil, an amount called for in several recipes we found. We used the vinaigrette to dress a simple salad of thinly sliced cabbage, shredded carrot, and sliced chicken. Not surprisingly, this much oil made the dressing heavy, dull, and too fatty for our lightened salad. With 2 tablespoons of oil, the dressing was reasonably light, but tasters were convinced we could go lower still. We found we could go as low as 2 teaspoons—this amount added the right degree of richness without obscuring the other flavors. Our next task was to nail down the other components of our dressing.

For the vinegar, we stuck with tradition and used rice vinegar; its mild acidity and slight sweetness were ideal for keeping this salad light and bright-tasting. Fresh ginger seemed like a natural addition and added a bright zing, and soy sauce contributed an earthy, malty richness. But our dressing still lacked depth and, because it contained so little oil, didn't cling to the cabbage. So we rummaged through our Asian pantry ingredients and spotted hoisin sauce. Hoisin added the sweetness and spiciness we were looking for, and its thick texture gave us a dressing with viscosity. A final drizzle (just ½ teaspoon) of sesame oil added a rich nuttiness without contributing too much extra fat.

Next, we moved on to the chicken. We wanted it to be fresh and moist, so leftover roast or grilled chicken wasn't an option. At the same time, we didn't want to make preparing the chicken a production, especially since we had determined that a single boneless, skinless breast—both lean and quick-cooking—was the right amount for a salad serving two. Considering cooking technique, we wanted the flavor and color of browning, but browning both sides of the chicken breast required more oil than we wanted to use. We found our answer in a half-sautéing, half-poaching method that required very little fat. First we browned the chicken on one side in just ½ teaspoon of oil, then we flipped the chicken over, added a small amount of water to the skillet, reduced the heat, and covered the skillet until the chicken was cooked through. This method yielded moist, flavorful chicken. So the chicken would be evenly distributed throughout the salad, we simply let it cool, then shredded it with two forks before combining it with the vegetables and dressing.

Now all we had left to do was decide which vegetables to include. Thinly sliced cabbage and shredded carrot were a given. To add color, texture, and a bit of sweetness, we added half a red bell pepper, cut into thin slices. Tasters also appreciated a few handfuls of bean sprouts for their fresh, crisp bite and earthy flavor; a single scallion and some minced cilantro contributed fresh, grassy notes. Finally, for a big crunch factor, we included some crispy chow mein noodles.

Our revamped Chinese chicken salad offered all the exciting textures and flavors we expected—but not the high fat count.

Chinese Chicken Salad
SERVES 2

Chow mein noodles can be found in most supermarkets with other Asian ingredients; La Choy is the most widely available brand. See page 63 for a recipe to use up the leftover cabbage.

1 (8-ounce) boneless, skinless chicken breast, trimmed of all visible fat
   Salt and pepper
2½ teaspoons canola oil
½ small head napa cabbage, shredded (4 cups)
1 small carrot, peeled and shredded
½ small red bell pepper, cut into ¼-inch-wide strips
1 ounce (½ cup) bean sprouts
¼ cup chow mein noodles
1 scallion, sliced thin on bias
2 teaspoons minced fresh cilantro
3½ tablespoons rice vinegar
2½ tablespoons hoisin sauce
2½ teaspoons low-sodium soy sauce
1½ teaspoons grated fresh ginger
½ teaspoon toasted sesame oil

1. Pat chicken dry with paper towels and season with ⅛ teaspoon salt and ⅛ teaspoon pepper. Heat ½ teaspoon canola oil in 8-inch nonstick skillet over medium-high heat until just smoking. Brown chicken well on first side, 5 to 7 minutes. Flip chicken, add ½ cup water, and reduce heat to medium-low. Cover and continue to cook until chicken registers 160 degrees, 5 to 7 minutes longer.

2. Transfer chicken to cutting board and let rest for 5 minutes. Using 2 forks, shred chicken into bite-size pieces.

3. In large bowl, combine shredded chicken, cabbage, carrot, bell pepper, sprouts, chow mein noodles, scallion, and cilantro. In small bowl, whisk remaining 2 teaspoons canola oil, vinegar, hoisin, soy sauce, ginger, and sesame oil together until combined. Drizzle dressing over salad and toss gently to coat. Season with salt and pepper to taste. Serve.

PER SERVING: Cal 340; Fat 12 g; Sat Fat 1.5 g; Chol 75 mg; Carb 29 g; Protein 29 g; Fiber 5 g; Sodium 1280 mg

SAUTÉED CHICKEN BREASTS WITH MANGO RELISH

✓ **WHY THIS RECIPE WORKS:** Sautéed chicken breasts are an easy answer to "What's for dinner?" when cooking for two. But too often, they make for a ho-hum meal. To liven up the weeknight dinner hour, we paired them with a sweet and spicy mango relish. To cook the lean chicken breasts, we coated them in flour and started them in a hot pan with a modicum of oil so they could take on some color, then turned down the heat so they could cook through more gently and evenly and stay moist. Fresh mango, tossed with Peppadew peppers, lime juice, and cilantro, gave our dinner a tropical feel and bright, fresh flavor.

SAUTÉED BONELESS CHICKEN BREASTS ARE A STAPLE not only in a healthy kitchen, but also in the for-two kitchen. This popular cut is packed with protein, virtually fat free, and frequently sold in convenient packages of two. Boneless chicken breasts also cook quickly and easily, needing only a skillet and a modicum of oil. The only problem? This simple supper can grow tiresome quite quickly, becoming a ho-hum go-to entrée, rather than a showcase for bright, bold flavors. To bring our chicken breasts back from the brink of boredom, we looked to pair them with a light and lively sauce that would wake up the palate. But before we got started, we wanted to make sure we had our sautéing technique nailed down—after all, turning out golden-brown, moist chicken breasts is half the battle.

We began by selecting our pan and preparing the chicken. After a few tests, we found that a large, heavy-bottomed skillet was best. Given that we were working with just two chicken breasts, we tried using an 8-inch pan first, but it crowded the chicken and caused it to steam. A 10-inch pan was clearly the way to go. Though we were using 6-ounce chicken breasts, we knew that no matter the total weight of each breast, the thin tip and the opposite end, which is much thicker, would cook at different rates. To remedy this problem, we pounded the chicken breasts to an even ½-inch thickness. Now we were ready to sauté.

In order for anything to brown properly in a skillet, at least some oil is necessary. To keep this dish on the lighter side, we didn't want to add a big pour of oil to the pan, but how much was really necessary to keep the chicken from sticking? We started with a single tablespoon of canola oil and tried dialing back 1 teaspoon at a time. It turned out that we could cut only 1 teaspoon before the chicken fused to the pan.

The problem we then found with our low-oil method was that the chicken took on very little browning—it had only spots of color—despite the fact that we heated the oil until it just started to smoke before adding the breasts. The smooth surface of the breast meat was going to need a little extra texture in order to turn golden brown. For our next test, we coated the chicken in a little flour to aid in browning (and to help protect the breasts from drying out). This worked like a charm, giving our chicken great color and a nice crust.

But even though our chicken now looked great, the finished product still needed some work. Although the chicken was cooked evenly, the exterior portions of the meat were dry and stringy. Up until this point, we had been sautéing the chicken over medium-high heat for the entire cooking time. Perhaps we needed to take a gentler tack. For our next test, we browned the chicken on the first side as before, but when we flipped the breasts, we reduced the heat to medium-low and let them finish cooking over the gentler heat level for just a few minutes. Perfect.

Having nailed the cooking technique, we had yet to develop a recipe for a light yet lively sauce to keep our dinner interesting. The idea of a fresh salsa or relish was appealing because we wouldn't have to add another pot to the stovetop or turn on the oven. We homed in on a fruit relish made from fresh, sweet mango, which would offer a bright-tasting, tropical counterpoint to our moist, golden-brown chicken. A few jarred Peppadew peppers packed just the right amount of heat, and their tangy bite contrasted perfectly with the sweetness of the mango. A tablespoon of fresh lime juice lent brightness, and a sprinkling of fresh cilantro added herbal complexity. We let our fresh relish chill for 30 minutes so that all the flavors could meld.

With that, we had a dish that boasted both fresh, bright flavor and savory depth—and though it had started with a kitchen standby, it was far from mundane.

Sautéed Chicken Breasts with Sweet and Spicy Mango Relish

SERVES 2

Pounding the thicker ends of the chicken breasts ensures even cooking.

- ½ mango, peeled and cut into ¼-inch pieces
- 5 jarred Peppadew peppers or pickled hot cherry peppers, chopped
- 1 tablespoon lime juice
- 2 teaspoons chopped fresh cilantro
   Salt and pepper
- ¼ cup all-purpose flour
- 2 (6-ounce) boneless, skinless chicken breasts, trimmed of all visible fat and pounded to even ½-inch thickness
- 2 teaspoons canola oil

1. In small bowl, combine mango, peppers, lime juice, and cilantro. Season with salt and pepper to taste. Cover and refrigerate until flavors meld, about 30 minutes.

USE IT UP: MANGO

Mango Lassi

SERVES 2

You may need to sweeten the drink with extra honey, depending on the sweetness of the mango. Be sure to use fresh mango; frozen mango will make a dull-tasting lassi.

- ½ mango, peeled and chopped
- 1 cup plain low-fat yogurt
- ½ cup ice water
- 2 teaspoons honey, plus extra as needed
- 2 teaspoons lime juice
   Pinch salt

Puree all ingredients together in blender until smooth, about 1 minute. Strain mixture through fine-mesh strainer, pressing on solids to extract as much liquid as possible; discard any solids left in strainer. Serve in chilled glasses.

PER 1-CUP SERVING: Cal 130; Fat 2 g; Sat Fat 1.5 g; Chol 10 mg; Carb 23 g; Protein 6 g; Fiber 1 g; Sodium 160 mg

---

2. Meanwhile, spread flour in shallow dish. Pat chicken dry with paper towels and season with ⅛ teaspoon salt and ⅛ teaspoon pepper. Lightly dredge chicken in flour and shake off excess.

3. Heat oil in 10-inch skillet over medium-high heat until just smoking. Add chicken and cook until well browned on first side, 6 to 8 minutes. Flip chicken, reduce heat to medium, and continue to cook until chicken registers 160 degrees, 6 to 8 minutes longer. Transfer to platter, tent loosely with aluminum foil, and let rest for 5 minutes. Serve with relish.

PER SERVING: Cal 340; Fat 9 g; Sat Fat 1.5 g; Chol 110 mg; Carb 24 g; Protein 38 g; Fiber 2 g; Sodium 880 mg

---

NOTES FROM THE TEST KITCHEN

POUNDING CHICKEN BREASTS

To ensure chicken breasts cook through evenly, simply pound the thicker end until the whole breast is roughly the same thickness. Though one breast may still be larger than the other, they will at least cook at a similar rate.

ALL ABOUT PEPPADEW PEPPERS

Peppadew is the brand name for the pickled grape-size red pepper known as Juanita. The Juanita plant was reportedly discovered in 1993 by Johannes Steenkamp, who found it growing in the garden of his vacation home in South Africa. His first bite of the pepper delivered a significant shot of heat. To capitalize on their spicy flavor profile, he pickled the peppers in a simple sugar and vinegar mixture.

Today, Peppadews are available in mild and hot varieties (the heat is adjusted by adding more or fewer dried, ground seeds to the pickling liquid), as well as in a new yellow Goldew variety, which has less heat.

While a comparison to these unusual peppers is hard to make, their closest competitor might be the pickled cherry pepper. When we compared hot Peppadews with hot cherry peppers, the biggest difference was the pronounced sweetness of the Peppadews, which made them the favorite of our tasters. We found that the subtleties of the Peppadew flavor were lost in cooked sauces, so we recommend eating them raw on antipasto platters and in salads and relishes, or in cooked dishes like pizza, where they can maintain their identity.

TURKEY TACO SALAD

TURKEY TACO SALAD

✔ **WHY THIS RECIPE WORKS:** For a lighter yet still flavorful taco salad for two, we skipped the deep-fryer and baked our tortillas instead, which gave us a pair of golden, ultracrisp taco shells with a lot less fuss and fat. Rather than use ground beef in the filling, we reached for leaner ground turkey; sautéed aromatics and tomato sauce added savory depth, and a hefty dose of chili powder lent heat and spicy flavor. For more heartiness, we included beans in our salad, along with cherry tomatoes and shredded romaine. Dressing the salad with a bit of lime juice ensured that it was both light and fresh-tasting.

ON PAPER, THE TACO SALAD SOUNDS LIKE A LIGHTER alternative to more indulgent Tex-Mex fare like quesadillas, burritos, or nachos. But once you consider the fried shell, the saucy, meaty filling, and the mountain of grated cheese piled on top, this dish becomes much less virtuous. Still, the idea of a healthier taco salad was intriguing. We decided to figure out how to slash the fat while keeping the bright flavors and great textures intact, so we would have the perfect main course for a fiesta for two.

As the edible bowl for our salad, the crunchy fried tortilla shell was the first fatty component we decided to tackle. Deep frying tortillas was obviously a no-go. Not only does frying increase the fat content of the tortilla to unacceptable levels, but it also requires cups of oil and can create a mess on the stovetop, making a simple salad for two into a big hassle. We tried serving our salad in a regular bowl and crumbling baked tortilla chips over the top, but tasters quickly turned up their noses at the idea. While the crunch was good, there wasn't enough of it. Plus, without the taco bowl, the salad seemed to have lost its identity. It was clear we couldn't do away with the taco shell. Instead, we explored ways that we could lighten it, while still retaining the ultracrisp, golden exterior.

When looking for a lighter snack option, we often make our own tortilla chips using store-bought flour tortillas; cut into wedges and spritzed with vegetable oil spray, the chips crisp nicely in a 425-degree oven. Perhaps this would be our answer. But how would we turn a flat tortilla into a bowl? We'd need a mold. After pulling out and tinkering with each and every oven-safe piece of equipment in the test kitchen, including ramekins and measuring cups, we finally landed on the obvious choice: soup bowls. To soften our two flour tortillas, we microwaved them briefly; we sprayed them with vegetable oil spray so they would turn golden and wouldn't dry out, then draped them over the bowls before popping them into the oven. Ten minutes later, we had incredibly crisp, golden taco shells that were much healthier than the deep-fried version.

Taco bowls in hand, we addressed the rest of the dish. We knew we wanted our salad topped with a hearty, saucy meat mixture, just like the taco salads found in restaurants. But since we were going for a lightened recipe, we bypassed the ground beef and turned instead to ground turkey. Six ounces, combined with our other salad components, gave us just the right amount for two. To ramp up its flavor, we sautéed the turkey with chopped onion, some garlic, and chili powder, then stirred in a bit of tomato sauce and chicken broth for moisture, sweetness, and savory depth. After the mixture simmered for a bit, tasters dug in with gusto, but they found the flavor a little dull. A splash of cider vinegar and a spoonful of brown sugar brightened things right up.

Moving on to the actual "salad" of the dish, we started with some shredded romaine lettuce, which offered a hearty base to support the saucy filling. Quartered cherry tomatoes provided sweetness and a pop of color, and a thinly sliced scallion and chopped cilantro added herbal, grassy notes. In our research we found that many recipes also included beans. We thought this would add heartiness to our dish, so we did a few tests with black beans, kidneys, and pintos. Each type of bean offered the same nutritional benefit—adding extra protein with very little additional fat—but we found that black beans stood up best to the turkey filling. Half a can (¾ cup) was just the right amount for two.

Cheese is standard when it comes to taco salads, but it adds a great deal of extra fat and calories. Clearly, we'd have to tread carefully here. We often turn to reduced-fat cheeses when lightening dishes, so we decided to give it a go here. First, we went for convenience and tried a preshredded Mexican cheese blend. Unfortunately, tasters found its flavor to be a little flat. Instead, we tried light cheddar, which we grated ourselves. Just 2 tablespoons per taco bowl, sprinkled over the salad and filling, provided the savory, cheesy flavor we were after.

Finally, we moved on to the dressing for the salad. Many taco salads are just topped with salsa, but we found it overwhelmed the lettuce and competed with the flavor of the saucy turkey mixture. Some recipes include a vinaigrette, but in our tests we found that oil-based dressings weighed down the salad. Moving in a more conservative direction, we tried simply tossing the lettuce, beans, and tomatoes with a tablespoon of lime juice. While subtle, the juice added just the right amount of acidity without overpowering our myriad ingredients or contributing much in the way of fat and calories.

At last, we had a taco salad that offered all the bright flavors and appealing textures of the full-fat restaurant version, but without any of the guilt.

USE IT UP: BLACK BEANS

Chunky Black Bean Dip
SERVES 2

You can substitute 1 minced small shallot for the scallion. Serve this dip with baked tortilla or pita chips.

- ¾ cup canned black beans, rinsed
- 1 teaspoon olive oil
- 1 tomato, cored, seeded, and cut into ½-inch pieces
- 2 scallions, minced
- 1 tablespoon lime juice
- 1 garlic clove, minced
- ⅛ teaspoon cumin
- Salt and pepper

Mash beans and oil together in medium bowl until coarsely mashed. Stir in tomato, scallions, lime juice, garlic, and cumin. Season with salt and pepper to taste. Serve.

PER ½-CUP SERVING: Cal 100; Fat 2.5 g; Sat Fat 0 g; Chol 0 mg; Carb 18 g; Protein 4 g; Fiber 4 g; Sodium 230 mg

---

Turkey Taco Salad
SERVES 2

Be sure to use ground turkey, not ground turkey breast (also labeled 99 percent fat free), in this recipe.

TACO BOWLS
- 2 (10-inch) flour tortillas
- Vegetable oil spray
- ½ teaspoon canola oil
- 1 small onion, chopped fine
- 2 teaspoons chili powder
- 1 garlic clove, minced
- 6 ounces 93 percent lean ground turkey
- ½ cup canned tomato sauce
- ¼ cup low-sodium chicken broth
- 1 teaspoon cider vinegar
- ½ teaspoon light brown sugar
- Salt and pepper

SALAD
- 1 romaine lettuce heart (6 ounces), shredded
- ¾ cup canned black beans, rinsed
- 4 ounces cherry or grape tomatoes, quartered
- 1 scallion, sliced thin
- 2 tablespoons chopped fresh cilantro
- 1 tablespoon lime juice
- Salt and pepper
- 1 ounce 50 percent light cheddar cheese, shredded (¼ cup)

1. **FOR THE TACO BOWLS:** Adjust oven rack to middle position and heat oven to 425 degrees. Arrange 2 ovensafe soup bowls upside down on rimmed baking sheet (or use 2 slightly flattened 3-inch aluminum foil balls). Place tortillas on plate, cover with damp paper towel, and microwave until warm and pliable, about 20 seconds.

2. Generously spray both sides of warm tortillas with oil spray. Drape tortillas over soup bowls, pressing top flat and pinching sides to create 4-sided bowl. Bake until tortillas are golden and crisp, 8 to 10 minutes, rotating sheet halfway through baking. Let cool upside down.

3. Meanwhile, heat oil in 10-inch nonstick skillet over medium-high heat until shimmering. Add onion and cook until softened, about 5 minutes. Stir in

MAKING TACO BOWLS

Warm tortillas in microwave until pliable, then spray with vegetable oil spray. Place 2 ovensafe soup bowls upside down on baking sheet; drape tortillas on top. Press tops flat and pinch sides to create two 4-sided bowls.

chili powder and garlic and cook until fragrant, about 30 seconds. Add turkey and cook, breaking up meat with wooden spoon, until almost cooked through but still slightly pink, about 2 minutes. Stir in tomato sauce, broth, vinegar, and sugar and simmer until slightly thickened, about 5 minutes; mixture will be saucy. Season with salt and pepper to taste.

4. FOR THE SALAD: Combine lettuce, beans, tomatoes, scallion, and 1 tablespoon cilantro in large bowl; toss with lime juice and season with salt and pepper to taste. Place tortilla bowls on individual plates. Divide salad between bowls and top with turkey mixture. Sprinkle with cheese and remaining 1 tablespoon cilantro. Serve.

PER SERVING: Cal 430; Fat 15 g; Sat fat 4.5 g; Chol 55 mg; Carb 46 g; Protein 30 g; Fiber 7 g; Sodium 1070 mg

SAUTÉED BONELESS PORK CHOPS WITH PORT WINE AND CHERRY SAUCE

✔ WHY THIS RECIPE WORKS: For a pair of juicy, tender pork chops, we had to sauté them over two different heat levels. First, we seared them on one side over medium-high heat for a nicely browned exterior, then we flipped them over and turned the heat down to let them finish cooking through. To dress up our chops, we created two effortless yet impressive pan sauces with the browned bits left behind in the pan.

BONELESS PORK CHOPS HAVE BECOME A POPULAR alternative for those looking to cook with leaner meat and wanting an option beyond chicken breasts. But as we began our research, we realized that most pork chop recipes out there were more likely to result in sad, poorly cooked chops with bland, heavy sauces (usually relying on lots of butter and cream) than something you would proudly bring to the table. Our goal was to create a pair of perfectly cooked pan-seared pork chops with a light pan sauce that would be flavorful, rich, and anything but boring.

First we focused on the pork. Boneless pork loin chops are a great option for a quick meal, since they cook relatively fast. After several tests with various sizes of pork chops, we discovered that extra-thick chops (those over 1 inch thick) required both the stovetop and the oven to cook properly; this felt like too much work for a weeknight meal for two. Thin chops (about ¼ inch), on the other hand, were impossible to keep juicy. A ¾-inch chop proved perfect: thick enough to stay moist during sautéing, but thin enough that we could cook it entirely on the stovetop.

Next, we experimented with cooking methods that would yield nicely browned chops without requiring a big pour of oil. The first technique we tried was browning the chops in a little oil, then covering them to finish cooking through. Doing this yielded a fairly moist piece of meat, but covering the pan created steam and ruined the chops' attractive and flavorful golden-brown exterior. The small amount of oil worked well (just a teaspoon did the trick), but a more traditional approach would be necessary. Unfortunately, the medium-high heat needed to properly brown the chops on the first side left us with dry, overcooked chops when we finished cooking them all the way through over that heat level. As with our Sautéed Chicken Breasts with Sweet and Spicy Mango Relish (page 177), we found it necessary to use two different heat levels. We seared the chops on one side over medium-high heat, and once they developed a deeply browned crust, we flipped the chops and reduced the heat to medium, allowing the chops to slowly reach 145 degrees. At this point, we removed them from the pan to rest for a few minutes, which allowed their juices to redistribute and the temperature to continue to rise (this is called carryover cooking) to the 150-degree mark. These chops were nicely browned and juicy.

During these tests, we found that a 10-inch skillet was necessary to build the exterior crust we desired; a pan that was any smaller crowded the chops and they simply steamed, while a pan that was larger scorched where the surface wasn't covered by meat. Testing both traditional and nonstick skillets, we were surprised to see that the two performed similarly well. We opted to use a traditional skillet, however, so that we could take advantage of the fond left behind—an opportunity to build our pan sauce.

Looking for flavors that best complemented the pork, we found that a broth-based sauce with a sweet component had the most potential. Tasters preferred chicken broth over beef for its unobtrusive nature, and dried cherries for their concentrated sweet-tart flavor. Shallot, rosemary, and port also helped to deepen the flavors of the sauce. To create an easy variation, we swapped in a chopped apple, cider, and freshly grated ginger for a quick chutney.

After just one bite, we realized we didn't miss the more typical (and higher-fat) ingredients we'd seen elsewhere, especially when we had such bold, flavorful options for topping our perfectly cooked chops.

Sautéed Boneless Pork Chops with Port Wine and Cherry Sauce

SERVES 2

Other dried fruit, such as figs (cut into slices), raisins, or cranberries, can be substituted for the cherries. There is no need to buy expensive port for this dish; less costly bottles will work fine.

- 2 (6- to 8-ounce) boneless pork chops, ¾ to 1 inch thick, trimmed of all visible fat
  Salt and pepper
- 1½ teaspoons canola oil
- 1 shallot, minced
- ½ teaspoon minced fresh rosemary
- ¾ cup low-sodium chicken broth
- ¼ cup ruby port
- ¼ cup dried cherries

1. Pat pork chops dry with paper towels and season with ⅛ teaspoon salt and ⅛ teaspoon pepper. Heat 1 teaspoon oil in 10-inch skillet over medium-high

heat until just smoking. Brown chops well on first side, about 3 minutes.

2. Flip chops over, reduce heat to medium, and continue to cook until chops register 145 degrees, 5 to 10 minutes longer. Transfer pork to platter, tent loosely with aluminum foil, and let rest while making sauce.

3. Add remaining ½ teaspoon oil, shallot, and rosemary to now-empty skillet and cook over medium heat until shallot is softened, about 2 minutes. Stir in broth, port, and cherries, scraping up any browned bits. Bring to simmer and cook until reduced to ¾ cup, about 5 minutes.

4. Add any accumulated meat juices to simmering sauce and cook until sauce has thickened slightly, about 2 minutes. Season with salt and pepper to taste. Spoon sauce over pork and serve.

PER SERVING: Cal 370; Fat 10 g; Sat Fat 2.5 g; Chol 110 mg; Carb 20 g; Protein 40 g; Fiber 2 g; Sodium 450 mg

Sautéed Boneless Pork Chops with Quick Ginger-Apple Chutney

SERVES 2

We like the flavor of Granny Smith apples here; however, any type of apple will work fine.

- 2 (6- to 8-ounce) boneless pork chops, ¾ to 1 inch thick, trimmed of all visible fat
  Salt and pepper
- 1½ teaspoons canola oil
- 1 Granny Smith apple, peeled, cored, and cut into ½-inch pieces

1 **shallot, minced**

1½ **teaspoons grated fresh ginger**

⅛ **teaspoon ground allspice**

½ **cup apple cider**

2 **tablespoons packed light brown sugar**

1. Pat pork chops dry with paper towels and season with ⅛ teaspoon salt and ⅛ teaspoon pepper. Heat 1 teaspoon oil in 10-inch skillet over medium-high heat until just smoking. Brown chops well on first side, about 3 minutes.

2. Flip chops over, reduce heat to medium, and continue to cook until chops register 145 degrees, 5 to 10 minutes longer. Transfer pork to platter, tent loosely with aluminum foil, and let rest while making chutney.

3. Add remaining ½ teaspoon oil, apple, and shallot to now-empty skillet, cover, and cook over medium-low heat until apple is softened, 8 to 10 minutes. Uncover, stir in ginger and allspice, and cook until fragrant, about 30 seconds. Stir in cider and brown sugar, scraping up any browned bits. Bring to simmer and cook until sauce has thickened slightly, about 4 minutes.

4. Add any accumulated meat juices to simmering sauce. Season with salt and pepper to taste. Spoon sauce over pork and serve.

PER SERVING: Cal 370; Fat 9 g; Sat Fat 2.5 g; Chol 110 mg; Carb 32 g; Protein 39 g; Fiber 1 g; Sodium 240 mg

CHILLED RICE NOODLES WITH SHRIMP

✔ **WHY THIS RECIPE WORKS:** Taking our inspiration from Japanese cuisine, we created a chilled noodle dish that boasted light, bright flavors. Though it's traditionally eaten with chopsticks, we transformed this dish into a fork-friendly supper for two by turning the standard dipping sauce into a deeply flavored dressing. A simple dashi (a sweet, briny broth) made with kombu and bonito flakes provided the basis for our dressing; soy sauce and ginger punched it up a bit. Steeping the rice noodles in hot water ensured that they were tender, and using the same water to poach shrimp streamlined our recipe and guaranteed our chilled noodle dish was refreshingly light yet satisfying.

A BOWL OF JAPANESE-STYLE CHILLED NOODLES CAN make a refreshing change of pace from the usual go-to Asian noodle dishes like pad thai and lo mein. As the name implies, these noodles are served in ice water with a bowl of dipping sauce and pickled ginger on the side. Traditionally, diners use chopsticks to dip the noodles a few at a time into the soy-based sauce, which is usually seasoned with dashi (a seafood broth) and ginger. With its delicate balance of Japanese flavors, this refreshing dish seemed like it would be perfect for our roster of lighter entrées for two. While we set out to develop our own recipe, we also hoped to make chilled noodles more approachable for the American dinner table—that meant putting away the chopsticks and transforming the dipping sauce into a dressing to pull the whole thing together for a fork-friendly dish.

First, we tackled the backbone of our dish, the dashi, or broth. Dashi is a simple seafood broth made from kombu (dried kelp), bonito flakes (dried, smoked fish flakes), and water. While the ingredient list might make dashi seem a complicated endeavor, the procedure is actually quite simple. Plus, most supermarkets now carry both kombu and bonito flakes in their international foods aisle. To make dashi, the water and kombu are brought slowly to a boil. Once the water bubbles, the pot is removed from the heat, and the bonito flakes are added and steeped for just a few minutes to infuse the liquid with their flavor. To finish, the kombu and bonito flakes are strained out, and the dashi is complete. Since this was a fairly easy, foolproof way to make our dashi, and neither kombu nor bonito flakes added any discernible fat or calories, we adhered to this method. In just a few minutes, we had an intensely flavored broth. However, it still needed a few flavor tweaks.

To ramp up our dashi, we added a handful of traditional seasonings. Soy sauce added rich, savory depth; a few spoonfuls of mirin, which is a tawny, sweetened Japanese rice wine, added distinctive flavor; some grated fresh ginger provided a fresher, less obtrusive flavor than the pickled ginger; and a small amount of sugar rounded out the other ingredients. With the dashi nicely seasoned and offering a rich taste, we moved it to the refrigerator to chill.

Next, we considered the noodles. Rice noodles are available in a variety of thicknesses, but for our dish, tasters preferred thin noodles, which offered a delicate feel that matched the tone of the subtle yet well-seasoned dashi. Like other noodles, rice noodles require an ample amount of water for cooking. We achieved the best results by boiling a pot full of water, then steeping the noodles in the pot (off the heat) until they were tender. When the noodles were tender, we found it best to quickly rinse them under cold water to stop their cooking and wash away any residual starches that might turn them gummy.

After the noodles were sufficiently cooled, we tossed them with our chilled broth and considered additional elements. To complement our broth and turn our noodle dish into a satisfying supper, we added 8 ounces of shrimp. Since we were already bringing out a pot of water to boil the noodles, we decided to poach the shrimp in the same pot before cooking the noodles; this step saved us both prep and dishwashing time. To add a little crunch, we topped our noodles with cucumber slices. A sprinkle of fresh scallions contributed a grassy, oniony quality that balanced the brininess of the shrimp and broth.

While not exactly identical to what you might find in Japan, our dish definitely captured the flavorful lightness of traditional chilled noodle dishes—and we didn't need any fancy chopstick skills to enjoy it.

Chilled Rice Noodles with Shrimp

SERVES 2

Bonito flakes are dried fish flakes found in the international aisle at the supermarket, or at Asian and natural foods markets; they add a distinct smoky flavor to this dish. Rice noodles can vary in sodium content; make sure you use a brand with the lowest amount of sodium possible.

    1⅓ cups water
    1   (3-inch) piece kombu
    2   tablespoons dried bonito flakes
    3   tablespoons low-sodium soy sauce
    3   tablespoons mirin
    1½ teaspoons grated fresh ginger
    ¾   teaspoon sugar
    8   ounces medium-large shrimp (31 to 40 per pound),
        peeled, deveined, tails removed, and sliced in half
        lengthwise
    4   ounces rice vermicelli
    ½   small cucumber, halved lengthwise and sliced thin
    2   scallions, sliced thin on bias

1. Bring water and kombu to boil in large saucepan over medium-low heat. Remove from heat, stir in bonito flakes, and let sit for 3 minutes. Strain broth through fine-mesh strainer into large bowl, pressing on solids to extract as much broth as possible; discard solids. Whisk in soy sauce, mirin, ginger, and sugar until sugar is dissolved. Cover and refrigerate until well chilled, about 3 hours.

2. Bring 4 quarts water to boil in large pot. Fill large bowl with ice water. Add shrimp to boiling water, remove pot from heat, and cover; let sit until shrimp are just cooked through, about 1 minute. Using slotted spoon, transfer shrimp to ice water and let chill; drain shrimp and pat dry with paper towels.

3. Off heat, add noodles to hot water in pot and stir to separate. Let noodles soak, stirring occasionally, until softened, pliable, and tender, 10 to 12 minutes. Drain noodles, rinse with cold water, and drain again. Toss noodles with chilled broth in large bowl. Divide noodles between 2 individual serving bowls. Top each bowl with broth, shrimp, cucumber, and scallions. Serve.

PER SERVING: Cal 350; Fat 1 g; Sat fat 0 g; Chol 105 mg; Carb 64 g; Protein 14 g; Fiber 2 g; Sodium 1300 mg

NOTES FROM THE TEST KITCHEN

ALL ABOUT KOMBU AND BONITO FLAKES

Kombu and bonito flakes give our Chilled Rice Noodles with Shrimp its authentic and distinctive flavor. You can usually find both ingredients in the international aisle at the supermarket, or at an Asian market or a natural foods market. Kombu is a type of seaweed sold in dried, whole sheets that are quite thick and often have a chalky white powder on the exterior. Bonito flakes are dried fish flakes; they have a notable smoky flavor.

SEAFOOD RISOTTO

✔ **WHY THIS RECIPE WORKS:** For an approachable and foolproof seafood risotto for two, we found we didn't need to constantly stir the pot as most recipes require; stirring every few minutes during the early stages of cooking worked just as well, ensuring a thick, creamy risotto. A quick seafood broth, made by simmering shrimp shells and aromatics with bottled clam juice, chicken broth, and water, gave our risotto deep yet balanced flavor in short order. For the seafood, we chose shrimp, squid, and bay scallops, which paired well with the rich, creamy rice.

SEAFOOD RISOTTO BEGINS WITH NATURALLY LOW-fat shellfish paired with Arborio rice and either broth or fish stock. So why does this healthy- and minimalist-sounding dish get such a bad rap? First of all, it tends to entail a lot of work, which is especially annoying when making only two servings. The standard procedure calls for adding ladles of hot broth to the pot in small amounts while the cook stirs almost constantly until the rice is tender but still maintains a slight bite. Add to that the fact that many seafood risotto recipes call for lots of butter and cheese to enhance the "creaminess" of the rice's naturally occurring starches, and it's easy to see how seafood risotto doesn't make it to the for-two table when lighter dishes are what you're after. Our goal was to create a rich-tasting weeknight seafood risotto without tipping the scale or leaving leftovers behind. We also wanted to keep dirty dishes to a minimum and develop a more hands-off approach.

We started with streamlining. Medium-grain rice, such as Arborio, is the best choice since it is higher than both short- and long-grain rice in an important starch called amylopectin, the key to what gives risotto a creamy consistency. Stirring the rice in hot broth releases the surface starches that dissolve into, and thicken, the broth. Since stirring is paramount to this technique, we knew that eliminating it entirely wasn't an option, but we were hopeful we could reduce the amount required.

To see how infrequently we could add broth and stir and still get the creamy results we desired, we made dozens of batches of risotto, tweaking both factors. Batches stirred roughly half of the time were hard to distinguish from those stirred constantly. In the end, we settled on a technique of adding almost half of the liquid at the beginning and stirring infrequently for the first 7 to 9 minutes. The remaining broth was then added in ½-cup increments, and the rice was stirred frequently (but not constantly) for the final 12 to 14 minutes. We found that ⅔ cup of Arborio rice was the right amount for two people, which required almost 3 cups of cooking liquid to achieve a fully cooked and creamy risotto.

While some seafood risotto recipes use plain water for the cooking liquid, our tasters found the resulting risotto thin and bland. Substituting bottled clam juice for a portion of the water was more promising, offering a welcome briny hit, but it came at a price: Bottled clam juice is high in sodium, and the two bottles we added sent our sodium numbers soaring. In addition, the broth still lacked depth. Stepping away from the sea for a moment, we tried substituting store-bought low-sodium chicken broth for some of the water. This was certainly our richest batch yet, but tasters were still missing a certain seafood essence.

At this point, a colleague pointed out that since we knew we wanted our risotto to include shrimp, we could use their shells to add the missing seafood flavor to the broth. We tried simmering the broth with the shells from 4 ounces of shrimp, along with a chopped onion, bay leaf, and peppercorns (a few classic broth additions). Simmering the shells for just 15 minutes infused the broth with a light but distinct seafood flavor that was potent enough to allow us to reduce the clam juice from two bottles to one, which got us into an appropriate range for sodium. Final touches of saffron and drained diced tomatoes added color and acidity to the rice.

Next, we focused on the seafood and when to add it to the pot. In addition to the shrimp, we decided to include 4 ounces of squid, which tasters liked for its mild flavor and gentle bite. We cut the bodies into rings but left the tentacles whole to showcase their unique texture and visual appeal. We excluded clams and mussels from the running (their steaming would require another pot, and we wanted to keep our risotto simple), but 4 ounces of scallops lent a gentle brininess and sweetness to the dish and, best of all, were easy to prepare. We chose small bay scallops over large sea scallops because they cooked quickly and fit on a fork with a bite of rice. Now we just needed to find the best way to cook the seafood.

SEAFOOD RISOTTO

We tested a number of recipes that called for adding the seafood to the rice as it stood off the heat for a few minutes. We liked the idea of relying on residual heat to gently cook the seafood, but we found it often produced undercooked shrimp and squid. We found it was necessary to keep the pot on the heat for about three minutes before taking it off. Stirring during this brief period ensured that every bite of seafood cooked at the same rate. With a richly flavored pot of perfectly cooked rice and seafood, we addressed a few final touches.

Since fish and cheese are rarely combined in Italian cooking, we weren't tempted to enrich this risotto with cheese, not to mention that it would add fat and calories. But we did want to add some richness. One minced anchovy added with the aromatics and just half a pat of butter stirred in at the end did the trick. The anchovy lent a savory character, and the butter gave the rice a voluptuous feel without weighing it down.

With just a few labor- and pot-saving techniques, we now had a deceptively light seafood risotto that was suitable for a healthy weeknight dinner for two, yet elegant enough to make it feel like a special occasion.

Seafood Risotto

SERVES 2

Do not buy peeled shrimp; you will need the shrimp shells in order to make the broth. You can substitute 4 ounces of sea scallops, quartered, for the bay scallops. If you cannot find squid or prefer to omit it, you can use 6 ounces each of shrimp and scallops. We recommend buying "dry" scallops, those without chemical additives. Dry scallops will look ivory or pinkish and feel tacky; "wet" scallops look bright white and feel slippery.

BROTH

1½ cups water
1 (8-ounce) bottle clam juice
1 cup low-sodium chicken broth
½ cup canned diced tomatoes, drained
   Shells from 4 ounces shrimp (see below)
1 small onion, chopped coarse
4 black peppercorns
1 bay leaf
   Pinch saffron threads, crumbled
   Hot water

RISOTTO

1 tablespoon unsalted butter
1 small onion, chopped fine
   Salt and pepper
2 garlic cloves, minced
½ anchovy fillet, rinsed and minced
¼ teaspoon minced fresh thyme or pinch dried
⅔ cup Arborio rice
⅓ cup dry white wine
4 ounces medium-large shrimp (31 to 40 per pound), peeled, deveined, and shells reserved
4 ounces small bay scallops
4 ounces squid, bodies cut crosswise into ½-inch rings, tentacles left whole
2 teaspoons minced fresh parsley
1 teaspoon lemon juice

1. FOR THE BROTH: Combine all ingredients except hot water in medium saucepan over medium-high heat and bring to boil. Reduce heat to medium-low and simmer for 15 minutes. Strain broth through fine-mesh strainer into large measuring cup, pressing on solids to extract as much liquid as possible. (You should have 3 cups broth; if not, add hot water as needed.) Discard solids and transfer broth to clean saucepan; return saucepan to lowest possible heat to keep broth warm.

2. FOR THE RISOTTO: Melt ½ tablespoon butter in large saucepan over medium-low heat. Add onion and ⅛ teaspoon salt, cover, and cook, stirring occasionally,

---

NOTES FROM THE TEST KITCHEN

THE BEST CLAM JUICE

When there's no time to shuck fresh littlenecks and cherrystones for a homemade seafood base, we reach for a jug of their juice. Clam juice is made by briefly steaming fresh clams in salted water and filtering the resulting broth before bottling. Of the three brands we tried in a basic seafood pasta dish, only one sample garnered criticism for tasting "too strong" and "too clammy"— perhaps because its sodium content was more than double that of the other brands. Our top brand, **Bar Harbor**, hails from the shores of clam country in Maine, is available nationwide, and brings a "bright" and "mineral-y" flavor to seafood dishes.

until softened, 6 to 8 minutes. Stir in garlic, anchovy, and thyme and cook until fragrant, about 30 seconds. Increase heat to medium, stir in rice, and cook, stirring frequently, until grains are translucent around edges, about 3 minutes.

3. Stir in wine and cook, stirring frequently, until fully absorbed, about 1 minute. Stir in 1 cup warm broth. Bring to simmer and cook, stirring about every 3 minutes, until broth is absorbed and bottom of pot is dry, 7 to 9 minutes.

4. Continue to cook rice, stirring frequently and adding more hot broth, ½ cup at a time (you may not need to add all of broth mixture), every few minutes as pan bottom turns dry, until rice is cooked through but still al dente, 12 to 14 minutes.

5. Stir in shrimp, scallops, and squid and continue to cook, stirring frequently, until seafood is just cooked through, about 3 minutes longer. Remove pot from heat, cover, and let sit for 5 minutes.

6. Stir in remaining ½ tablespoon butter, parsley, and lemon juice and season with salt and pepper to taste. If desired, add remaining broth, 1 tablespoon at a time, to loosen consistency of risotto before serving.

PER SERVING: **Cal** 530; **Fat** 9 g; **Sat fat** 4.5 g; **Chol** 220 mg; **Carb** 73 g; **Protein** 31 g; **Fiber** 4 g; **Sodium** 1380 mg

BRAISED COD PEPERONATA

✔ WHY THIS RECIPE WORKS: Braising mild-tasting cod in a sauce made from tomatoes, red bell pepper, onion, and garlic gave us a simple yet richly flavored supper for two that was on the table in a flash. The fish fillets absorbed the bright, bold flavors of the sauce in just minutes and were protected from the heat of the pan so they stayed moist and tender. Chopped basil and a dash of balsamic vinegar, stirred into the sauce at the end, amped up the freshness of the dish and kept with our Mediterranean theme.

WHILE BRAISING IS USUALLY ASSOCIATED WITH cooking tough pieces of meat over a long period of time, it can also be a great way to add deep flavor and complexity to mild-tasting fish in a short amount of time. To that end, we looked to use this cooking method to deliver two moist, tender, and flavor-packed cod fillets, for a lighter, fresher alternative to the standard, less healthful offerings of fish baked and topped with buttery bread crumbs or deep-fried in a big vat of oil. Taking our inspiration from the Italian dish *peperonata*, we looked to pair our cod with a mixture of sautéed tomatoes, peppers, onions, and garlic for a lively-tasting dish that didn't taste like it was light. And to keep our recipe easy and quick—making it the perfect go-to dish for two on a busy weeknight—we wanted to keep all the cooking to one pan.

After gathering a handful of recipes uncovered in our research, we commenced testing, but we were soon disappointed to find that most produced tough, dry cod and dull sauces that were either too thick or too thin, too sweet or too greasy. The biggest challenge would be cooking the cod to perfection, as it is meaty but lean and prone to drying out. We had our work cut out for us.

First, we focused on the sauce in which the cod would be braised; it would need to be slightly thick so we could nestle our pair of fish fillets in it to protect them from the heat of the pan. We started by sautéing a sliced onion in olive oil, then added two cloves of garlic and sautéed them briefly to bring out their flavor. Bell peppers are a given in peperonata; after testing both the green and red varieties, tasters exhibited a clear preference for the latter, which offered more sweetness and less of a vegetal taste. A single pepper was ample for our two-person dish, and adding it to the pan with the onion gave it plenty of time to soften. Slicing it thinly, rather than chopping it, helped give our sauce more substance.

Turning next to the tomatoes, which would add not only flavor but also more volume and liquid for braising, we considered the most likely options: crushed, diced, or pureed canned tomatoes, or fresh tomatoes. Both crushed and pureed canned tomatoes produced a thick, sweet, overbearing sauce reminiscent of bad Italian restaurant food. Fresh tomatoes, though more promising, offered inconsistent results depending on the juiciness of the tomato. Canned diced tomatoes were the clear winner. Just ½ cup of drained diced tomatoes provided sufficient acidity and the right amount of boldness and presence to complement the pepper and onion.

At this point, tasters were happy with the texture of the sauce, but the flavor was somewhat lacking. A few additions remedied the problem. A splash of white wine gave our sauce a much-needed boost of brightness and complexity. Fresh thyme contributed a sweet, woodsy quality, and paprika offered a slight kick and reinforced the peppery notes of the dish. With our sauce in good shape, we turned our attention to cooking the cod.

We found the key to braising our fish was twofold: Low heat ensured that nothing burned, and a skillet with a tight-fitting lid trapped the heat so the fish partially steamed and partially simmered in the aromatic stew of vegetables. We nestled the cod into the simmering sauce and basted it quickly with the mixture to ensure that it was infused with flavor, then cooked it over medium-low heat, covered, for just 10 minutes. The fish emerged succulent and moist, and the sauce had good body.

For last touches, we stirred a dash of balsamic vinegar and a bit of chopped basil into the sauce once the fish was cooked. These two additions ramped up the brightness and freshness of the finished sauce, guaranteeing our one-pan braise offered not only moist, tender bites of fish, but also vibrant, intense flavor.

Braised Cod Peperonata
SERVES 2

Halibut, snapper, tilapia, bluefish, monkfish, and sea bass fillets are all good substitutions for the cod. If your fillets have skin on them, follow the instructions at right to remove it. Smoked paprika is a nice substitution for the paprika here.

- 2 (6-ounce) skinless cod fillets, 1 inch thick
  Salt and pepper
- 2 teaspoons olive oil
- 1 red bell pepper, stemmed, seeded, and cut into ¼-inch-wide strips
- 1 small onion, sliced thin
- 1 teaspoon paprika
- 2 garlic cloves, minced
- ½ teaspoon minced fresh thyme or ¼ teaspoon dried
- ½ cup canned diced tomatoes, drained
- ¼ cup dry white wine
- 1 tablespoon chopped fresh basil
- 1 teaspoon balsamic or sherry vinegar

1. Pat cod dry with paper towels and season with ¼ teaspoon salt and ¼ teaspoon pepper.

2. Heat oil in 10-inch nonstick skillet over medium heat until shimmering. Add bell pepper, onion, paprika, and ¼ teaspoon salt and cook until vegetables have softened and browned, 8 to 10 minutes. Stir in garlic and thyme and cook until fragrant, about 30 seconds. Stir in tomatoes, wine, and ⅛ teaspoon pepper and bring to simmer.

3. Nestle cod into pan and spoon sauce mixture over fish. Cover, reduce heat to medium-low, and cook until fish flakes apart when gently prodded with paring knife and registers 140 degrees, about 10 minutes.

4. Gently transfer fish to individual plates. Off heat, stir basil and vinegar into sauce in pan and season with salt and pepper to taste. Spoon sauce over fish and serve.

PER SERVING: Cal 260; Fat 6 g; Sat Fat 1 g; Chol 75 mg; Carb 13 g; Protein 32 g; Fiber 4 g; Sodium 840 mg

NOTES FROM THE TEST KITCHEN

SKINNING FISH FILLETS

1. Using tip of boning knife (or sharp chef's knife), begin to cut skin away from fish at corner of fillet.

2. When enough skin is exposed, grasp it firmly with paper towel, hold it taut, and carefully slice flesh off skin.

RUSTIC CHICKEN TART WITH SPINACH AND GOAT CHEESE

CHAPTER 7

EXPRESS LANE

PUTTING ROTISSERIE CHICKEN TO WORK

A SUPERMARKET ROTISSERIE CHICKEN MAKES A good emergency dinner on its own, but we wondered if there were more interesting ways we could put it to work. Once we got in the kitchen, we found there are countless ways to press this tender meat into service to make all sorts of quick and easy dishes.

We started out with an elegant tart that only looks like it took hours to make. We combined rotisserie chicken, a few carefully chosen ingredients, and a store-bought pie crust. These timesaving ingredients made it possible to assemble and bake the tart in just half an hour. Hearty, healthy spinach added color and helped make this tart a satisfying meal, and toasted chopped walnuts added crunch and nutty flavor. Creamy, flavorful goat cheese pulled double duty, imparting richness and binding the filling together.

Next, to make a practically effortless weeknight baked pasta dish for two, we relied on a simple no-cook red bell pepper sauce that we whirled together in the food processor. To brighten and balance the sauce, we added plenty of fresh parsley, Parmesan, shallot, and garlic along with a good amount of extra-virgin olive oil. After tossing our richly flavored, colorful sauce with cooked pasta, we stirred in the shredded chicken and briny olives. Dollops of ricotta mixed with Parmesan cheese made for a creamy topping that browned beautifully in the oven in about 10 minutes.

For comfort food in no time, we wanted to streamline chicken and biscuits. This Southern classic is usually a time-consuming labor of love, making it completely impractical for two, but we beat the clock by using our rotisserie chicken and Bisquick baking mix to speed up the process. We focused most of our time and effort on making a rich, creamy sauce with sweet leeks and meaty mushrooms that would add deep flavor and heft to the dish. For the crowning glory, we doctored up the baking mix by adding Gruyère and tarragon for cheesy, flavorful biscuits that tasted like they were made from scratch. To avoid gummy biscuits, we parbaked them before adding them to our casserole. After just 10 minutes in the oven, this down-home comfort food was a table-worthy treat.

Finally, we put our rotisserie chicken to use south of the border. For a quick Southwestern-inspired quiche for two, we mixed a batter of eggs, milk, flour, and baking powder with a classic quesadilla filling. Our creative "crust" is simply a flour tortilla, which we cut down to size and spritzed with vegetable oil spray to ensure that it didn't dry out or crack during baking. We made a hearty, tasty filling that required no extra cooking with rotisserie chicken, cheese, corn, cilantro, and pickled jalapeños; we simply mixed the ingredients and spread them in the pie dish. Once baked, this pie boasted a rich, creamy filling with a crust so crispy that we made two mini pies so we wouldn't have to share.

With so many easy options to make a simple rotisserie chicken into something special, it definitely won't be just a last-minute resort in our kitchens anymore.

Rustic Chicken Tart with Spinach and Goat Cheese

SERVES 2

Our favorite store-bought pie dough is made by Wholly Wholesome. It is sold frozen and requires 3 hours of defrosting. This is best done on the counter rather than in the refrigerator; microwave the dough for up to 10 seconds if the center is not fully thawed. You can use an inverted bowl with a 10-inch diameter to cleanly cut out the circle of pie dough.

- 1 cup shredded rotisserie chicken
- 4 ounces frozen chopped spinach, thawed and squeezed dry
- 2 ounces goat cheese, crumbled (½ cup)
- 2 tablespoons toasted and chopped walnuts
- 2 tablespoons water
- Salt and pepper
- 1 store-bought pie crust

1. Adjust oven rack to middle position and heat oven to 475 degrees. Combine chicken, spinach, goat cheese, walnuts, water, ⅛ teaspoon salt, and ⅛ teaspoon pepper in bowl and microwave until heated through, about 1 minute. Stir mixture to recombine and season with salt and pepper to taste.

2. Line rimmed baking sheet with parchment paper. Trim pie crust to 10-inch round and place on prepared sheet. Spread chicken filling in center of crust, leaving 1½-inch border around edge. Fold edge of dough over filling, pleating it every 1 to 2 inches as needed.

3. Bake tart until crust is golden and filling is hot, about 15 minutes, rotating sheet halfway through baking. Let cool slightly and serve.

Baked Pasta with Chicken, Olives, and Roasted Red Pepper Sauce

SERVES 2

You will need two 12-ounce ramekins for this recipe (see page 3). Other pasta shapes can be substituted for the penne; however, their cup measurements may vary (see page 88).

- 4 ounces (1¼ cups) penne
  Salt and pepper
- 2 ounces (¼ cup) whole-milk ricotta cheese
- 1½ ounces Parmesan cheese, grated (¾ cup)
- 3 tablespoons extra-virgin olive oil
- 1 cup jarred roasted red peppers, rinsed, patted dry, and chopped coarse
- 2 tablespoons fresh parsley leaves
- 1 shallot, minced
- 1 garlic clove, minced
- 1 cup shredded rotisserie chicken
- ¼ cup pitted kalamata olives, chopped

1. Adjust oven rack to middle position and heat oven to 450 degrees. Bring 4 quarts water to boil in large pot. Add pasta and 1 tablespoon salt and cook, stirring often, until nearly al dente. Reserve ¼ cup cooking water, then drain pasta and return it to pot.

2. Meanwhile, mix ricotta, ¼ cup Parmesan, 1½ teaspoons oil, ⅛ teaspoon salt, and ⅛ teaspoon pepper together in bowl; set aside. Process remaining ½ cup Parmesan, remaining 2½ tablespoons oil, red peppers, parsley, shallot, garlic, ⅛ teaspoon salt, and ⅛ teaspoon pepper together in food processor until smooth, scraping down bowl as needed, about 20 seconds.

3. Add red pepper sauce, chicken, olives, and reserved cooking water to pasta and toss to combine. Season with salt and pepper to taste. Divide pasta evenly between two 12-ounce ramekins. Dollop ricotta mixture evenly over top. Bake until filling is bubbling and cheese is spotty brown, 10 to 15 minutes. Let cool slightly and serve.

Chicken and Biscuits

SERVES 2

You will need a 3-cup baking dish (measuring approximately 7¼ by 5¼ inches) or a similar-size dish for this recipe (see page 3).

- ½ cup Bisquick original mix
- 1¼ cups low-sodium chicken broth
- 2 ounces Gruyère cheese, shredded (½ cup)
- 1 tablespoon minced fresh tarragon
  Salt and pepper
- 1 tablespoon vegetable oil
- 4 ounces white mushrooms, trimmed and sliced thin
- 1 small leek, white and light green parts only, halved lengthwise, sliced thin, and washed thoroughly

NOTES FROM THE TEST KITCHEN

MAKING A RUSTIC CHICKEN TART

1. Trim pie crust into 10-inch circle and place on parchment-lined baking sheet. Spread chicken filling in center of dough, leaving 1½-inch border at edges.

2. Fold edge of dough in over the filling, pleating it every 1 to 2 inches as needed.

THE BEST ROASTED RED PEPPERS

Whether you're cooking for two or more, we recommend keeping a jar of good roasted red peppers on hand at all times. Roasted red peppers are an easy way to quickly give dishes bold, deep flavor, such as in our Baked Pasta with Chicken, Olives, and Roasted Red Pepper Sauce. Just be sure to rinse and pat the peppers dry before using them. To determine which brand of jarred roasted red peppers is best, we rounded up eight nationally available brands and tasted them plain and in a hummus. Peppers that were packed with flavorful ingredients like garlic, herbs, and vinegar tasted good plain, but those flavors weren't appreciated when incorporated into a sauce. In the end, our tasters' favorite roasted red peppers were **Dunbars Sweet Roasted Red Peppers**; the label lists only red bell peppers, water, salt, and citric acid in the ingredients list. These peppers were great on their own, and their sweet, earthy, unmarred essence made for a terrific sauce.

2 tablespoons all-purpose flour

1 garlic clove, minced

⅓ cup heavy cream

1 cup shredded rotisserie chicken

⅓ cup frozen peas

1. Adjust oven rack to middle position and heat oven to 450 degrees. Line baking sheet with parchment paper. Stir Bisquick, ¼ cup broth, Gruyère, 1½ teaspoons tarragon, and ⅛ teaspoon pepper together in bowl until combined. Using 2 greased spoons, scoop out and drop 4 even mounds of dough onto prepared sheet. Bake until biscuits are puffed and lightly browned on bottom, 8 to 10 minutes.

2. Meanwhile, heat oil in 10-inch skillet over medium-high heat until shimmering. Add mushrooms and leek and cook, stirring occasionally, until softened and lightly browned, 5 to 7 minutes. Stir in flour and garlic and cook, stirring often, until lightly browned, about 1 minute. Gradually whisk in remaining 1 cup broth and cream, scraping up any browned bits and smoothing out any lumps. Simmer, stirring occasionally, until mixture is thickened, 3 to 5 minutes. Stir in remaining 1½ teaspoons tarragon, shredded chicken, and peas and season with salt and pepper to taste.

3. Grease shallow 3-cup baking dish. Transfer chicken mixture to prepared dish and arrange biscuits on top. Bake until filling is bubbling and biscuits are browned, about 10 minutes. Let cool slightly and serve.

Chicken and Cheese Quesadilla Pies

SERVES 2

You will need two 6-inch pie plates for this recipe (see page 3). Serve with sour cream and fresh tomato salsa, if desired.

  Vegetable oil spray

2 (8-inch) flour tortillas

1 cup shredded rotisserie chicken

3 ounces sharp cheddar cheese, shredded (¾ cup)

¼ cup frozen corn, thawed

2 tablespoons minced fresh cilantro

1½ tablespoons minced jarred jalapeños

  Salt and pepper

1 large egg

½ cup whole milk

⅓ cup all-purpose flour

¼ teaspoon baking powder

NOTES FROM THE TEST KITCHEN

PREPARING LEEKS

1. Trim and discard root and dark green leaves.

2. Slice trimmed leek in half lengthwise, then cut it into pieces as directed. Rinse cut leeks thoroughly to remove dirt and sand.

ASSEMBLING CHICKEN QUESADILLA PIES

1. After trimming each tortilla to 7-inch round, press into pie plates, and spray tortillas with vegetable oil spray to ensure crust does not dry out or crack during baking.

2. Evenly pour batter over chicken mixture and sprinkle with cheese.

CHICKEN AND CHEESE QUESADILLA PIES

1. Adjust oven rack to middle position and heat oven to 450 degrees. Spray two 6-inch pie plates with vegetable oil spray. Trim each tortilla to 7-inch round, press into prepared pie plates, and spray with oil spray. Toss shredded chicken in bowl with ½ cup cheese, corn, cilantro, jalapeños, ¼ teaspoon salt, and ⅛ teaspoon pepper. Divide mixture evenly between pie plates and transfer plates to rimmed baking sheet.

2. Whisk egg, milk, flour, baking powder, and ⅛ teaspoon salt together in bowl until smooth. Slowly pour mixture into pie plates, dividing mixture evenly, then sprinkle with remaining ¼ cup cheese. Bake until surface is golden brown, about 20 minutes. Let cool slightly and serve.

PUTTING CHICKEN SAUSAGE TO WORK

CHICKEN SAUSAGE IS A LIFESAVER FOR A BUSY COOK; it is already well seasoned, so it contributes rich flavor to a dish and cuts down on the amount of additional seasonings needed. And because it is precooked, it needs just a few minutes in a skillet or oven to brown and warm through. We set out to develop some interesting, creative recipes that would spice up our weeknights.

To start, we wanted to put our chicken sausage to work in a simple, hearty pasta dish. Roasted garlic has a sweet, intensely aromatic flavor that's great for punching up pasta, but we weren't about to roast a head of garlic for over an hour for a quick dinner for two. To speed up the process, we needed to get creative. First, we found we could roast the garlic more quickly when the cloves were separated, and cranking the oven up to 425 degrees cut the roasting time to just 20 minutes. Covering the garlic was essential to keep the cloves from turning tough and overly brown during roasting. Once our garlic was soft and browned, we mashed it into a paste. Crumbled goat cheese and a little of the pasta cooking water were all we needed to turn the roasted garlic into a thick and creamy sauce for our campanelle. We lightly browned the chicken sausage and added some fresh baby arugula to round out the dish.

For our next dish, we combined tender bites of meaty sausage, delicate pasta, and hearty greens for a warming Italian-style soup. We browned the sausage to create a flavorful fond on the bottom of our pot, then sautéed an onion and some garlic. The fond and aromatics gave us deeper flavor than that of a simple broth-based soup you'd get out of a can. Red pepper flakes infused the soup with a subtle heat. Cooking orzo pasta right in the broth streamlined the dish, and the starch from the pasta gave the broth more body and substance. Finally, we stirred in some chopped escarole—a green related to the endive family but with a slightly less bitter flavor—to simmer with the sausage and orzo.

Kebabs are a great way to put dinner on the table quickly and with minimal cleanup, and using precooked chicken sausage made them a snap. To make our kebabs for two even faster, we skipped firing up the grill, relying on our broiler to do the job instead. We combined flavorful, precooked chicken sausage with sweet pineapple and crunchy bell pepper for a fresh, delicious meal that came together in just 25 minutes. For an added flavor boost, we brushed the skewers with hoisin sauce, a richly flavored Asian condiment made of soybeans, sugar, vinegar, garlic, and chiles. The sugar in the hoisin glaze also helped speed up the browning—after just 10 minutes under the broiler, our kebabs were perfect.

Like rice and pasta, polenta is a great vehicle for flavorful sauces. We wanted to incorporate its unique creaminess and hearty corn flavor into an Italian-inspired casserole. What we didn't want was the endless stirring that preparing our own polenta from scratch would entail. With simplicity in mind, we turned to precooked polenta. We cut the polenta into thick slices, layered them on the bottom of a small casserole dish, and topped them with a simple sausage-packed tomato sauce. Switching from regular diced tomatoes to fire-roasted tomatoes imparted a pleasant smokiness that paired perfectly with the sausage. A layer of cheese, which browned beautifully in the oven, topped off our casserole.

As quick and easy as our simple chicken sausage dinners were, they definitely didn't taste like convenience food. And because chicken sausage comes in a variety of flavors, we had endless options to change up the recipes.

Campanelle with Roasted Garlic, Sausage, and Arugula

SERVES 2

Chicken sausage is available in a wide variety of flavors; feel free to choose a flavor that you think will pair well with the other flavors in this dish. Other pasta shapes can be substituted for the campanelle; however, their cup measurements may vary (see page 88).

- 8 garlic cloves, peeled
- 2 tablespoons olive oil
  Salt and pepper
- 6 ounces (2 cups) campanelle
- 2 (3-ounce) links cooked chicken sausage, sliced ½ inch thick
- 2 ounces baby arugula (2 cups)
- 2 ounces goat cheese, crumbled (½ cup)

1. Adjust oven rack to middle position and heat oven to 425 degrees. Combine garlic, 1 tablespoon oil, and ¼ teaspoon salt in 10-inch ovensafe skillet. Cover and roast until garlic is soft and lightly browned, 15 to 20 minutes. Transfer to small bowl and mash into paste with back of spoon.

NOTES FROM THE TEST KITCHEN

THE BEST GARLIC PEELER
When you need to peel garlic, you can either whack the clove with the side of a knife blade (which works beautifully, but you get a crushed clove) or you can use a garlic peeler. Garlic peelers are simply silicone or rubber tubes (or sheets that you shape into tubes); you roll them with the garlic inside, and they gently tug the papery skins off the cloves, leaving the cloves intact. Garlic peelers are perfect for recipes that call for whole or sliced garlic cloves. We tried three models priced from $6.50 to $8.79, peeling both single cloves and multiple cloves, and evaluated them on their peeling performance, ease of use, and cleanup. While all were easy to wash in the dishwasher or by hand, the differences lay in how comfortable they were to press down on and roll and how quickly and effectively they removed the peels. Our winner, the **Zak! Designs E-Z Rol Garlic Peeler**, lived up to its name. It was the thickest and most well cushioned, and its grippy silicone surface thoroughly and speedily removed the skins from cloves of all sizes without bruising them. It's our new favorite way to peel garlic.

2. Bring 4 quarts water to boil in large pot. Add pasta and 1 tablespoon salt and cook, stirring often, until al dente. Reserve ½ cup cooking water, then drain pasta and return it to pot.

3. Meanwhile, heat remaining 1 tablespoon oil in now-empty skillet over medium-high heat until shimmering. Add sausage and cook, stirring occasionally, until browned, about 5 minutes.

4. Add roasted garlic, sausage, arugula, goat cheese, and ¼ cup cooking water to pasta and stir until goat cheese is melted and arugula is slightly wilted. Season with salt and pepper to taste. Before serving, add remaining cooking water as needed to adjust consistency. Serve.

Escarole, Sausage, and Orzo Soup

SERVES 2

Chicken sausage is available in a wide variety of flavors; feel free to choose a flavor that you think will pair well with the other flavors in this dish.

- 1 tablespoon olive oil
- 2 (3-ounce) links cooked chicken sausage, sliced ½ inch thick
- 1 small onion, chopped fine
- 1 garlic clove, minced
- ⅛ teaspoon red pepper flakes
- 3 cups low-sodium chicken broth
- 2 ounces escarole, chopped coarse (2 cups)
- ¼ cup orzo
- ¼ cup grated Parmesan cheese
- 1 tablespoon minced fresh parsley
  Salt and pepper

1. Heat 2 teaspoons oil in large saucepan over medium-high heat until shimmering. Add sausage and cook, stirring occasionally, until browned, about 5 minutes. Transfer to bowl, cover, and set aside.

2. Add remaining 1 teaspoon oil and onion to now-empty saucepan and cook over medium heat, stirring occasionally, until onion is softened and just beginning to brown, 5 to 7 minutes. Stir in garlic and pepper flakes and cook until fragrant, about 30 seconds.

3. Stir in sausage, broth, escarole, and orzo and simmer until orzo is tender, 10 to 12 minutes. Off heat, stir in Parmesan and parsley and season with salt and pepper to taste. Serve.

ALOHA KEBABS

Aloha Kebabs

SERVES 2

Chicken sausage is available in a wide variety of flavors; feel free to choose a flavor that you think will pair well with the other flavors in this dish. You will need four 12-inch metal skewers for this recipe. Serve with rice, if desired.

- 3 (3-ounce) links cooked chicken sausage, sliced 1 inch thick
- 1 cup 1-inch pineapple pieces
- 1 red or green bell pepper, stemmed, seeded, and cut into 1½-inch pieces
- ¼ cup hoisin sauce

1. Adjust oven rack 6 inches from broiler and heat broiler. Line rimmed baking sheet with aluminum foil.

2. Thread sausage, pineapple, and bell pepper onto four 12-inch metal skewers. Brush skewers evenly with hoisin sauce. Transfer skewers to sheet and broil, turning every few minutes, until vegetables are softened and well browned, 10 to 15 minutes. Serve.

Smoky Sausage and Polenta Bake

SERVES 2

Chicken sausage is available in a wide variety of flavors; feel free to choose a flavor that you think will pair well with the other flavors in this dish. You will need a 3-cup baking dish (measuring approximately 7¼ by 5¼ inches; see page 3).

- 1 (14.5-ounce) can diced fire-roasted tomatoes
- 1 tablespoon olive oil
- 2 (3-ounce) links cooked chicken sausage, sliced ½ inch thick
- 1 small onion, chopped fine
- 1 garlic clove, minced
- ⅛ teaspoon red pepper flakes
  Salt and pepper
- ½ (18-ounce) tube cooked polenta, sliced into ½-inch-thick rounds
- 1 ounce shredded Italian cheese blend (¼ cup)

1. Adjust oven rack to middle position and heat oven to 450 degrees. Place tomatoes in bowl and mash with potato masher until mostly smooth. Heat oil in 10-inch skillet over medium-high heat until shimmering. Add sausage and

PREPPING BELL PEPPER

1. Slice off top and bottom of pepper and remove seeds and stem.

2. Slice down through side of pepper.

3. Lay pepper flat, trim away remaining ribs and seeds, then cut into pieces or strips as desired.

ALL ABOUT PRECOOKED POLENTA

We generally prepare raw polenta from scratch when we want to serve it as a traditional Italian-style cornmeal mush, but for some recipes, such as our Smoky Sausage and Polenta Bake, we like to use the firmer precooked polenta sold in supermarkets. These shelf-stable tubes are handy to have in your pantry; all that is required is slicing, heating, and serving. You can cut the polenta into rounds and grill or broil them, ladle beef stew over warmed rounds, or top a slice with a fried egg for breakfast. You can find precooked polenta near the dried pasta in most supermarkets.

cook, stirring occasionally, until browned, about 5 minutes. Add onion and cook until softened, about 5 minutes.

2. Stir in garlic and pepper flakes and cook until fragrant, about 30 seconds. Add mashed tomatoes and simmer until slightly thickened, 8 to 10 minutes. Season with salt and pepper to taste.

3. Place polenta rounds in bottom of 3-cup baking dish. Top with sausage mixture and sprinkle evenly with cheese. Bake until hot, 10 to 15 minutes. Serve.

PUTTING PRECOOKED SHRIMP TO WORK

WHEN YOU'RE TIGHT ON TIME, FROZEN, PRECOOKED shrimp are a great way to pull a delicious meal out of thin air. Because they're frozen, the quality is consistent, and it's easy to keep them on hand. And because they come fully cooked and peeled, they don't require any prep work. You can simply stir them into chilled dishes, or, to use them in warm dishes, add them at the end of the cooking time so that they are just warmed through.

To put our shrimp to work, first we wanted something light and easy. Sandwiches can be a frequent default dinner in a two-person household: They are filling and easy, and when they are good, they are definitely crave-worthy—but they can quickly become dull if you aren't thinking creatively. For a one-of-a-kind sandwich wrap with fresh, bright flavors, we developed a shrimp salad recipe that boasted plenty of garden-fresh herbs, convenient precooked shrimp, and a creamy, piquant dressing. For the salad, we tossed chopped shrimp and red bell pepper in a mixture of mayonnaise, lemon juice, cayenne, paprika, and garlic. To brighten things up, we added a hefty amount of chopped cilantro and mint, folding half of the herb mixture into the shrimp salad, then topping the salad with the remaining herbs before wrapping it up in soft flour tortillas.

Next, we wanted to come up with a simple shrimp stir-fry packed with flavor. We got started by quickly scrambling an egg in a nonstick skillet, then we used the same skillet to fry leftover rice, shrimp, and a little garlic. Prep-free peas added freshness, and scallions lent the dish color and crunch as well as a light onion flavor. Our precooked and peeled shrimp made this dish super-simple; all we needed to do was stir them in with the rice to heat them through. A combination of soy and oyster sauces imparted an *umami*-rich complexity that complemented our simple ingredients.

To transform risotto into a simple weeknight recipe for two, we avoided the laborious process of constant stirring by relying on a stovetop-to-oven method. For a little more flavor and color, we sautéed a zucchini until it was lightly browned and tender. We used the same skillet to soften a chopped onion in some butter, then added the Arborio rice and lightly toasted it for a couple of minutes before adding liquid. White wine and chicken broth added bright, rich flavor without overwhelming the dish. We needed to stir the rice for only a minute before moving it to the oven to cook through. Once the rice was tender, we stirred in Parmesan, parsley, the sautéed zucchini, and precooked shrimp for a light but satisfying meal.

For our final simple shrimp recipe we made a refreshing Mediterranean-style pasta salad. Thanks to our easy precooked shrimp, the dish came together in minutes. We cooked some farfalle pasta, then rinsed it under cold water to cool it quickly. For the dressing, we combined rich, flavorful extra-virgin olive oil with sharp red wine vinegar, bright, citrusy lemon juice, and a little oregano to amplify the Mediterranean flavors. Along with pasta and shrimp, we chose sweet cherry tomatoes and salty kalamata olives to round out the dish and tossed in some briny feta cheese and fresh parsley just before serving.

For easy weeknight meals that go beyond boneless, skinless chicken breasts, precooked shrimp are a great way to break out of the box.

Spicy Shrimp and Herb Salad Wraps

SERVES 2

Parsley is a good alternative to the cilantro in this recipe.

- 1 cup coarsely chopped fresh cilantro
- ½ cup coarsely chopped fresh mint
- ¼ cup mayonnaise
- 1 garlic clove, minced
- 1 teaspoon lemon juice
- ¼ teaspoon paprika
- ¼ teaspoon cayenne pepper
   Salt and pepper
- 12 ounces cooked and peeled medium shrimp (41 to 50 per pound), cut into ½-inch pieces
- 1 red bell pepper, stemmed, seeded, and cut into 2-inch-long matchsticks
- 2 (10-inch) flour tortillas

1. Combine cilantro and mint in small bowl. In separate large bowl, whisk mayonnaise with half of herb mixture, garlic, lemon juice, paprika, cayenne, ¼ teaspoon salt, and ⅛ teaspoon pepper until combined. Fold shrimp and bell pepper into mayonnaise mixture. Season with salt and pepper to taste.

ASSEMBLING SHRIMP AND HERB SALAD WRAPS

1. After spreading shrimp mixture on bottom half of each tortilla, leaving 2-inch border at bottom edge of tortilla, sprinkle half of reserved herb mixture on top.

2. Fold sides of tortilla over filling, then tightly roll bottom edge of tortilla up over filling, and continue to roll into wrap.

2. Lay tortillas on clean counter. Divide shrimp mixture evenly between tortillas, leaving 2-inch border at bottom. Sprinkle remaining half of chopped herbs evenly over shrimp mixture. Working with 1 tortilla at a time, fold sides of tortilla over filling, then tightly roll bottom edge of tortilla up over filling, and continue to roll into wrap. Cut each wrap in half on bias. Serve.

Shrimp Fried Rice
SERVES 2

You can use leftover or precooked rice here; our favorite precooked brand is Minute Ready to Serve White Rice.

- 4 teaspoons vegetable oil
- 1 large egg, lightly beaten
- 2½ cups cooked rice
- 8 ounces cooked and peeled medium shrimp (41 to 50 per pound)
- 1½ tablespoons soy sauce
- 1 tablespoon oyster sauce
- 1 garlic clove, minced
- ⅓ cup frozen peas, thawed
- 4 scallions, sliced thin on bias

1. Heat 1 teaspoon oil in 10-inch nonstick skillet over medium-high heat until shimmering. Add egg and cook, stirring often, until scrambled and barely moist, about 2 minutes; transfer to bowl.

2. Heat remaining 1 tablespoon oil in now-empty skillet over high heat until just smoking. Add rice, shrimp, soy sauce, oyster sauce, and garlic and cook, stirring constantly, until heated through, about 3 minutes. Off heat, stir in cooked egg, peas, and scallions. Cover and let sit until egg and peas are heated through, about 2 minutes. Serve.

Baked Risotto with Shrimp and Zucchini
SERVES 2

RiceSelect Arborio Rice is the test kitchen's winning brand.

- 2¼ cups low-sodium chicken broth
- 2 tablespoons unsalted butter
- 1 small zucchini (6 ounces), quartered lengthwise and sliced ½ inch thick
- 1 small onion, chopped fine
- Salt and pepper
- ¾ cup Arborio rice
- 1 garlic clove, minced
- ¼ cup dry white wine
- 6 ounces cooked and peeled medium shrimp (41 to 50 per pound)
- 1 ounce Parmesan cheese, grated (½ cup)
- 2 tablespoons minced fresh parsley

1. Adjust oven rack to middle position and heat oven to 400 degrees. Bring broth to simmer in small saucepan over medium-high heat. Reduce heat to low and cover to keep hot.

2. Meanwhile, melt 1 tablespoon butter in 10-inch ovensafe skillet over medium heat. Add zucchini and cook until tender and lightly browned, 8 to 10 minutes. Transfer zucchini to bowl and cover to keep warm. Melt remaining 1 tablespoon butter in now-empty skillet over medium-high heat. Add onion and ⅛ teaspoon salt and cook, stirring occasionally, until softened, about 5 minutes. Add rice and stir until edges begin to turn translucent, about 2 minutes. Stir in garlic and cook until fragrant, about 30 seconds. Add wine and cook, stirring constantly, until completely absorbed, about 1 minute.

3. Pour 2 cups broth over rice mixture, cover, and transfer to oven. Bake until rice is tender and liquid is mostly absorbed, about 15 minutes. Stir in zucchini, shrimp, Parmesan, and parsley. Add remaining ¼ cup broth as needed to adjust consistency. Season with salt and pepper to taste. Serve.

Mediterranean Pasta Salad with Shrimp and Feta

SERVES 2

Other pasta shapes can be substituted for the farfalle; however, their cup measurements may vary (see page 88).

4	ounces (1⅔ cups) farfalle
	Salt and pepper
2	tablespoons extra-virgin olive oil
1	tablespoon red wine vinegar
1	tablespoon lemon juice
1	small shallot, minced
⅛	teaspoon sugar
	Pinch dried oregano
6	ounces cooked and peeled medium shrimp (41 to 50 per pound)
3	ounces cherry tomatoes, quartered
¼	cup pitted kalamata olives, chopped coarse
2	tablespoons crumbled feta cheese
1	tablespoon minced fresh parsley

1. Bring 4 quarts water to boil in large pot. Add pasta and 1 tablespoon salt and cook, stirring often, until al dente. Drain pasta and rinse under cold water until cool, then drain pasta well.

2. Meanwhile, whisk oil, vinegar, lemon juice, shallot, sugar, oregano, and ⅛ teaspoon pepper together in medium bowl until combined. Add drained pasta, shrimp, tomatoes, olives, feta, and parsley to bowl and toss to combine. Season with salt and pepper to taste, cover, and refrigerate for at least 10 minutes. Serve.

PUTTING CHEESE TORTELLINI TO WORK

IF YOU THINK STORE-BOUGHT TORTELLINI IS ONLY a vehicle for jarred pasta sauce on a busy night, think again. Store-bought tortellini offers both good flavor and tender texture in a fraction of the time of homemade. Tortellini can be found at the supermarket refrigerated, frozen, or dried.

To start, we wanted to use our cheesy tortellini in a warm, satisfying soup. Tomato and tortellini soup can be a perfect comfort food on a cold winter day, but when tomatoes aren't in season, good luck getting ripe tomato flavor. Canned tomatoes are available all year round, but they require a long simmer to get rid of the tinny taste. We got around these problems by using a rather unusual ingredient: V8 juice. It lent the soup a surprisingly rich, fresh tomato flavor without tasting harsh and canned. To boost its flavor, we rendered a little pancetta, then added an onion, tomato paste to deepen the tomato flavor, brown sugar for balance, and garlic to boost the savory qualities. We simmered the dried tortellini in the soup until tender, then we stirred in some baby spinach for a hearty dose of fresh leafy greens. Our substantial soup had all the warmth and complexity we wanted—any time of year.

For a super-easy pasta salad that would impress any picnic date, we paired convenient store-bought cheese tortellini with sweet red bell pepper and a simple yet bold dressing made of extra-virgin olive oil, lemon juice, and shallot. To give the salad a little more flavor and some crunch, we added a handful of chopped basil and stirred in toasted pine nuts at the end. The fresh basil and toasty pine nuts gave this simple salad the flavors of a classic Italian pesto.

Next, we found the velvety texture of a cream sauce to be a good complement for our cheesy store-bought tortellini, especially when paired with meaty cremini mushrooms. For a simple pasta sauce that came together in minutes, we first cooked the mushrooms in some butter in a skillet. Covering the cremini until they released their liquid sped up the cooking process and concentrated their flavor. A shallot and some garlic infused the sauce with aromatic flavor. Some corn lent color as well as a subtle sweetness that complemented the earthy mushrooms. After simmering the tortellini and mushroom mixture with chicken broth until tender, we added some heavy cream. For a cheesy finish, we folded in grated Parmesan just before serving, along with a sprinkle of fresh parsley.

Finally, for a weeknight supper that is as delicious as it is fast, we kept the cheesy premade tortellini but made our own quick tomato sauce by sautéing an onion until golden brown, then adding a can of fire-roasted diced tomatoes. The tomatoes gave our sauce a smoky complexity, and we fortified the flavors with a little smoked paprika and garlic. We reduced the sauce on the stovetop to concentrate its flavor, then tossed it with the tortellini, spread the mixture in two individual gratin dishes, and topped the dishes with cheese. We broiled them just long enough to melt and brown the topping. A sprinkle of fresh chopped basil rounded out the flavors and made this simple weeknight supper far from ordinary.

Once we looked beyond the jarred tomato sauce, we found store-bought tortellini to be a great way to make a dinner for two that is quick, easy, and delicious.

Tomato Florentine Soup
SERVES 2

We like to serve this soup drizzled with a little extra-virgin olive oil.

- 1 tablespoon olive oil
- 1 ounce pancetta, chopped fine
- 1 small onion, chopped fine
- 1 teaspoon tomato paste
- 1 teaspoon brown sugar
- 2 garlic cloves, minced
- 1½ cups V8 juice
- 1½ cups low-sodium chicken broth
- 3 ounces dried cheese tortellini
- 3 ounces (3 cups) baby spinach
- Salt and pepper
- Grated Parmesan cheese

1. Heat oil in large saucepan over medium-high heat until shimmering. Add pancetta and cook until fat begins to render, about 2 minutes. Add onion, tomato paste, and sugar and cook, stirring occasionally, until onion is softened, about 5 minutes. Stir in garlic and cook until fragrant, about 30 seconds.

2. Whisk in V8 juice and broth, scraping up any browned bits. Stir in tortellini, bring to simmer, and cook until tender, about 10 minutes. Stir in spinach and let wilt, about 1 minute. Season with salt and pepper to taste. Serve with Parmesan.

Pasta Salad with Red Bell Pepper, Pine Nuts, and Basil
SERVES 2

Cooking the tortellini until it is completely tender and leaving it slightly wet after rinsing are important for the texture of the finished salad. You can substitute one 9-ounce package of fresh cheese tortellini for the dried tortellini.

- 6 ounces dried cheese tortellini
- Salt and pepper
- 2 tablespoons extra-virgin olive oil
- 2 tablespoons lemon juice
- 1 small shallot, minced
- 1 small red bell pepper, stemmed, seeded, and cut into ¼-inch-wide strips
- ¼ cup coarsely chopped fresh basil
- 2 tablespoons pine nuts, toasted

NOTES FROM THE TEST KITCHEN

THE BEST TORTELLINI
Making tortellini by hand is a delicious, albeit time-consuming, kitchen project. Store-bought tortellini is a great runner-up, offering both good flavor and tender texture in a fraction of the time. To find the best brand, we recently sampled seven supermarket varieties of cheese tortellini, including two refrigerated, two dried, and three frozen. Surprisingly, our winner was a dried brand: **Barilla Three Cheese Tortellini**. It was praised for a filling that tasters called "creamy," "pungent," and "tangy," thanks to its bold mixture of ricotta, Emmentaler, and Grana Padano cheeses. Another factor in Barilla's win was the texture of the pasta. The delicate wrapper of these petite tortellini was strong enough to contain the filling during boiling, but not overly gummy or prone to blowouts like other brands.

SKILLET TORTELLINI WITH MUSHROOM CREAM SAUCE

1. Bring 4 quarts water to boil in large pot. Add tortellini and 1 tablespoon salt and cook, stirring often, until tender. Drain tortellini, rinse with cold water, and drain again, leaving tortellini slightly wet.

2. Meanwhile, whisk oil, lemon juice, shallot, ⅛ teaspoon salt, and ⅛ teaspoon pepper together in medium bowl. Add tortellini, bell pepper, and basil to bowl and toss to combine. Cover and let sit for 10 minutes. Stir in pine nuts and season with salt and pepper to taste. Serve.

Skillet Tortellini with Mushroom Cream Sauce

SERVES 2

You can substitute one 9-ounce package of fresh cheese tortellini for the dried tortellini; increase the broth to 2½ cups and simmer for an additional 3 to 5 minutes.

- 1 tablespoon unsalted butter
- 6 ounces cremini mushrooms, trimmed and sliced thin
- 1 shallot, minced
- ¼ cup fresh or frozen corn
- 1 garlic clove, minced
- 1¾ cups low-sodium chicken broth
- 6 ounces dried cheese tortellini
- ¼ cup heavy cream
- ¼ cup grated Parmesan cheese
- 1 tablespoon minced fresh parsley
  Salt and pepper

NOTES FROM THE TEST KITCHEN

STORING MUSHROOMS

Gourmet markets usually sell loose mushrooms, but most of the time you'll find mushrooms prepackaged in amounts that are too much for two people. Because of their high moisture content, raw mushrooms are very perishable. Packaged mushrooms, unopened, can be stored in their original containers, which are designed to "breathe," balancing the retention of moisture and the release of ethylene gas. If you open a sealed package of mushrooms but don't use all the contents, simply rewrap the remaining mushrooms in the box with plastic wrap. If your market has loose mushrooms, store these in a partially open zipper-lock bag, which maximizes air circulation (and allows for the release of ethylene gas) without drying out the mushrooms.

1. Melt butter in 10-inch nonstick skillet over medium-high heat. Add mushrooms and shallot, cover, and cook until mushrooms have released their liquid, about 4 minutes. Uncover, stir in corn, and cook, stirring often, until mushrooms are browned, about 5 minutes. Stir in garlic and cook until fragrant, about 30 seconds.

2. Stir in broth and tortellini and bring to rapid simmer. Cook, stirring often, until tortellini is tender, about 10 minutes.

3. Reduce heat to medium-low and stir in cream. Cook, stirring constantly, until sauce is slightly thickened and tortellini is coated with sauce, 2 to 3 minutes. Off heat, stir in Parmesan and parsley and season with salt and pepper to taste. Serve.

Tortellini Gratin with Fire-Roasted Tomatoes

SERVES 2

You will need two shallow 2-cup gratin dishes (measuring approximately 9 by 6 inches; see page 3). You can substitute one 9-ounce package of fresh cheese tortellini for the dried tortellini.

- 8 ounces dried cheese tortellini
  Salt and pepper
- 1 tablespoon olive oil
- 1 small onion, chopped fine
- 1 garlic clove, minced
- ¼ teaspoon smoked paprika
- 1 (14.5-ounce) can diced fire-roasted tomatoes
- 2 ounces shredded Italian cheese blend (½ cup)
- 1 tablespoon chopped fresh basil

1. Adjust oven rack 6 inches from broiler and heat broiler. Bring 4 quarts water to boil in large pot. Add pasta and 1 tablespoon salt and cook, stirring often, until tender. Reserve ¼ cup cooking water, then drain pasta and return it to pot.

2. Meanwhile, heat oil in 8-inch skillet over medium heat until shimmering. Add onion and pinch salt and cook, stirring occasionally, until browned, 8 to 10 minutes. Stir in garlic and paprika and cook until fragrant, about 30 seconds. Stir in tomatoes and simmer, mashing tomatoes with back of spoon, until slightly thickened, about 5 minutes.

3. Add tomato sauce and reserved cooking water to pasta and toss to combine. Season with salt and pepper to taste. Divide pasta mixture evenly between 2 shallow 2-cup gratin dishes (measuring approximately 9 by 6 inches) and sprinkle evenly with cheese. Broil until cheese is melted and spotty brown, about 3 minutes. Sprinkle with basil and serve.

PUTTING CANNED BEANS TO WORK

DRIED BEANS OFTEN OFFER SUPERIOR FLAVOR AND texture, but most require presoaking and long cooking times—not a great option for the weeknight table. Canned beans are a convenient alternative, and we've had success using them in a variety of recipes. They're the perfect choice for last-minute soups, salads, and chilis because they require only a few minutes of simmering to heat through and meld with the flavors in the pot.

First we wanted to make a hearty vegetarian meal. Crispy on the outside and creamy on the inside, pan-fried black bean cakes make a satisfying supper, and canned beans make this supper a snap. We found that mashing most of the beans but leaving a portion of them whole made a cake that was neither too crumbly nor too dense and pasty. To ensure that the cakes would hold together once cooked, we added a little beaten egg and bread crumbs, ingredients often used to bind meat in meatloaf and meatball recipes. Scallions, garlic, and cumin spiked the cakes with warm, savory flavor. We simply mixed everything together, shaped the patties, quickly breaded them, and fried them in a skillet until nicely browned. For a tangy, spicy accompaniment, we mixed sour cream, lime juice, and minced canned chipotle chile in adobo for a dipping sauce that helped to round out our bold Southwestern flavor profile.

For a hearty, flavorful Tuscan-inspired white bean soup, we started by browning pancetta in a large saucepan, then added an onion and carrot for depth and sweetness. To get the maximum amount of flavor from only a few ingredients, we sautéed the vegetables until brown, then stirred in an ample amount of garlic and a pinch of red pepper flakes for a little heat. Earthy and aromatic rosemary infused the soup with Italian flavor. Convenient canned white beans needed to simmer in chicken broth for only 10 minutes. Once the beans were hot and the soup slightly thickened, we had a hearty, flavorful soup perfect for devouring with crusty bread.

For another Italian-influenced meal, we took inspiration for a quick, fresh salad from northern Italy, where hearty portions of white beans and tuna are lightly dressed with olive oil and citrus for an easy summer dinner. To make this dish convenient for a two-person table, we used canned white beans and oil-packed tuna, which boasts a taste and texture far superior to those of the usual canned tuna packed in water. We tossed the beans and tuna with oil-cured olives, grape tomatoes, and peppery watercress. For our dressing, we reduced orange and lemon juice to pack a refreshing flavor punch. The bright citrus brought all the flavors of the rich tuna, salty olives, and sweet tomatoes into perfect balance.

When it comes to cooking with beans, it's hard to beat a good, meaty chili. Whether you like your chili spicy or mild, with or without tomatoes, a bowl of chili should always taste rich, thick, and hearty. But chili typically takes hours to thicken to that perfect consistency, so we set out to streamline the process for two. First, a sautéed onion, minced garlic, and enough chili powder to pack a punch served as our building blocks to a quick, flavorful chili. Once our aromatics were softened, we

---

NOTES FROM THE TEST KITCHEN

THE BEST CANNED WHITE BEANS
We sampled four brands of canned white beans in our search for the best beans. Because so few brands of canned cannellini beans are distributed nationwide, we broadened our taste test to include alternative white beans with widespread distribution, such as great Northern and navy beans. We tasted each contender twice: straight from the can (after being rinsed) and prepared in soup. **Westbrae Organic Great Northern Beans**, described as "creamy" but "firm," came in first in both tastings. Tasters complained that other brands of beans were mealy, bland, and mushy in comparison.

added ground chicken and cooked it until no longer pink. To give our chili body and a touch of smoky sweetness, we added some store-bought barbecue sauce. A can of diced tomatoes lent a nice acidity to the chili, and creamy canned pinto beans ensured that our chili was hearty and substantial.

Whether we were in the mood for a light summer supper or a hearty, warming winter meal, all we needed was a couple of cans of beans in the pantry to get dinner on the table.

Crispy Black Bean Cakes with Chipotle Sour Cream

SERVES 2

Canned chickpeas are a good alternative to the black beans in this recipe.

- ¼ cup sour cream
- 2 teaspoons lime juice
- 1 teaspoon minced canned chipotle chile in adobo sauce
- 1 (15-ounce) can black beans, rinsed
- 3 scallions, sliced thin
- 2 tablespoons plus ½ cup vegetable oil
- 1 garlic clove, minced
- ½ teaspoon ground cumin
     Salt and pepper
- 2 eggs, lightly beaten
- ¾ cup panko bread crumbs

1. Whisk sour cream, lime juice, and chipotle together in bowl until combined; set aside. Mash 1 cup beans, scallions, 2 tablespoons oil, garlic, cumin, ¼ teaspoon salt, and ¼ teaspoon pepper together in medium bowl until mostly smooth. Gently stir in remaining beans, 2 tablespoons beaten egg, and ¼ cup panko. Divide bean mixture into 4 equal portions and lightly pack into 1-inch-thick cakes.

2. Place remaining egg in shallow dish and remaining ½ cup panko in second shallow dish. Working with 1 bean cake at a time, dip cake in egg, allowing excess to drip off, then coat with panko, pressing gently to adhere.

3. Heat remaining ½ cup oil in 10-inch skillet over medium-high heat until shimmering. Carefully place cakes in skillet and cook until golden brown on both sides, 2 to 3 minutes per side. Transfer cakes to paper towel–lined plate to drain briefly. Serve with chipotle sour cream.

Tuscan White Bean Soup

SERVES 2

We like to serve this soup with crusty Italian bread.

- 2 teaspoons olive oil
- 1 ounce pancetta, cut into ¼-inch pieces
- 1 small onion, chopped fine
- 1 carrot, peeled, halved lengthwise, and cut into ¼-inch-thick pieces
- 3 garlic cloves, minced
- ¼ teaspoon minced fresh rosemary
     Pinch red pepper flakes
- 2 cups low-sodium chicken broth
- 1 (15-ounce) can white beans, rinsed
     Salt and pepper
     Grated Parmesan cheese

1. Heat oil in large saucepan over medium-high heat until shimmering. Add pancetta and cook, stirring occasionally, until browned, 3 to 5 minutes. Add onion and carrot and cook until lightly browned, 5 to 7 minutes.

2. Stir in garlic, rosemary, and pepper flakes and cook until fragrant, about 30 seconds. Add broth and beans and bring to simmer. Reduce heat to medium-low and simmer until soup is slightly thickened, about 10 minutes. Season with salt and pepper to taste. Serve with Parmesan.

White Bean and Tuna Salad

SERVES 2

We prefer more flavorful oil-packed tuna in this salad, but you can substitute water-packed tuna.

- 2 (2-inch) strips orange zest, sliced thin, plus ½ cup juice
- 2 tablespoons lemon juice
- 3 tablespoons extra-virgin olive oil
- 1 teaspoon minced fresh thyme

THE BEST PREMIUM CANNED TUNA

The imported European equivalent of sushi-grade *toro*, *ventresca* tuna is cut from the fatty belly of either the *bonito del norte* or yellowfin species, and the buttery, tender, olive oil–packed slices make a luxe addition to any tuna salad or Spanish tapas spread.

Most of the six brands we tasted (priced from $1.20 to $4.72 per ounce, plus shipping) stood head and shoulders above regular supermarket canned tuna. One in particular, **Nadrin Bonito Del Norte Ventresca Fillets**, left tasters swooning over its "creamy, delicate" meat boasting "full, rich tuna flavor." We think it's worth the occasional splurge, but since it costs $35 for 8.5 ounces before shipping, we gladly elected a more frugal alternative: The "firm-fleshed," "briny" **Tonnino Tuna Ventresca Yellowfin** was our Best Buy at one-quarter the price ($7.99 for 6.7 ounces) and can be found in some supermarkets.

THE BEST BOTTLED BARBECUE SAUCE

Whether you use it to baste, dip, or slather, chances are you have a bottle of barbecue sauce tucked into the door of your refrigerator. But is it the best-tasting brand? To find out, we gathered eight national brands and asked tasters to sample each sauce on its own, as a dip for chicken nuggets, and broiled on chicken thighs.

Barbecue styles vary greatly by region, but we'd argue there's an all-American supermarket style. It's on the sweet side and balances tang, smoke, and tomato flavor. The sauces that fit that profile rated better than those closer to regional barbecue styles, which tasters often thought weren't sweet enough. Total sugars proved the determining factor in our tasting; the sauces with more total sugars rated better than the sauces with less. But not all sugars are created equal.

Our two favorite sauces were the only two in our lineup that list molasses as their third ingredient. When the robust, distinct flavor of molasses was in short supply, the sauces fell flat. Moreover, our winner contains no high-fructose corn syrup; white sugar is its primary sweetener. In the end, **Bull's-Eye Original Barbecue Sauce** won tasters over with its tangy, tomatoey, robust and spicy flavor; tasters thought it was "almost perfect," with "a good balance of smoky and sweet."

Salt and pepper

4 ounces (4 cups) watercress

1 (15-ounce) can white beans, rinsed

6 ounces grape tomatoes, halved

¼ cup pitted oil-cured olives, halved

5 ounces oil-packed solid white tuna, drained and flaked

1. Combine orange zest and juice and lemon juice in small saucepan and bring to boil over medium-high heat. Reduce heat to medium-low and simmer until reduced by half, 4 to 6 minutes. Strain juice through fine-mesh strainer set over large bowl. Whisk in oil, thyme, pinch salt, and pinch pepper.

2. Add watercress, beans, tomatoes, and olives and toss to coat. Season with salt and pepper to taste. Divide salad between 2 serving plates, then arrange tuna evenly on top of each portion. Serve.

Smoky Chicken Chili

SERVES 2

Serve with your favorite chili toppings.

1 tablespoon vegetable oil

1 small onion, chopped fine

1 garlic clove, minced

1 tablespoon chili powder

8 ounces ground chicken

1 (15-ounce) can pinto or kidney beans, rinsed

1 (14.5-ounce) can diced tomatoes

¾ cup water

⅓ cup barbecue sauce

1 tablespoon minced fresh cilantro

Salt and pepper

1. Heat oil in large saucepan over medium-high heat until shimmering. Add onion and cook, stirring occasionally, until softened, about 5 minutes. Stir in garlic and chili powder and cook until fragrant, about 30 seconds. Add ground chicken and cook, breaking up meat with spoon, until no longer pink, 3 to 5 minutes.

2. Add beans, tomatoes, water, and barbecue sauce and bring to simmer. Reduce heat to medium-low and simmer until thickened, about 10 minutes. Off heat, stir in cilantro and season with salt and pepper to taste. Serve.

SMOKY CHICKEN CHILI

SLOW-COOKER RED WINE-BRAISED SHORT RIBS

SLOW-COOKER FAVORITES

SLOW-COOKER RED LENTIL STEW

✔ WHY THIS RECIPE WORKS: For a satisfying, flavorful lentil stew for two, we looked to Indian cuisine for inspiration. Red lentils, a handful of warm spices, and coconut milk gave us a rich, creamy stew with vibrant flavor, even after hours in the slow cooker. Fork-friendly bites of carrot, chopped tomatoes, sweet peas, and minced cilantro ensured that our stew was plenty hearty and offered colorful bursts of flavor.

WHILE WE'RE BIG FANS OF TRADITIONAL LENTIL soup, sometimes it can seem a little ho-hum. Casting about for a more exciting way to enjoy this legume, we looked to Indian cuisine for inspiration. Deeply flavored, exotically spiced *dal* are comforting, hearty lentil dishes that have a thick, almost porridgelike consistency when cooked. Red lentils, sold under the Indian name *masoor dal*, are one of the most popular legumes of India. These mild, slightly nutty-tasting lentils are small and break down easily, so we thought they would cook down nicely in the moist environment of the slow cooker. We also expected that the potent mix of Indian spices would keep our lentils richly flavored, even after hours of cooking. Our goal, then, was a deeply flavored, perfectly thickened lentil stew for two from the slow cooker.

We started with the foundation of our stew: the spices. We weeded through our spice pantry to determine our favorite mix. In an attempt to streamline our ingredient list, we tried using only garam masala—an Indian spice blend that includes coriander, cloves, cardamom, cumin, cinnamon, black pepper, and nutmeg—but found that this didn't produce the complex flavor we expected. Instead we reached for individual spices to create our own mix. Not wanting to make our lentil stew overly spicy, we sought to build a basic blend of warm spices that offered just a punch of subtle heat. After a number of tests, we settled on a combination of coriander, cumin, cinnamon, turmeric, and a pinch of red pepper flakes. Together the spices yielded fragrance and flavor that were rich and complex, but not overpowering.

Many recipes we researched called for adding the aromatics raw or skipping them altogether, relying entirely on the spices and additional garnishes such as chutney for flavor. We felt this dish would benefit from the addition of onion, garlic, and ginger, but adding them to the slow cooker raw gave us a harsh-tasting stew. For our next test, we reached for a skillet and sautéed them quickly in a small amount of oil. Since we already had our pan out, we decided to bloom, or cook, the spices as well in order to deepen their flavors.

Though it took just 10 minutes to cook our aromatics and spices, we wondered if we could speed up the process. To keep things easy and to cut back on dirty dishes, we simply combined our onion, garlic, and ginger with the spices and 2 teaspoons of vegetable oil in a bowl, popped it into the microwave, and hit the start button. Just a few minutes worked to enhance the flavor of our spices and mellow the harshness of our aromatics, leading to a dish with more complexity. For even more vegetal presence, we added some chopped carrots to the slow cooker; they added to the heartiness of our stew and contributed a slightly sweet, earthy quality.

Next, it was time to address the texture of the cooked stew. Traditional dal has a porridgelike consistency, almost bordering on a puree; this consistency comes from cooking the lentils for the appropriate amount of time with the correct amount of water. This was easier said than done in the slow cooker, and it took us several tries to get the lentils to their ideal consistency. Too much water and the dish wound up thin and soupy; too little and it was thick and pasty. We found that 2 cups of liquid to ½ cup of lentils worked best, giving our stew just the right texture (and ensuring that we had no leftovers). But though it had the right texture, tasters found it somewhat lean-tasting. Luckily, we found an easy solution to this problem. We simply swapped out a portion of the water for coconut milk. Now our stew was not only properly thickened; it was rich and creamy as well.

With our lentils perfectly cooked, we considered final additions. Chopped plum tomatoes contributed freshness and acidity; to ensure that they didn't break down too much, we added them to the slow cooker for the last 10 minutes of cooking. Frozen peas, stirred in at the end just to heat through, offered sweetness and a pop of color. Minced cilantro added herbal, citrusy notes.

Miles away from ordinary, our slow-cooked red lentil stew was not only richly flavored, but it was also incredibly hearty and satisfying—and we didn't even have to dirty a pot to make it.

SLOW-COOKER RED LENTIL STEW

Slow-Cooker Red Lentil Stew

SERVES 2

Do not substitute light coconut milk here. Do not substitute brown lentils for the red lentils in this recipe; red lentils have a very different texture. See page 12 for a recipe to use up the leftover coconut milk. *Cooking time: 4 to 5 hours on low or 2 to 3 hours on high*

- 1 small onion, chopped fine
- 2 garlic cloves, minced
- 2 teaspoons vegetable oil
- 1 teaspoon grated fresh ginger
- ¼ teaspoon ground coriander
- ¼ teaspoon ground cumin
- ¼ teaspoon ground cinnamon
- ¼ teaspoon ground turmeric
   Pinch red pepper flakes
- 1¼ cups water, plus extra as needed
- ¾ cup coconut milk
- ½ cup red lentils, picked over and rinsed
- 2 carrots, peeled and cut into ¼-inch pieces
- 2 plum tomatoes, cored and chopped medium
- ⅓ cup frozen peas
- 1 tablespoon minced fresh cilantro
   Salt and pepper

1. Lightly spray inside of slow cooker with vegetable oil spray. Microwave onion, garlic, oil, ginger, coriander, cumin, cinnamon, turmeric, and pepper flakes in bowl, stirring occasionally, until onion is softened, about 3 minutes; transfer to slow cooker.

NOTES FROM THE TEST KITCHEN

ALL ABOUT LENTILS
Lentils come in various sizes and colors, and the differences in flavor and texture are surprisingly distinct. Though both red and yellow lentils are frequently used in Indian cooking, we prefer red lentils in our slow-cooked stew. They are very small, have an orange-red hue, and break down completely when cooked. Yellow lentils are also small, brightly colored, and cook down completely. Brown and green lentils are the most common varieties. Brown lentils are larger than red and yellow lentils and have a uniform brown color and a "mild yet light and earthy flavor"; green lentils are similar in size to the brown but are greenish brown in color and have a very "mild flavor." *Lentilles du Puy* are smaller than the brown and green varieties and take their name from the city of Puy in France. They are dark olive green, almost black, in color and are praised for their "rich, earthy, complex flavor" and "firm yet tender texture."

2. Stir water, coconut milk, lentils, and carrots into slow cooker. Cover and cook until lentils are very tender and broken down, 4 to 5 hours on low or 2 to 3 hours on high.

3. Stir in tomatoes, cover, and cook on high until heated through, about 10 minutes. Stir in peas and let sit until heated through, about 5 minutes. (Adjust stew consistency with additional hot water as needed.) Stir in cilantro and season with salt and pepper to taste. Serve.

SLOW-COOKER BLACK BEAN SOUP

✔ WHY THIS RECIPE WORKS: To create an easy black bean soup for two that offered robust flavor even after hours in the slow cooker, we cooked the beans in a mixture of chicken broth and water for a flavorful backbone and simmered the soup with a few slices of bacon (we removed the bacon at the end of cooking). Onion, garlic, and a good amount of chili powder amped up the flavor and heat level, and mashing some of the cooked beans and stirring them back into the finished soup provided excellent body and a nicely thickened texture.

GOOD BLACK BEAN SOUP IS ROBUST, HEARTY, AND earthy-tasting, with a creamy texture and jet-black color. Most black bean soups we've sampled, however, are not so good—their flavor is dull and washed out, and their color is a drab and murky gray. Add the moist cooking environment of the slow cooker to the mix, and things don't improve much. Plus, most recipes serve a hungry crowd. We thought the appeal of a hands-off black bean soup that served just two was undeniable and resolved to not only scale down our soup, but also infuse it with as much flavor as possible. We set out to create a black bean soup for two that we could walk away from for part of the day, but it had to be rich and full-flavored when we returned.

We started out with dried beans in hand. Usually we prefer to soak beans in a saltwater solution prior to cooking. This softens the tough bean skins and prevents the beans from bursting during cooking. However, we weren't convinced that soaking would be necessary given the long cooking time. After a few tests, we knew our instincts were right. The unsoaked beans were just as flavorful and tender as the beans that had been soaked. A few of them had burst open, but these beans would only contribute to the thick, rich texture we were after.

Moving on to the liquid component of our soup, we needed to determine the right amount to properly cook the beans—too much and the soup was dull and watery; too little and we ended up with sludge. To serve two people, we found that ¾ cup of beans and 2½ cups of liquid produced perfectly cooked beans with just the right texture. To ensure well-seasoned beans, the liquid component also needed to impart flavor. Because we were working with a slow cooker, using a flavorful liquid was even more important, as there would be no opportunity for the liquid to reduce and concentrate in flavor. We tried using chicken broth first, but the resulting soup was (not surprisingly) too chicken-y in flavor. Water alone left the soup bland and one-dimensional. We tested various combinations of chicken broth and water and settled on a ratio of 1½ cups of chicken broth to 1 cup of water for soup with a balanced flavor.

Now we could focus on developing the flavor profile. We began with chopped onion and minced garlic. For heat and depth, we included some chili powder. Taking a cue from our Slow-Cooker Red Lentil Stew (page 214), we microwaved these ingredients with a small amount of oil rather than sautéing them on the stovetop. This worked to mellow the raw, harsh taste of the aromatics and intensify the flavor of the chili powder. Chopped celery and carrot, which we added to the slow cooker with the beans and cooking liquid, contributed more heartiness and vegetal notes.

The soup was coming together nicely, but tasters agreed it was missing a certain meaty quality traditionally imparted by salt pork or ham hocks. Keeping an eye on convenience in the for-two kitchen, we tested cooking the beans with a few slices of bacon, a thin ham steak from the deli counter, and some kielbasa. We liked all three for different reasons, but the familiar smoky and salty flavor of the bacon ultimately won out. However, we didn't care for the slippery, unappetizing texture of the bacon after a few hours in the slow cooker, so we opted to remove the slices right before serving.

This slow-cooked soup boasted perfectly cooked beans and rich, deep flavor, but the texture was still lacking a certain creaminess. Yes, some of the beans had broken down during cooking, but the soup still remained brothy. To solve the problem, we decided to mash a small portion of the beans and stir the smooth paste back into the soup. This worked like a charm and gave us the velvety texture we were after. Finished with minced cilantro for color and freshness, our Slow-Cooker Black Bean Soup was richly flavored, utterly satisfying—and practically effortless.

Slow-Cooker Black Bean Soup

SERVES 2

If cooking this soup on low, you may need to adjust the consistency with additional warm broth before serving. Serve this soup with minced red onion, sour cream, and hot sauce. *Cooking time: 10 to 12 hours on low or 4 to 5 hours on high*

- **1 onion, chopped fine**
- **3 garlic cloves, minced**
- **2 teaspoons vegetable oil**
- **2 teaspoons chili powder**
- **1½ cups low-sodium chicken broth**
- **1 cup water**
- **¾ cup dried black beans, picked over and rinsed**
- **3 slices bacon**
- **1 celery rib, cut into ½-inch pieces**
- **1 small carrot, peeled and cut into ½-inch pieces**
- **1 bay leaf**
- **1 tablespoon minced fresh cilantro**
- **Salt and pepper**

NOTES FROM THE TEST KITCHEN

THE BEST DRIED BLACK BEANS

In the cooking-for-two kitchen, canned beans offer the ultimate in convenience. But for dishes in which the beans truly take center stage, we prefer the flavor and texture provided by dried beans. To find the best dried black beans, we sampled three brands cooked plain and in a recipe for black beans and rice. Surprisingly, the single mail-order variety, a pricey heirloom bean, became mushy, while the beans from the two national supermarket brands were perfectly creamy. Our favorite was **Goya Dried Black Beans**, which offered "nutty," "buttery" bean flavor and a reliably uniform texture.

1. Lightly spray inside of slow cooker with vegetable oil spray. Microwave onion, garlic, oil, and chili powder in bowl, stirring occasionally, until onion is softened, about 4 minutes; transfer to slow cooker.

2. Stir broth, water, beans, bacon, celery, carrot, and bay leaf into slow cooker. Cover and cook until beans are tender, 10 to 12 hours on low or 4 to 5 hours on high.

3. Let soup settle for 5 minutes, then remove fat from surface using large spoon. Discard bacon and bay leaf.

4. Transfer ½ cup cooked beans to bowl and mash until smooth with potato masher. Stir mashed beans into soup and let sit until heated through, about 5 minutes. Stir in cilantro and season with salt and pepper to taste. Serve.

SLOW-COOKER CHICKEN PROVENÇAL

✔ WHY THIS RECIPE WORKS: A French classic, chicken Provençal calls for slow-simmering chicken with a bold mix of tomatoes, herbs, and olives. For a more hands-off version for two, we moved ours to the slow cooker and traded the whole bird for chicken thighs. Removing the skin prior to cooking kept the sauce from becoming greasy, and a spoonful of tomato paste amped up the rich, savory notes of the dish in lieu of browning the meat. Canned whole tomatoes, processed until smooth, gave us the makings of a bright-tasting, nicely clingy sauce. A potent blend of garlic, oregano, white wine, and niçoise olives rounded out our homage to simple yet satisfying French fare.

CHICKEN PROVENÇAL REPRESENTS THE BEST OF French peasant cooking—chicken on the bone is slowly simmered with tomatoes, garlic, herbs, and olives, making for an appealing, satisfying supper. Given that this dish traditionally calls on low, slow heat to produce chicken that's fall-off-the-bone tender and a sauce that's thick and rich-tasting, we thought it would be the perfect candidate for the slow cooker. We wanted a simple recipe for slow-cooked chicken Provençal, for an easy yet flavorful dinner for two.

In our research we found a handful of recipes and commenced testing. Most of them began with browning a cut-up chicken, then removing it from the pot; sautéing some aromatics; deglazing the pot with white wine or dry vermouth; adding stock, tomatoes, olives, and herbs; and finally simmering the chicken in the slow cooker until done. Though they sounded promising, the results were disastrous. Our sample recipes produced rubbery, dry chicken, dull and muddy flavors, and a sauce that was either too thick or too thin, too sweet or too salty. We had to find a way to turn out moist, tender chicken, even after hours in the slow cooker, and a boldly flavored yet balanced sauce with a nice, clingy texture, without the aid of any evaporation. We knew we could do better.

Since a whole chicken is overkill for just two servings, our first move was to ditch the bird in favor of bone-in chicken thighs. Experience has taught us that chicken breasts tend to dry out and become tough in the slow cooker, so we knew dark meat was the way to go. We also knew we'd have to remove the skin prior to cooking; otherwise we would end up with a greasy sauce. We did a trial run with our chicken thighs (skin removed) and a simple sauce (we could finesse the amounts and seasonings later) and were pleased with the results. The meat came out tender, moist, and flavorful, and the sauce had just a modicum of fat on the surface.

Though searing the chicken is usually the first step in most slow-cooker recipes, our skinless thighs stuck to the pan during searing, the outer layer of the chicken becoming tough and dry from browning. The skin, it turns out, acts as a necessary cushion between the meat and the pan, and without it searing wasn't a viable option. We'd have to find another way to instill our dish with deep flavor because we wouldn't have a flavorful fond, or the browned bits left behind from searing our chicken, available to us. In the test kitchen we often turn to tomato paste, which is high in glutamates, to add depth and savory complexity to recipes. Here, it was just the ticket. A single teaspoon, cooked with our aromatics, contributed subtle depth to our dish.

Our final tests with the chicken focused on the timing. Chicken is notorious for drying out with extended cooking, even in the moist environment of a slow cooker. After several rubbery results, we found that the optimal cooking time and temperature were three to four hours on low in a standard slow cooker. Any longer and the chicken overcooked, and cooking the chicken on high for half that time turned out inconsistent results and negated using a slow cooker in the first place. This was reversed, however, when we used a small (3-quart) slow cooker. Because of the smaller size of the slow-cooker insert, the chicken was covered by more of the sauce, so it was insulated from the heat of the cooker and we were able to achieve perfectly tender chicken on the high setting.

With the chicken squared away, we turned our attention to the sauce. Onion, a healthy dose of garlic, and tomato paste were set as the foundation. As in our Slow-Cooker Black Bean Soup (page 215), we enlisted the help of our microwave to jump-start the cooking of the aromatics and intensify the flavor of the tomato paste. Recipes we researched had included either dry white wine or dry vermouth, but in our sauce wine turned out to be the favorite among tasters; the vermouth seemed to exaggerate the acidity of the tomatoes. We tested a variety of tomato products to round out our sauce. Both tomato sauce and pureed canned tomatoes produced thick, sweet, overbearing sauces reminiscent of bad Italian restaurant fare. Canned diced tomatoes, though more promising, presented the opposite problem: Even when drained they contain a fair amount of liquid, and the resulting sauce was too thin. We found a happy medium in canned whole tomatoes, which we quickly pulsed in the food processor until smooth. This improved the sauce dramatically, and it easily coated the chicken.

Whole niçoise olives appeared in nearly every recipe we found, but tasters complained that whole olives cooked with the chicken overpowered the dish. No problem—we coarsely chopped a few olives and stirred them in near the end of cooking. Now they added a salty contrast to the slightly sweet sauce. As for seasonings, tasters liked a combination of fresh oregano and parsley. To maximize the brightness of the parsley we stirred it in just before serving.

A couple of other last-minute additions brought the whole dish together. We considered extra-virgin olive oil to be essential (after all, it's a signature ingredient of Provençal cuisine), and drizzling a little over the sauce at the end perfumed the dish. Finally, a spritz of lemon contributed brightness. This slow-cooker chicken Provençal was every bit as hearty and homey as the original, and though it required a lot less work, it still offered all the big flavors.

NOTES FROM THE TEST KITCHEN

SLOW COOKING FOR TWO

Using a slow cooker is a great way for the time-pressed cook to get supper on the table—no close monitoring of the stovetop or oven necessary. But most slow-cooker recipes make enough food to feed a crowd. In this chapter you'll find an array of slow-cooker recipes scaled down to serve just two. We developed these recipes with an oval 3- to 3½-quart slow cooker because we found it to be easier to maneuver and clean, more affordable, and less space-hogging than larger slow cookers, but this collection of recipes works equally well in a standard 6-quart slow cooker. After developing lots of slow-cooker recipes over the years, we've learned a few tricks for ensuring success, no matter the size of your slow cooker.

SPRAY YOUR SLOW COOKER: Spraying the sides of the insert with vegetable oil spray, before adding food, eliminates any sticking (or burning) and makes cleanup easier. This is especially important when you are cooking a smaller amount of food, as with our scaled-down recipes for two.

USE THE MICROWAVE: When there is no need to get out a skillet to brown meat, use the microwave to cook the aromatics and bloom the flavors of any spices. We also use the microwave in place of the oven to infuse rib bones with "roasted" flavor in our Slow-Cooker Red Wine–Braised Short Ribs (page 228).

BROWN YOUR MEAT—SOMETIMES: In recipes that use a lot of spicy or aromatic ingredients, we've found that we can get away with not browning meat. But when a deep flavor base is required, we need to get out the skillet and brown the meat.

INCLUDE FLAVOR-AMPLIFYING INGREDIENTS FOR DEPTH: We've found that a handful of key ingredients, such as tomato paste and soy sauce, can increase meaty richness and depth of flavor substantially, especially when we're not browning meat.

ADD A THICKENER: Since there is no opportunity for sauces and stews to thicken naturally in the moist environment of the slow cooker, thickeners are necessary for many recipes. We've found that tapioca, cornstarch, and flour all work well according to the application. When we don't need to sauté aromatics or brown meat, we opt for tapioca or cornstarch; they require no precooking and can simply be stirred into the slow cooker. Flour, on the other hand, must be cooked briefly to rid it of its raw flavor, so that's our thickener of choice when we're sautéing or browning.

SLOW-COOKER CHICKEN PROVENÇAL

Slow-Cooker Chicken Provençal

SERVES 2

We like serving this dish with polenta, but rice or crusty bread also make good accompaniments. *Cooking time: 3 to 4 hours on low in a 6-quart slow cooker, or 3 to 4 hours on high in a 3- to 3½-quart slow cooker*

- 1 onion, chopped fine
- 4 garlic cloves, minced
- 2 teaspoons extra-virgin olive oil, plus extra for serving
- 1 teaspoon tomato paste
- ¾ teaspoon minced fresh oregano or ⅛ teaspoon dried
- 1 (14.5-ounce) can whole peeled tomatoes
- 3 tablespoons dry white wine
- 1 bay leaf
- 4 (6-ounce) bone-in chicken thighs, skin removed, trimmed
    Salt and pepper
- 2 tablespoons pitted niçoise olives, chopped coarse
- 1½ tablespoons minced fresh parsley
    Lemon wedges

1. Lightly spray inside of slow cooker with vegetable oil spray. Microwave onion, garlic, oil, tomato paste, and oregano in bowl, stirring occasionally, until onion is softened, about 4 minutes; transfer to slow cooker.

2. Pulse tomatoes and their juice in food processor until almost smooth, about 10 pulses. Stir tomatoes, wine, and bay leaf into slow cooker. Season chicken with salt and pepper and nestle into slow cooker. Cover and cook until chicken is tender, 3 to 4 hours on low in 6-quart slow cooker (or 3 to 4 hours on high in 3- to 3½-quart slow cooker).

3. Transfer chicken to serving platter and tent loosely with aluminum foil. Let braising liquid settle for 5 minutes, then remove fat from surface using large spoon. Discard bay leaf. Stir in olives and parsley and season with salt and pepper to taste. Spoon 1 cup sauce over chicken and serve with additional olive oil, lemon wedges, and remaining sauce.

SLOW-COOKER MOROCCAN CHICKEN STEW

✔ WHY THIS RECIPE WORKS: For a slow-cooked Moroccan chicken stew for two that delivered authentic flavor, we started with chicken thighs and added chickpeas and dried apricots, which softened during the long cooking time and permeated the stew with their flavor. Onion and garlic provided a flavorful backbone, and tomato paste added depth to our slow-simmered sauce. A small amount of tapioca ensured that the sauce thickened nicely. Narrowing down the spice list to just the essentials—paprika, cardamom, and cayenne—gave us a dish that tasted like a true tagine but didn't require seeking out obscure ingredients.

DRAWING ON INFLUENCES FROM DIVERSE surrounding cultures, Moroccan stews (or tagines, as they're commonly called) are highly aromatic and flavorful. Characterized by brilliant, earthy hues and a blend of sweet and savory ingredients, they can be at once intriguing and intimidating—traditional recipes call for a laundry list of spices, plus they make enough food to feed a small village. We wanted to develop a

---

NOTES FROM THE TEST KITCHEN

PITTING OLIVES

We prefer buying unpitted olives and pitting them ourselves since olives sold already pitted tend to be mushier and saltier and have less flavor than their unpitted counterparts. Buy olives from the refrigerated or salad bar section of the supermarket, rather than purchasing the jarred, shelf-stable variety.

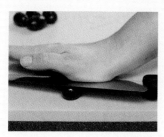

To pit olives, place them on cutting board; hold flat edge of knife over one olive. Press blade firmly with your hand to loosen olive meat from pit, then remove pit with your fingers and repeat.

recipe for an authentic-tasting Moroccan stew featuring bites of moist, tender chicken that was prepared in the slow cooker and didn't require much advance work (read: no seeking out specialty ingredients). And it had to make just enough to serve two.

We started with chicken thighs as the base for our stew, which we chose because their flavor is more robust than that of chicken breasts and would stand up to the bold mix of spices we planned to include. For our first pass, we chopped boneless, skinless thighs into bite-size pieces before cooking, but after a few hours in the slow cooker the chicken had dried out despite the moist cooking environment. To keep the chicken moist, we decided to cook the thighs whole and then shred the meat and stir it back into the stew after cooking. This gave us tender meat that, when shredded, dispersed evenly throughout the stew.

Knowing that the choice of spices would be critical, we addressed seasonings next. We tested a number of options that appear often in Moroccan stews but in the end kept only two that tasters deemed essential: cardamom and paprika. Cardamom is a pungent, aromatic spice with lemony undertones and is available in whole pods or in ground form, which we used in this recipe to keep things simple. Paprika can range in potency from sweet to hot. We opted for sweet paprika and supplemented it with a pinch of cayenne pepper to give our stew a vibrant and piquant flavor.

Moving on to the aromatics, we selected onion and garlic. A teaspoon of tomato paste offered depth of flavor to our long-cooked stew. To temper the sharp spices, we cooked them together with our aromatics in the microwave for just a few minutes before adding them to the slow cooker. For a touch of sweetness, we added dried apricots, another common tagine ingredient, and used chicken broth and a small amount of white wine for the cooking liquid. Now we had a stew packed with big flavors.

Tasters were satisfied with our chicken stew thus far but wanted more heartiness, so we decided to add chickpeas, a common ingredient in Moroccan cuisine. Their creamy texture and nutty flavor added yet another dimension to the stew. Canned chickpeas proved a more convenient option than the dried variety, so we opted for canned. When stirred in at the onset of cooking, the chickpeas absorbed the complex flavors of the stew, and their firm texture had softened slightly by the time the stew finished cooking.

Our last challenge was to address the consistency of our stew, which had been on the loose side in our initial tests. Many slow-cooker stew recipes turn to a slurry of either flour or cornstarch, combined with broth or water, which has to be stirred in at the end of the cooking time. While both of these options worked to thicken the sauce, they imparted a starchy taste and required extra cooking time to thicken the liquid. We found a substitute, however, in instant tapioca; this ingredient was ideal because it thickened the sauce without making it gloppy or contributing any off-flavors.

Finishing the stew with cilantro and lemon juice gave it the fresh, bright flavor we sought. With its exotic flavors and heady aromas, this simple stew had all the intrigue and complexity of a true tagine.

NOTES FROM THE TEST KITCHEN

SHREDDING CHICKEN OR PORK

Hold 1 fork in each hand, with tines facing down. Insert tines into meat and gently pull forks away from each other, breaking meat into bite-size pieces or large chunks.

CHOPPING DRIED FRUIT

Dried fruits, especially apricots (or dates), very often stick to the knife when you try to chop them. Here's an easy way to avoid this problem.

Coat the blade of the knife with a thin film of vegetable oil spray before chopping the dried fruit. The chopped fruit won't cling to the blade, and the knife will stay relatively clean.

Slow-Cooker Moroccan Chicken Stew

SERVES 2

This stew can be served on its own or over couscous or basmati rice. *Cooking time: 3 to 4 hours on low in a 6-quart slow cooker, or 3 to 4 hours on high in a 3- to 3½-quart slow cooker*

1	small onion, chopped fine
3	garlic cloves, minced
1	teaspoon tomato paste
1	teaspoon vegetable oil
¾	teaspoon sweet paprika
¼	teaspoon ground cardamom
	Pinch cayenne
1⅔	cups low-sodium chicken broth, plus extra as needed
¾	cup canned chickpeas, rinsed
¼	cup dry white wine
3	tablespoons chopped dried apricots
2	teaspoons Minute tapioca
1	bay leaf
12	ounces boneless, skinless chicken thighs, trimmed
	Salt and pepper
1	tablespoon minced fresh cilantro
	Light brown sugar
	Lemon wedges

1. Lightly spray inside of slow cooker with vegetable oil spray. Microwave onion, garlic, tomato paste, oil, paprika, cardamom, and cayenne in bowl, stirring occasionally, until onion is softened, about 4 minutes; transfer to slow cooker.

2. Stir broth, chickpeas, wine, apricots, tapioca, and bay leaf into slow cooker. Season chicken with salt and pepper and nestle into slow cooker. Cover and cook until chicken is tender, 3 to 4 hours on low in 6-quart slow cooker (or 3 to 4 hours on high in 3- to 3½-quart slow cooker).

3. Transfer chicken to cutting board, let cool slightly, then shred into bite-size pieces. Let stew settle for 5 minutes, then remove fat from surface using large spoon. Discard bay leaf.

4. Stir shredded chicken into stew and let sit until heated through, about 5 minutes. Adjust stew consistency with additional hot broth as needed. Stir in cilantro, season with salt, pepper, and sugar to taste, and serve with lemon wedges.

SLOW-COOKER PORK CHOPS WITH CRANBERRIES AND ORANGE

✔ **WHY THIS RECIPE WORKS:** To keep a pair of pork chops from drying out in the slow cooker, we chose thick-cut blade chops, which have plenty of dark meat and fat to keep them tender and juicy. But even with this cut, we had to limit their exposure to the heat and found it best to stick to the low setting on the slow cooker. Dried cranberries and orange juice gave us the makings of a brightly flavored sauce that we reduced briefly on the stovetop until it was nicely thickened and clung perfectly to our tender chops.

PORK CHOPS ARE ONE OF OUR GO-TO CUTS IN THE cooking-for-two kitchen. But given that they are fairly lean, they can overcook easily, resulting in a dry, flavorless dinner. We wanted to take advantage of the convenience of the slow cooker to prepare this supermarket staple so we could have a satisfying supper waiting in the wings when we were ready to eat, but we'd have to figure out how to keep the pork moist and tender for the duration of cooking. Since pork chops and fruit pair perfectly, we decided to incorporate bright, citrusy orange and tangy, sweet cranberries into our dish to create a simple sauce for our slow-cooked pork chops for two.

First we had to figure out which cut of chop would stay tender in the slow cooker. Rib chops are a common cut for braising, so that's where we started. We made sure they were about ¾ inch thick, thinking anything thinner would overcook quickly in the slow cooker. For a quick sauce (we'd finesse the flavors later on), we combined canned cranberry sauce and orange juice. We moved this mixture to the slow cooker, added our pork chops, and set the cooker on low. When we pulled them from the slow cooker 4 hours later, the chops were dry and stringy. It appeared that thin was not in, and we'd need to consider thicker chops.

For our next test we used 1½-inch-thick rib chops, but to our dismay, 4 hours later these chops were also overcooked. We were thinking of cutting back on the cooking time when a test kitchen colleague suggested blade chops, which are cut from the shoulder end of the loin and contain a significant amount of fat and connective tissue, both of which make them ideal for long cooking times. When we tried them, the fat melted into the meat, keeping it moist and tender, and the connective tissue all but disappeared over the long stint in the slow cooker. Though we often sear meat prior to braising, we found that in this case, searing sped up the cooking process, leading to the dry meat we were trying to avoid, so we crossed this extra step off the list. We tested cooking the chops on the low and high settings in the slow cooker and found that high heat, even for just a couple of hours, was too intense and dried out our chops. For this recipe, only low would do.

But while our chops were now in great shape, our sauce was definitely not up to par. The canned cranberry sauce, while easy, turned far too sweet and one-dimensional. It was clear that the canned stuff wouldn't cut it, so we ditched it in favor of an equally no-prep ingredient: dried cranberries. But simply braising our chops in orange juice with some dried cranberries gave us a thin, runny sauce that tasted way too tart. For deeper, more complex flavor and a thicker sauce, we swapped some of the orange juice for chicken broth, which amped up the savory notes, and added a tablespoon of maple syrup, which offered a more sophisticated sweetness than white or brown sugar. With a few more refinements—a minced shallot contributed some aromatic backbone, and a sprinkling of fresh thyme offered a woodsy herbal quality—our sauce boasted a complex, multidimensional flavor.

Our last challenge was to finesse the texture of the sauce—the dried fruit had absorbed some of the liquid, but overall it was still a bit thin. While the chops rested after cooking, we transferred the sauce to a small saucepan and simmered it briefly on the stovetop until it had reduced to the perfect consistency. At last, we had a bright-tasting sauce that clung nicely to our tender, juicy chops.

Slow-Cooker Pork Chops with Cranberries and Orange

SERVES 2

Be sure to use blade-cut pork chops (that are at least 1½ inches thick), which are cut from the shoulder end of the loin and contain a significant amount of fat and connective tissue. *Cooking time: 3 to 4 hours on low*

⅓   cup low-sodium chicken broth
¼   cup dried cranberries
1   shallot, minced
3   tablespoons orange juice
1   tablespoon maple syrup
½   teaspoon minced fresh thyme
2   (12- to 14-ounce) bone-in blade-cut pork chops, 1½ inches thick, trimmed
     Salt and pepper

1. Lightly spray inside of slow cooker with vegetable oil spray. Stir broth, cranberries, shallot, orange juice, maple syrup, and thyme into slow cooker.

2. Cut 2 slits about 2 inches apart through fat around outside of each pork chop. Pat chops dry with paper towels and season with salt and pepper. Nestle chops into slow cooker. Cover and cook until pork is tender and fork easily slips in and out of meat, 3 to 4 hours on low.

3. Transfer pork chops to serving platter, tent loosely with aluminum foil, and let rest for 5 to 10 minutes. Let sauce settle for 5 minutes, then remove fat from surface using large spoon. Transfer sauce to small saucepan, bring to simmer, and cook until reduced to ¾ cup, about 10 minutes. Season with salt and pepper to taste. Spoon ⅓ cup sauce over meat and serve with remaining sauce.

NOTES FROM THE TEST KITCHEN

PREVENTING CURLED PORK CHOPS

To prevent pork chops from curling, cut 2 slits about 2 inches apart through fat around outside of each raw chop. This method works with both thin and thick pork chops.

SLOW-COOKER TOMATILLO CHILI WITH PORK AND HOMINY

✔ **WHY THIS RECIPE WORKS:** We wanted an easier, more streamlined take on classic Mexican green chili, *posole*, which stars tender pork, tangy tomatillos, and earthy hominy, and started by moving the dish to our slow cooker. To make it for-two friendly, we traded the traditional pork shoulder for boneless country-style pork ribs. To achieve the bold flavor of authentic recipes, we broiled the tomatillos, along with our aromatics and spices; once charred, the vegetables and spices took on an earthy, smoky flavor. Canned hominy added sweet, "corny" flavor, and a bit of tapioca helped give our chili just the right consistency.

WANTING TO SPICE UP THE DINNER HOUR FOR TWO, we looked south of the border for inspiration and hit on posole, which is the Mexican name for both hominy (dried field corn kernels treated with lime and boiled until tender but still chewy) and a stew made with hominy and pork. While this dish is made throughout Mexico in several distinct incarnations, we thought the appeal of *posole verde* (green posole), which is chock-full of bright, fresh tomatillos (tangy little tomato-like fruits common in Mexican cuisine) and chiles, was undeniable. With its long simmering time, posole seemed a natural choice for our slow cooker. Our goal was to create our own take on this dish using the slow cooker, not the stovetop, and keep all the bold, bright flavors intact, while also making just enough to serve two.

We started with the foundation of our chili: the meat. Traditional recipes start with a pork shoulder roast, which is simmered for hours before being shredded and returned to the pot. Since a roast isn't practical in the for-two kitchen, we turned to boneless country-style ribs, not only because of their availability but because they require little trimming. We chose ribs with a lot of dark meat and fat and cut them into bite-size pieces, which became juicy and tender during the long cooking time.

With the pork ready to go, we addressed the tomatillos and decided on fresh for the bright, tangy flavor they would impart. (That said, fresh tomatillos can be difficult to locate, so canned can be substituted.) In authentic posole verde, tomatillos are traditionally dry-roasted whole in a cast-iron pan and then ground to a puree using a mortar and pestle before being added to the pot. This cooking method works to impart smokiness and concentrate flavor, but it also requires close monitoring, as cooking the tomatillos for just a few seconds too long can make them unusable. Looking for an easier and more hands-off method, we tried broiling the tomatillos along with our aromatics (onion and garlic) and a little oil. The tomatillos could be broiled whole, but this required more frequent turning, and ultimately we found that cutting them in half helped them blacken more evenly. One taste, and we knew that we'd hit the jackpot: Broiling was quick and easy, and it tempered the tartness of the tomatillos. Plus, it added charred, smoky flavor to the aromatics, too. To puree the broiled vegetables, we tossed them into the food processor. After a few pulses, we had a coarsely chopped mixture that closely approximated the texture produced by a mortar and pestle.

Moving on to the chiles, which are another defining ingredient of this dish, we tested the usual suspects: poblanos, serranos, and jalapeños. Tasters preferred the poblanos, which have a mild to moderate heat and a deep herbal flavor that is more complex than the straightforward heat of jalapeños and serranos. Just two provided ample flavor, and we found we could chop them finely and add them right to the slow cooker.

Next, it was time to decide on the liquid and other seasonings. We tested water and canned chicken broth. Although the water was fine, the broth was superior, adding not only depth of flavor but body to the stewing liquid. In addition to the onion and garlic that we broiled with the tomatillos, oregano and cumin provided an earthy backbone. To balance the acidity of the tomatillos, we also stirred in some sugar.

With the chili's flavor balanced and the pork on its way to being fall-apart tender, we could now consider the other star ingredient—the hominy. There were two options: freshly rehydrated hominy, which takes hours

SLOW-COOKER TOMATILLO CHILI WITH PORK AND HOMINY

to prepare, and canned hominy, which we simply had to drain and rinse. We prepared a batch of chili using each and gathered tasters. The chili made with freshly cooked hominy was superb, but the chili with canned hominy was still really good. The hominy was chewy (as hominy should be) and relatively sweet, so we decided it was well worth using canned to save a significant amount of prep time.

Canned hominy comes in white and yellow varieties, depending on the type of field corn used. In our tests we found that both types are fine. Flavor isn't much of an issue, as both are sweet and "corny"-tasting. We determined that adding the canned hominy at the beginning of cooking allowed it to soak up some of the flavorful broth as well as infuse the chili with big corn flavor. Though the starch from the hominy helped to thicken the chili slightly, we found it necessary to add a tablespoon of tapioca, which had also worked well to bring our Slow-Cooker Moroccan Chicken Stew (page 221) to the right thickness.

Finally, a generous sprinkling of minced cilantro emphasized the fresh, clean flavor of this Mexican-inspired chili. Our recipe delivered a uniquely bright but still rich chili with all the hallmark flavors of an authentic posole verde—but without all the work.

Slow-Cooker Tomatillo Chili with Pork and Hominy

SERVES 2

If you can't find fresh tomatillos, you can substitute one 11-ounce can of tomatillos, drained, rinsed, and patted dry; broil as directed in step 1. Serve with your favorite chili garnishes. *Cooking time: 5 to 6 hours on low or 3 to 4 hours on high*

  6 ounces tomatillos (3 to 4 medium), husks and stems removed, rinsed well, dried, and halved
  ½ onion, cut into 1-inch pieces
  1 garlic clove, minced
  1 teaspoon minced fresh oregano or ¼ teaspoon dried
  ¼ teaspoon ground cumin
  1 tablespoon vegetable oil
  ¾ cup canned white or yellow hominy, rinsed
  ¾ cup low-sodium chicken broth
  2 poblano chiles, stemmed, seeded, and minced
  1 tablespoon Minute tapioca
  ½ teaspoon sugar
  1 bay leaf
 12 ounces boneless country-style pork ribs, cut into ¾-inch pieces
     Salt and pepper
  1 tablespoon minced fresh cilantro

1. Lightly spray inside of slow cooker with vegetable oil spray. Adjust oven rack 6 inches from broiler element and heat broiler. Line rimmed baking sheet with aluminum foil. Toss tomatillos, onion, garlic, oregano, and cumin with oil and spread on prepared sheet. Broil until vegetables are blackened and begin to soften, 5 to 10 minutes, rotating pan halfway through broiling.

2. Let vegetables cool slightly. Pulse vegetables with accumulated juices in food processor until almost smooth, about 10 pulses; transfer to slow cooker.

3. Stir hominy, broth, chiles, tapioca, sugar, and bay leaf into slow cooker. Season pork with salt and pepper and nestle into slow cooker. Cover and cook until pork is tender, 5 to 6 hours on low or 3 to 4 hours on high.

4. Let chili settle for 5 minutes, then remove fat from surface using large spoon. Discard bay leaf. Stir in cilantro and season with salt and pepper to taste. Serve.

NOTES FROM THE TEST KITCHEN

ALL ABOUT TOMATILLOS

Called *tomates verdes* (green tomatoes) in much of Mexico, tomatillos have a tangier, more citrusy flavor than true green tomatoes. When choosing tomatillos, look for pale green orbs with firm flesh that fills and splits open the fruit's outer papery husk, which must be removed before cooking. The flavor of canned tomatillos is less bright, but they make a fine substitute when fresh are not available.

SLOW-COOKER SOUTHWESTERN PORK

✔ **WHY THIS RECIPE WORKS:** For a hearty, richly flavored slow-cooker pork dish for two, we turned to country-style pork ribs, which gave us just the right amount of meat and stayed moist and tender in the slow cooker. For a Southwestern-inspired supper, we applied a combination of chili powder, cumin, and oregano to the pork as a rub; we also included a small amount of the rub in the sauce for robust flavor. Chicken broth and pulsed whole tomatoes formed the base of the sauce, and tomato paste, soy sauce, and chipotle chiles contributed depth and heat. Tapioca, plus mashed sweet potato, ensured that it was plenty thick.

YOU'D THINK A HEARTY, RICH CUT OF PORK WOULD make the perfect candidate for slow cooking, but too often its flavor turns washed out after hours in the appliance. We wanted a satisfying yet scaled-down pork supper worthy of the Sunday-night dinner table, with fork-tender meat and big flavors. For the flavor profile, we quickly settled on the spicy, smoky notes of Southwestern cuisine—we thought these bold flavors would enliven the mild-tasting meat and make for one robustly flavored meal for two.

As we set out to bring our vision to reality, we first considered the cut of pork that would work best. Well-marbled boneless pork butt stays tender in the slow cooker as the fat melts and keeps the meat moist, but it's an unwieldy size when cooking for two. Pork tenderloin and center- or rib-cut pork chops are our go-to cuts when cooking for two, but they were far too lean and dried out easily. Blade chops worked much better, but the light meat didn't quite stand up to the bold flavor profile of the dish. In the end, we opted for country-style ribs, which have a good amount of fat and dark meat and turned silky and fall-apart tender.

Working with the Southwestern theme, we seasoned the meat with a potent mix of chili powder, cumin, and oregano. To create a flavorful sauce in which to braise our pork, we started with the aromatics—a chopped onion and some minced garlic—and added a bit of tomato paste for savory depth. Chicken broth and processed canned tomatoes provided the bulk of the sauce, and a small amount of tapioca was selected as the thickening agent. We added everything to the slow cooker and nestled the pork into the sauce.

After a few hours of cooking, the meat was tender and flavorful, but the onion was a tad soggy. As we'd done in other recipes, we opted to precook the onion (and garlic and tomato paste) in the microwave to soften it and prevent it from becoming soggy in the slow cooker.

Another problem we faced was that the sauce tasted washed out. Since we were mixing up spices to rub on the pork, we tried adding some of the rub to the onion before microwaving it so the spices could bloom and deepen in flavor. This was a big improvement. A tablespoon of canned chipotle chile further emboldened the sauce; reserving a portion and stirring it in at the end provided another hit of potent, smoky flavor. We also added a couple of spoonfuls of soy sauce, which lent deep, savory notes. The flavor was definitely more robust, but the sauce tasted a little harsh and out of balance. And there was a bigger problem—it was too thin.

Sure, we could reduce the sauce on the stovetop, but we hoped to avoid dirtying another pan. Adding more tapioca made the sauce too thick and did nothing for the flavor. We needed something that fit with the Southwestern theme of our pork dinner that could both round out the flavor of the sauce and help thicken it. Thankfully, orange-hued inspiration struck: We sometimes thicken sauces with cooked potato, so what about sweet potato? Adding half of a sweet potato, peeled and cut into wedges, to the slow cooker with the pork deepened the flavor of the cooking liquid. And, when mashed into a paste, the cooked sweet potato thickened the sauce beautifully.

To finish the dish, we stirred in some lime juice and sprinkled minced cilantro over the top to reinforce the Southwestern angle. Tasters not only approved of the fork-tender meat, enlivened with our boldly flavored sauce—they devoured it.

Slow-Cooker Southwestern Pork

SERVES 2

Try to buy country-style pork ribs with lots of fat and dark meat, and stay away from ribs that look overly lean with pale meat. Serve with mashed potatoes or rice. *Cooking time: 5 to 6 hours on low or 3 to 4 hours on high*

- 1½   teaspoons chili powder
- 1   teaspoon ground cumin
- 1   teaspoon minced fresh oregano or ¼ teaspoon dried
     Salt and pepper
- 1   pound boneless country-style pork ribs, trimmed
- 1   small onion, chopped fine
- 1½   teaspoons tomato paste
- 1½   teaspoons vegetable oil
- 2   garlic cloves, minced
- 1   (14.5-ounce) can whole tomatoes
- ½   cup low-sodium chicken broth
- 1½   tablespoons soy sauce
- 1   tablespoon Minute tapioca
- 1   teaspoon minced canned chipotle chile in adobo sauce
- ½   small sweet potato, peeled and cut into 6 wedges
- 1½   teaspoons lime juice
- 1   tablespoon minced fresh cilantro

1. Lightly spray inside of slow cooker with vegetable oil spray. Combine chili powder, cumin, oregano, ¾ teaspoon salt, and ½ teaspoon pepper in bowl. Rub pork ribs with half of spice mixture.

2. Combine remaining half of spice mixture, onion, tomato paste, oil, and garlic in bowl and microwave, stirring occasionally, until onion is softened, about 5 minutes; transfer to slow cooker.

3. Pulse tomatoes, with their juice, in food processor until almost smooth, about 10 pulses. Add tomatoes, broth, soy sauce, tapioca, and ½ teaspoon chipotle to slow cooker. Nestle ribs and sweet potato into slow cooker. Cover and cook until pork is tender, 5 to 6 hours on low or 3 to 4 hours on high.

4. Transfer ribs to serving platter, tent loosely with aluminum foil, and let rest for 10 minutes. Transfer sweet potato to medium bowl. Let braising liquid settle for 5 minutes, then remove fat from surface using large spoon. Add 2 tablespoons cooking liquid to sweet potato and whisk to smooth paste. Whisk sweet potato, lime juice, and remaining ½ teaspoon chipotle into sauce. Season with salt and pepper to taste.

5. Top pork with ⅓ cup sauce and sprinkle with cilantro. Serve, passing remaining sauce separately.

SLOW-COOKER RED WINE–BRAISED SHORT RIBS

✔ WHY THIS RECIPE WORKS: Beef short ribs usually require hours to become meltingly tender. To make this hearty dish a more accessible option for the for-two household, we moved them to the slow cooker. To build deep flavor from the outset, we cut away the bones and "roasted" them in the microwave, which not only ratcheted up the flavor of the sauce but also helped to render excess fat. Browning the meat and reducing our sauce in a skillet before moving everything to the slow cooker ensured deep, savory flavor after hours of cooking.

THERE MAY BE NO CUT OF MEAT BETTER SUITED for braising than the rich, beefy short rib. Thanks to copious amounts of fat and gnarly sinews of connective tissue, these "short" portions cut from a cow's ribs start out tough and chewy but are transformed into soft, succulent morsels through lengthy braising. But though it may be the ultimate in comfort food, the downside is the prep and cooking time involved. Most recipes call for an hours-long stint in the oven, and some even have you start a day ahead—traits that make this dish unreasonable when cooking for two. We wanted to streamline this time-intensive recipe for the for-two household by moving it to the slow cooker, where it could simmer unattended for hours until the meat was fall-apart tender and richly flavored.

In the test kitchen, we typically turn to English-style ribs for braises. Their single bone and thick layer of meat make for hefty, uniform portions. Browning the ribs in a skillet first is standard protocol to intensify the meat's flavor, but in an effort to streamline prep we tried skipping this step and simply stirred all our ingredients into the slow cooker. This was a big mistake. After hours of cooking, our ribs were tender but the sauce was thin and dull. This was one case where we definitely needed the flavor imparted by fond, or the browned bits left behind from searing the meat.

To easily and quickly brown our meat, we decided to remove it from the bones first; this would also work to give us more surface area for browning. But we'd learned from many past recipes that the bones contribute irreplaceable flavor and body to dishes, so we reserved them and stirred them into the slow cooker along with our seared meat. After browning the meat, we sautéed chopped onion, celery, and carrot in the drippings left behind in the pan and stirred in a small amount of flour to help thicken the sauce and give it some body. Then we deglazed the surface with a generous cup of red wine to bring up all the flavorful browned bits and reduced the mixture to a thick, concentrated sauce that would hold its flavor through hours of cooking.

The only trouble now was that we didn't have enough braising liquid to keep the meat partway submerged in the slow cooker. We tried adding more wine, but it made our sauce overly acidic. After testing additions of water and chicken broth, we settled on the broth, which won out for its ability to reinforce the meaty flavors of our dish. After another stint in the slow cooker the flavor had improved but was still missing the rich depth and body we had hoped for.

Restaurant chefs know that roasting bones is key to making flavorful stock, since bones carry lots of flavor and roasted bones carry even more. Could we brown the bones as well to add more flavor to our braise? Roasting the bones in the oven would take more time than we wanted, but we wondered if we could "roast" them in the microwave. We spread the bones in a dish, popped it into the microwave, and hit the start button. After about 10 minutes, the bones looked as if they'd spent hours in the oven, and this process had also rendered some unwanted fat. We added them to the slow cooker. To further intensify and balance our flavor profile, we added two powerhouse flavor components to our sauce mixture, tomato paste and balsamic vinegar, along with thyme for its herbal complexity.

At this point, only one problem remained: Short ribs ooze fat as they cook, and after another 7 hours in the slow cooker we had a slick of grease on the surface of our sauce. To remedy this, many recipes include a step of chilling the cooked ribs overnight so that the jelled fat can be scraped from the cooking liquid and discarded. Adding a day to our cooking time wasn't an option, so we simply fished out the ribs and set them aside, discarded the bones, let the sauce settle, and skimmed as much fat as we could from the top before pouring everything through a fine-mesh strainer. What we were left with was a sauce that had incredible body and layers of flavor.

Our slow-cooked short ribs were unbelievably tender and now were smothered in a luxurious sauce that boasted just the right amount of rich wine flavor. This was one ultrasatisfying dinner for two that we knew we'd be making again and again.

Slow-Cooker Red Wine–Braised Short Ribs
SERVES 2

Buy English-style short ribs that have at least 1 inch of meat on top of the bone; avoid ribs that have little meat or large bones. This dish is equally good served over mashed potatoes or noodles. *Cooking time: 7 to 9 hours on low or 5 to 6 hours on high*

2½ pounds bone-in English-style short ribs, trimmed, meat and bones separated
    Salt and pepper
1 tablespoon vegetable oil
1 onion, chopped
1 small carrot, peeled and chopped
1 small celery rib, chopped
1 tablespoon tomato paste
1½ teaspoons minced fresh thyme or ½ teaspoon dried
1½ tablespoons all-purpose flour
1 cup dry red wine
1 tablespoon balsamic vinegar
1 cup low-sodium chicken broth
1 bay leaf
1 tablespoon minced fresh parsley

1. Lightly spray inside of slow cooker with vegetable oil spray. Arrange beef bones on dish and microwave until well browned, about 10 minutes; transfer to slow cooker.

2. Pat short ribs dry with paper towels and season with salt and pepper. Heat oil in 10-inch skillet over medium-high heat until just smoking. Brown short ribs well on all sides, 7 to 10 minutes; transfer to slow cooker.

3. Add onion, carrot, celery, tomato paste, and thyme to fat in skillet and cook over medium-high heat until onion is softened and lightly browned, 8 to 10 minutes. Stir in flour and cook for 1 minute. Slowly whisk in wine and vinegar, scraping up any browned bits and smoothing out any lumps. Bring to simmer and cook until reduced and thickened, about 5 minutes; transfer to slow cooker.

4. Stir broth and bay leaf into slow cooker. Cover and cook until beef is tender, 7 to 9 hours on low or 5 to 6 hours on high.

5. Transfer short ribs to serving platter and tent loosely with aluminum foil. Let braising liquid settle for 5 minutes, then remove fat from surface using large spoon. Strain braising liquid through fine-mesh strainer, discarding solids. Stir in parsley and season with salt and pepper to taste. Spoon ½ cup sauce over short ribs and serve with remaining sauce.

NOTES FROM THE TEST KITCHEN

BUYING BEEF SHORT RIBS

Short ribs are just that: fatty ribs (cut from any location along the length of the cow's ribs) that are shorter than the more common, larger beef ribs. Short ribs come in two styles: "English," which contain a single rib bone, and "flanken," which have several smaller bones. After cooking both, we found the two options to be equally tender and flavorful. However, the flanken-style ribs are more expensive, and you typically have to buy them from a butcher. We prefer the cheaper and more readily available English-style ribs.

ENGLISH   **FLANKEN**

PREPARING SHORT RIBS FOR THE SLOW COOKER

Insert knife between rib and meat and, staying as close to bone as possible, slice meat off bone.

SLOW-COOKER SMOTHERED STEAK

✔ **WHY THIS RECIPE WORKS:** Smothered steak, with its tender meat and rich, oniony gravy, sounds perfect for the slow cooker, but we had our work cut out for us if we wanted to avoid the common pitfalls of washed-out meat and a watery, flavorless sauce. For fork-tender steaks and perfectly cooked onion, we devised a simple two-step process for preparing each component. First, we marinated the meat and onion separately in soy sauce prior to cooking. Then we briefly microwaved the onion to soften its texture, draw out some of its liquid, and deepen its flavor. For the steaks, rather than sear them in a pan on the stovetop, we simply dusted them with cornstarch to help them brown and develop flavor in the steamy environment of the slow cooker.

IN CULINARY TERMS, "SMOTHERED" MEANS BRAISED and served with gravy. Hearty and satisfying, smothered steak typically starts with a cheap cut (usually lean, tough beef from the round) that's slowly cooked with onions in broth until the meat is tender and the onions break down to create a rich, savory gravy. We looked to bring this dish home for two and wanted to use the slow cooker to deliver all the appealing flavors and textures we expected; that way we wouldn't need to spend hours monitoring the stovetop.

While we were researching recipes for slow-cooker smothered steak, we discovered that they fell into two camps. There are the easy "dump and cover" recipes in which the seasoned meat, chopped onions, and broth (or a can of condensed soup) go into the slow cooker with little upfront prep. The other style of recipe takes the time to brown the meat, sauté the onions, and reduce the sauce before everything goes into the cooker. We prepared three examples of each style (five of them called for round steaks, and one called for blade steaks) and 7 hours later eagerly opened the slow cookers.

Unfortunately, none of our test recipes contained the succulent beef and rich, oniony gravy we sought. Though the round steaks all resembled rawhide, the blade steaks were somewhat tender (albeit bland and dry), so at least we had somewhere to start. The pale appearance of both meat and onions in the recipes in

SLOW-COOKER SMOTHERED STEAK

which ingredients were simply added to the slow cooker was offputting; the recipes that called for precooking looked much better, but we wanted easy *and* a nicely browned exterior. As for the sauce, all the steaks swam in watery juices, not the thick, rich gravy we were after, but reducing the sauce at the end was an extra step we hoped to avoid.

To improve the texture of the blade steaks, we reduced the cooking time from 7 to 4 hours on high and placed the steaks on top of the sliced onion; this meant that the beef wouldn't be immersed in liquid and, thus, would cook more gently and emerge more moist. In order to avoid the lake of watery "sauce," we needed to understand how much liquid the onion and blade steaks threw off during cooking. So we made a batch with no added liquid. To our surprise, the onion and beef released almost enough liquid for a sauce. But that liquid was sour and unpleasantly oniony. We needed to find a way to get rid of some of the raw onion flavor and juices upfront; to ensure that the sauce had the right volume and texture, we could simply add some moisture back to the slow cooker.

After several tests, we came up with a simple method for bold but not sour onion flavor: We macerated the onion in a little brown sugar and salt for a half-hour and then microwaved it for a few minutes before adding it to the slow cooker. The brown sugar brought out the onion's natural sweetness, and microwaving softened it and kick-started the cooking process so all the raw onion juices didn't end up in our sauce. A small amount of chicken broth ensured that there was enough moisture in our slow cooker.

To further finesse our sauce, we stirred some cornstarch into the precooked onion before adding the steaks and broth to the slow cooker; the cornstarch helped to thicken the mixture. To deepen the flavor of the sauce, we introduced garlic and thyme. For enhanced seasoning (and color), we added a little soy sauce, a test kitchen secret weapon when we want to infuse dishes with savory flavor. To make the most of its deep, *umami*-rich flavors, we decided to use soy sauce instead of salt when we macerated the onion. Using a small amount of soy sauce to marinate the meat also worked to amp up the savory flavor of the dish.

Now the gravy was well balanced and flavorful, and the meat was much better seasoned and tasted beefier. But it still looked unappetizingly gray. As we stirred the cornstarch into the next batch of onion slices, a colleague reminded us of a recent discovery made with a pot roast recipe: During testing, it was revealed that cornstarch reacts with meat juices to form sugars that brown at low temperatures and in moist environments. For our next test, we rubbed the tops of the blade steaks with an extra teaspoon of cornstarch; they emerged from the slow cooker with enough browning that tasters were fooled into thinking we'd seared them first.

But though cornstarch worked to give our steaks a nicely browned exterior when they were cooked on the high setting, our rubbed steaks never passed the gray and unappetizing state when cooked on low heat. It seemed that high heat was our only option here—luckily, it worked beautifully.

With just a few flavor-boosting tricks, and the right heat level, we had deeply flavored, almost effortless smothered steaks we couldn't wait to dig into.

Slow-Cooker Smothered Steak

SERVES 2

Do not cook this recipe on the low setting. If using a 3- to 3½-quart slow cooker, omit the chicken broth in step 3. Arrange the steaks so the cornstarch-rubbed sides face up during cooking to ensure adequate browning. Blade steaks have a thin line of gristle running through the center. Some people eat it; others eat around it. *Cooking time: 4 to 5 hours on high*

1	onion, halved and sliced ½ inch thick
1½	teaspoons packed dark brown sugar
1	tablespoon soy sauce
2	(6- to 8-ounce) blade steaks, ¾ to 1 inch thick, trimmed
	Salt and pepper
1	tablespoon cornstarch
1	garlic clove, minced
¼	teaspoon dried thyme
½	cup low-sodium chicken broth

1. Toss onion, sugar, and 1 teaspoon soy sauce together in large bowl and let sit for 30 minutes. Combine steaks, remaining 2 teaspoons soy sauce, and ¼ teaspoon salt in large zipper-lock bag and let sit for 30 minutes, turning once.

2. Lightly spray inside of slow cooker with vegetable oil spray. Microwave onion mixture until onion is softened and beginning to dry around edges, about 3 minutes, stirring halfway through cooking. Transfer onion mixture to slow cooker and stir in 2 teaspoons cornstarch, garlic, thyme, and ¼ teaspoon pepper.

3. Pat steaks dry with paper towels and rub 1 side with remaining 1 teaspoon cornstarch. Gather onion mixture in center of slow cooker and arrange steaks, cornstarch side up, in single layer on onion mixture. Pour broth around steaks in slow cooker (if using 6-quart slow cooker). Cover and cook until steaks are completely tender, 4 to 5 hours on high.

4. Transfer steaks to platter, tent loosely with aluminum foil, and let rest for 5 to 10 minutes. Let liquid settle in slow cooker for 5 minutes, then remove fat from surface using large spoon. Strain onion mixture through fine-mesh strainer set over large liquid measuring cup. Season sauce with salt and pepper to taste. Top steaks with onion mixture and ¼ cup sauce and serve with remaining sauce.

NOTES FROM THE TEST KITCHEN

"SEARING" STEAKS WITHOUT A SKILLET
Searing meat in a hot skillet gives it a tasty browned crust. To avoid the work of searing the blade steaks before putting them in the slow cooker, we devised a technique that allows the meat to brown in the moist environment of the slow cooker.

For a nicely browned exterior, we rub the meat with cornstarch, which breaks down into sugars that react with the meat juices to cause browning in the slow cooker.

SLOW-COOKER BEER BRATS

✔ **WHY THIS RECIPE WORKS:** We wanted to use the slow cooker to deliver the flavor of great grilled beer brats—plump, juicy bratwurst topped with sweet onion and crisp sauerkraut—any time of year, and for just two. Microwaving the onion with soy sauce and sugar before adding it to the slow cooker ensured that it cooked up tender and flavorful. Elevating the brats from the bottom of the slow cooker allowed for gentler cooking and ensured a perfect texture. And adding the sauerkraut at the end of cooking maintained its appealing flavor and texture.

ON GAME DAYS, THERE'S NOTHING LIKE CLASSIC tailgating fare to get you ready to root for the home team. We're big fans of burgers and dogs, wings, and especially beer brats—grilled sausages cooked in a flavorful concoction of beer, onions, and sauerkraut and served on rolls with mustard. But sometimes we want a recipe that serves two rather than the whole team, so we set out to re-create beer brats in the slow cooker. That way, we could prepare just enough for two any time we had a hankering for this hearty dish, even if it wasn't grilling season.

Not surprisingly, we found several slow-cooker recipes for beer brats in cookbooks and online. We ordered a case of bratwurst and several types of beer, plugged in a number of slow cookers, and got to work. The recipes were all similar: Dump in the brats, shower them with sliced onions and sauerkraut, pour beer over them, cover, and cook. But the results were dismal; the brats were mealy and gray, the onions raw and crunchy, the kraut barely detectable, and the whole dish wan and practically flavorless. Clearly, we had our work cut out for us.

We started with the beer. Our test recipes had led us to believe that the type of beer we used didn't matter much. But we quickly discovered that was not the case. When the beer simmered in the slow cooker for several hours, its flavor really made a difference. We tested batches of beer brats made with stout, porter, a hoppy IPA, American lager, red ale, wheat beer, and even fruity lambics. Darker, malty beers (like stout, porter, and red ales) became bitter when cooked, and the flavor of wheat and hops got cooked out. The lambic didn't taste right, but old-fashioned American lager was perfect. Its clean, mild flavor could withstand hours in the slow cooker without becoming bitter. Adding mustard and a sprinkling of caraway seeds to the beer before it went into the slow cooker helped bump up the flavor and was a nod to the German heritage of the dish.

Next, we tackled the brats themselves. Although they had good flavor, the brats emerged from the cooker dry and mealy by the time they were cooked through (about 4 hours on high). Plus, they were missing that signature "snap" in the casing. Because the brats were immersed in liquid at the bottom of the slow cooker, they cooked at a fast simmer. This caused the casings to rupture and the juices that they normally contain to leak out, making the brats dry. Rearranging the order in which they went into the slow cooker—the onion and kraut first, followed by the brats—slightly elevated the bratwursts out of the simmering liquid so they cooked more gently without breaking and drying out. The drier environment also helped the casings retain their snap.

Although moving the onion to the bottom of the cooker helped the brats, the sauerkraut was still washed out, and the onion was stringy and raw tasting. The kraut fix was easy. We held off on adding it until the end of cooking; it just needed to be warmed through for a few minutes in the slow cooker. As for the onion, we decided to try precooking the slices in the microwave. Since we were taking this extra step, we saw it as another opportunity to add flavor (and color) by microwaving the onion with some soy sauce and brown sugar, a trick we'd learned when developing our recipe for Slow-Cooker Smothered Steak (page 231). This worked perfectly, softening the onion and giving it a helpful injection of flavor that lasted throughout the

hours of cooking. After we removed the brats from the slow cooker, we stirred in the sauerkraut and let it warm through, then drained the mixture of excess moisture so our buns wouldn't become soggy. Finally, we nestled the brats into buns, topped them with our flavorful onion-kraut mixture, and enjoyed a perfect game-day dish for two.

Slow-Cooker Beer Brats

SERVES 2

Light-bodied American lagers, such as Budweiser, work best in this recipe. *Cooking time: 5 to 6 hours on low or 3 to 4 hours on high*

- ½ onion, sliced into ¼-inch-thick rings
- 2 teaspoons soy sauce
- 1¼ teaspoons packed brown sugar
- 2 (4-ounce) bratwurst sausages
- ¾ cup beer
- 2 teaspoons Dijon mustard, plus extra for serving
- ¼ teaspoon caraway seeds
- ⅓ cup sauerkraut
- 2 hot dog buns

1. Combine onion, soy sauce, and sugar in bowl and microwave until just softened, about 4 minutes, stirring halfway through cooking. Spread onion rings and their liquid in bottom of slow cooker. Arrange bratwursts on top of onion.

2. Whisk beer, mustard, and caraway seeds together in bowl and add to slow cooker. Cover and cook until bratwursts are tender, 5 to 6 hours on low or 3 to 4 hours on high.

3. Transfer bratwursts to platter and tent loosely with aluminum foil. Stir sauerkraut into onion mixture in slow cooker and let sit until warmed through, about 5 minutes. Strain onion-sauerkraut mixture through colander, discarding liquid, and transfer to serving bowl. Serve bratwursts on buns, topped with onion-sauerkraut mixture and mustard.

PARMESAN-CRUSTED ASPARAGUS

CHAPTER 9

SIDE DISHES

SOUTHERN-STYLE GREEN BEANS

✔ **WHY THIS RECIPE WORKS:** Southern cooks simmer green beans with pork for up to 4 hours to give them an irresistibly silky texture and intense flavor, but simmering beans for that long to make just two servings hardly makes sense. For a quicker take on this dish, we created a flavorful broth with a sliced onion and a strip of bacon. Removing the pot lid for the last few minutes of cooking gave the liquid a chance to reduce and deepen in flavor. Salt, pepper, and a bit of sugar ensured well-seasoned beans, and a sprinkling of crisp bacon provided more pork flavor and a crunchy contrast.

GENERATIONS OF SOUTHERN COOKS HAVE GOTTEN the most out of their green beans by tossing pork—oftentimes a ham hock left over from Sunday dinner—into the pot. After a long, gentle simmer, the beans emerge satiny soft and saturated with rich, pork-infused broth—delicious proof that not all green beans are meant to be snappy and bright green. But when you're cooking for two, it's rare to have an extra ham hock lying around and 4 hours to spend monitoring the stovetop. We hoped to find another way to deliver the same rich flavor and tender texture of the authentic Southern dish, and we wanted to do it in an hour or less.

Since we couldn't count on having a spare ham hock on hand, we did our first trial with a small chunk of salt pork. We simmered our green beans in water with the salt pork and some sliced onion (a standard addition), but it was a huge disappointment; the salt pork didn't give up its flavor quickly enough, and long-simmered green beans without pork flavor just weren't worth the effort.

After considering our options, we decided to try a two-pronged approach using bacon instead. We cooked one slice until it was crisp and removed it from the pot. Then we softened an onion in the fat, added 8 ounces of green beans, covered them with water, and tossed in another slice of raw bacon. We brought the pot to a boil, then covered it and lowered the heat to a simmer. (We knew from experience that we couldn't boil the beans because they'd turn to mush.)

In most recipes the simmering time is dragged out to 2, even as many as 4, hours. We waited a mere 45 minutes, at which point a peek inside the pot revealed a battalion of army-green beans that certainly looked like what we were after. We discarded the bacon slice, which was now soggy, and called our tasters to dig in. They were pleased that the texture was spot-on—almost, but not quite, falling apart. But the much shorter simmering time left both beans and broth short on flavor. To fix that, we tried swapping the water for chicken broth in our next batch. The broth only muddied the flavor.

For the next test, we took the cover off the pot and turned up the heat for a few minutes after the beans had simmered for 45 minutes. This allowed the liquid to reduce, which, by concentrating, intensified the pork flavor. To reinforce that and add crunch, we crumbled the crisped bacon and sprinkled it on top before serving.

With a little salt, pepper, and sugar for a gentle sweetness, our Southern-Style Green Beans both looked and tasted the part—even though they were ready in a fraction of the time.

Southern-Style Green Beans

SERVES 2

The long-simmered beans will easily break apart; be sure to stir them gently when seasoning and serving.

- 2 slices bacon
- 1 small onion, halved and sliced thin
- 8 ounces green beans, trimmed
- ⅔ cup water
- Salt and pepper
- ⅛ teaspoon sugar

NOTES FROM THE TEST KITCHEN

TRIMMING GREEN BEANS QUICKLY

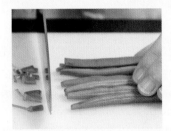

Line up several green beans in row on cutting board. Trim about ½ inch from each end, then cut beans as directed in recipe.

1. Cook 1 slice bacon in medium saucepan over medium heat until crisp, 6 to 8 minutes. Transfer bacon to paper towel–lined plate, leaving fat in pot. Add onion to now-empty pot and cook until softened, 5 to 7 minutes. Add remaining 1 slice uncooked bacon, green beans, water, ¼ teaspoon salt, and sugar and bring to boil. Cover, reduce heat to medium-low, and simmer, stirring occasionally, until green beans are very tender, about 40 minutes.

2. Remove lid and discard bacon. Increase heat to medium-high and continue to cook until liquid is reduced slightly, 3 to 5 minutes. Season with salt and pepper to taste. (Stir carefully to avoid breaking beans apart.) Transfer to serving bowl. Crumble reserved bacon over top. Serve.

PARMESAN-CRUSTED ASPARAGUS

✔ WHY THIS RECIPE WORKS: A crunchy, flavorful coating of bread crumbs and grated Parmesan promised to jazz up our roasted asparagus, but only if we could figure out how to get rid of the vegetable's excess moisture. Poking holes in the asparagus and salting it worked wonders, driving off the extra moisture that would have made our asparagus rubbery and prevented the topping from sticking. From there, we dipped the spears in a combination of honey and egg white whipped to soft peaks and then coated them with a mixture of panko bread crumbs, Parmesan, melted butter, and a pinch of cayenne. Finally, to reinforce the Parmesan flavor, we topped the spears with an extra dose of cheese halfway through roasting.

WE LOVE THE SWEET, INTENSELY CONCENTRATED flavor of roasted asparagus, but we wanted a more exciting take on this vegetable to liven up the dinner hour for two. We thought a nice coating of bread crumbs and freshly grated Parmesan would elevate this side to something more that would pair well with simply prepared steaks or chops. Our goal was an amped-up asparagus dish that delivered rich, roasted flavor plus an ultracrispy, cheesy coating.

From the outset, we thought it would be a simple matter of tossing raw spears with olive oil, seasonings, and a cheese and bread-crumb mixture. But when we tried this, we found that as the asparagus roasted, it released moisture. That's no problem when the spears roast on their own—the moisture simply evaporates. But now that we'd coated them with crumbs and cheese, the moisture turned the topping soggy, so it fell off in large clumps.

Clearly we had to get rid of some of the moisture before adding the crumb topping. For the next test, we tried roasting the stalks in a 450-degree oven until the moisture evaporated, about 10 minutes, and then topping them with the cheese-crumb mixture. We gave everything a few more minutes to crisp in the oven. The finished asparagus was dehydrated and leathery, and the coating didn't adhere. We tried parcooking the asparagus in the microwave, but after this go-around the spears were limp by the time the moisture was gone.

What about salt? We often salt vegetables like tomatoes, eggplant, and cucumbers to draw out their moisture. We sprinkled ¼ teaspoon of salt over the raw asparagus and let it sit on paper towels to drain. Thirty minutes later, the towels were sodden with exuded liquid. We tossed the asparagus with oil, sprinkled on the bread-crumb topping, and then let the spears roast for 20 minutes. This batch was markedly better. We saw further improvement when we poked the spears with a fork before salting to facilitate the release of moisture.

But the cheese-crumb mixture still refused to stick. So we decided that, rather than tossing the crumbs onto the spears, we'd need to "glue" them on. We moistened each spear in lightly beaten egg and pressed them in the cheese-crumb mixture before roasting. Unfortunately, this topping was too heavy for the delicate vegetable. To lighten it, we ditched the egg yolk and used only the white. To ensure that the cheese-crumb combo would stay put, we mixed the white with the stickiest (edible) thing we could think of: honey. The fact that tasters liked its subtle sweetness was a bonus; its adhesive properties won us over from the start.

For the coating, we pitted ordinary bread crumbs against extra-crunchy panko crumbs. Not surprisingly, we preferred the latter. Ultimately, we determined that ⅓ cup of crumbs to ¾ cup of Parmesan worked best. We also found that if we set aside ¼ cup of the cheese to sprinkle over the coated asparagus partway through roasting, we got the crispiest coating and best cheese flavor.

With each test, the asparagus was improving, yet tasters continued to ask for more crunch. If we whipped the egg white before coating the asparagus, might it help form peaks and valleys to grip the most possible bits of crunchy coating? In a word, yes. With this one simple change, each spear now delivered loads of crunch, cheese, salt, and roasty asparagus sweetness.

NOTES FROM THE TEST KITCHEN

MAKING THE COATING STICK

1. Use fork to poke holes in asparagus spears, then toss with salt and let drain on paper towel–lined baking sheet to draw out excess moisture that could saturate bread-crumb coating.

2. Gently toss asparagus spears in whipped egg white–honey mixture, which helps crumbs adhere.

3. Working with 1 spear at a time, dredge spears in panko bread-crumb mixture.

THE BEST PANKO

Light and flaky, panko bread crumbs, which originated in Japan, add big crunch and a neutral flavor to recipes. Once the domain of specialty shops and Asian markets, panko bread crumbs are now available in most supermarkets. We tested four supermarket brands, as a coating for baked chicken and pan-fried pork cutlets, to find the best one. While we couldn't distinguish differences in taste among brands, our test kitchen tasting did reveal differences in texture. Our favorite is **Ian's Panko Bread Crumbs**, which provided a much more substantial crunch than the other brands.

Parmesan-Crusted Asparagus

SERVES 2

Avoid pencil-thin asparagus for this recipe. Since the recipe involves just one egg white, we recommend using a hand-held electric mixer to whip it rather than a stand mixer. Work quickly when tossing the asparagus with the egg white, as the salt will rapidly begin to deflate the white.

1 **pound (½ inch thick) asparagus, trimmed**
    Salt and pepper
1½ **ounces Parmesan cheese, grated (¾ cup)**
⅓ **cup panko bread crumbs**
½ **tablespoon unsalted butter, melted and cooled**
    Pinch cayenne
1 **large egg white**
½ **teaspoon honey**

1. Adjust oven rack to middle position and heat oven to 450 degrees. Line rimmed baking sheet with aluminum foil and spray with vegetable oil spray. Using fork, poke holes up and down stalks of asparagus. Toss asparagus with ¼ teaspoon salt and let stand for 30 minutes in single layer on large paper towel–lined platter.

2. Meanwhile, combine ½ cup Parmesan, panko, butter, ⅛ teaspoon salt, pinch pepper, and cayenne in bowl. Transfer half of panko mixture to shallow dish and reserve remaining mixture. Using electric mixer, whip egg white and honey together on medium-low speed until foamy, about 1 minute. Increase speed to medium-high and whip until soft peaks form, 2 to 3 minutes. Scrape egg white mixture into medium baking dish, then gently toss asparagus in mixture. Working with 1 spear at a time, dredge half of asparagus spears in panko and transfer to prepared baking sheet. Refill shallow dish with reserved panko mixture and repeat with remaining asparagus.

3. Bake asparagus until just beginning to brown, 6 to 8 minutes. Sprinkle with remaining ¼ cup Parmesan and continue to bake until cheese is melted and bread crumbs are golden brown, 6 to 8 minutes longer. Transfer to platter. Serve.

EASY CREAMED SPINACH

✔ **WHY THIS RECIPE WORKS:** We wanted super-easy, one-pot creamed spinach that still offered the rich flavor and creamy texture of the authentic steakhouse versions. After wilting our spinach in a covered pot, we set it aside and used the same pot to make the sauce. We bypassed the usual béchamel and started with creamy Boursin cheese, flavored with garlic and herbs. Just 2 tablespoons of cream ensured that our sauce was the right thickness and coated our spinach nicely.

A STALWART OF STEAKHOUSES, WHERE IT RIDES shotgun to a juicy rib eye or T-bone, creamed spinach offers big flavor in spite of its homely appearance. Then again, when a vegetable comes cloaked in a velvety cheese sauce, who's complaining about aesthetics? We were much more interested in finding a way to streamline this recipe into an easy weeknight side dish for two. Most versions call for at least two pots: one to cook the spinach, and another to prepare the sauce. In the interest of ease, we set out to make a one-pot creamed spinach that cut back not only on dirty dishes but also on leftovers.

First, we tackled the greens. Though for salads we prefer bagged baby spinach or bundled tender flat-leaf spinach, curly-leaf spinach sold in cellophane bags has one distinct advantage: Most of the dirt has already been removed, so it requires only a quick rinse. In our testing, it also retained its structure after being sautéed and mixed with the cream sauce. Flat-leaf spinach was a close second when it came to hearty texture, but because it comes in bunches, it is almost always sandy and requires multiple soakings before it can be used. Baby spinach, for all its popularity raw, wilted away to nothing and left us with a pool of cream sauce. Curly-leaf spinach, it seemed, was the clear choice for our creamed spinach.

Although we tried blanching, steaming, and microwaving, we achieved the best results when we wilted the spinach in a covered pot; this technique yielded the best texture in a short amount of time. We heated some olive oil over high heat in a large saucepan, then added the stemmed leaves, still damp from rinsing, to the pot by the handful. The water clinging to the leaves was enough to cook the spinach, which broke down from the seemingly large volume of raw leaves (we used 10 ounces) to a manageable quantity of cooked spinach in about a minute. To make sure the spinach wilted evenly, we stirred the leaves constantly, then transferred the wilted spinach to a colander to drain off excess liquid.

With our spinach cooked, we turned to the cream sauce. Most recipes for creamed spinach start with a béchamel, which is a white sauce made by stirring milk into a butter and flour roux. Cheese is then stirred in before the sauce and spinach are combined. To streamline our recipe, we looked to bypass the béchamel and build a quick creamy sauce in the saucepan we were already using.

Looking through the ingredients in creamed spinach sauces, we came back to the same basic players: milk or heavy cream, cheese, salt, aromatics such as shallot or garlic, and flour to thicken the sauce. Instead of adding cheese to the cream sauce, what if we started with a creamy cheese that would melt and turn into a rich, velvety sauce? Cream cheese was an obvious first choice, but although it melted nicely, it lacked the rich texture of a béchamel. We tried adding other varieties of cheese and a few types of dairy to give it the intense

creaminess we were after, but to no avail. That's when we hit on Boursin cheese, a soft, spreadable cheese that comes in a few different varieties.

The Boursin melted like a champ, and the garlic-and-herb variety offered big flavor, allowing us to nix the aromatics from our ingredient list. To ensure that the sauce was the right consistency, we added 2 tablespoons of heavy cream. After just a couple of minutes in the pan, our sauce was nicely thickened.

Finally, we tossed the still-warm spinach with the warm sauce until it was coated. In about 10 minutes and with just a handful of ingredients, our for-two take on this steakhouse classic offered all the rich flavor and silky texture we were craving—and we weren't left with a pile of dishes or leftovers to deal with afterward.

Easy Creamed Spinach

SERVES 2

Leave some water clinging to the spinach leaves to help encourage steam when cooking. One pound of flat-leaf spinach (about 1½ bunches) can be substituted for the curly-leaf spinach, but do not use baby spinach because it is much too delicate.

- 1½ teaspoons olive oil
- 10 ounces curly-leaf spinach, stemmed and chopped coarse
- ½ (5.2-ounce) package Boursin Garlic and Fine Herbs cheese
- 2 tablespoons heavy cream
   Salt and pepper

1. Heat oil in large saucepan over high heat until shimmering. Add spinach in handfuls, stirring and tossing each handful to wilt slightly before adding next. Continue to cook spinach, stirring constantly, until uniformly wilted, about 1 minute. Transfer spinach to colander and squeeze between tongs to release excess liquid.

2. Wipe saucepan dry with paper towels. Whisk Boursin and cream together in now-empty saucepan and simmer over medium-high heat until thickened, about 2 minutes. Off heat, stir in spinach until evenly coated. Season with salt and pepper to taste and serve.

BROCCOLI SALAD

✔ WHY THIS RECIPE WORKS: Most recipes for this potluck favorite make enough for a crowd, but we wanted a scaled-down dish for two. Rather than leaving the broccoli raw, we found that cooking it briefly in boiling water improved both its flavor and its texture and kept it bright green. Adding the hardier stems to the cooking water first ensured that they were tender at the same time as the quick-cooking florets. Drying the broccoli in a salad spinner got rid of the excess moisture, so the dressing—a tangy mayo-and-vinegar mixture—didn't get watered down. Crisped bacon, toasted walnuts, and raisins brought crunch and a salty-sweet balance to this salad.

FOR SOME FOLKS, BROCCOLI SALAD IS A POTLUCK and block party mainstay. Its combination of ingredients—chopped broccoli, crumbled bacon, raisins, and chopped walnuts in a mayonnaise-based dressing—is surprising. Even more surprising is how unexpectedly delicious the components can be together. But did we have to wait for the next picnic to enjoy it? We hoped to scale this potluck favorite down to two servings and still keep the appealing mix of textures and flavors intact.

We collected a number of recipes and headed into the test kitchen. The problems in our test salads were quickly evident: The raw broccoli tasted woody, the dressing was way too sweet, and the recipes used so much mayonnaise that not much else registered. Since the name is broccoli salad, shouldn't you be able to taste the broccoli? Most of these recipes called for raw broccoli, but we were grateful to find one that called for cooking it. When the broccoli was briefly blanched in boiling water and then shocked in cold to stop the cooking, the woodiness disappeared. These pretty green florets had a softer crunch and a clearer broccoli flavor. There was no need to smother them in mayonnaise now, so we cut back to a reasonable ¼ cup for 12 ounces of broccoli. The stems, however, remained tough, even though we'd peeled them. To fix that, we gave them a minute's head start in the boiling water. Now stems and florets were cooked to a perfect, tender crunch.

BROCCOLI SALAD

The dressing itself is usually little more than mayonnaise, sugar, and vinegar. We tested an assortment of vinegars and liked the sweet-tart quality contributed by 1½ teaspoons of balsamic. Its slight sweetness was really all the salad needed, so we cut the sugar out of the recipe altogether. We seasoned the dressing with salt and pepper and tossed it with the blanched broccoli. Unfortunately, after the salad sat, even for a few minutes, we noticed that the dressing had thinned and pooled in the bottom of the bowl. Now that we were blanching the broccoli, it was obvious we needed to dry it. So we whirled the blanched broccoli in a salad spinner, which shook off any water that still clung to it and restored the dressing's creamy consistency.

At this point, our dish just needed a couple of minor tweaks. Most recipes for broccoli salad include raw walnuts, but we found that toasting the nuts was a small step with a large positive impact. Plumping the raisins in hot water for a few minutes to soften them also upgraded the salad; to make things easy, we simply used the water we were already boiling to blanch the broccoli. Now, the juicy raisins—golden tasted slightly fruitier—were a good counterpoint to the crunchy broccoli.

We combined all the components, tossed them together, and dug in. We were thrilled with this new take on an old favorite, which now offered the perfect combination of big, crunchy bites and fresh flavor.

Broccoli Salad

SERVES 2

When prepping the broccoli, keep the stems and florets separate. If you don't own a salad spinner, lay the broccoli on a clean dish towel to dry in step 3.

- **2 slices bacon, chopped fine**
- **3 tablespoons golden raisins**
- **½ bunch broccoli (12 ounces), florets cut into 1-inch pieces, stalks peeled and sliced ¼ inch thick**
- **¼ cup mayonnaise**
- **1½ teaspoons balsamic vinegar**
- **Salt and pepper**
- **3 tablespoons coarsely chopped toasted walnuts**
- **1 small shallot, minced**

1. Cook bacon in 8-inch skillet over medium heat until crisp, 6 to 8 minutes. Using slotted spoon, transfer bacon to paper towel–lined plate.

2. Combine 2 cups water and 2 cups ice in large bowl. Bring 2 quarts water to boil in large saucepan. Remove ¼ cup boiling water and combine with raisins in small bowl. Let sit, covered, for 5 minutes, then drain.

3. Meanwhile, add broccoli stalks to boiling water and cook for 1 minute. Add florets and cook until slightly tender, about 1 minute. Drain broccoli and place in ice water to cool, about 2 minutes. Drain again, transfer broccoli to salad spinner, and spin dry.

4. Whisk mayonnaise, vinegar, ¼ teaspoon salt, and ⅛ teaspoon pepper together in large bowl. Add broccoli, raisins, walnuts, and shallot to bowl with dressing and toss to combine. Season with salt and pepper to taste. Sprinkle with bacon and serve.

ROASTED BRUSSELS SPROUTS

✓ **WHY THIS RECIPE WORKS:** For a streamlined recipe for roasted Brussels sprouts for two, we tossed the halved sprouts with a bit of water and oil before roasting them, covered, in the oven. The water worked to create a steamy environment, which cooked the sprouts through, and the oil ensured that they didn't stick. Uncovering the pan allowed the exteriors to dry out and caramelize, giving us perfectly tender Brussels sprouts with a nicely browned exterior.

ACHIEVING PERFECTLY COOKED BRUSSELS SPROUTS is usually a two-part process. To ensure that the interiors of this dense vegetable get sufficiently tender, the sprouts are often blanched or steamed before being roasted or pan-seared. The latter process lightly crisps the outer leaves and creates the nice browning that mellows the sprouts' bitter kick. But when you're cooking for two, this two-step approach can be a little fussy. We wanted to streamline the preparation of this side dish but still enjoy nicely tender, richly flavored Brussels sprouts with a well-caramelized exterior when we were done.

Since roasting seemed like the most hands-off option, we elected to focus our efforts in the oven, rather than on the stovetop. We started out with 8 ounces of sprouts, which offered just enough for two servings, looking for same-size specimens about 1½ inches long.

With parcooking ruled out, the obvious first step was to halve the sprouts, which would help ensure that they cooked through and would create a flat surface for browning. We then tossed them in a bowl with a bit of olive oil, salt, and pepper.

To maximize browning and to jump-start cooking, we often preheat the baking sheet before roasting vegetables. We did precisely this, placing the sprouts cut side down on the hot sheet before moving it back into a 500-degree oven. But when we pulled the vegetables out 20 minutes later, they were dry, chewy, and even burnt in spots on the outside, while practically crunchy on the inside. Switching to a cool baking sheet didn't improve matters, and turning down the heat merely meant that it took a little longer for the sprouts to reach the same unsatisfactory state.

To prevent the outer leaves from drying out too much before the center achieved the ideal tender-firm texture, it seemed clear that we needed to introduce moisture into the equation. We wondered if just covering the sprouts with aluminum foil as they roasted would trap enough steam to do the trick. Once again, we arranged the sprouts cut side down on the baking sheet, but this time we covered the pan tightly with foil before placing it in the oven. After 10 minutes we removed the foil so that the slightly softened sprouts could brown and get just a little crisp. Ten minutes later, the Brussels sprouts were perfectly browned on the outside. But they were still undercooked on the inside and a bit dry and chewy all around.

Before we addressed the chewiness factor, we needed to examine our sheet pan: It was a mess. While perfectly appropriate for a bigger batch of vegetables, the sheet pan was simply too much surface area for our small batch of sprouts; excess olive oil began to burn in unappealing (and hard-to-clean) spots on the uncovered parts of the pan. For the next test, we reached for our favorite 12-inch skillet. With less empty surface area, the skillet was the perfect size to give our sprouts room to cook, but not enough empty space to burn. Plus, since we had a tightly fitting lid, there was no need to use foil to retain moisture.

The sheet pan problem solved, we returned to the dry, chewy sprouts and reluctantly considered lowering the oven temperature—but that would almost certainly increase the cooking time, and we wanted a side dish that would be done when our chicken breasts or pork chops finished resting. The solution was as simple as tossing the sprouts with 4 teaspoons of water along with the oil and seasonings before we put them in the oven. With the lid forming a moisture seal for the skillet, each halved sprout acted like its own little steam chamber, holding on to a tiny bit of water to finish cooking its interior even as its outside began to brown. The results were perfect: tender, sweet insides and caramelized exteriors.

Now that we'd made perfectly cooked Brussels sprouts in one easy step, we devised two quick variations. For an Italian-inspired dish, we tossed our roasted sprouts with garlicky, peppery olive oil and grated Parmesan. And to play up their nuttiness, we created a second variation with toasted pecans and crisped bacon.

Roasted Brussels Sprouts

SERVES 2

If you are buying loose Brussels sprouts, select those that are about 1½ inches long. Quarter Brussels sprouts that are longer than 2½ inches; don't cut sprouts shorter than 1 inch. You will need a 12-inch ovensafe skillet with a tight-fitting lid for this recipe.

- **8 ounces Brussels sprouts, trimmed and halved**
- **4 teaspoons water**
- **1 tablespoon olive oil**
- **Salt and pepper**

1. Adjust oven rack to upper-middle position and heat oven to 500 degrees. Toss Brussels sprouts, water, oil, ⅛ teaspoon salt, and pinch pepper in bowl until sprouts are coated. Transfer sprouts to 12-inch skillet and arrange so cut sides are facing down.

2. Roast sprouts, covered, for 10 minutes. Uncover and continue to cook until sprouts are well browned and tender, 10 to 12 minutes longer. Transfer sprouts to serving platter, season with salt and pepper to taste, and serve.

VARIATIONS

Roasted Brussels Sprouts with Garlic, Red Pepper Flakes, and Parmesan

While Brussels sprouts roast, heat 2 teaspoons olive oil in 8-inch skillet over medium-low heat until shimmering. Add 1 small minced garlic clove and pinch red pepper flakes; cook until garlic is golden and fragrant, about 1 minute. Remove from heat. After transferring sprouts to platter, toss with garlic oil and season with salt and pepper to taste. Sprinkle with 1 tablespoon grated Parmesan cheese before serving.

Roasted Brussels Sprouts with Bacon and Pecans
While Brussels sprouts roast, halve 1 slice bacon crosswise and cook in 8-inch skillet over medium heat until crisp, 6 to 8 minutes. Using slotted spoon, transfer bacon to paper towel–lined plate and reserve bacon fat. Finely chop bacon. After transferring sprouts to platter, toss with 1½ teaspoons olive oil, reserved bacon fat, chopped bacon, and 2 tablespoons finely chopped toasted pecans. Season with salt and pepper to taste and serve.

SKILLET-FRIED CORN

✔ **WHY THIS RECIPE WORKS:** This traditional Southern side dish normally requires constant stirring to achieve a rich, creamy texture. We wanted an easier, more hands-off recipe. First, we let the corn brown for about 10 minutes before we added water to the pan. Then we supplemented the corn's natural starch, which adds significant body, with a teaspoon of flour. A little sugar brought out the sweetness of the corn and further enhanced browning, and a small pat of butter ensured that our creamy side dish tasted plenty rich.

SKILLET-FRIED CORN, A POPULAR SIDE DISH IN THE South, is a cousin of creamed corn, and it's just as simple: Add corn kernels to a skillet with water, fat of some sort (often lard), corn "milk" (the starchy white liquid that can be scraped from the cob), and lots of salt and pepper. Then cook, stirring constantly, for upwards of 30 minutes to encourage the corn's starch to release. It's slightly creamy although it has no cream, plus it tastes like sweet corn amplified. Though it sounds pretty good, we weren't excited about the prospect of standing over the stove for half an hour, so we set out to come up with an easier version of this Southern staple, and it had to be scaled down to serve just two.

We began by considering the ingredients and started with the fat. We quickly rejected lard—few people keep

it around. We tried butter but it burned, and bacon fat overshadowed the sweet, nutty corn flavor. In the end, we decided to go with neutral vegetable oil. We also found that ½ teaspoon of sugar enhanced the natural sweetness of our two ears of corn (which provided just enough for two). With that, we turned to technique.

For a baseline, we made the dish following the traditional recipe but stirring it just enough to keep the corn from burning. That batch lacked the slightly caramelized, lightly coated, porridgelike quality that is the hallmark of skillet-fried corn. Luckily, further testing showed that if we staggered the ingredients instead of adding them all at once, we had better results. We learned to let the corn brown in the oil for some 10 minutes before adding the water. That one step helped us reduce the time of steady stirring by more than half—to about 10 minutes—with no harm done. We also discovered that the dish improved if we added the water in two parts, almost as if we were making risotto.

Unfortunately, less time stirring meant less time for the corn to release its starch, which meant the dish had less body. We tried adding some cornstarch, but it lost its thickening power after being cooked for more than a few minutes. Happily, a single teaspoon of flour ensured that our dish had the proper texture.

Satisfied with the texture, we dug in for a taste and found our corn was lacking in richness. We finished it by stirring in half a pat of butter. At last, we'd reached our goal: an easy, creamy, sweet-tasting skillet-fried corn with all the satisfying flavor and texture of the authentic versions that have been prepared for many years in kitchens across the South.

NOTES FROM THE TEST KITCHEN

CUTTING CORN KERNELS FROM THE COB

Standing corn upright inside large bowl, carefully cut kernels from cob using paring knife.

Skillet-Fried Corn

SERVES 2

Do not use frozen corn for this recipe.

2 ears corn, kernels cut from cobs, cobs reserved
1 teaspoon all-purpose flour
½ teaspoon sugar
¼ teaspoon salt
⅛ teaspoon pepper
2 teaspoons vegetable oil
⅔ cup water
½ tablespoon unsalted butter

1. Place kernels in bowl. Holding cobs over bowl, use back of butter knife to firmly scrape any pulp and liquid into bowl. Combine flour, sugar, salt, and pepper in second bowl.

2. Heat oil in 10-inch nonstick skillet over medium-high heat until shimmering. Add corn and cook, stirring occasionally, until beginning to brown, 8 to 10 minutes. Reduce heat to medium-low. Stir flour mixture into corn and cook for 1 minute. Stir in ⅓ cup water and cook, stirring constantly, until water evaporates, about 5 minutes. Add remaining ⅓ cup water and cook, stirring constantly, until corn is tender, about 5 minutes. Remove from heat and stir in butter. Serve.

CAULIFLOWER GRATIN

✔ WHY THIS RECIPE WORKS: We wanted an effortless version of this casserole that would serve two, not 10. Cooking the cauliflower in the microwave gave us a big head start (no need to drag out a pot to steam it on the stovetop) and meant that our gratin needed just a short stint in the oven. For a speedy cheese sauce, we microwaved garlic-and-herb Boursin cheese with a small amount of heavy cream; after a minute, it had thickened to the right consistency. Toasted panko bread crumbs ensured that our easy cauliflower gratin offered the same golden, crisp topping as the traditional versions.

MAKING A CHEESY CAULIFLOWER GRATIN SEEMS like a surefire way to entice even the pickiest eaters to eat their vegetables, but all too often the plan backfires: The gratin contains mushy or undercooked vegetables and an unappetizing and curdled or gloppy sauce. We set out to fix these problems while also scaling down this classic casserole to serve just two. And to up the ante, we hoped to streamline the traditional process, which calls for a few pots and pans to cook the cauliflower and make the sauce, so we could put the tender florets, crisp topping, and rich, cheesy sauce within reach on even the busiest of weeknights.

We began by looking for the easiest way to cook the cauliflower and started out on the stovetop. We tried boiling and steaming 10 ounces of florets, which seemed just the right amount for two diners. Given the vegetable's porous nature, boiling it resulted in a waterlogged veggie that tasted bland and dull; regardless of the cooking time, all we could taste was the cooking water. Steaming the cauliflower, on the other hand, produced evenly cooked florets with a clean, bright, sweet flavor. We wondered if microwaving would do as good a job, thereby shrinking our pile of dirty pots; indeed, it did. After just a minute in the microwave, our florets were still crisp but on their way to tender; a little time in the oven would ensure that they finished cooking through properly. To guarantee that they didn't make our gratin a watery mess, we set them in a colander for a few minutes so the excess moisture could drain off.

We turned our attention to the sauce. Most gratins rely on a béchamel, a white sauce that is made by stirring milk into a butter-flour roux, but that would require getting out a pan. We wondered if we could cut down on the extra time and effort by taking a cue from our Easy Creamed Spinach (page 240), for which we skipped the béchamel and created a sauce with Boursin cheese and heavy cream. We gave it a whirl here, microwaving a couple of ounces of Boursin with ¼ cup of heavy cream until the cheese melted, then whisking it together to form a thick, creamy sauce. We added our cauliflower to the bowl and tossed the lot together. The sauce was a bit on the thick side, but we anticipated the cauliflower would release more liquid as it finished cooking in the oven.

Sure enough, the sauce thinned out to just the right consistency as it baked. We did find, however, that the parcooked cauliflower florets did not soften appreciably during their stint in the oven. Would giving them a couple of extra minutes in the microwave solve this problem?

For our next test, we microwaved the cauliflower until it was tender, which took about three minutes. We set it aside to drain; wiped out the bowl; added the Boursin, cream, and some salt and pepper; and popped the sauce into the microwave to heat through. After combining our drained florets with the rich, creamy sauce and sprinkling on a few bread crumbs (we could finesse the topping later), we moved our casserole to the oven. As we'd expected, we were able to cut down on the baking time; our gratin needed only long enough for a golden-brown, crisp crust to form on top.

While some gratins achieve that appealing top layer with melted cheese, others rely on buttered bread crumbs. Since we already had plenty of cheese in the sauce, we opted for a crunchy bread-crumb topping. Bypassing fresh bread crumbs, we reached for ultracrisp panko, or Japanese-style bread crumbs, and toasted them in a skillet until they were golden. Scattered on top of the casserole, the panko browned further in the oven. Just seven minutes later, the crust was perfect, and the casserole was bubbling lightly around the edges.

This cauliflower gratin offered everything we wanted—tender florets, rich, cheesy sauce, and a satisfying crunch—but without all the work.

Cauliflower Gratin

SERVES 2

If buying a head of cauliflower rather than cauliflower florets, you will need half of a 2-pound head of cauliflower in order to yield 10 ounces of florets. You will need an 8½ by 5½-inch baking dish for this recipe (see page 3).

- ½ cup panko bread crumbs
- 1½ teaspoons olive oil
- 10 ounces cauliflower florets, cut into 1-inch pieces
- 1 tablespoon water
- ½ (5.2-ounce) package Boursin Garlic and Fine Herbs cheese
- ¼ cup heavy cream
- ¼ teaspoon salt
- ⅛ teaspoon pepper

1. Adjust oven rack to middle position and heat oven to 450 degrees. Toss panko with oil and place in 8-inch nonstick skillet. Toast panko over medium-high heat, stirring often, until golden, about 3 minutes.

2. Microwave cauliflower and water together in covered bowl until tender, about 3 minutes. Drain cauliflower in colander; set aside.

3. Wipe bowl dry with paper towels; add Boursin, cream, salt, and pepper; and microwave, uncovered, until cheese is melted, about 1 minute. Whisk Boursin mixture until smooth, then add drained cauliflower and toss to coat.

4. Transfer cauliflower mixture to 8½ by 5½-inch baking dish and sprinkle with toasted panko. Bake until hot and lightly bubbling around edges, about 7 minutes. Transfer gratin to wire rack and let cool slightly before serving.

TOMATO GRATIN

✓ WHY THIS RECIPE WORKS: Most tomato gratins end up waterlogged and flavorless—not ours. We solved the problem of a watery gratin by salting the tomatoes for 30 minutes before taking them for a spin in a salad spinner to remove excess moisture. Sautéed onion, flavored with garlic and fresh thyme, amped up the savory notes of the dish, and panko plus grated Parmesan cheese delivered a crispy, cheesy topping. Since the panko browned before the tomatoes were cooked, we gave the tomatoes a head start in the oven before sprinkling on the topping.

RIDING HIGH ON THE SUCCESS OF OUR CAULIFLOWER Gratin, we set our sights on another popular variation on this dish: tomato gratin. But what makes a good tomato great—lots of flavorful juices—can also wreak havoc on this humble casserole. At its simplest, tomato gratin is made by layering sliced tomatoes under a mixture of bread crumbs and grated cheese. Fancier recipes include other vegetables, like cooked onions or grilled eggplant. The gratin is then baked or broiled until the topping turns golden. But if making it were as simple as it sounds, the topping wouldn't be soggy and

TOMATO GRATIN

the tomatoes wouldn't taste washed out—problems we encountered with almost all of the recipes we tested. We resolved to bring both a crisp topping and full, distinct tomato flavor to our tomato gratin for two, for a boldly flavored side dish that would go well with any number of entrées.

We knew from the outset that too much moisture was the enemy, so we decided on plum tomatoes, which are less watery than other varieties. Even with these, though, we found it necessary to employ a test kitchen technique for drying watery vegetables: Slice, salt and sugar (the sugar enhances the tomatoes' natural sweetness), wait, then drain. After a half-hour, a good amount of liquid had drained from the tomatoes, so we whirled them in a salad spinner. Then we put together and baked a gratin, using a basic topping from our first tests. Combined, these tactics mitigated the moisture pretty well, and we added insurance by cranking up the oven to 450 degrees. At that temperature, any remaining tomato juices cooked off.

We liked the taste of onions in one of the gratins from the first tests we'd done, and we figured we could sauté them (with a bit of garlic and thyme for flavor) to soften them as the tomatoes drained. We spread the sautéed onions in a baking dish, layered the drained tomatoes on top, and turned to the topping.

Parmesan is the traditional choice for gratins, and it's a classic for a reason: It adds big flavor without melting into a gooey mess. We stuck with it. We tested the cheese mixed with three sorts of crumbs: uncooked sandwich bread crumbs, fried bread crumbs, and panko (which we liked in our Cauliflower Gratin). To promote browning, we stirred in a little olive oil. Baked atop the gratin, both the uncooked and the fried crumbs tasted slightly sandy. Panko, however, lent a nice crunch. And thanks to our diligent salting and spinning of the tomatoes, the topping wasn't soggy at all.

Unfortunately, a new problem emerged: In the hot oven, the topping browned before the tomatoes had time to cook. To get the components in harmony, we'd need to adjust the baking method. For the next test, we started by cooking the onion and tomato layers together in the baking dish without the topping. After 15 minutes—with the dish on the lower-middle oven rack—they began to gently meld and bubble. At that point, we sprinkled on the crumbs, moved the dish to the upper-middle oven rack for better browning, and cooked our casserole for another 10 minutes.

After the gratin had cooled for 10 minutes, we eagerly dug in. We were thrilled: The tomatoes were moist but not wet, and their flavor was concentrated. The onions added a savory undertone, and the beautifully browned topping had great toasty Parmesan flavor and offered a big crunch factor. Our Tomato Gratin was a resounding success.

Tomato Gratin

SERVES 2

You will need an 8½ by 5½-inch baking dish for this recipe (see page 3).

12	ounces plum tomatoes, cored and sliced into ¼-inch-thick rings
	Salt and pepper
⅛	teaspoon sugar
¼	cup panko bread crumbs
¼	cup grated Parmesan cheese
4	teaspoons extra-virgin olive oil
1	small onion, halved and sliced thin
1	small garlic clove, minced
½	teaspoon minced fresh thyme

1. Adjust oven racks to lower-middle and upper-middle positions and heat oven to 450 degrees. Toss tomatoes, ½ teaspoon salt, and sugar together in bowl until combined; let sit for 30 minutes. Combine panko, Parmesan, 2 teaspoons oil, ⅛ teaspoon salt, and pinch pepper in second bowl.

2. Heat remaining 2 teaspoons oil in 8-inch skillet over medium-high heat until shimmering. Add onion and cook until softened, 5 to 7 minutes. Stir in garlic and thyme and cook until fragrant, about 30 seconds. Season with salt and pepper to taste. Spread onion mixture in bottom of 8½ by 5½-inch baking dish.

3. Transfer tomatoes to salad spinner and spin to remove excess moisture. Arrange tomatoes in even layer over onion mixture and sprinkle with pinch pepper. Transfer baking dish to lower-middle oven rack and bake until tomatoes are tender and starting to bubble, about 15 minutes. Sprinkle evenly with panko mixture, transfer to upper-middle oven rack, and bake until topping is golden brown, about 10 minutes longer. Transfer gratin to wire rack and let cool for 5 to 10 minutes before serving.

ROASTED SALT-AND-VINEGAR POTATOES

✓ **WHY THIS RECIPE WORKS:** We wanted a side dish that delivered spuds with a bold, vinegary tang and crisp exterior. Cooking small red potatoes in a super-saturated salt solution ensured that they had an incredibly creamy, well-seasoned interior. After the potatoes were parcooked, we smashed them to expose some of the potato flesh, brushed them with malt vinegar, and roasted them in a well-oiled skillet until the exposed surface was golden and crispy. A final brush with more vinegar when the potatoes came out of the oven reinforced the addictive salty-sour flavor of these spuds.

GERMAN POTATO SALAD, SALT-AND-VINEGAR potato chips, and English "chips" sprinkled with malt vinegar all offer an addictively appealing salty-sour flavor combination. Inspired by this unique flavor profile, we set out to come up with a crispy potato side dish that was easy and satisfying and made just enough for two.

This dish was more of a concept than an established dish, but we did discover a few recipes online. We followed two of the recipes we found: For one, we boiled potatoes in a mixture of vinegar and lightly salted water. We couldn't taste the vinegar or the salt, and obviously the spuds had no crunch. For the other recipe, we roasted seasoned potato quarters and doused them in vinegar when they came out of the oven. The vinegar tasted raw and harsh, and the salt was barely skin-deep. Clearly we had our work cut out for us.

Moving on, we abandoned these half-baked efforts in favor of a technique we've used in the past: boiling small red potatoes in very heavily salted water. In previous tests, we've found that the concentrated salt solution cooks the potato starch more completely than usual, resulting in extremely creamy flesh. At the same time, these potatoes develop an amazingly salt-encrusted exterior and a well-seasoned interior; the potato skin protects the interior from being inedibly salty. Salt solved, the vinegar challenge lay ahead.

At this point, we knew that, first, we'd need to roast the potatoes for crispness and, second, sprinkling vinegar on cooked potatoes was not the answer. So for our next batch, after boiling the potatoes in the super-saturated salt solution, we cut them into quarters, brushed them with vinegar, and roasted them in an extremely hot oven. This was a definite step forward.

But had we gone overboard? The whole idea of baking the vinegar into the roasting potatoes was to mellow it, but now we missed its brightness. While the roasted potatoes were still very hot, we brushed them with extra vinegar. We got a nice jolt of pleasing sourness, with none of the harshness that had ruined earlier versions. Why? Our science editor explained that as the water molecules rising from the hot potatoes evaporate, they carry some acetic acid molecules from the vinegar along with them. This technique worked better when we replaced the neat wedges with a "smash": We pressed the potatoes with the bottom of a measuring cup to about a ½-inch thickness. The interiors of the smashed potatoes stayed soft when roasted, so they could better absorb the vinegar brush.

Cider vinegar was our default vinegar, but was it the best choice? We tried white vinegar, only to find it too harsh. Cider and red wine vinegars were perfectly fine, but balsamic vinegar was better. Unfortunately, it turned the potatoes the color of mud. Hoping for the same sweetness but a more appealing color, we tried malt vinegar, a sweet, mild vinegar popular in Britain. Now both color and flavor hit the mark.

Roasted Salt-and-Vinegar Potatoes
SERVES 2

Use small red potatoes, measuring 1 to 2 inches in diameter. If you prefer to use kosher salt, you will need ¾ cup of Morton kosher salt or 1¼ cups of Diamond Crystal kosher salt. Cider vinegar works here, too.

- 3 tablespoons olive oil
- 1 pound small red potatoes
- ½ cup plus 2 tablespoons salt
- 1½ tablespoons malt vinegar
  Pepper

1. Adjust oven rack to upper-middle position and heat oven to 500 degrees. Set wire rack inside rimmed baking sheet. Brush 12-inch ovensafe skillet evenly with oil. Bring 4 cups water to boil in medium saucepan over

SMASHING OUR SPUDS

Use bottom of 1-cup dry measuring cup to evenly flatten potatoes to ½-inch thickness. Then brush potatoes with half of vinegar and pepper.

medium-high heat. Stir in potatoes and salt and cook until just tender and paring knife slips easily in and out of potatoes, 20 to 25 minutes. Drain potatoes and transfer to wire rack; let dry for 10 minutes.

2. Transfer potatoes to oiled skillet. Flatten each potato with bottom of measuring cup until ½ inch thick. Brush potatoes with half of vinegar and season with pepper. Roast until potatoes are well browned, 25 to 30 minutes. Brush with remaining vinegar. Transfer potatoes to platter, smashed side up. Serve.

POTATO CASSEROLE WITH BACON AND CARAMELIZED ONION

✔ **WHY THIS RECIPE WORKS:** In the old days, this rich potato and onion casserole got its deep flavor from the drippings of a meaty roast. For an easier take on this luxurious dish, minus the roast, we started by rendering a small amount of bacon, which lent the dish a meaty flavor. Browning the onions in the rendered bacon fat gave the dish remarkable complexity. A mix of chicken broth and beef broth provided a savory backbone, and the step of reducing it on the stovetop, in addition to the potatoes' natural starch, ensured that the sauce was nicely thickened by the time it came out of the oven.

IN THE FRENCH DISH KNOWN AS *POMMES DE TERRE boulangère*, or "baker's potatoes," incredibly tender potatoes nestle in a rich, meaty sauce beneath a delicately browned crust. The name dates to a time when villagers used the residual heat of the baker's oven to cook dinner at the end of the day. Chicken, pork, or beef would roast on an upper oven shelf while this casserole of thinly sliced potatoes and onions bubbled away underneath, seasoned by the savory fat and juices dripping from above.

Today French chefs no longer cook this dish beneath a blistering roast, but they impart the same unctuous flavor, deep brown color, and supreme tenderness using hearty meat stock and a well-calibrated oven. While we could spend hours making stock from scratch, that was too much time and effort for a side dish for two. We wanted a potato casserole with deep flavor and a super-tender texture—without spending all day in the kitchen.

Since we were seeking a creamy consistency, only one potato variety would do: the moderately starchy, buttery-tasting Yukon Gold. For our casserole for two, 1 pound of potatoes seemed ample. A mandoline was the ideal tool for slicing the peeled spuds since we wanted them to be wafer-thin (about ⅛ inch)—any thicker and the casserole would be too chunky, losing its refined nature. We added a thinly sliced onion to the Yukons, packed the mixture into a small baking dish, poured in 1½ cups of store-bought beef broth, and slid the casserole into a 350-degree oven. It was no surprise when this test batch revealed two big flaws. First, the sauce was bland and tasted tinny from the canned broth. And second, its consistency was soupy, lacking the requisite creaminess.

We tackled the flavor issue first. To temper the beef broth's undesirable qualities, we diluted it with an equal amount of commercial chicken broth. This mellowed the flavor of both, for a blend that didn't taste processed. But that didn't mean it tasted meaty. For more depth and meaty notes, we turned to flavor-packed pork options like ham hocks, pancetta, and bacon. We simmered a hock briefly in the broth, expecting it to impart smokiness, but the effect was negligible. (We could have cooked it longer but we wanted a quick fix.) For the pancetta and bacon, we simply rendered them until crisp and then tossed the pieces with the potatoes and onion. Both were much more effective at boosting meatiness than the ham hock was, but in the end, tasters preferred the smoky bacon; a single slice was all we needed.

Next up: the onion. We found inspiration in another French classic: onion soup, in which onions are deeply caramelized to concentrate their flavor. Cooking the sliced onion to a deep molasses-y brown made it too sweet for this dish, but sautéing it in some of the leftover bacon fat until golden brown was enough to bring out remarkable complexity.

With a scattering of fresh thyme, sprinkles of salt and pepper, plus a few pats of butter, the flavor of our potatoes was in really good shape. But we still needed to improve the too-thin sauce and somehow make the overall texture silkier and more luscious.

Our first attempt to remedy the consistency of the sauce was twofold: We decreased the amount of broth to 1 cup and increased the oven temperature to 425 degrees so that more liquid would evaporate during baking. When we started to see an improvement, we took things one step further by bringing the broth to a simmer in the pot used to cook the onion, giving it a jump start on reducing in the oven. As a bonus, this deglazing step captured all of the flavorful fond left behind by the bacon and caramelized onion.

The broth had now cooked down, but it was still neither thick nor creamy. Then it became clear: We had been submerging the sliced potatoes in water to keep them from discoloring while we prepped the remaining ingredients—a common practice, but one that also washes away most of the spuds' starch. Without enough starch, the sauce couldn't thicken up. We tried again with unsoaked potatoes and witnessed a striking difference. The sauce now glazed the potatoes and onion in a velvety cloak. As a final measure, we made sure to allow the casserole to rest for a good 20 minutes before serving it. This went a long way toward developing a silky, creamy texture, since the starch granules in the potatoes continued to absorb moisture and swell as they cooled.

With a few modifications, we had been able to achieve a satisfying version of a rustic French dish within a reasonable time frame. It was now much more accessible for kitchens of two, and it still delivered all of the hearty appeal and great flavors of the original casserole.

Potato Casserole with Bacon and Caramelized Onion

SERVES 2

Do not rinse or soak the potatoes, as this will wash away their starch, which is essential to the dish. A mandoline makes slicing the potatoes much easier. For the proper texture, make sure to let the casserole sit for 20 minutes before serving. You will need an 8½ by 5½-inch baking dish for this recipe (see page 3).

1 slice bacon, cut into ¼-inch pieces
1 small onion, halved and sliced thin
½ teaspoon chopped fresh thyme
½ teaspoon salt
⅛ teaspoon pepper
1 pound Yukon Gold potatoes, peeled
½ cup low-sodium chicken broth
½ cup beef broth
½ tablespoon unsalted butter, cut into 4 pieces

1. Adjust oven rack to lower-middle position and heat oven to 425 degrees. Grease 8½ by 5½-inch baking dish.

2. Cook bacon in small saucepan over medium heat until crisp, 6 to 8 minutes. Using slotted spoon, transfer bacon to paper towel–lined plate. Return now-empty saucepan to medium heat and add onion; cook, stirring frequently, until onion is soft and golden brown, about 20 minutes, adjusting heat and adding water 1 tablespoon at a time if onion or bottom of pot becomes too dark. Transfer onion to bowl; add bacon, thyme, salt, and pepper.

3. Slice potatoes ⅛ inch thick. Transfer to bowl with onion mixture and toss to combine. Transfer to prepared baking dish. Firmly press down on mixture to compress into even layer.

4. Add broths to now-empty saucepan and bring to simmer over medium-high heat, scraping bottom of pan to loosen any browned bits. Carefully pour hot broth over top of potatoes. Dot surface evenly with butter.

5. Bake, uncovered, until potatoes are tender and golden brown on edges and most of liquid has been absorbed, 40 to 45 minutes. Transfer to wire rack and let stand for about 20 minutes to fully absorb broth before cutting and serving.

CHEESY SCALLOPED POTATOES

CHEESY SCALLOPED POTATOES

✔ WHY THIS RECIPE WORKS: Casserole-style scalloped potatoes can take up to an hour to cook through, plus they usually serve a small crowd. We not only wanted a version suitable for two, but we wanted it on the table as quickly as possible. We began by sautéing onion, garlic, and thyme in a small skillet before adding chicken broth and cream. To ensure that our casserole was ready in short order, we simmered the potatoes in the aromatic liquid until they were nearly tender, then moved the skillet to the oven so they could finish baking. A mix of cheddar and Parmesan gave our spuds big cheesy flavor, and a bit of cornstarch prevented the dish from becoming greasy.

IN MANY HOUSEHOLDS, SCALLOPED POTATOES ARE reserved for a large crowd. We suspect it's because the dish bakes for as long as 90 minutes, so people think the time commitment isn't worth it for a smaller group. We disagree: This bubbling casserole of sliced potatoes in a luscious, creamy sauce oozing with cheese is too good to save for company. We set out to both scale down and speed up this satisfying dish.

We made several versions to figure out our starting point. All of the recipes required layering thinly sliced raw potatoes in a casserole dish, pouring cream or milk (sometimes mixed with chicken broth) over the slices, sprinkling the dish with cheese, and setting it in the oven to bake. After assimilating tasters' comments, we cherry-picked aspects of the different versions to put together a basic dish. Our working recipe used a combination of cream and chicken broth, with cheddar for the cheese. Now we whittled down the proportions to serve two; the potatoes and sauce fit neatly in a pie plate.

We expected that with so much less bulk, the dish would cook faster, but our scaled-down scalloped potatoes still required an hour of baking time to tenderize. Clearly, the spuds needed a head start. For the next test, we parcooked the sliced potatoes in boiling water before following the recipe as usual. These potatoes were tender after just 15 minutes in the oven. But they tasted watery, and the sauce was now thin. Too late,

we realized that we'd forgotten a key advantage of the traditional method: The potatoes release starch into the liquid as they bake, which helps thicken it. By parboiling and then draining the potatoes, we were pouring all that starch—and thickening power—down the drain. We had a better idea.

We turned to a technique that the test kitchen has used that not only takes advantage of the potatoes' natural starch but also gets flavor deep inside the spuds. We pulled out a saucepan and simmered the raw potatoes on the stovetop right in the cream and broth. After 10 minutes, we emptied everything into the pie plate and baked our potatoes. Barely 15 minutes later, we had tender potatoes nestled in velvety sauce. Since we were now using a saucepan to get the potatoes started, it seemed like an easy opportunity to introduce more flavor. We sautéed chopped onion, garlic, and thyme in butter for a few minutes, only then adding the potatoes, cream, and broth. It was a winning flavor combination.

But by this point, the pie plate seemed unnecessary (unless we had a burning desire to wash more dishes). We ditched the pie plate and exchanged the saucepan for a small ovensafe skillet to allow the potatoes to bake more quickly and evenly. As we'd hoped, the skillet proved a talented multitasker, letting us sauté the vegetables, simmer the potatoes and cream, bake, and serve—all in a single dish.

Most of our test cooks would agree that half of the pleasure of scalloped potatoes is the cheese. The ¼ cup of cheddar we'd been sprinkling on top wasn't adding much, so we doubled that amount and mixed it right into the sauce. Then, for nutty flavor, we sprinkled on Parmesan. The flavor was great, but there was too much grease. Here in the test kitchen, we've figured out how to solve that problem: by tossing the cheese with cornstarch, which absorbs the fat (or grease) that the melting cheese releases.

Because the scalloped potatoes were baking comparatively quickly, they didn't have time to develop a deep-golden crust. Fortunately, raising the oven rack so that the top potatoes could brown where the oven was warmest was an easy work-around.

We baked one final test batch—and were thrilled with the outcome. The potatoes were tender, the sauce creamy and oozing, the top golden and crisp around the edges—and it was just enough to serve two.

Cheesy Scalloped Potatoes

SERVES 2

Don't use preshredded cheese, which contains added starch that will interfere with the sauce. You'll need two small potatoes or one extra-large one.

        2   ounces mild cheddar cheese, shredded (½ cup)
     1½   teaspoons cornstarch
        1   ounce Parmesan cheese, grated (½ cup)
        1   teaspoon vegetable oil
        ½   cup finely chopped onion
        1   garlic clove, minced
        ¼   teaspoon dried thyme
        ⅓   cup low-sodium chicken broth
        ⅓   cup heavy cream
     12   ounces russet potatoes, peeled and sliced ¼ inch thick
        ½   teaspoon salt
        ¼   teaspoon pepper

1. Adjust oven rack to upper-middle position and heat oven to 425 degrees. Toss cheddar and 1 teaspoon cornstarch together in bowl until well combined. Toss Parmesan and remaining ½ teaspoon cornstarch together in second bowl until well combined.

2. Heat oil in 8-inch nonstick ovensafe skillet over medium heat until shimmering. Add onion and cook until browned, about 5 minutes. Stir in garlic and thyme and cook until fragrant, about 30 seconds. Add broth, cream, potatoes, salt, and pepper and bring to boil. Reduce heat to medium-low, cover, and simmer until potatoes are nearly tender, 10 to 12 minutes.

3. Off heat, stir in cheddar mixture and press potatoes into even layer. Sprinkle Parmesan mixture evenly over top and bake until golden brown, 12 to 14 minutes. Let potatoes cool on wire rack for 10 minutes. Serve.

NOTES FROM THE TEST KITCHEN

JUMP-STARTING OUR SPUDS

To get dinner on the table faster and infuse our spuds with flavor, we simmered the slices in the sauce on the stovetop, then moved everything to the oven, where the potatoes could finish cooking through in about 10 minutes.

CRISP ROASTED FINGERLING POTATOES

✓ **WHY THIS RECIPE WORKS:** Roasted potatoes should be easy enough, but too often the results are disappointing: chewy, leathery skins and a mealy interior. Fingerlings present an even bigger problem because they're lacking in starch, which helps facilitate browning for a crisp exterior. Boiling our spuds in a mixture of salt and baking soda was our first step toward perfectly roasted fingerlings; the salt made the potatoes fluffy, and the baking soda brought any potato starch to the surface. After boiling the potatoes, we let them cool to vent steam and then roasted them, cut side down, in a hot skillet so that the now-starch-covered potatoes would become crispy.

FINGERLING POTATOES ARE PRIZED FOR THEIR good flavor, ultrathin skins, and creamy texture. Plus, they can be purchased in smaller quantities, which makes them ideal for the for-two kitchen. Though they're usually cooked gently to showcase their delicate nature, we had a tougher treatment in mind: We wanted roasted fingerling potatoes that were still fresh-tasting and creamy but had a crisp edge. The problem? It's the starch that facilitates crisp browning, and diminutive fingerlings have little of it. Could we find a way to deliver small spuds with the perfect creamy interior and a nicely browned exterior to match?

Early tests proved that putting fingerlings (halved lengthwise to create a flat surface to brown) on an oiled sheet pan in a hot oven was a nonstarter: The potatoes were leathery by the time they picked up any color. We tried covering them with aluminum foil for half of the cooking time to trap the steam, but that didn't work either. From previous recipes we learned that boiling potatoes in super-salty water helps season them throughout and maximizes a creamy interior. Also, with potato salad recipes we've added vinegar to the boil to halt the release of starch. Could we do the reverse here, making the water more alkaline (with baking soda) to encourage maximum starch release—and better browning?

Our science editor thought it would work, explaining that adding baking soda to boiling potatoes starts a chain reaction in which the pectin molecules that strengthen cell walls are unzipped, releasing the starch molecule amylose (a potato starch that facilitates browning) to the potatoes' surface. So we gave it a try and added lots of salt and a little baking soda to the boiling water. Once the fingerlings were drained in the colander, we could see a thin layer of sticky starch on them. As we shook the potatoes dry in the colander, the starch became more abundant. We arranged the dried potatoes, cut side down, on a preheated, oiled sheet tray and roasted them at 500 degrees for about 15 minutes.

These spuds came out of the oven tender and crisp but became soggy as they cooled because they continued to release steam even after a seared crust had formed. Clearly, we needed to cool the potatoes before roasting them, so in our next test we spread the boiled potatoes out on a large platter. After 5 minutes they'd stopped steaming. Now we placed them on a hot, oiled sheet tray and roasted them as before. These fingerlings were just as tender and creamy as boiled ones, but this time they had a crisp, flavorful crust.

Only one problem remained. Since we were cooking such a small quantity of potatoes (just 1 pound to serve two people), we were left with a lot of empty space on the sheet pan, which caused the oil to burn and leave a black, crusty mess behind. Transferring the potatoes to a 12-inch ovensafe skillet was a better option; the size was just right for the potatoes, and the resulting cleanup made for a dish that was a snap both to prepare—and to devour.

Crisp Roasted Fingerling Potatoes
SERVES 2

Using fingerlings of uniform size will ensure that the potatoes cook at the same rate and fit in the skillet in an even layer. Be sure to press the potatoes so that the cut side is flush against the bottom of the pan for even browning. If you prefer to use kosher salt, you will need ¼ cup plus 2 tablespoons of Morton kosher salt or ½ cup of Diamond Crystal kosher salt.

- 1 **pound fingerling potatoes, halved lengthwise**
- ¼ **cup salt**
- ¼ **teaspoon baking soda**
- 1 **tablespoon olive oil**
- ⅛ **teaspoon pepper**

1. Adjust oven rack to lowest position, place 12-inch ovensafe skillet on rack, and heat oven to 500 degrees. Bring 4 cups water to boil in medium saucepan over

NOTES FROM THE TEST KITCHEN

COAXING OUT THE STARCH

Boiling the potatoes with salt helps guarantee a creamy interior and seasons the spuds, and adding baking soda to the water breaks down pectin, draws starch to the surface, and encourages browning.

medium-high heat. Stir in potatoes, salt, and baking soda and cook until potatoes are tender but centers offer slight resistance when pierced with paring knife, 8 to 10 minutes. Drain potatoes in colander and shake vigorously to roughen edges. Transfer potatoes to large platter lined with dish towel and arrange cut side up. Let sit until no longer steaming and surface is tacky, about 5 minutes.

2. Transfer potatoes to large bowl and toss with 1 teaspoon oil and pepper. Working quickly, carefully remove skillet from oven, add remaining 2 teaspoons oil to skillet, and swirl to coat. Carefully arrange potatoes in skillet, cut sides down, in even layer, pressing potatoes to ensure that cut sides are flush with bottom of pan. Return skillet to oven and bake until cut sides are crisp and skins are spotty brown, 15 to 18 minutes. Flip potatoes cut sides up and let cool in pan for 5 minutes. Serve.

WHITE BEAN SALAD

✔ **WHY THIS RECIPE WORKS:** To liven up canned white beans for a boldly flavored bean salad for two, we started by steeping the namesake ingredient in a garlicky broth. This infused the beans with deep flavor in short order, and sautéing the garlic first brought a toasty element to the salad. Marinating our shallot in vinegar worked to tame its raw, harsh notes. Some red bell pepper added color and crunch, and chopped parsley and chives ramped up the freshness of the salad.

COME SUMMER, WE LOVE WHITE BEAN SALAD WITH a simple vinaigrette—the creamy, mild beans offer a nice counterpoint to the boldly flavored dressing. But when you're cooking for two, it doesn't make sense to start with dried beans, which require an overnight soak prior to being cooked for a good amount of time in order to develop their deep, savory flavor. In the test kitchen, we turn to canned beans often when they're playing a supporting role or are gussied up with lots of big flavors. But here they'd be the main attraction, and there wouldn't be many distractions. Could we find a way to deliver the rich flavor of long-simmered beans in our white bean salad for two, but use the convenient canned variety?

In the past, the test kitchen has found that simmering canned beans for at least 30 minutes with strong flavors like garlic and onion improves their flavor significantly. But it also causes the beans to soften and break apart—which is fine for a soup that you're going to puree, but a nonstarter for salad. We'd need to flavor them yet keep them intact.

To get our bearings, we threw together an easy salad: We minced garlic and chopped a small shallot (a vinaigrette staple) and tossed them with a can of drained, rinsed beans and oil and vinegar. The verdict? The shallot and garlic tasted harsh, and the beans were dull. To fix the beans, we tried steeping them with smashed garlic. We experimented with letting the beans rest in hot garlicky water for 10, 20, and 30 minutes. Then we drained them, discarded the garlic, and tossed them with vinaigrette. After 20 minutes, the beans emerged intact and with good garlic flavor. It was a solid start.

Typically, sautéing garlic in fat both mellows and deepens its flavor. So rather than using raw garlic, we switched to sautéing smashed cloves in olive oil for a couple of minutes, until they began to brown. We added salt and water to the saucepan, brought everything to a simmer, and introduced the beans to this flavored water. Tasters were pleased; we'd drawn out the garlic flavor and added a toasty dimension to the salad. To further boost the flavor, we experimented with soaking the beans in chicken broth and vegetable broth in place of water. But the broths didn't add enough to justify their inclusion, especially since we'd have to discard them after the steeping was done.

The bean salad already tasted much better, but our work was only half done; now for the shallot. Since we had 20 minutes to kill while the beans steeped, we'd use that time to quickly pickle the shallot. We minced it and soaked it in sherry vinegar until the beans were ready. The shallot's raw, oniony harshness was transformed. Tasters liked its milder flavor, and we especially liked the fact that the timing lined up so neatly.

After that, the salad came together quickly. We drained the steeped beans and threw away the garlic. Then we tossed the beans with olive oil and the shallot-vinegar mixture, adding red bell pepper for crunch and color, as well as fresh chives, chopped parsley, and salt and pepper. We used more vinegar than called for in a classic vinaigrette to counter the sweet starchiness of the creamy beans; that jolt of acid kept the flavors bright. Then we let the salad sit so the flavors could meld briefly. We were thrilled with the results: The beans were garlicky, creamy, and intact, and the pickled shallot vinaigrette brought everything together. After just a forkful, we knew canned beans had earned a permanent spot in our pantry.

White Bean Salad

SERVES 2

Make sure you rinse the white beans thoroughly before adding them to the pot to get rid of excess salt. The salad can be served chilled or at room temperature.

- 2 tablespoons extra-virgin olive oil
- 2 garlic cloves, peeled and smashed
  Salt and pepper
- 1 (15-ounce) can cannellini beans, rinsed
- 1 tablespoon sherry vinegar
- 1 small shallot, minced
- ½ red bell pepper, stemmed, seeded, and cut into ¼-inch pieces
- 2 tablespoons chopped fresh parsley
- 2 tablespoons chopped fresh chives

1. Heat 1½ teaspoons oil and garlic in small saucepan over medium-high heat until garlic just begins to brown, about 2 minutes. Slowly add ⅔ cup water and ¼ teaspoon salt and bring to simmer. Off heat, add beans, cover, and let sit for 20 minutes. Combine vinegar and shallot in large bowl and let sit for 20 minutes.

2. Drain beans and remove garlic. Add beans, remaining 1½ tablespoons oil, bell pepper, parsley, and chives to shallot mixture and toss to combine. Season with salt and pepper to taste. Cover and let sit for 20 minutes. Serve.

TABBOULEH

✓ **WHY THIS RECIPE WORKS:** For a bright, balanced, and fresh-tasting tabbouleh, we started by salting the tomatoes to rid them of excess moisture that would have made our salad soggy. Soaking the bulgur wheat in some of the drained tomato liquid and lemon juice, rather than water, ensured that it was flavorful. For the herbs, we included lots of bright, peppery parsley and a good amount of mint. Chopped tomato and a sliced scallion rounded out the mix, and a bit of cayenne pepper added zing. We added the mix-ins while the bulgur was still soaking so the components had time to mingle, resulting in a perfectly balanced dish.

TABBOULEH HAS LONG BEEN A MEZE STAPLE IN THE Middle East, but these days it can be found in the refrigerator case of virtually every American supermarket. Its brief (and healthful) ingredient list explains its popularity: Chopped fresh parsley and mint, tomatoes, onion, and bits of nutty bulgur are tossed with lemon and olive oil for a refreshing appetizer or side dish. It all sounds easy enough, but following a recipe or picking up a pint at the market reveals that most versions are hopelessly soggy, with flavor that is either too bold or too bland.

Another problem is that there's no agreement on the correct proportions for tabbouleh. Middle Eastern cooks favor loads of parsley (75 to 90 percent of the salad), employing only a sprinkle of bulgur as a texturally interesting garnish. Most American recipes, on the other hand, invert the proportions, transforming the green salad into an insipid pilaf with a smattering of herbs. We were after a balanced dish that featured a hefty amount of parsley as well as a decent amount of bulgur. It had to offer the bright, fresh flavors lacking in the supermarket versions, and it had to yield just enough for two.

For our scaled-down tabbouleh, we started with the bulgur. Bulgur is made by boiling, drying, and grinding wheat kernels, so it only needs to be reconstituted in cool water. But specific advice on how to prepare the grains is all over the map. Rehydration times range from a cursory 5 minutes all the way up to several hours. And then there's the amount of liquid: Some recipes call for just enough to plump the grains; others employ the "pasta method," soaking the bulgur in lots of water and then squeezing out the excess.

Working with ¼ cup of medium-grind bulgur (the easiest size to find) and first rinsing the grains to remove any detritus, we experimented with innumerable permutations of time and amount of water. Our initial findings: First, the grains required at least 90 minutes to tenderize fully. Second, the less liquid we used, the better the texture was. Soaking the bulgur in excess water only made it heavy, damp, and bland. In the end, a mere 2 tablespoons of liquid was enough for ¼ cup of dried bulgur. The grains absorbed the liquid almost instantly and then slowly swelled into ½ cup of tender, fluffy grains as they rested.

With the method settled, we switched to soaking the bulgur in lemon juice instead of water, as some cookbooks recommend. This was a no-brainer—eliminating water only made sense for a salad that can taste washed out.

Next, we moved on to the parsley. To our ½ cup of reconstituted bulgur we added ¾ cup of chopped parsley and ¼ cup of chopped mint. These quantities still put the emphasis on the bright, peppery parsley but didn't discount the lemony bulgur and refreshing mint.

As for the rest of the salad, 3 tablespoons of extra-virgin olive oil tempered the tart lemon juice, and a chopped ripe tomato and a single sliced scallion (preferred over red or white onion) rounded out the mix. A pinch of cayenne pepper along with the usual salt and pepper added zing. Finally, we considered garlic and cucumbers. Tasters soundly rejected these additions, complaining that they detracted from the salad's clean flavor (in the case of the former) and overall texture (in the case of the latter).

We set out pita bread wedges and romaine lettuce leaves (traditional accompaniments) and summoned tasters for feedback. They were happy enough with the texture, but the flavors of the salad, they lamented, weren't cohesive—tabbouleh features bold ingredients, and our method wasn't giving them time to blend. This was easy to resolve: We simply reworked the method to give the bulgur a chance to absorb the liquids—namely, olive oil and juices from the tomato—in the salad. Soaking the bulgur for 30 to 40 minutes, until it began to soften, and then combining it with the remaining ingredients and letting it sit for an hour until fully tender gave everything time to mingle, resulting in a perfectly well-balanced dish.

We had just one final issue to deal with. Over the course of testing, we had noticed that depending on variety, the tomato contributed different amounts of liquid to the tabbouleh, sometimes diluting its flavor and making it soupy. The solution? Salting. Tossing the chopped tomato with salt and letting it drain in a colander drew out its moisture, precluding sogginess. We were about to break out the bubbly when a light bulb went on: By discarding the tomato juice, we were literally pouring flavor down the drain. What if we reserved this savory liquid and used it to soak the bulgur? For our next try, we put a bowl under the colander to catch the juices and prepared a salad using 1 tablespoon of the tomato liquid (along with an equal amount of lemon juice) to soak the bulgur, whisking the remaining 1 tablespoon of lemon juice with oil for the dressing. At last, here was tabbouleh with fresh, penetrating flavor and a light texture that would make cooks—from anywhere around the globe—proud.

Tabbouleh

SERVES 2

Serve the salad with the crisp inner leaves of romaine lettuce and wedges of pita bread.

- 1 tomato, cored and cut into ½-inch pieces
  Salt and pepper
- ¼ cup medium-grind bulgur
- 2 tablespoons lemon juice
- 3 tablespoons extra-virgin olive oil
  Pinch cayenne pepper
- ¾ cup chopped fresh parsley
- ¼ cup chopped fresh mint
- 1 scallion, sliced thin

1. Toss tomato with ⅛ teaspoon salt in medium bowl. Transfer to fine-mesh strainer, set strainer in bowl, and let sit for 30 minutes, tossing occasionally.

2. Rinse bulgur in fine-mesh strainer under cold running water. Drain well and transfer to second bowl. Stir in 1 tablespoon juice from drained tomatoes and 1 tablespoon lemon juice. Let stand until grains are beginning to soften, 30 to 40 minutes.

3. Whisk remaining 1 tablespoon lemon juice, oil, cayenne, and ⅛ teaspoon salt together in large bowl.

Add drained tomatoes, soaked bulgur, parsley, mint, and scallion; toss gently to combine. Cover and let sit at room temperature until flavors have blended and bulgur is tender, about 1 hour. Toss to recombine, season with salt and pepper to taste, and serve immediately.

LENTIL SALADS

✔ **WHY THIS RECIPE WORKS:** We wanted a bright-tasting lentil salad in which the lentils retained their shape and boasted a firm-tender bite. Brining the lentils in warm salt water was our first move. With brining, the lentils' skins soften, which leads to fewer blowouts. Then we cooked the lentils in the oven to heat them gently and uniformly. Once we had perfectly cooked lentils, all we had left to do was to pair the earthy beans with a tart vinaigrette and boldly flavored additions.

LENTILS MAY NOT GET POINTS FOR GLAMOUR, BUT when properly cooked and dressed up in a salad with a bright vinaigrette and herbs, nuts, and cheeses, the legumes' earthy, almost meaty depth and firm-tender bite make a satisfying side dish that's a nice break from the norm and the perfect partner to a variety of main courses, such as simply prepared chicken breasts or fish fillets.

The trouble is, perfectly cooked lentils are never a given. Too often, either their skins burst and their flesh disintegrates into starchy mush, or they don't cook through completely and retain chewy skin and a hard, crunchy core. Before we started adding accoutrements, we had to nail down a reliable way to produce tender, buttery lentils with soft, unbroken skins. And because the tiny, shape-retaining French green lentils we favor in the test kitchen, known as *lentilles du Puy*, can be hard to come by, we were also determined to develop an approach that would yield perfect results with whatever lentil variety our supermarket had to offer.

Fortunately, the test kitchen's previous work with bean cookery gave us a good idea of how to improve the skins. We've discovered that brining beans overnight softens their outer skins and makes them less likely to burst. The explanation is twofold: As the beans soak, the sodium ions from the salt replace some of the calcium and magnesium ions in the skins. By replacing some of the mineral ions, the sodium ions weaken the pectin in the skins, allowing more water to penetrate and leading to a more pliable, forgiving texture. But with beans, brining requires an overnight rest to be most effective. Fortunately, due to the lentils' smaller, flatter shape, we found that just a few hours of brining dramatically cuts down on blowouts. We also had another idea for hastening the process: Since heat speeds up all chemical reactions, we managed to reduce that time to just an hour by using warm water in the salt solution.

Another way to further reduce blowouts would be to cook the lentils as gently as possible. But we could see that even our stovetop's low setting still agitated the lentils too vigorously. We decided to try the oven, hoping that its indirect heat would get the job done more gently—and it did. And while the oven did increase the cooking time from less than 30 minutes to up to an hour, the results were worth the wait: Virtually all of the lentil skins were tender yet intact.

Despite the lentils' soft, perfect skins, their insides tended to be mushy, not creamy. It occurred to us to try another very simple trick with salt: adding it to the cooking water. Many bean recipes (including ours) shy away from adding salt during cooking because it produces firmer interiors that can be gritty. Here's why: While a brine's impact is mainly confined to the skin, heat (from cooking) affects the inside of the bean, causing sodium ions to move to the interior, where they slow the starches' ability to absorb water. But a firmed-up texture was exactly what our mushy lentils needed. Could a problem for beans prove to be the solution for lentils? Sure enough, when we added ¼ teaspoon of salt to the cooking water, the lentils went from mushy to firm yet creamy.

We had just two remaining tasks to tackle: enriching the flavor of the lentils and creating a couple of salad variations. Swapping some of the cooking water for chicken broth solved the first problem, and tossing the lentils with tart vinaigrettes and bold mix-ins—feta, olives, and mint in one salad; hazelnuts and goat cheese in another—brightened and balanced their rich, earthy flavor.

Lentil Salad with Olives, Mint, and Feta
SERVES 2

French green lentils, or lentilles du Puy, are our preferred choice for this recipe, but it works with any type of lentil except red or yellow. Brining helps keep the lentils intact, but if you don't have time, they'll still taste good without it. The salad can be served warm or at room temperature.

½ cup lentils, picked over and rinsed
    Salt and pepper
3 cups warm water (about 110 degrees)
1 cup low-sodium chicken broth
2 garlic cloves, lightly crushed and peeled
1 bay leaf
2½ tablespoons extra-virgin olive oil
1½ tablespoons white wine vinegar
¼ cup coarsely chopped pitted kalamata olives
¼ cup chopped fresh mint
1 shallot, minced
2 tablespoons crumbled feta cheese

1. Place lentils and ½ teaspoon salt in bowl. Cover with 2 cups warm water and soak for 1 hour. Drain well.

2. Adjust oven rack to middle position and heat oven to 325 degrees. Place drained lentils, remaining 1 cup water, broth, garlic, bay leaf, and ¼ teaspoon salt in medium saucepan. Cover and bake until lentils are tender but remain intact, 40 to 60 minutes. Meanwhile, whisk oil and vinegar together in large bowl.

3. Drain lentils well; remove garlic and bay leaf. Add drained lentils, olives, mint, and shallot to dressing and toss to combine. Season with salt and pepper to taste. Transfer to serving dish, sprinkle with feta, and serve.

VARIATION

Lentil Salad with Hazelnuts and Goat Cheese
Substitute red wine vinegar for white wine vinegar and add 1 teaspoon Dijon mustard to dressing in step 2. Omit olives and substitute 2 tablespoons chopped fresh parsley for mint. Substitute 1 ounce crumbled goat cheese for feta and sprinkle with 2 tablespoons coarsely chopped toasted and skinned hazelnuts before serving.

EASY APPLE GALETTE

BAKED GOODS AND DESSERTS

CRANBERRY-NUT MUFFINS

✔ WHY THIS RECIPE WORKS: We wanted cranberry-nut muffins for two punctuated by zingy but not harsh cranberries and rich-tasting, crunchy nuts. Our first job was to tame the bite of the cranberries, so we chopped them in a food processor with a little confectioners' sugar and salt. For big, nutty flavor, we supplemented the all-purpose flour with our own nut flour (made by grinding pecans in a food processor). Letting the batter rest for 30 minutes ensured that the small amount of flour became more hydrated, resulting in a properly thickened batter that baked up perfectly domed. A pecan-streusel topping added even more nuttiness and a nice crunch.

MOST RECIPES FOR CRANBERRY-NUT MUFFINS follow the same course as those for any fruit-studded muffin: Just toss fresh berries and coarsely chopped nuts into the batter and bake. It's an approach that works well enough when using ripe, sweet blueberries or raspberries, but the method is never as successful with cranberries. That's because the cranberries' ultrasour burst completely overwhelms the delicate flavor of the muffin. And as for the nuts, after they've steamed in the moist batter, their rich, toasty flavor has washed away. Then there's the usual problem of unevenly distributed mix-ins. Depending on where you bite, you might get a mouthful of sour berries, a cluster of nuts, or plain old cake. Hankering for a well-balanced breakfast pastry, we decided to reinvent the concept. Our muffin would feature a moist crumb with plenty of its own flavor, punctuated by zingy but not harsh cranberries and rich-tasting, crunchy nuts. And it would make just enough for breakfast for two, plus an afternoon snack, so we didn't have muffins hanging around for days.

First things first: We had to create a muffin that could stand up to the heft of two mix-ins. We could choose one of two options: either the creaming method or the hand-mixed "quick bread" method. In this case, only the latter's coarser, sturdier crumb would do. We whisked together sugar, an egg, melted butter, and milk in one bowl, and flour, baking powder, and salt in another. Then we gently combined the two components with a generous fistful each of whole cranberries and rich, buttery pecans before putting the muffins into

a 375-degree oven. About 18 minutes later, we had a good-looking quartet of muffins—nicely domed and sturdy enough to accommodate the fruit and nuts. But that's all this batch had going for it, as the nuts offered nothing but a little crunch and the cake's ho-hum flavor was no match for the sour berries.

One idea was to trade some of the all-purpose flour for a heartier grain like cornmeal or whole-wheat flour, but when we tried it, the resulting batches baked up gritty and dense, respectively. It then dawned on us that the magic ingredient to replace some of the flour had been sitting under our noses the whole time: nuts. What if we ground some in the food processor to create our own nut flour? We knew the trade would mean losing some of the wheat's gluten-forming proteins and, in turn, some of the muffins' tall, sturdy structure, but we decided to worry about that later. We processed the toasted pecans into a coarse, sandlike meal, which we then substituted for regular flour in varying amounts—from 2 tablespoons all the way up to ½ cup.

Our suspicions were correct: These batches of muffin batter looked looser and runnier than those made with regular flour, and rather than baking up tall and self-contained, they spread out—particularly those with more nut flour. But once our tasters took a bite, we knew the trade-off hadn't been for naught. Despite their now-disappointing structure, these nut-based muffins boasted a richer-tasting, heartier crumb that helped counter the cranberries' acidity. As for how much nut flour to put in the batter, tasters were definitive: the more, the better.

Moving on to another batch, we decided to compensate for the nut flour's inability to form gluten and committed what some in the baking community would call treason: We overmixed the batter, to overdevelop the gluten strands in the flour and toughen up the final product. But instead of the domed tops that we wanted, we got squat, chewy muffins with stunted peaks—two classic signs of overworking.

But if a lack of gluten wasn't the problem, what was? After whipping up another batch of batter, we were called across the kitchen to another tasting. When we returned 30 minutes later, a curious thing had happened: The batter had thickened up considerably. Intrigued, we baked the muffins and were rewarded with the best batch yet. The batter hadn't spread across the pan, and the muffins were symmetrical, with gently rounded tops. When we hit the science books for an explanation, we discovered that although the rest allowed a little more gluten to form, its main effect was to hydrate the batter. Because this batter contained relatively little flour, there were very few starch granules to absorb the liquid and thicken the batter. Letting the batter rest allowed what starch granules were available to more fully absorb the free water, which, in turn, resulted in batter with more body.

It was time to temper the berries' sour punch. Sugar was the obvious go-to ingredient, but further sweetening the batter wouldn't help once the whole berries burst and released their sharp juice. The more effective solution was chopping the berries to expose some of their inner flesh—a fix that also helped distribute the fruit more evenly throughout the batter—and tossing them with sugar. We pulsed the berries in the food processor with a little confectioners' sugar (which dissolves more quickly than granulated sugar). The sugar took the edge off, and a pinch of salt tamed any residual bitterness.

NOTES FROM THE TEST KITCHEN

RAMPING UP NUTTINESS, TONING DOWN TANG

1. Processing toasted pecans with sugar results in pecan "flour" that makes for muffins with a richer, heartier flavor.

2. Processing the berries with confectioners' sugar sweetens them, while adding a dash of salt masks their bitter edge.

3. Finally, sprinkling a classic nut streusel over the top of the muffins provides a rich, buttery crunch and just a hint of sweetness.

These muffins were in good shape, but our tasters wanted more nut flavor. They also wanted to get back the crunchy element that had been eliminated when we switched from chopped to ground pecans. To meet the first request, instead of grinding the nuts by themselves, we processed them with the granulated sugar. The sugar's abrasiveness helped the nuts break down further, releasing more of their flavorful oils and preventing clumping. Recovering some of the crunchy texture was as simple as creating a topping. A mixture of flour, sugar, butter, and chopped pecans worked perfectly.

Finally, with its crunchy topping and the pop of tart berries against the nutty-tasting crumb, this was a cranberry muffin we could go nuts for.

Cranberry-Pecan Muffins

MAKES 4 MUFFINS

Any size muffin tin will work here, and the batter can be placed in any of the muffin cups. If fresh cranberries aren't available, you can substitute frozen; simply microwave them in a bowl until they're partially but not fully thawed, 30 to 45 seconds.

STREUSEL TOPPING

- 2½ tablespoons all-purpose flour
- 1½ tablespoons unsalted butter, cut into ½-inch pieces and softened
- 1 tablespoon brown sugar
- 1 tablespoon granulated sugar
  - Pinch salt
- 3 tablespoons chopped pecans

MUFFINS

- 6 tablespoons (1¾ ounces) all-purpose flour
- ¼ teaspoon baking powder
  - Salt
- ½ cup pecans, toasted and cooled
- ¼ cup granulated sugar
- 1 large egg
- 1½ tablespoons unsalted butter, melted and cooled
- 3 tablespoons whole milk
- ½ cup cranberries
- 1 teaspoon confectioners' sugar

1. FOR THE STREUSEL TOPPING: Adjust oven rack to upper-middle position and heat oven to 375 degrees. Mix together flour, butter, brown sugar, granulated sugar, and salt with fingers in small bowl until mixture resembles wet sand. Stir in pecans and set aside.

2. FOR THE MUFFINS: Spray 4 cups of muffin tin with baking spray with flour. Whisk flour, baking powder, and ¼ teaspoon salt together in bowl; set aside.

3. Process pecans and granulated sugar together in food processor until mixture resembles coarse sand, 10 to 15 seconds. Transfer to large bowl and whisk in egg, melted butter, and milk until combined. Whisk flour mixture into egg mixture until just moistened and no streaks of flour remain. Set aside for 30 minutes to thicken.

4. Pulse cranberries, confectioners' sugar, and pinch salt together in food processor until very coarsely chopped, 3 to 5 pulses. Gently fold cranberries into batter and divide batter evenly among prepared muffin cups. Sprinkle streusel topping over muffins, gently pressing into batter to adhere. Bake until muffin tops are golden and just firm, 18 to 20 minutes, rotating pan halfway through baking. Let muffins cool in muffin tin on wire rack for 10 minutes. Remove muffins from tin and cool for at least 10 minutes before serving.

CINNAMON STREUSEL COFFEE CAKE

✔ WHY THIS RECIPE WORKS: For a well-balanced coffee cake for two that delivered both tender cake and a crunchy, cinnamon-y topping, we started by building a simple cake with the right amount of moisture and structure. We cut back on the butter so our cake wouldn't be greasy, but we needed to find another ingredient to bump up the moistness and richness. Buttermilk solved the problem, guaranteeing that our cake was sturdy enough to support the crumb topping. A generous amount of pecan- and cinnamon-laced streusel topping made the perfect finishing touch.

ORDER A SLICE OF COFFEE CAKE AT A CAFÉ AND you'll inevitably be disappointed. Most versions we've seen offer a heavy, grease-laden cake with an achingly sweet crumb topping. And recipes for this popular brunch treat result in far too much for a small household to consume before it dries out. We wanted to develop

a tasty, old-fashioned coffee cake that was nicely sweetened but wouldn't give us a toothache. It had to have just enough of the appealing crumb topping, and it had to make the perfect amount for two (with just a little left over for a snack, of course).

After digging up a few recipes in our research, we baked up a number of cakes but ended up being disappointed with all of them. First of all, there was not nearly enough streusel, although this problem could be remedied easily by just scaling up. The bigger issue was the mediocre texture of both the batter and the topping. What should be a moist, tender crumb with a crunchy topping was in fact a dry, crumbly cake with a soggy, scant topping. Starting with the cake itself, we vowed to fix these recurring problems so we'd have a recipe for a coffee cake that we'd want to start our day with.

Most coffee cake is nothing more than buttery yellow cake topped with a crumbly streusel. But it's essential that the cake be sturdy enough to support the streusel. To that end, we started with a simple yellow cake recipe and made adjustments along the way. All-purpose flour provided the proper structure; a single egg helped reinforce that structure. Though we wanted our cake to be rich and moist, we also didn't want it to leave us with greasy fingertips. Cutting back on the butter solved the greasiness issue, but now we were left with a dry, lean coffee cake. To stave off dryness, we tried including a handful of dairy ingredients. Sour cream and yogurt created a batter that was slightly too thick. Buttermilk, on the other hand, worked much better, imparting a flavorful tang and ample moisture.

For final tweaks, we added baking powder and baking soda to take some of the leavening burden off the lone egg and ensure that the cake would rise evenly. The duo of granulated sugar and brown sugar added a moderate amount of sweetness that had a deeper flavor than granulated sugar on its own but didn't put our cake into cavity-inducing territory. A small amount of cinnamon offered subtle warmth.

With the cake figured out, it was time to analyze what most would consider the most important part of a good coffee cake: the topping. Crispy, crunchy, yet melt-in-your-mouth streusel requires a careful balance of sugar, flour, and butter; spices and nuts also warrant careful scrutiny. As in the cake, we liked the flavor contributed by both granulated and brown sugar; the former added a nice sweetness, and the latter contributed rich, caramel-like undertones. Just 1½ tablespoons

CINNAMON STREUSEL COFFEE CAKE

of flour was necessary to keep the sugar from melting into shards, and a single pat of butter helped hold the topping together without making it greasy. A hefty dose of cinnamon gave our streusel a bold flavor and echoed the warm notes in the cake. For more textural interest, we decided to include nuts. Chopped pecans added a big crunch factor that tasters loved.

About 30 minutes in the oven at 350 degrees proved to be the best and easiest option for baking; at higher temperatures, the streusel became too dark, requiring an aluminum foil shield to protect it from the heat. After a brief rest so the cake could cool, we dug in. Our coffee cake was perfectly moist and tender, with a crumbly, crunchy, cinnamon-spiked streusel on top. In short, this was a morning treat worth getting out of bed for.

Cinnamon Streusel Coffee Cake

SERVES 2

You will need a 6-inch round cake pan for this recipe (see page 3). You can substitute 3 tablespoons of plain whole-milk or low-fat yogurt mixed with 1 tablespoon of milk for the buttermilk if necessary.

TOPPING

- 1½ tablespoons all-purpose flour
- 1½ tablespoons granulated sugar
- 1½ tablespoons packed light brown sugar
- 1 tablespoon unsalted butter, softened
- ¾ teaspoon ground cinnamon
- ⅓ cup pecans or walnuts, chopped

CAKE

- ¾ cup (3¾ ounces) all-purpose flour
- ¼ teaspoon baking powder
- ¼ teaspoon baking soda
- ¼ teaspoon ground cinnamon
- Pinch salt
- ¼ cup buttermilk
- ¼ cup (1¾ ounces) granulated sugar
- ¼ cup (1¾ ounces) packed light brown sugar
- 1 large egg
- 2 tablespoons unsalted butter, melted and cooled

1. FOR THE TOPPING: Adjust oven rack to middle position and heat oven to 350 degrees. Grease 6-inch round cake pan, line with parchment paper, grease parchment, then flour pan. Using your fingers, mix flour, granulated sugar, brown sugar, butter, and cinnamon together in medium bowl until mixture resembles wet sand. Stir in pecans and set aside.

2. FOR THE CAKE: Whisk flour, baking powder, baking soda, cinnamon, and salt together in medium bowl. Whisk buttermilk, granulated sugar, brown sugar, egg, and melted butter together in small bowl until smooth. Gently fold egg mixture into flour mixture until combined.

3. Scrape batter into prepared pan and smooth top. Sprinkle topping evenly over top of cake. Bake until top is golden and toothpick inserted in center comes out with few moist crumbs attached, about 30 minutes. Let cake cool on wire rack for 15 minutes before serving.

MAPLE-PECAN SCONES

✔ WHY THIS RECIPE WORKS: To infuse our scones with deep maple flavor throughout, we replaced the sugar in the dough with maple syrup, which offered sweetness without being cloying. To amp up the maple flavor a little more, we made a glaze with maple syrup and confectioners' sugar, then drizzled it over our baked and cooled scones. Because we had only four scones on the baking sheet, they came out burnt when baked at the higher temperatures suggested by most recipes. We found the middle ground—and perfectly golden-brown scones—at 375 degrees.

WHEN FALL ROLLS AROUND AND WE SEE MAPLE scones at the local coffeehouse, we hope for a tender and buttery pastry that will be subtly infused with maple flavor. Unfortunately, what we usually get is a dense, dry, and bland rock, topped with a sickly sweet maple topping. We wanted a maple scone that was not only light and delicate but also tasted like maple through-out—not just in the topping. We set out to develop our own recipe for maple scones for two; four seemed like a good number, providing enough for breakfast and to satisfy an afternoon craving.

Most recipes we surveyed used similar amounts of flour—about 2 cups—to produce eight scones, but they used different types of flour. We figured we'd need to cut the amount of flour down to 1 cup for our batch of four scones, but we'd have to do some legwork to figure out which type of flour to use. We tested bread flour, cake flour, and all-purpose flour, and the differences in outcome were astonishing. The scones made with bread flour were heavy and tough. Cake flour produced scones that were doughy in the center, with a raw taste and poor texture. All-purpose flour was the clear winner, resulting in scones that were light and tender.

For the butter, we tested varying amounts, ending up at 2½ tablespoons for rich scones with a tender texture. Any more, and the dough was too soft; any less, and the scones baked up dry and tough.

Not surprisingly, the choice of liquid also profoundly affected the flavor of our scones. Scones made with milk were bland and dry. Buttermilk gave us scones with plenty of flavor, but they were too flaky and biscuitlike. Scones made with cream were both light in texture and flavorful, making it the clear winner.

Conventional recipes tend to call for a good amount of granulated sugar for sweetness. After a number of tests, we determined that just a tablespoon and a half provided a nice level of sweetness. But, at this point, our scones were still lacking in rich maple flavor. What if we swapped the sugar for maple syrup? Indeed, this provided the maple notes we were looking for. Our scones weren't tooth-achingly sweet but instead had a slightly sweet, maple-y flavor.

To enhance their appeal, scones are often either coated with a sweet glaze or filled with chopped fruit or nuts. We definitely wanted a glaze to enhance the subtle maple flavor we had in the dough, but we also wanted to add a little more textural interest. When we threw in dried fruit such as raisins and cherries, their sweetness overpowered the delicate maple notes. Pecans, on the other hand, offered up a sweet, toasty flavor that played off the maple syrup nicely.

The quickest and easiest way to mix the dough was in a food processor. We found the food processor to be more reliable than hand mixing, since hand mixing can overheat the butter and soften it. For shaping the scones, many recipes suggest using a 9-inch round cake pan as a mold before cutting the dough into wedges. But with so little dough, we did away with the cake pan entirely and simply pressed the dough into a 5-inch circle of even thickness before cutting it into four wedges.

The biggest problem we encountered in our scaled-down recipe arose when we put the scones in the oven. Without the extra scones to absorb the heat from our 450-degree oven (the temperature stipulated by a number of recipes), our scones began to darken before they completely baked through, resulting in moist, gummy centers. Reducing the heat to 425 degrees merely bought us a few more minutes before the scones began to burn—but it still wasn't enough to fully bake them. We turned the oven knob down to 400 degrees—still no luck. Finally, at the gentler temperature of 375 degrees, we were able to bake the scones for about 20 minutes, long enough to ensure that the centers were fully baked and the crusts were just the right shade of light golden brown. Once they had cooled, we drizzled a simple glaze of confectioners' sugar and maple syrup over the top; this easy topping reinforced the subtle flavor of our tender scones nicely.

At last, we had flaky, tender, rich-tasting scones with just enough maple flavor to satisfy all of our cold-weather cravings.

Maple-Pecan Scones

MAKES 4 SCONES

Be sure to let the scones cool for at least 20 minutes before glazing.

- ½ **cup heavy cream**
- 2½ **tablespoons maple syrup**
- 1 **cup (5 ounces) all-purpose flour**
- 1½ **teaspoons baking powder**
- ¼ **teaspoon salt**
- 2½ **tablespoons unsalted butter, cut into ¼-inch pieces and chilled**
- ¼ **cup pecans, toasted and chopped**
- 3 **tablespoons confectioners' sugar**

1. Adjust oven rack to middle position and heat oven to 375 degrees. Line rimmed baking sheet with parchment paper. Combine cream and 1½ tablespoons maple syrup in small bowl and set aside.

2. Pulse flour, baking powder, and salt together in food processor until combined, about 3 pulses. Scatter butter evenly over top and continue to pulse until mixture resembles coarse cornmeal with some slightly larger butter lumps, about 6 pulses. Transfer mixture to large bowl and stir in pecans. Stir in cream mixture until dough begins to form, about 30 seconds.

3. Turn out dough and any floury bits onto lightly floured counter and knead until rough, slightly sticky ball forms, 5 to 10 seconds. Shape dough into 5-inch round of even ¾-inch thickness and cut into 4 wedges.

4. Place wedges on prepared baking sheet. Bake until tops are golden brown, 20 to 25 minutes, rotating pan halfway through baking. Transfer scones to wire rack and let cool to room temperature, about 20 minutes. Whisk remaining 1 tablespoon maple syrup and confectioners' sugar together in bowl until combined. Drizzle glaze over scones and let glaze set for 5 to 10 minutes before serving.

NOTES FROM THE TEST KITCHEN

MAKING MAPLE-PECAN SCONES

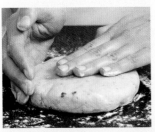

1. Pat dough into 5-inch round, about ¾ inch thick.

2. Using metal bench scraper or knife, cut dough into 4 evenly sized wedges.

OUR FAVORITE BENCH SCRAPER

Here in the test kitchen, we find that there is one incredibly simple and inexpensive piece of equipment that is invaluable for baking: a bench scraper. A bench scraper is a rectangular blade with a wood or plastic handle affixed to one side. Bench scrapers are ideal for countless baking tasks, like dividing dough for scones or cleaning up a messy counter. Our favorite scraper is the **OXO Good Grips Stainless Steel Multi-Purpose Scraper and Chopper**, $8.95, which has a sturdy blade and comfortable handle. We also like the ruler marked along the blade, which is helpful for accurate measuring.

SKILLET OLIVE BREAD

✔ **WHY THIS RECIPE WORKS:** Most savory breads serve a crowd and require long rest periods and kneading. Not ours. We stirred together an effortless quick bread and baked it in a small cast-iron skillet, which gave us just enough for two (plus a little extra). We started with all-purpose flour and added whole milk and sour cream for a clean, creamy flavor and rich, moist texture. A whole egg lent richness and structure. Coarsely grated Parmesan, minced garlic, chopped kalamata olives, and fresh basil ensured that our bread was robustly flavored, and our cast-iron pan guaranteed a golden-brown, crisp crust.

A HEARTY, RUSTIC BREAD MAKES THE PERFECT partner to a steaming-hot bowl of chili or stew. But if you're a household of two, chances are that a store-bought loaf will go stale before you're able to finish it. We wanted a richly flavored bread that yielded just enough for two and came together in a flash—no long rises or kneading necessary. A skillet bread spiked with salty, nutty Parmesan and briny olives seemed just the ticket, as it would stand up to any number of robustly flavored dishes, while providing just the right amount for a couple of diners.

The recipes we found all followed a simple formula: Just stir together flour, cheese, salt, milk, and baking powder; scrape the batter into a preheated skillet; and bake. Unfortunately, there were a lot of problems with the recipes we tested. Many loaves were about as flavorful as a saltine, and others were as dense and heavy as a hockey puck. And some breads were so greasy that we had to pass out extra napkins after each tasting. Clearly, we had our work cut out for us.

In search of a light but hearty crumb, we experimented with different flours, making one loaf with all-purpose flour, another with bread flour, and yet another with half bread and half all-purpose flour. A few tasters noticed that the breads made with all or part of the higher-protein bread flour were slightly rubbery, but the difference was not all that dramatic. Still, all-purpose flour was clearly the best, and most convenient, choice.

Moving on to the liquid component, we considered our options. Buttermilk is a common ingredient in

SKILLET OLIVE BREAD

quick breads, and it produced a decent loaf. Skim milk was too watery and produced a crumbly, dry bread. The whole-milk version was the best, with a creamier flavor.

Several recipes omitted the butter in favor of olive oil, which was preferred for its subtler, cleaner flavor. Starting with 4 tablespoons, we worked our way down to a mere 2, putting an end to the slick hands and lips we'd been experiencing after eating a piece of the greasier samples. The single egg we had been using turned out to be just right. When we once mistakenly omitted it, the loaf failed to rise properly and had little structure. Skillet bread made with more than one egg had a beautiful golden hue but tasted more like quiche than a hearty, rustic bread.

We had made progress, but we were falling short in the texture department. Because we wanted a rich loaf with a light texture, we replaced a portion of the milk in each of two breads with scoops of yogurt and sour cream, respectively. Tasters preferred the sour cream–based bread; it was rich and moist without being greasy. The sour cream also added a nip of tartness to the bread, offsetting the richness of the milk.

It was time to decide on the leavening: baking soda or baking powder. To do its job, baking soda needs an acidic ingredient (such as the lactic acid in sour cream), while baking powder is self-reliant, essentially composed of baking soda plus one or two acids. We made two breads, one with baking powder and a second with baking soda. Both breads rose perfectly evenly, but the bread made with baking powder was preferred, due to its more complex flavor. A discussion with our science editor helped us understand why: The baking soda had neutralized the lactic acid in the sour cream, whereas the baking powder, which brings its own acid to the mix, had not. The acid was giving the bread more flavor.

Although we were on the right track, and we knew the cheese and olives would bring our bread squarely into savory territory, we still wanted to add a bit more savory flavor to the crumb itself. For the next test, we flavored the olive oil with a minced garlic clove before adding part of it to the batter. This worked wonders, adding just the right aromatic background. Using the rest of the garlic oil to coat the bottom of the skillet ensured that our bread developed a golden-brown, ultraflavorful crust on the bottom.

Finally, it was time to consider the mix-ins. We loved the sharp, nutty flavor and moistness contributed by a good amount of grated Parmesan, but it wasn't doing anything for the texture of the bread. We discovered that coarsely shredding the cheese, instead of grating it fine, was better, as it melted into luscious, cheesy pockets. For rich color and flavor on the top crust, we sprinkled the bread with shredded Parmesan before moving it to the oven. Turning to the olives, we decided to chop them for even distribution. To play up the decidedly Mediterranean tone of our bread even further, we added a tablespoon of freshly chopped basil, which infused the bread with a bright, herbaceous note.

At last, we had a recipe for an easy, fast, and incredibly flavorful skillet bread that would pair well with any number of entrées—or be enjoyed all on its own.

Skillet Olive Bread

SERVES 2

Coarsely grating the Parmesan adds a nice texture to the bread and helps prevent the cheese from burning. To grate the cheese coarsely, use the large holes of a box grater. Do not substitute finely grated or pregrated Parmesan. We prefer to use an 8-inch cast-iron skillet here because it makes the best crust; however, an 8-inch ovensafe skillet will also work, but you will need to increase the baking time by 10 to 15 minutes.

1   **cup (5 ounces) all-purpose flour**

1   **tablespoon chopped fresh basil**

1   **teaspoon baking powder**

¼   **teaspoon salt**

1¾   **ounces Parmesan cheese, grated coarse (½ cup)**

½   **cup whole milk**

3   **tablespoons sour cream**

1   **large egg**

2   **tablespoons olive oil**

1   **garlic clove, minced**

¼   **cup pitted kalamata olives, chopped**

1. Adjust oven rack to lower-middle position and heat oven to 450 degrees.

2. Whisk flour, basil, baking powder, and salt together in large bowl. Stir in ⅓ cup Parmesan, breaking up any clumps, until coated with flour. In separate bowl, whisk milk, sour cream, and egg together until smooth.

3. Heat oil in 8-inch cast-iron skillet over medium-high heat until shimmering. Add garlic and cook until fragrant, about 30 seconds. Pour all but 2 teaspoons garlic oil into milk mixture and whisk to incorporate. Gently fold milk mixture into flour mixture with rubber spatula until just combined, then fold in olives. Batter will be heavy and thick; do not overmix.

4. Working quickly, scrape batter into hot skillet and smooth top. Sprinkle with remaining Parmesan. Bake until golden brown and toothpick inserted into center comes out clean, 15 to 20 minutes, rotating skillet halfway through baking. Let bread cool slightly in skillet before removing. Serve warm or at room temperature.

SOUR CREAM BISCUITS

✓ WHY THIS RECIPE WORKS: Instead of a big batch of biscuits, we wanted just enough for two. They had to give us from-scratch flavor, but without the hassle of cutting butter into flour or rolling and stamping out dough. Sour cream drop biscuits, which are simply stirred together, fit the bill nicely. Though most recipes call for self-rising flour or baking mix, we didn't like the flavor these contributed and swapped in all-purpose flour. We then upped the amount of sour cream so the tangy flavor came through. Adding melted butter to the batter kept the biscuits tender and moist, and brushing melted butter on top helped them brown and crisp nicely.

WE LOVE A GOOD BISCUIT—WITH A TENDER texture and rich flavor—as much as anyone. But pulling out the food processor to work the butter and flour into a coarse meal; then mixing in buttermilk; and finally rolling, stamping, and baking just doesn't make sense when preparing a smaller batch. When we came across sour cream biscuits, which require neither cutting the butter into the flour nor (at least for the drop biscuit version) rolling and stamping and boast an appealingly tangy flavor, we thought we might have the ultimate easy biscuit recipe for two on our hands.

To get our bearings, we collected a number of recipes and headed into the test kitchen. Most called for combining sour cream with either self-rising flour or biscuit mix, but tasters complained that these versions tasted either soapy or salty, so they were out of the running. Recipes that used standard flour instead of the self-rising kind or a biscuit mix varied primarily in the ratio of sour cream to flour. Unfortunately, even those

that used the highest ratio had none of the characteristic tang of sour cream. And strangely, despite the sour cream, most of our samples came out tough and lean.

Since we had ruled out biscuit mix and self-rising flour, we looked over some of the test kitchen's plain biscuit recipes and decided to follow their lead on the ratios for dry ingredients to make four biscuits. In accordance with the directions, we whisked together all-purpose flour, baking powder, and salt; dumped in as much sour cream as it took to form a cohesive dough; and baked a batch of biscuits. Finally, these biscuits really tasted like sour cream. But, sadly, they didn't taste buttery at all.

We thought the solution would be to just add butter. We hoped this would pull double duty and fix the lean texture (sour cream has about 20 percent fat to butter's 80 percent) while also introducing buttery flavor. The key, obviously, was to get the right balance. At 1 cup of sour cream and 4 tablespoons of butter (melted to maintain the ease of drop biscuits) to ¾ cup of flour, we were making progress, but now the biscuits were too fat: They were greasy and flat. We gradually reduced the butter and the sour cream. At 2 tablespoons of butter and ¾ cup of sour cream, the interior was fluffy, moist, and tender. For more flavor, we brushed the biscuits with a little more melted butter before baking.

About 20 minutes later, we pulled our biscuits from the oven and let them cool before we dug in. The golden-brown, light biscuits were tender and buttery, and the flavor was rich and tangy. And the best part: They were so easy to throw together—just stir, scoop, and bake—that we knew we'd be making them again and again.

Sour Cream Biscuits
MAKES 4 BISCUITS

For easy portioning, grease the ¼-cup measure with vegetable oil spray.

- ¾ cup (3¾ ounces) all-purpose flour
- ¾ teaspoon baking powder
- ¼ teaspoon salt
- ¾ cup sour cream
- 2½ tablespoons unsalted butter, melted and cooled

1. Adjust oven rack to middle position and heat oven to 425 degrees. Line rimmed baking sheet with parchment paper. Combine flour, baking powder, and salt in bowl. Add sour cream and 2 tablespoons melted butter and stir until just combined.

2. Using greased ¼-cup measure, scoop out and drop 4 mounds of dough onto prepared baking sheet, spacing them about 2 inches apart. Brush with remaining 1½ teaspoons melted butter and bake until golden brown, 20 to 25 minutes, rotating pan halfway through baking. Let biscuits cool on sheet on wire rack for 15 minutes. Serve warm.

EASY APPLE GALETTE

✔ WHY THIS RECIPE WORKS: For an ultraeasy apple galette for two, we bypassed the labor-intensive, time-consuming homemade pastry and reached for store-bought frozen puff pastry instead. Forming an attractive crust was as easy as folding over the edges of the pastry. We found the best variety of apple to be the Granny Smith; it stayed moist in the oven and maintained its shape throughout cooking. Once we doctored up the apple slices with some sugar to lock in moisture and a simple glaze for an attractive sheen and fruity tartness, our scaled-down apple galette was ready to be served.

CLASSICALLY FRENCH BUT FAR FROM COMPLICATED, an apple galette marries buttery, flaky pastry with sweet, tender slices or chunks of apple. But though the galette itself is a simple dessert, making the pastry from scratch is truly a labor of love, requiring a serious investment of time, not to mention dexterity with a rolling pin. But we didn't want to write this elegant dessert off the menu for households of two. We hoped to keep the crisp, flaky texture and fruity flavors intact, while scaling down and speeding up this dessert so it could be on the menu even on a busy weeknight.

During our research, we found that galettes come in all shapes and sizes—from ones in which the dough is folded over the apples, to others that feature layers of sweet pastry, almond filling, and meticulously layered apples. But it was a simpler version that caught our eye: This galette has a thin, flaky crust topped with a layer of thinly sliced apples; there really wasn't much to this galette after all, besides the puff pastry and fruit. Now that we knew what style of galette we were after, we could get to work.

Though we considered store-bought pie dough and phyllo dough, subsequent tests told us that neither one was ideal here; the pie dough was too thick, and the phyllo dough, even when layered, was too thin. Instead, we turned to commercial puff pastry for our base; half of a sheet provided just enough for a dessert for two. After letting the dough thaw, we created a border by simply folding over the edges, then baked it, topped with a simple layer of sliced apples, until golden brown. It came out as tender and sturdy as a homemade dough would, and tasters were happy with the rich, buttery flavor. With our dough problems figured out, we moved on to the fruit.

Because this style of galette has no top crust to seal in moisture, our apple slices could easily dry out during baking. Obviously, the variety of apple used here would be key. We gathered some of the most commonly available apple varieties, including Granny Smith, Gala, McIntosh, Braeburn, Fuji, and Red and Golden Delicious, and tested each type in our galette. In every case but one, the apples cooked up tough, dry, and leathery. The exception was the McIntosh, which baked to the other extreme; they were so moist that they turned to mush. Of the varieties tested, we found that Granny Smith and Golden Delicious showed the most promise and had the best flavor after cooking. When we tried parcooking the Granny Smith slices before layering them in the tart, in the hope that they might retain some moisture, the apples turned mushy and we lost all of the pure apple flavor we wanted to preserve (not to mention it was a slippery mess trying to arrange them attractively on the puff pastry).

So we returned to our original method—layering raw apple slices into the tart. The thin slices were more moist but still not perfect. That's when a colleague suggested that we sprinkle the apples with sugar. This turned out to be our saving grace—the sugar prevented the apples from drying out in the oven and also helped them brown nicely.

Last, the ideal galette should have both a crust and apples that are deep golden brown in color. After several tests, most tasters felt that 400 degrees struck the right balance between intensely caramelized and simply burnt. Now our galette was perfect—almost.

Although not all galette recipes called for it, in many that we found the hot-out-of-the-oven tart was brushed with apricot preserves. After just one test, we could see why. This glaze provided an attractive sheen and fruity tartness that brought out the flavor of the apples, taking our Easy Apple Galette from good to great.

MAKING EASY APPLE GALETTE

1. Slice apples ⅛ inch thick so they are easy to shingle.

2. Fold edges of dough over by ¼ inch and crimp to create ¼-inch-thick border.

3. Starting in 1 corner, shingle sliced apples to form even row across dough, overlapping each slice by about half.

Easy Apple Galette

SERVES 2

Be sure to let the puff pastry thaw completely before using; otherwise it can crack and break apart. To thaw frozen puff pastry, let it sit either in the refrigerator for 24 hours or on the counter for 30 to 60 minutes. Apple jelly can be substituted for the apricot preserves; omit straining in step 3.

- ½ **(9½ by 9-inch) sheet frozen puff pastry, thawed**
- 1 **large Granny Smith apple (8 ounces), peeled, cored, and sliced ⅛ inch thick**
- ½ **tablespoon unsalted butter, cut into ¼-inch pieces**
- 2 **teaspoons granulated sugar**
- 1 **tablespoon apricot preserves**
- 1 **teaspoon water**

1. Adjust oven rack to middle position and heat oven to 400 degrees. Line rimmed baking sheet with parchment paper. Transfer puff pastry to prepared baking sheet and fold edges over by ¼ inch; crimp to create ¼-inch-thick border.

2. Starting in 1 corner of tart, shingle apple into crust in tidy, diagonal rows, overlapping each slice by about half, until surface is completely covered. Dot apple slices with butter and sprinkle evenly with sugar. Bake until bottom of tart is deep golden brown and apple has caramelized, 40 to 45 minutes.

3. Combine apricot preserves and water in bowl and microwave until mixture begins to bubble, about 30 seconds. Strain mixture through fine-mesh strainer to remove any large apricot pieces. Brush baked galette with glaze and cool sheet on wire rack for 15 minutes. Serve.

USE IT UP: PUFF PASTRY

Coffeehouse Breakfast Twists

MAKES 4

Be sure to let the puff pastry thaw completely before using; otherwise it can crack and break apart. To thaw frozen puff pastry, let it sit either in the refrigerator for 24 hours or on the counter for 30 to 60 minutes.

- 2 **teaspoons sugar**
- ½ **teaspoon ground cinnamon**
- ½ **(9½ by 9-inch) sheet frozen puff pastry, thawed**
- 1 **tablespoon unsalted butter, melted and cooled**

1. Adjust oven rack to middle position and heat oven to 425 degrees. Line rimmed baking sheet with parchment paper. Combine sugar and cinnamon in bowl.

2. Lay puff pastry on clean counter, brush with half of melted butter, then sprinkle with half of cinnamon sugar. Flip dough over and brush with remaining butter and sprinkle with remaining cinnamon sugar. Fold dough in half, creating 4½-inch square. Cut dough into 4 equal strips. Working with 1 strip at a time, pinch ends together and twist strip few times to create spiral; transfer to prepared baking sheet.

3. Bake twists until fully puffed and golden, 12 to 15 minutes, rotating sheet halfway through baking. Transfer twists to wire rack and let cool slightly. Serve warm or at room temperature.

PEACH MELBA CRISP

✓ **WHY THIS RECIPE WORKS:** For a new spin on classic peach Melba, we decided to combine peaches and raspberries in a warm crisp for two. Fruit juiciness varies based on ripeness, so to even the playing field, we macerated and drained the peaches before assembling the crisp in a small baking dish, avoiding a runny filling and soggy topping. We added back a measured amount of the peach juice, which we thickened with ground tapioca, to create a perfectly thickened, flavorful filling. Layering the raspberries on top of the peaches instead of folding them in prevented them from turning to mush. Finally, using oats, flour, and nuts in our topping guaranteed that it was ultracrisp.

WE LOVE THE CLASSIC FLAVORS OF PEACH MELBA, in which poached peach halves and vanilla ice cream are drizzled with a luscious raspberry sauce. But we hoped to update this retro dessert by transforming it into a rustic, homey crisp for two. It had to boast all the lively sweet and tart flavors of the traditional dish, but we would take things up a notch by adding a crunchy, nutty topping.

After doing diligent research, we realized we weren't the first to have thought of morphing peach Melba into a crisp, so we assembled a few recipes we stumbled across and baked them to assess the territory. While the flavor combo was predictably delicious, these crisps shared several problems: The peaches released so much juice that the fillings were soupy and the toppings soggy. And, just as bad, the raspberries disintegrated with baking.

In an effort to right these wrongs, we threw together a standard topping from butter, flour, oats, pecans, sugar (brown and white), and cinnamon (we later spiced it up with ginger) and set the topping aside as we combined the peach slices and raspberries with more sugar. In a handful of recipes the fruit wasn't thickened at all (no wonder those were soupy), but most called for a few tablespoons of either flour or cornstarch. We tried these options, plus ground tapioca, which we've used in the past to thicken fruit fillings. The tapioca won out, producing a jammy filling with the clearest fruit juices and brightest flavor. To boost the flavor further, we stirred in vanilla extract and lemon juice.

As we were working through these thickener tests, we noticed that no matter how carefully we folded the berries in with the peaches, they fell apart in the oven. To avoid smashing them, we scattered the berries on the bottom of the baking dish and gently placed the sweetened peaches and the topping over them. While more berries than before survived this test, it wasn't a rousing success. But if we put the peaches on the bottom and the raspberries in the middle, the delicate berries were jostled less, protected from the direct heat of the baking dish, and remained intact.

Thinking our work was about done, we made another crisp for good measure. We peeled, sliced, topped, and baked. A half-hour later, we were staring at a soupy mess. Had we forgotten the tapioca? We didn't think so. Aggravated, we baked another crisp. The results were just as bad. We rummaged through our notes and studied our recipe, trying to figure out what had gone wrong. Suddenly, it dawned on us: During the week of testing, the firm, slightly underripe peaches had softened and become deliciously juicy: perfect for eating, but problematic for cooking. We would need to standardize them so that no matter how variable the fruit, the recipe would always work.

Clearly, we would need to get rid of some juice before the crisp ever went into the oven. Macerating fruit draws off liquid, so we combined the peaches with sugar and salt (to season them deeply), let them sit for 30 minutes, and drained them. Then we made the recipe as before, this time with our drained peaches and 2 teaspoons of their juice (during tests the peaches released as much as 2 tablespoons or as little as 2 teaspoons of juice). We also raised the oven temperature from 350 to 400 for extra browning and, we hoped, extra crispness.

After letting the baked crisp cool, we reached for our spoons. We were thrilled: The berries were fresh and bright, the peaches tender but not mushy, the topping crisp, and the balance of sweet, tart, and buttery exactly right. Our new take on peach Melba was perfect for the modern-day dinner table for two.

Peach Melba Crisp
SERVES 2

You will need a 3-cup baking dish, measuring approximately 7¼ by 5¼ inches, for this recipe (see page 3). Do not use quick or instant oats in this recipe. Measure the tapioca before grinding it.

FILLING

- 2 teaspoons instant tapioca
- 2 peaches (6 ounces each), peeled, halved, pitted, and cut into ½-inch wedges, or 8 ounces frozen sliced peaches, thawed
- 1½ tablespoons granulated sugar
- Pinch salt
- 1 teaspoon lemon juice
- ¼ teaspoon vanilla extract
- 3 ounces (⅔ cup) raspberries

TOPPING

- 3 tablespoons all-purpose flour
- 1 tablespoon packed light brown sugar
- 1 tablespoon granulated sugar
- ⅛ teaspoon ground ginger
- Pinch ground cinnamon
- Pinch salt
- 2 tablespoons unsalted butter, cut into ½-inch pieces and chilled
- 3 tablespoons old-fashioned rolled oats
- 3 tablespoons chopped pecans

1. FOR THE FILLING: Grind tapioca in spice grinder to fine powder, about 30 seconds; set aside. Gently toss peaches with sugar and salt in bowl and let sit, stirring occasionally, for 30 minutes. Drain peaches through colander set inside bowl; reserve 2 teaspoons peach juice. Return drained peaches to original bowl and toss with reserved peach juice, ground tapioca, lemon juice, and vanilla. Transfer to 3-cup baking dish measuring approximately 7¼ by 5¼ inches and press gently into even layer. Top peaches with raspberries.

2. FOR THE TOPPING: While peaches are macerating, combine flour, brown sugar, granulated sugar, ginger, cinnamon, and salt in food processor and process until combined, about 5 seconds. Add butter and pulse until mixture resembles wet sand, about 5 pulses. Add oats and pecans and pulse until mixture forms marble-size clumps and no loose flour remains, 8 to 10 pulses. Chill mixture for at least 15 minutes. Adjust oven rack to upper-middle position and heat oven to 400 degrees.

3. Distribute topping evenly over fruit. Bake until topping is well browned and fruit is bubbling around edges, about 30 minutes, rotating dish halfway through baking. Cool on wire rack for at least 15 minutes before serving.

CREAM CHEESE POUND CAKE

✔ **WHY THIS RECIPE WORKS:** We wanted a tender, fine-crumbed pound cake flavored with tangy cream cheese. For the richest flavor, we let the butter, cream cheese, and egg take center stage, adding only vanilla and a moderate amount of sugar. For a velvety texture, cutting back to just one egg and swapping all-purpose flour for lower-protein cake flour were key. And to achieve a tight, fine crumb, we left the leavener out altogether. Finally, though a low oven took a little longer, we found it produced a golden-brown crust and a moist, tender interior.

WITH ITS RICH, BUTTERY FLAVOR, MOIST, TENDER crumb, and bronzed exterior, pound cake makes a nice treat after dinner, or an equally good pick-me-up in the afternoon with coffee. And its versatility doesn't end there. This simple cake takes well to any number of flavorings, from lemon and poppy seeds to chocolate. But one issue we have is that no matter the flavor, pound cake tends to serve at least eight. We wanted a scaled-down cake that would make enough for just two so we wouldn't be tempted by the leftovers for a week. And, for a slight twist on the classic, we looked to make ours a cream cheese pound cake; the cream cheese would give it a slightly tangy flavor and an especially velvety texture.

To start, we gathered a few recipes for cream cheese pound cake and headed into the test kitchen. Following these recipes, we baked and then ate our way through a half-dozen samples. We had plenty of help in the eating department, but the reviews were mixed. Overall, we agreed that while the cream cheese added a pleasant tang, most of the cakes were either dense and gummy or coarse and marred by tunnels. A coarse, open crumb suits white layer cake, but pound cake should be fine-crumbed, lusciously tender, and rich. As for flavor, tasters voted for simplicity. Classic pound cake, we felt, is defined by pure flavors: butter, vanilla, and, in this case, cream cheese. We also preferred the cakes that weren't cloyingly sweet.

Informed by those tests and armed with a favorite test kitchen recipe for plain pound cake, we cobbled together a working recipe as a place to begin our testing. We beat half a stick of butter (this *is* a pound cake, after all) with ½ cup of sugar and 4 ounces of cream cheese. Then we added two eggs and a dash of vanilla extract, followed by ½ cup of all-purpose flour mixed with baking powder and salt. We scraped the batter into a 5½ by 3-inch loaf pan and baked the cake. An hour later, we tasted. The verdict: too cakey. On top of that, we spied the occasional tunnel worming its way through the cake.

Our experience has taught us that tunnels can be caused by overleavening. For our next test, we cut the baking powder in half (to ⅛ teaspoon), which alleviated but didn't eliminate the tunneling. Maybe baking powder wasn't necessary in the first place.

We knew from our research that older recipes for pound cakes don't call for leaveners. When cakes are made, air is beaten into batter during the creaming stage, when the butter and sugar are beaten together until fluffy. This forms small holes that eventually make the cake's crumb. The job of the leavener is to enlarge those holes. So if we wanted a tighter crumb, eliminating the baking powder might get us there. Indeed it did: The tunnels disappeared. But we still hadn't achieved the ideal velvety texture.

Cake flour was the obvious next thing to try: It's a little more acidic than all-purpose flour. Acidity lowers the temperature at which proteins coagulate and at which starches gelatinize, in turn making for a tighter crumb. Our years in the test kitchen had taught us that cake flour absorbs more moisture than all-purpose flour does. To account for that, we replaced some of the cream cheese that we had been using with a tablespoon of neutral-tasting milk. These changes in place, we baked another pound cake. We were definitely on the right track: This latest version was more tender, fine-crumbed, and velvety than any other we had baked thus far.

Encouraged, we moved down the ingredient list, looking for more ways to improve the cake. That's when we spied eggs. Egg yolks tenderize, but the whites actually have a drying effect. After several more tests, we decided to cut an egg; including just one in our recipe gave us the fine crumb that we had been after all along.

Our cream cheese pound cake was getting better and better, but now a layer of gumminess on top stood between us and a perfect pound cake. A gummy top is a telltale sign of an underbaked cake. But if we baked the cake any longer, the sides of the cake burned—unless we decreased the oven temperature. We inched the dial down to 325 degrees (from 350).

One hour later, we knew we'd hit the sweet spot. This cake was moist, tender, golden brown, and very velvety. It had all the richness (more, actually) and pure buttery flavor of classic pound cake, but with a delicate tang—and, as a boon to the for-two kitchen, none of the leftovers.

Cream Cheese Pound Cake

SERVES 2

You will need a 5½ by 3-inch loaf pan or a pan of similar size for this recipe (see page 3). Make sure to give the batter a final stir by hand before transferring it to the loaf pan.

- ½ **cup (2 ounces) cake flour**
- ⅛ **teaspoon salt**
- 1 **large egg, room temperature**
- 1 **tablespoon milk**
- ½ **teaspoon vanilla extract**
- ½ **cup (3½ ounces) sugar**
- 4 **tablespoons unsalted butter, softened**
- 1½ **ounces cream cheese, softened**

NOTES FROM THE TEST KITCHEN

THE BEST VANILLA EXTRACT

Vanilla extract is sold in pure and imitation varieties. So which should you buy? If you're buying only one bottle of vanilla for cooking, baking, and making cold and creamy desserts, our top choice is a real extract—real vanilla has around 250 flavor compounds compared to imitation vanilla's one, giving it a complexity tasters appreciated in certain applications. Our favorite pure vanilla is **McCormick Pure Vanilla Extract**. But if you use vanilla only for baking, we have to admit there's still not much of a difference between a well-made synthetic vanilla and the real thing (the flavor and aroma compounds in pure vanilla begin to bake off at higher temperatures, so the subtleties are lost). Tasters liked the "well-balanced and full" vanilla flavor and budget-friendly price of our top-rated imitation vanilla, **Gold Medal**.

1. Adjust oven rack to middle position and heat oven to 325 degrees. Grease and flour 5½ by 3-inch loaf pan.

2. Combine flour and salt in bowl and set aside. Whisk egg, milk, and vanilla together in 1-cup liquid measuring cup. Using stand mixer fitted with paddle, beat sugar, butter, and cream cheese together on medium-high speed until pale and fluffy, about 3 minutes. Reduce speed to low and very slowly add egg mixture until incorporated (batter may look slightly curdled). Add flour mixture in 3 additions, scraping down bowl as needed. Give batter final stir by hand.

3. Scrape batter into prepared pan and gently tap pan on counter to release air bubbles. Bake until toothpick inserted into center comes out clean, about 1 hour, rotating pan halfway through baking.

4. Let cake cool in pan on wire rack for 15 minutes. Remove cake from pan and let cool completely, about 1 hour. Serve.

BANANA CREAM PIE

✔ **WHY THIS RECIPE WORKS:** This layered concoction of pastry cream and sliced bananas topped with whipped cream is utterly addictive—but it serves a crowd. For a smaller pie, we reached for a 6-inch pie plate. Using cornstarch instead of flour gave us a nicely thickened pastry cream that held up to slicing. For big banana flavor, rather than relying on banana extract (which tasted artificial) or liqueur (which was an impractical purchase when we needed only a splash) as most recipes do, we got far better results by infusing the pastry cream with sautéed bananas. To keep the fresh banana slices from browning, we tossed them with orange juice. And relying on our favorite store-bought pie crust made this recipe a no-brainer for the for-two household.

WE CAN THINK OF FEW MORE INDULGENT DESSERTS than banana cream pie. But leftover cream pie is never as appealing as it is the first time it hits the plate, so we set out to scale down this dessert so that smaller households could enjoy all the addictive flavors and textures, too.

Before getting to work on our for-two version, we sampled a number of recipes, looking for some insight into what would produce the very best banana cream pie. These initial tests revealed problems with every aspect of the pie. The creamiest versions were unsliceable, and the tidiest slices were starchy and gloppy. To reinforce the banana flavor, some recipes include banana extract or banana liqueur in the pastry cream. We liked the idea, but the extract tasted artificial, and buying a bottle of liqueur for the small amount we'd need seemed crazy. Pies with cookie-crumb crusts were too sweet, and those with from-scratch dough took a good portion of the day to make. And the sliced bananas in every last test pie turned brown by the time the pastry cream set. In truth, the pie needed more work than just being scaled down.

First things first: We focused on the "cream" of banana cream pie. To make pastry cream, you combine egg yolks, flour or cornstarch, and sugar; whisk in hot half-and-half; stir over low heat until thick; and then add vanilla and a little butter. (The butter melts in the hot pastry cream but resolidifies and stiffens the cream as it cools.) Hoping to strike a compromise between starchy and runny, we made pastry cream again and again over a series of days, adjusting each component. Eventually, we figured out our ratios and settled on cornstarch, which proved to be a more foolproof thickener than flour.

With our working pastry cream, we assembled a test pie. We arranged a sliced banana between two layers of the pastry cream in a prebaked pie shell (we used store-bought pie dough for convenience). After chilling the pie, we sliced into it and served a couple of pieces. Though the pie sliced nicely, the bananas were turning brown.

To investigate without the trouble of baking more pies, we decided to toss banana slices with various ingredients alleged to protect them from browning, then left them out on the counter, checking in periodically to see which browned the slowest. Sugar and vodka were a bust. Salt, vinegar, and lemon juice slowed browning but tasted either salty or sour. Orange juice, however, slowed browning and left the mellow, fruity banana flavor alone, so we assembled a pie, this time tossing our banana with orange juice. Tasters approved.

Next, we turned to bumping up the banana flavor. Since banana extract and liqueur were out, we tried smashing up a banana in the pastry cream. No dice: It turned the pastry cream brown. A colleague recommended banana baby food—great idea, but another failure: It made the pastry cream runny. So we borrowed an idea from a banana pudding recipe, using pureed

BANANA CREAM PIE

roasted bananas to flavor our pastry cream. This pie was delicious. Unfortunately, it was also loose and turned brownish gray. Now we tried sautéing the bananas in butter, and again we pureed them into the cream.

Once more, delicious—and gray. We were starting to get really frustrated when the solution occurred to us: Maybe we could infuse the half-and-half with banana flavor and then strain out the fruit. Just one sautéed banana gave the pastry cream a big banana-y boost, and straining minimized the unappealing color change.

For the pie shell, we decided to stick with our favorite store-bought pie crust instead of laboring with our own homemade version; this was much more practical for our scaled-down dessert, and tasters were plenty satisfied.

With a creamy yet sliceable banana-boosted pastry cream, mellow and (finally) yellow sliced bananas, and a light and stable whipped cream, this pie now had it all.

Banana Cream Pie

SERVES 2

You will need a 6-inch pie plate for this recipe (see page 3). Use all-yellow to lightly spotted bananas for this recipe (not green-topped or all-brown). Peel and slice the bananas just before using to prevent browning. When straining the half-and-half mixture in step 2, do not press on the bananas or the custard will turn gray as it sits. The pie can be made up to 24 hours in advance; note that it should be chilled for a minimum of 5 hours. Our favorite pie dough is made by Wholly Wholesome, which has two crusts in a box; you will need only one for this recipe. This pie dough is sold frozen and requires 3 hours of defrosting. This is best done on the counter rather than in the refrigerator; you may microwave the dough for up to 10 seconds if the center is not fully thawed.

- 2   ripe bananas
- 2   tablespoons unsalted butter
- 1¼ cups half-and-half
- ¼   cup (1¾ ounces) plus 1 tablespoon granulated sugar
- 3   large egg yolks
- ⅛   teaspoon salt
- 1   tablespoon cornstarch
- ¾   teaspoon vanilla extract
- ½   package store-bought pie dough
- 1   tablespoon orange juice
- ¼   cup heavy cream, chilled
- 2   teaspoons confectioners' sugar

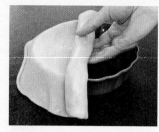

1. Peel 1 banana and slice into ½-inch-thick pieces. Melt 1 tablespoon butter in small saucepan over medium-high heat. Add banana slices and cook until they begin to soften, about 2 minutes. Add half-and-half, bring to boil, and boil for 30 seconds. Remove pot from heat, cover, and let sit for 40 minutes.

2. Whisk granulated sugar, egg yolks, and salt together in medium bowl until smooth. Whisk in cornstarch. Strain half-and-half mixture through fine-mesh strainer into yolk mixture—do not press on bananas—and whisk until incorporated; discard cooked bananas.

3. Transfer mixture to clean saucepan. Cook over medium heat, whisking constantly, until thickened to consistency of warm pudding (180 degrees), 4 to 6 minutes. Remove pan from heat; whisk in remaining 1 tablespoon butter and ½ teaspoon vanilla. Transfer to bowl, press greased parchment paper directly against surface, and let cool for about 1 hour.

4. Gently unroll dough onto 6-inch pie plate, letting excess hang over edge. Ease dough into plate by gently lifting edge of dough with 1 hand while pressing into plate bottom with other hand. Leave any dough that overhangs plate in place. Trim overhang to ½ inch beyond lip of pie plate. Tuck overhang under itself; folded edge should be flush with edge of pie plate. Crimp dough evenly around edge of pie using your fingers. Wrap dough-lined pie plate loosely in plastic wrap and place in freezer until dough is fully chilled and firm, about 20 minutes.

5. Adjust oven rack to lower-middle position and heat oven to 375 degrees. Line chilled crust with sheet of lightly greased aluminum foil, folding foil over edges of dough. Fill with pie weights. Bake until pie dough looks dry and is light in color, about 20 minutes. Carefully remove foil and weights, rotate plate, and continue baking until crust is golden brown, 10 to 12 minutes longer. Let cool to room temperature.

6. Peel remaining banana, slice into ¼-inch-thick rounds, and toss with orange juice. Whisk pastry cream briefly, then spread half over bottom of pie shell. Arrange sliced bananas on pastry cream. Top with remaining pastry cream. Whip cream, confectioners' sugar, and remaining ¼ teaspoon vanilla together in bowl until soft peaks form. Spread whipped cream attractively over center of pie and refrigerate until set, at least 5 hours or up to 24 hours. Serve.

CRÈME CARAMEL

✔ **WHY THIS RECIPE WORKS:** Our crème caramel for two had to be creamy and tender, yet firm enough to unmold without collapsing on the plate. Nailing the custard came down to figuring out the right proportion of whole eggs to yolks. Selecting half-and-half for the dairy ensured that the custard was plenty rich and creamy, but not over the top. Creating a custard that's creamy and smooth also depends on maintaining a gentle heating environment; this was provided by baking our ramekins in a water bath. Once inverted, our custards were coated by a nicely sweetened caramel, which gave them a picture-perfect appearance and worked to balance their richness.

CRÈME CARAMEL IS A DECEPTIVELY SIMPLE CLASSIC French dessert. Made with just a few ingredients that are readily available (sugar, eggs, and milk or cream), it is similar in construction and flavor to other baked custards from around the world. Slightly lighter and a little less sweet than a standard baked custard, this dessert really stands out thanks to the caramel sauce, which bakes underneath the custard. Once the dessert is baked and the custard inverted for serving, the caramel sauce spills over the top and onto the plate, making for one showstopping finish to any special-occasion dinner. We thought this fancy dessert would be the perfect addition to our lineup of scaled-down sweets.

Since eggs are integral to the structure of crème caramel, we started there. In doing our research, we learned that not all recipes agreed on the number of eggs or the proportion of egg yolks to egg whites. Here's what we learned: Too many whites produced a custard that was almost solid and rubbery; too few egg whites, on the other hand, and our custard collapsed. After much tinkering, we came up with what we consider the ideal ratio: 2 tablespoons of lightly beaten egg (roughly half of a large egg) and one yolk. The resulting custard was tender yet not overly rich, and firm enough to unmold easily.

Next, we examined the question of what liquid to use. Since we were making a classic crème caramel, our choices were limited to milk, heavy cream, and half-and-half. We made our initial custard using milk alone, but it tasted far too thin. The custard made with heavy cream, on the other hand, was creamy but too rich. This left us wanting something in between, and half-and-half solved the problem, giving us just that extra edge of richness, creamy enough to satisfy our tasters.

As for the sugar, we knew that a crème caramel custard should be less sweet than a custard meant to be eaten unadorned. We initially used 2 tablespoons of sugar for ¾ cup of liquid in the recipe and were quite satisfied, but some tasters felt that this custard was too bland. Bumping up the sugar to 4 tablespoons ensured that our custards were nicely sweetened, but not cloying.

Now that our custard base was settled, we got to work on the caramel. We had two techniques to choose from. In the dry method, you use only sugar, cooking it slowly until it melts and caramelizes. The wet method uses a combination of water and sugar. The sugar begins to dissolve in the water, then the mixture is simmered until the water evaporates and the sugar caramelizes. The dry method can be tricky to pull off, so we opted for the wet method.

Once our caramel was done, we poured it directly into our lightly greased 4-ounce ramekins. We then followed common advice to coat the bottom evenly and tilt the ramekins to coat the sides. But an accident with hot caramel burning our fingers while the ramekins were tilted caused us to question this particular bit of advice. We started to coat only the bottoms of the molds, reasoning that the caramel sinks to the bottom while baking anyway. When we unmolded the custards, the caramel still poured evenly over the tops of the custards, and we didn't have to worry about burnt fingertips.

How you bake crème caramel and how long you bake it can make all the difference between a great dessert and a mediocre, or even disappointing, one. After considerable experimentation, we determined that baking the custards at 350 degrees in a water bath, in order to maintain an even, gentle heating environment, worked best, producing custards that were creamy and smooth.

As a final experiment, we decided to try lining the baking pan with a towel before adding the ramekins or the water. We found this step in a couple of recipes and thought it was worth a try, given that our custards still had bubbles from overcooking near the bottom. We reasoned that the towel might absorb some of the heat from the bottom, preventing the custards from overcooking in this area. Custards baked with the towel contained significantly fewer bubbles, so we decided to throw in the towel (no pun intended).

Just one spoonful revealed that we'd succeeded. Our pair of perfect crème caramels not only looked elegant and refined, but they also tasted that way, too, with their rich, creamy texture and sophisticated sweetness from the caramel.

Crème Caramel

SERVES 2

You will need two 4-ounce ramekins for this recipe (see page 3). Note that the custards will look barely set once they are ready to be removed from the oven. You will need a candy thermometer or another thermometer that registers high temperatures for this recipe.

- 2 tablespoons water
- 6 tablespoons (2⅔ ounces) sugar
- 2 tablespoons lightly beaten egg, plus 1 large yolk
- ¼ teaspoon vanilla extract
  Pinch salt
- ¾ cup half-and-half

1. Adjust oven rack to middle position and heat oven to 350 degrees. Bring kettle of water to boil. Place dish towel in bottom of metal 8-inch square baking pan. Grease two 4-ounce ramekins and place on towel.

2. Pour 2 tablespoons water into small saucepan, then pour 4 tablespoons sugar into center of pan (don't let it hit sides of pan). Gently stir sugar with clean heatproof spatula to wet thoroughly. Bring to boil over medium-high heat and cook, without stirring, until sugar has dissolved completely and liquid has faint golden color and registers 300 degrees, 3 to 4 minutes.

3. Reduce heat to medium-low and continue to cook, stirring occasionally, until caramel has dark amber color and registers 350 degrees, 1 to 2 minutes longer. Carefully divide caramel between ramekins and let cool slightly until hardened.

4. Whisk remaining 2 tablespoons sugar, 2 tablespoons lightly beaten egg, egg yolk, vanilla, and salt together in large bowl. Heat half-and-half in medium saucepan over medium heat until steaming, then whisk into egg mixture until just combined. Strain custard through fine-mesh strainer into liquid measuring cup. Pour custard evenly into ramekins on top of caramel.

5. Place baking pan in oven and carefully pour enough boiling water into pan to reach halfway up sides of ramekins. Bake custards until small knife inserted halfway between center and edge comes out clean, 25 to 30 minutes.

6. Carefully remove ramekins from water bath using tongs and sturdy spatula and let custards cool to room temperature, 1 to 2 hours. Set ramekins on plate, cover tightly with plastic wrap, and refrigerate until cold, at least 2 hours.

7. Run small knife around 1 ramekin to loosen custard. Place inverted serving plate over top and quickly flip custard onto plate, drizzling any extra caramel sauce over top (some caramel will remain stuck in ramekin). Repeat with remaining ramekin and serve.

NOTES FROM THE TEST KITCHEN

UNMOLDING CRÈME CARAMEL

1. Slide small knife around custard to loosen it, pressing knife against side of dish.

2. Hold individual serving plate over top of ramekin and swiftly invert.

3. Set plate on counter and shake ramekin gently to release custard and caramel (some caramel will remain in ramekin).

INDIVIDUAL CHOCOLATE FUDGE CAKES

✔ **WHY THIS RECIPE WORKS:** To bring this bistro favorite home for two, we started by building a rich, brownielike cake with an intense chocolate flavor. Moderate amounts of vegetable oil and chocolate ensured that our cakes were plenty moist and boasted a good jolt of chocolaty flavor. Half an egg also contributed to our cakes' moistness and richness, and a small amount of flour gave our cakes more structure and lift. Finally, for a gooey center, we pressed a square of chocolate into each ramekin before baking, giving us individual cakes with a big burst of chocolate and a rich, fudgy center.

WARM, GOOEY, AND UBER-CHOCOLATY, INDIVIDUAL chocolate cakes are a mainstay on most bistro menus—and it's not hard to understand why. With their rich, fudgy centers and dense, brownielike exteriors, these individual desserts are incredibly satisfying—and not just for diehard chocoholics. But we didn't want to have to go out to enjoy the decadent, intense richness and big chocolate flavor of this dish, so we set out to develop our own recipe to make this restaurant favorite at home. And because we'd be preparing just two desserts—not a whole fleet of individual cakes—we were already well on our way to ensuring that these were easy enough to make, bake, and serve that we could indulge any night of the week.

Our first step was to gather several recipes that we had encountered in our research and test them out. We found that most followed one of two paths. The fussier version called for beating the egg yolks and whites separately and then folding them together before baking the cakes in a hot-water bath to produce a soufflélike cake that sat above a layer of fudgy sauce. Then there were the absurdly simple recipes that started with melting the chocolate before stirring in everything else, dividing the batter among the ramekins, and baking the cakes. But though the latter method was much easier and more foolproof, not all of the recipes delivered fudgy cakes with the flavor and texture we were after.

Instead of offering deep, chocolaty flavor, some tasted shallow and mild. And instead of providing a molten fudgy center, some were dry, while others were just

INDIVIDUAL CHOCOLATE FUDGE CAKES

plain soupy or severely underbaked. But we weren't about to give up on the notion of an effortless recipe for cakes with intense flavor and a gooey center.

For our next move, we cobbled together a working recipe based on our test cakes. It consisted of chocolate, oil, milk, eggs, and flour, plus brown sugar (which provided more depth than granulated sugar) and leaveners (both baking powder and baking soda). After considerable testing, we decided that just 2 tablespoons of vegetable oil and 2 ounces of bittersweet chocolate made the dessert moist enough and delivered a good jolt of intense chocolate flavor. A quarter-cup of whole milk further amped up the moistness and richness of our cakes.

Moving on to the eggs, we quickly realized that nailing down the right amount was perhaps even more crucial, as it affected the texture, richness, and moisture of our cakes. We tested cakes made with one whole egg (these had a light and spongy texture), one large yolk (these were moist and dense), and half of a beaten egg (these were rich but light, moist, intense, and dark). Half an egg gave us the best cakes overall, with both the flavor and texture we were after.

Although some recipes use very little or no flour, we found after some testing that 6 tablespoons gave the cakes some structure and lift—making them less fudgelike and more cakelike.

But though we liked a more cakey exterior, we still wanted the center of the cakes to have a soft, fudgy texture. Underbaking our cakes prevented the outside of the dessert from setting up, so to get the gooey center we were after, we tried adding plain chocolate to the batter. Chocolate chips melted into the cake, but a single square of bittersweet chocolate, pressed right into the center of each ramekin, melted perfectly and made for a delicious molten center.

To bake the cakes, we greased two 6-ounce ramekins and dusted them with flour to ensure that the cakes wouldn't stick to the sides. With the dishes ready and the batter portioned, we turned our attention to oven temperatures, baking our cakes at 350, 400, and 450 degrees. At the two higher temperatures, we found that the tops were slightly burned and the centers were too runny. At 350 degrees, our cakes had a nicely set, cakey perimeter surrounding a saucy surprise in the middle.

With a scoop of ice cream on top, these ultrachocolaty cakes delivered the richness, intensity, and flavor we expected—and we didn't have to tip our server afterward.

Individual Chocolate Fudge Cakes

SERVES 2

You will need two 6-ounce ramekins for this recipe (see page 3). Serve these cakes warm in their ramekins and top them with vanilla ice cream, if desired.

- 6 tablespoons (1¾ ounces) all-purpose flour
- ¼ teaspoon baking powder
- ⅛ teaspoon baking soda
- ⅛ teaspoon salt
- 3 ounces bittersweet chocolate, 2 ounces chopped and 1 ounce broken into 2 (½-ounce) squares
- ¼ cup whole milk
- 3 tablespoons packed light brown sugar
- 2 tablespoons vegetable oil
- 2 tablespoons lightly beaten egg
- ¼ teaspoon vanilla extract

1. Adjust oven rack to middle position and heat oven to 350 degrees. Grease and flour two 6-ounce ramekins and arrange on rimmed baking sheet. Whisk flour, baking powder, baking soda, and salt together in bowl; set aside.

2. Microwave 2 ounces chopped chocolate and milk together in medium bowl, stirring occasionally, until melted and smooth, 1 to 2 minutes. Stir in sugar until dissolved; let cool slightly. Whisk oil, egg, and vanilla

---

NOTES FROM THE TEST KITCHEN

THE BEST DARK CHOCOLATE
Semisweet and bittersweet chocolate, also called dark chocolate, must contain at least 35 percent chocolate liquor (a combination of chocolate solids and cocoa butter), although most contain more than 55 percent and some can go as high as 99 percent. Many brands have distinctive flavors that tasters liked in particular desserts, but two brands, **Callebaut Intense Dark Chocolate L-60-40NV** and **Ghirardelli Bittersweet Chocolate Baking Bar**, consistently produced great results in all types of baked goods. Note that both of these chocolates contain 60 percent cacao—the type most recipes calling for dark have been developed to use. (Chocolates containing 70 percent or more cacao usually require recipe adjustments to get good results.)

into melted chocolate mixture until combined. Slowly whisk in flour mixture until just combined.

3. Divide batter between prepared ramekins and gently tap ramekins on counter to release air bubbles. Gently press 1 square chocolate into center of each ramekin to submerge. Bake until tops are just firm to touch and center is gooey when pierced with toothpick, about 15 minutes, rotating sheet halfway through baking. Let cool for 2 to 3 minutes before serving.

CREAMY CHOCOLATE PUDDING

✔ WHY THIS RECIPE WORKS: For a rich and creamy homemade chocolate pudding for two that was worlds better than a snack pack, we found that using a moderate amount of bittersweet chocolate in combination with unsweetened cocoa and espresso powder helped us to achieve maximum chocolate flavor. For thickening, cornstarch proved the right choice, and using mostly milk and just ¼ cup of heavy cream, along with one egg yolk, ensured that our pudding had a silky-smooth texture. Salt and vanilla enhanced the chocolate flavor even more.

SOMETIMES WE MISS THE SIMPLICITY—AND THE restraint—of a good homemade chocolate pudding: that wonderfully smooth, dense, yet light marriage of chocolate and dairy thickened with cornstarch and maybe a couple of egg yolks. We can manage only a few bites of dense, ganachelike *pot de crème*, but we can easily devour a generous serving of chocolate pudding. Though it might be viewed as a kids' dessert, we think this classic is worthy of the adult dinner table and looked to bring back this simple pleasure in a recipe that made just enough for two.

When we went to the test kitchen library to gather recipes, we were happily reminded that making chocolate pudding from scratch couldn't be easier: Simmer dairy and sugar with cornstarch, whisk in chocolate and (sometimes) egg yolks, add vanilla extract, and chill. If we weren't already excited about scaling this recipe down for two, its sheer simplicity sealed the deal.

That said, when we gave the recipes a closer look, the variety among them was startling for a dish with so few steps and ingredients. Some called for unsweetened chocolate, others bittersweet. Amounts ranged from a modest ounce to more than 10 times that amount. Still others ditched the solid chocolate for cocoa powder. As for the egg yolks, many recipes didn't include them, instead opting for a heftier dose of cornstarch to thicken things up. Then there was the dairy question: Should it be milk, cream, half-and-half—or some combination? And would adding butter be a good thing or overkill?

We decided to start conservatively, scaling down and preparing a pudding from an old recipe that called for 1 ounce of unsweetened chocolate, milk, cornstarch, and no eggs. No surprise: Tasters panned this pudding for its wan flavor and loose consistency. Trying our hand at a more modern recipe, we made a version that kicked everything up a notch, increasing the unsweetened chocolate to 3 ounces, swapping in some half-and-half for the milk, and adding a few tablespoons of butter. But still, our pudding had no fans.

Putting the lackluster recipes aside, we went for a more drastic change and tried a bittersweet chocolate pudding recipe we'd found. This formula—2 ounces of bittersweet chocolate, milk, and no eggs—produced a markedly richer, more complex chocolate pudding. But we hadn't hit the mark yet. Sure, this pudding's chocolate flavor had more oomph and dimension, but according to our tasters, we had yet to reach the chocolate ceiling. Upping our chocolate to 3 ounces only gave us a grainy pudding, which we figured was from the high proportion of chocolate solids.

Thinking back to our research, one unusual recipe had called for cocoa powder, but no bar chocolate. We decided to give it a try, although we thought the gritty cocoa particles would equal gritty pudding that didn't taste very rich. Sure enough, our tasters thought this pudding's flavor was just OK, but to our surprise, they raved about its silky texture—by far the smoothest pudding we had turned out to date.

Turning back to our working recipe that used 2 ounces of solid chocolate, we began adding cocoa powder to it, stopping when we got to 1 tablespoon. This pudding boasted not only deep chocolate flavor but also perfect smoothness.

How was it that more chocolate contributed to a gritty texture, while cocoa didn't adversely affect the pudding's smoothness? A chat with our science editor helped clarify things. He explained that the culprit in causing grittiness is cocoa butter—and solid chocolate has far more of it than cocoa powder. Solid chocolate is manufactured so that its cocoa butter remains solid at room temperature but melts precisely at human body temperature. But when the same chocolate is melted and then allowed to re-solidify, the crystalline structure of the cocoa butter is reorganized; it becomes more stable and melts at higher temperatures. If present in high enough amounts, this more-stable form of cocoa butter creates a grainy texture. The upshot: For a pudding with both potent chocolate flavor and a supremely smooth texture, a combo of bittersweet chocolate and cocoa powder was definitely the way to go.

With that mystery solved and the chocolate flavor exactly where we wanted it, we had just a few more tweaks to make. Thus far, we hadn't used egg yolks in our recipe, but the pudding was lacking a certain richness and body that yolks would surely provide. After a few tests, we determined that one yolk did the trick. Tasters also liked the extra creaminess brought about by adding ¼ cup of heavy cream.

And yet something was still missing—some depth and roundness to the chocolate flavor. We often turn to espresso powder to add richness and depth to chocolate desserts, and here it worked perfectly. Just ⅛ teaspoon did the trick.

At long last—and with the help of two kinds of chocolate—we had achieved pudding perfection.

Creamy Chocolate Pudding

SERVES 2

For this recipe, we recommend using one of our favorite dark chocolates—Callebaut Intense Dark Chocolate L-60-40NV or Ghirardelli Bittersweet Chocolate Baking Bar. If you like, garnish the pudding with whipped cream and chocolate shavings.

- ¾ teaspoon vanilla extract
- ⅛ teaspoon instant espresso powder
- 3 tablespoons sugar
- 1 tablespoon unsweetened cocoa powder
- 2½ teaspoons cornstarch
- ⅛ teaspoon salt
- ¼ cup heavy cream
- 1 large egg yolk

- 1 cup whole milk
- 2 tablespoons unsalted butter, cut into 8 pieces
- 2 ounces bittersweet chocolate, chopped fine

1. Combine vanilla and espresso powder in bowl; set aside. Whisk sugar, cocoa, cornstarch, and salt together in small saucepan. Whisk in cream and egg yolk until fully incorporated, making sure to scrape corners of saucepan. Add milk and whisk until combined.

2. Heat milk mixture over medium heat and cook, whisking constantly, until mixture is thickened and bubbling over entire surface, 5 to 8 minutes. Cook 30 seconds longer, remove from heat, add butter, chocolate, and vanilla mixture, and whisk until chocolate is melted and smooth.

3. Pour pudding through fine-mesh strainer into bowl. Press lightly greased parchment paper against surface of pudding and refrigerate until completely cool, at least 4 hours. Briefly whisk pudding before serving.

QUICKER TURTLE BROWNIES

✔ WHY THIS RECIPE WORKS: With their rich caramel and crunchy nuts, turtle brownies up the ante when it comes to your standard brownie—but they also up the ante when it comes to the amount of work involved. For an easier path to turtle brownie heaven for two, we first created a simple yet flavor-packed brownie. Bypassing the homemade caramel, we doctored up caramel candies with heavy cream. Placing a layer of caramel in the brownies, rather than just on top, ensured that it stayed put, and parbaking the bottom layer first kept the caramel from sinking. Using a loaf pan to bake our brownies delivered just enough for two (with a little extra left over for a snack).

DARK CHOCOLATE BROWNIES, RICH AND CHEWY caramel, and sweet pecans—it's hard to go wrong with turtle brownies. In the test kitchen, we recently developed a recipe for this amped-up brownie, but scaling it down for two seemed like a nonstarter. Even though they are incredibly decadent and rich, that wasn't enough to justify buying a few different types of chocolate and making caramel from scratch. We wanted a recipe that would be every bit as tempting and rich tasting but would require a little less shopping, time, and effort.

Looking for a more streamlined take on the turtle brownie, we started with a more basic recipe for brownies. First, we melted butter and unsweetened chocolate (for maximum chocolate flavor) together until smooth, then whisked in granulated sugar, an egg, and vanilla. Finally, we added the flour (cake flour gave our brownies a more tender texture than all-purpose flour), baking powder, and salt. After baking our brownies—a loaf pan made the perfect mini baking pan—and letting them cool, we topped one batch with jarred caramel sauce and the other with melted caramel candies. The jarred sauce was a goopy mess, and the melted caramels, although tasty, were waxy and created a skin that peeled off in a single leathery layer. Worse, the brownies were soggy because the sugar in the caramel added too much moisture. Cutting back on the sugar and increasing the flour in the brownie batter seemed to fix the moisture level, but we still had to fix the caramel.

To prevent waxiness in the melted caramels, we melted them with a little cream. But the solidified caramel layer still peeled off in one big strip. What if we put the caramel layer inside the brownies instead? We poured half of the batter into our loaf pan, layered on the melted caramel, topped it with the rest of the batter, and baked it. Sadly, the caramel disappeared into the bottom brownie layer. Maybe parbaking the bottom layer would help, so the caramel wouldn't have a chance to sink into the batter.

For our next test, we mixed together our brownie batter, spread half of it in the pan, and then parbaked the bottom while making the caramel sauce. After just 10 minutes, the bottom layer was set. Next, we sprinkled on the nuts, poured on the caramel, and topped it with the remaining batter and more pecans. When the brownies were done, we gave them a finishing drizzle of a little more caramel. Finally, the caramel stayed put, and each bite was met with tender brownie, crunchy nuts, and rich caramel flavor.

Our streamlined turtle brownies now both looked and tasted the part. And though they were ready in record time, they disappeared from the plate even faster.

Quicker Turtle Brownies
MAKES 4 BROWNIES

You will need an 8½ by 4½-inch loaf pan, or a pan of similar size, for this recipe (see page 3).

  6 **tablespoons (1½ ounces) cake flour**
  ¼ **teaspoon baking powder**
     Salt
  3 **tablespoons unsalted butter, cut into 1-inch pieces**
  1½ **ounces unsweetened chocolate, chopped fine**
  ½ **cup (3½ ounces) sugar**
  1 **large egg**
  1 **teaspoon vanilla extract**
 10 **soft caramels**
  1½ **tablespoons heavy cream**
  ½ **cup pecans, toasted and chopped**

1. Adjust oven rack to middle position and heat oven to 325 degrees. Make aluminum foil sling for 8½ by 4½-inch loaf pan by folding 2 long sheets of foil; first sheet should be 8½ inches wide and second sheet should be 4½ inches wide. Lay sheets of foil in pan perpendicular to each other, with extra foil hanging over edges of pan. Push foil into corners and up sides of pan and smooth foil flush to pan. Spray with vegetable oil spray.

2. Combine flour, baking powder, and ⅛ teaspoon salt in bowl. Microwave butter and chocolate together in large bowl, stirring occasionally, until smooth, about 1 minute. Whisk sugar, egg, and ½ teaspoon vanilla into chocolate mixture. Add flour mixture in two additions, mixing until combined. Scrape approximately half of batter into prepared pan and spread into even layer. Bake until center is just set, 10 to 12 minutes.

3. Meanwhile, microwave caramels, cream, remaining ½ teaspoon vanilla, and ⅛ teaspoon salt together in bowl, stirring occasionally, until smooth, 1 to 2 minutes. Reserve 1 tablespoon caramel mixture for topping. Sprinkle parbaked brownies with ¼ cup pecans; pour remaining caramel mixture evenly over pecans. Top with remaining brownie batter and remaining ¼ cup pecans. Bake until toothpick inserted in center comes out with few moist crumbs attached, 30 to 35 minutes.

4. Let brownies cool in pan on wire rack for 1 hour. Reheat reserved 1 tablespoon caramel mixture in microwave for 30 seconds, drizzle over brownies, and let sit for 30 minutes. Using foil overhang, lift brownies from pan and cut into 4 pieces. Serve.

Conversions & Equivalencies

SOME SAY COOKING IS A SCIENCE AND AN ART. We would say that geography has a hand in it, too. Flour milled in the United Kingdom and elsewhere will feel and taste different from flour milled in the United States. So we cannot promise that the loaf of bread you bake in Canada or England will taste the same as a loaf baked in the States, but we can offer guidelines for converting weights and measures. We also recommend that you rely on your instincts when making our recipes. Refer to the visual cues provided. If the bread dough hasn't "come together in a ball," as described, you may need to add more flour—even if the recipe doesn't tell you to. You be the judge.

The recipes in this book were developed using standard U.S. measures following U.S. government guidelines. The charts below offer equivalents for U.S., metric, and imperial (U.K.) measures. All conversions are approximate and have been rounded up or down to the nearest whole number.

EXAMPLE:

1 teaspoon	=	4.9292 milliliters, rounded up to 5 milliliters
1 ounce	=	28.3495 grams, rounded down to 28 grams

VOLUME CONVERSIONS

U.S.	METRIC
1 teaspoon	5 milliliters
2 teaspoons	10 milliliters
1 tablespoon	15 milliliters
2 tablespoons	30 milliliters
¼ cup	59 milliliters
⅓ cup	79 milliliters
½ cup	118 milliliters
¾ cup	177 milliliters
1 cup	237 milliliters
1¼ cups	296 milliliters
1½ cups	355 milliliters
2 cups	473 milliliters
2½ cups	591 milliliters
3 cups	710 milliliters
4 cups (1 quart)	0.946 liter
1.06 quarts	1 liter
4 quarts (1 gallon)	3.8 liters

WEIGHT CONVERSIONS

OUNCES	GRAMS
½	14
¾	21
1	28
1½	43
2	57
2½	71
3	85
3½	99
4	113
4½	128
5	142
6	170
7	198
8	227
9	255
10	283
12	340
16 (1 pound)	454

CONVERSIONS FOR INGREDIENTS COMMONLY USED IN BAKING

Baking is an exacting science. Because measuring by weight is far more accurate than measuring by volume, and thus more likely to achieve reliable results, in our recipes we provide ounce measures in addition to cup measures for many ingredients. Refer to the chart below to convert these measures into grams.

INGREDIENT	OUNCES	GRAMS
Flour		
1 cup all-purpose flour*	5	142
1 cup cake flour	4	113
1 cup whole-wheat flour	5½	156
Sugar		
1 cup granulated (white) sugar	7	198
1 cup packed brown sugar (light or dark)	7	198
1 cup confectioners' sugar	4	113
Cocoa Powder		
1 cup cocoa powder	3	85
Butter†		
4 tablespoons (½ stick, or ¼ cup)	2	57
8 tablespoons (1 stick, or ½ cup)	4	113
16 tablespoons (2 sticks, or 1 cup)	8	227

* U.S. all-purpose flour, the most frequently used flour in this book, does not contain leaveners, as some European flours do. These leavened flours are called self-rising or self-raising. If you are using self-rising flour, take this into consideration before adding leavening to a recipe.

† In the United States, butter is sold both salted and unsalted. We generally recommend unsalted butter. If you are using salted butter, take this into consideration before adding salt to a recipe.

OVEN TEMPERATURES

FAHRENHEIT	CELSIUS	GAS MARK (imperial)
225	105	¼
250	120	½
275	135	1
300	150	2
325	165	3
350	180	4
375	190	5
400	200	6
425	220	7
450	230	8
475	245	9

CONVERTING TEMPERATURES FROM AN INSTANT-READ THERMOMETER

We include doneness temperatures in many of our recipes, such as those for poultry, meat, and bread. We recommend an instant-read thermometer for the job. Refer to the table above to convert Fahrenheit degrees to Celsius. Or, for temperatures not represented in the chart, use this simple formula:

Subtract 32 degrees from the Fahrenheit reading, then divide the result by 1.8 to find the Celsius reading.

EXAMPLE:

"Roast chicken until thighs register 175 degrees."
To convert:

$$175°F - 32 = 143°$$
$$143° \div 1.8 = 79.44°C, \text{ rounded down to } 79°C$$

Index

F

Fajitas, Skillet Chicken, *44*, 46–48
Farmhouse Vegetable and Barley Soup, 118–20, *119*
Fennel
    Olive, and Goat Cheese Tarts, 124–27, *125*
    and Parsnips, Pan-Roasted Chicken Breasts with, 50
    preparing, 122
    Vegetable Pot Pie, *116*, 121–22
Feta
    Grilled Spicy Shrimp Masala with Zucchini and Couscous Salad, 165–67, *166*
    and Herbs, Greek Meatballs with, 32–34
    Moroccan-Style Quinoa with Chickpeas and Kale, 128–29
    Olives, and Mint, Lentil Salad with, 258–59
    Roasted Garlic, and Shrimp, Campanelle with, 89–90
    and Shrimp, Mediterranean Pasta Salad with, 202
    and Spinach, Skillet Chicken and Orzo with, 55–57
Figs and Port, French-Style Pot-Roasted Pork with, 19
Filipino Chicken Adobo, 11–13
Fish
    Baked, with Crisp Bread Crumbs, 39–42, *41*
    Braised Cod Peperonata, *168*, 188–89
    Chili-Glazed Salmon with Bok Choy, 76–78
    and Couscous Packets, Moroccan, 73–76, *75*
    Fillets, Poached, with Crispy Artichokes and Tomato-Sherry Vinaigrette, *36*, 37–39
    Fillets, Poached, with Crispy Jalapeños and Spicy Vinaigrette, 39
    Fillets, Poached, with Crispy Scallions and Miso-Ginger Vinaigrette, 39
    fillets, skinning, 189
    Grill-Smoked Salmon with Cucumber, Radish, and Watercress Salad, 160–62, *161*
    Olive Oil Sauce with Anchovy and Parsley, 99
    poaching in oil, note about, 38
    premium canned tuna, taste tests on, 208
    White Bean and Tuna Salad, 207–8
    see also Shellfish
Five-Alarm Chili, 71–73
Five-Spice and Scallions, Chicken and Rice with, 53
French-Style Pot-Roasted Pork, *16*, 17–19
French-Style Pot-Roasted Pork with Port and Figs, 19
Fresh Pasta with Olive Oil Sauce with Anchovy and Parsley, 99
Fresh Pasta without a Machine, 97–99
Fresh Pasta with Walnut Cream Sauce, *96*, 99–100
Fruit
    dried, chopping, 220
    see also Berries; *specific fruits*

G

Galette, Easy Apple, *260*, 272–73
Garam masala, taste tests on, 167
Garlic
    Aïoli, 108
    -Parsley Butter, Minute Steaks with, 25–26
    Picada, 71

Garlic *(cont.)*
    prepeeled vs. fresh, 90
    Roasted, Sausage, and Arugula, Campanelle with, 196–97
    Roasted, Shrimp, and Feta, Campanelle with, 89–90
    Sauce, Sichuan Stir-Fried Pork in, 63–66, *64*
Garlic peelers, ratings of, 197
Ginger
    -Apple Chutney, Quick, Sautéed Boneless Pork Chops with, 182–83
    Chili-Glazed Salmon with Bok Choy, 76–78
    -Miso Vinaigrette and Crispy Scallions, Poached Fish Fillets with, 39
    Moroccan Fish and Couscous Packets, 73–76, *75*
Glazed Caribbean Tofu with Rice and Pigeon Peas, 135–37, *136*
Gnocchi, Potato, with Browned Butter and Sage, 100–103, *101*
Goat Cheese
    Campanelle with Roasted Garlic, Sausage, and Arugula, 196–97
    Fennel, and Olive Tarts, 124–27, *125*
    and Hazelnuts, Lentil Salad with, 259
    and Spinach, Rustic Chicken Tart with, *190*, 192
Grains
    Cajun-Style Eggs in Purgatory with Cheesy Grits, 57–59, *58*
    Farmhouse Vegetable and Barley Soup, 118–20, *119*
    Moroccan-Style Quinoa with Chickpeas and Kale, 128–29
    precooked polenta, about, 199
    quinoa, about, 129
    Smoky Sausage and Polenta Bake, 199
    Tabbouleh, 257–58
    see also Rice
Gratin dishes, small, 3
Gratins
    Cauliflower, 245–46
    Tomato, 246–48, *247*
    Tortellini, with Fire-Roasted Tomatoes, 205–6
Greek Meatballs with Herbs and Feta, 32–34
Green Beans
    Southern-Style, 236–37
    trimming quickly, 236
Greens
    Campanelle with Roasted Garlic, Sausage, and Arugula, 196–97
    Cheese Ravioli with Kale and Sunflower Seed Pesto, 94
    Escarole, Sausage, and Orzo Soup, 197
    Moroccan-Style Quinoa with Chickpeas and Kale, 128–29
    Spaghetti al Vino Bianco, 83–84
    Spicy Asian Soy and Rice Lettuce Wraps, 137–38, *139*
    Turkey Taco Salad, *178*, 179–81
    White Bean and Tuna Salad, 207–8
    see also Spinach
Grilled dishes
    Bacon-Wrapped Scallops with Radicchio and Gorgonzola Salad, 163–64
    Barbecued Pulled Chicken with Warm Cabbage Slaw, 146–49, *147*
    Chinese-Style Glazed Pork Tenderloin with Sesame Bok Choy, 149–51

N

Noodles
Beef Lo Mein with Broccoli and Bell Pepper, 113–14
Chinese, fresh, about, 114
Chinese Chicken Salad, 174–75
Drunken, with Chicken, 111–12
rice, about, 112
Rice, Chilled, with Shrimp, 183–84
Rice, Coconut, with Shrimp and Pineapple, 108–11, *109*
soba, about, 115
Soba, with Roasted Eggplant and Sesame, 114–15

Nut(s)
Broccoli Salad, 240–42, *241*
Cheese Ravioli with Roasted Red Pepper and Pistachio Pesto, 92–93
Cheese Ravioli with Sage, Walnut, and Browned Butter Pesto, 93–94
Cinnamon Streusel Coffee Cake, 264–66, *265*
-Cranberry Muffins, 262–64
Fresh Pasta with Walnut Cream Sauce, *96,* 99–100
Lentil Salad with Hazelnuts and Goat Cheese, 259
Maple-Pecan Scones, 266–68
Moroccan-Style Quinoa with Chickpeas and Kale, 128–29
Peach Melba Crisp, 274–75
Pine, Red Bell Pepper, and Basil, Pasta Salad with, 203–5
Quicker Turtle Brownies, 286–87
Roasted Brussels Sprouts with Bacon and Pecans, 244
toasting, 84
see also Almond(s)

O

Oklahoma Fried Onion Burgers, 30–32, *31*

Olive Oil
extra-virgin, taste tests on, 172
Sauce with Anchovy and Parsley, 99

Olive(s)
Bread, Skillet, 268–71, *269*
Chicken, and Roasted Red Pepper Sauce, Baked Pasta with, 193
Chicken and Chorizo Paella, 53–55
Chicken Marbella, 8–11, *9*
Fennel, and Goat Cheese Tarts, 124–27, *125*
Green, Almond, and Orange Pesto, Cheese Ravioli with, 94
Mediterranean Pasta Salad with Shrimp and Feta, 202
Mint, and Feta, Lentil Salad with, 258–59
pitting, 219
Slow-Cooker Chicken Provençal, 216–19, *218*
and Tomatoes, Quick Braised Chicken Thighs with, 14–15
White Bean and Tuna Salad, 207–8

Onion(s)
Caramelized, and Bacon, Potato Casserole with, 250–51
Fried, Burgers, Oklahoma, 30–32, *31*
Skillet Chicken Fajitas, *44,* 46–48
Slow-Cooker Beer Brats, 232–33
Slow-Cooker Smothered Steak, 229–32, *230*

Onion(s) *(cont.)*
Southern-Style Green Beans, 236–37
Tomato Gratin, 246–48, *247*
Orange, Green Olive, and Almond Pesto, Cheese Ravioli with, 94

P

Paella, Chicken and Chorizo, 53–55
Pancetta
Spaghetti al Vino Bianco, 83–84
White Beans, and Rosemary, Penne with, 84–87
Panko bread crumbs, taste tests on, 238
Pan-Roasted Chicken Breasts with Fennel and Parsnips, 50
Pan-Roasted Chicken Breasts with Root Vegetables, 48–50
Parmesan
Baked Pasta with Chicken, Olives, and Roasted Red Pepper Sauce, 193
Baked Risotto with Shrimp and Zucchini, 201–2
Cheesy Scalloped Potatoes, *252,* 253–54
-Crusted Asparagus, *234,* 237–38
Garlic, and Red Pepper Flakes, Roasted Brussels Sprouts with, 243–44
Grilled Pesto Chicken with Corn on the Cob, *140,* 142–44
pregrating, note about, 95
Risotto Primavera, *130,* 131–32
Shaved, and Zucchini Ribbons, Grilled Marinated Skirt Steak with, 153–56, *154*
shaving, 156
Skillet Olive Bread, 268–71, *269*
Tomato Gratin, 246–48, *247*
Parsley
-Garlic Butter, Minute Steaks with, 25–26
Picada, 71
Tabbouleh, 257–58
Parsnips
Farmhouse Vegetable and Barley Soup, 118–20, *119*
and Fennel, Pan-Roasted Chicken Breasts with, 50
Pasta
Baked, with Chicken, Olives, and Roasted Red Pepper Sauce, 193
Campanelle with Roasted Garlic, Sausage, and Arugula, 196–97
Campanelle with Roasted Garlic, Shrimp, and Feta, 89–90
cheese ravioli, taste tests on, 94
Cheese Ravioli with Green Olive, Almond, and Orange Pesto, 94
Cheese Ravioli with Kale and Sunflower Seed Pesto, 94
Cheese Ravioli with Roasted Red Pepper and Pistachio Pesto, 92–93
Cheese Ravioli with Sage, Walnut, and Browned Butter Pesto, 93–94
cooking instructions, 88
Escarole, Sausage, and Orzo Soup, 197
Fresh, with Olive Oil Sauce with Anchovy and Parsley, 99